The Complete Scotland FC 1872-2020

Dirk Karsdorp

British Library Cataloguing in Publication Data
A catalogue record for this book is available from the British Library

ISBN 978-1-86223-442-0

Copyright © 2020, SOCCER BOOKS LIMITED. (01472 696226)
72 St. Peter's Avenue, Cleethorpes, N.E. Lincolnshire, DN35 8HU, England

All rights are reserved. No part of this publication may be reproduced, stored in a retrieval system or transmitted, in any form or by any means, electronic, mechanical, photocopying, recording, or otherwise, without the prior written permission of Soccer Books Limited.

Printed in the UK by Severn

FOREWORD

Three years ago we published a book covering the international games played by Scotland from the very first international match against England in 1872 through to 2017. This new edition brings these statistics right up to date to the end of 2020 and, as before, lists full team line-ups and goalscorers for both Scotland and their opponents.

Only officially-recognised full international games are included in this book and other titles updated to 2020 in this series are also available for England, Wales, Northern Ireland and the Republic of Ireland. We have also published new books containing complete statistics for the international matches of Belgium, Italy and the Netherlands.

Although we have endeavoured to include statistics which are as complete as possible, inevitably there are omissions with one or two small pieces of information missing for a handful of games. Most notably, the times at which goals were scored were not recorded for a number of the earliest games although the goalscorers themselves are known. In such cases, the following symbol has been used to indicate that the time of the goal is not known: "#".

1. 30.11.1872
SCOTLAND v ENGLAND 0-0

West of Scotland Cricket Ground, Glasgow

Referee: William Keay (Scotland)   Attendance: 3,000

SCOTLAND: Robert W. Gardner (Cap), Joseph Taylor, William Ker, James J. Thomson, James Smith, William Muir MacKinnon, James Begg Weir, Robert Leckie, David N. Wotherspoon, Robert Smith, Alexander Rhind.

ENGLAND: Robert Barker, Ernest Harwood Greenhalgh, Reginald de Courtenay Velch, Frederick Brunning Maddison, William John Maynard, John Brockbank, John Charles Clegg, Arnold Kirke Smith, Cuthbert John Ottaway (Cap), Charles John Chenery, Charles John Morice.

2. 08.03.1873
ENGLAND v SCOTLAND 4-2 (2-0)

Kennington Oval, London

Referee: T. Lloyd (England)   Attendance: 3,000

SCOTLAND: Robert W. Gardner (Cap), Joseph Taylor, William Ker, James J. Thomson, Robert Smith, William Muir MacKinnon, Henry Waugh Renny-Tailyour, Arthur Fitzgerald Kinnaird, John Edward Blackburn, William Gibb, David N. Wotherspoon.

ENGLAND: Alexander Morten (Cap), Ernest Harwood Greenhalgh, Leonard Sidgwick Howell, Alfred George Goodwyn, Robert Walpole Sealy Vidal, Pelham George Von Donop, Charles John Chenery, William Edwin Clegg, Alexander George Bonsor, William Kenyon-Slaney, George Hubert Hugh Heron.

Goals: William Kenyon-Slaney (1, 75), Alexander George Bonsor (10), Charles John Chenery (85) / Henry Waugh Renny-Tailyour (25), William Gibb (70)

3. 07.03.1874
SCOTLAND v ENGLAND 2-1 (1-1)

West of Scotland Cricket Ground, Glasgow

Referee: Archibald Rae (Scotland)   Attendance: 7,000

SCOTLAND: Robert W. Gardner, John Hunter, Joseph Taylor, Charles Campbell, James J. Thomson (Cap), James Begg Weir, John Ferguson, Henry McNeil, William Muir MacKinnon, Angus McKinnon, Frederick Anderson.

ENGLAND: Reginald de Courtenay Velch, Robert Andrew Muter MacIndoe Ogilvie, Alfred Hugh Stratford, Cuthbert John Ottaway (Cap), Francis Hornby Birley, Charles Henry Reynolds Wollaston, Robert Kennett Kingsford, John Hawley Edwards, Charles John Chenery, George Hubert Hugh Heron, John Robert Blayney Owen.

Goals: Frederick Anderson (42), Angus McKinnon (47) / Robert Kennett Kingsford (28)

4. 06.03.1875
ENGLAND v SCOTLAND 2-2 (1-1)

Kennington Oval, London

Referee: Francis Arthur Marindin (England)   Att: 2,000

ENGLAND: William Henry Carr, Edward Brownlow Haygarth, William Stepney Rawson, Francis Hornby Birley, Pelham George Von Donop, Charles Henry Reynolds Wollaston, Charles William Alcock (Cap), Herbert Edward Rawson, Alexander George Bonsor, George Hubert Hugh Heron, Richard Lyon Geaves.

SCOTLAND: Robert W. Gardner, John Hunter, Joseph Taylor (Cap), Alexander Kennedy, Alexander McLintock, James Begg Weir, William Muir MacKinnon, Henry McNeil, Thomas Cochrane Highet, Peter Andrews, John McPherson.

Goals: Charles Wollaston (5), Charles William Alcock (70) / Henry McNeil (30), Peter Andrews (75)

5. 04.03.1876
SCOTLAND v ENGLAND 3-0 (3-0)

West of Scotland Cricket Ground, Glasgow

Referee: William C. Mitchell (Scotland)   Attendance: 15,000

SCOTLAND: Alexander McGeoch, Joseph Taylor (Cap), John Hunter, Alexander McLintock, Alexander Kennedy, Henry McNeil, William Muir MacKinnon, Thomas Cochrane Highet, William Miller, John Ferguson, John Campbell Baird.

ENGLAND: Arthur Henry Patrick Savage, Thomas Frederick Green, Edgar Field, Ernest Henry Bambridge, Beaumont Griffith Jarrett, George Hubert Hugh Heron, Arthur William Cursham, Charles Francis William Heron (Cap), Charles Eastlake Smith, Walter Scott Buchanan, William John Maynard.

Goals: William Muir MacKinnon (8), Henry McNeil (12), Thomas Cochrane Highet (16)

6. 25.03.1876
SCOTLAND v WALES 4-0 (1-0)

West of Scotland Cricket Ground, Glasgow

Referee: Robert Gardner (Scotland)   Attendance: 17,000

SCOTLAND: Alexander McGeoch, Joseph Taylor, Robert W. Neill, Alexander Kennedy, Charles Campbell (Cap), Thomas Cochrane Highet, John Ferguson, James J. Lang, William Muir MacKinnon, Moses McLay McNeil, Henry McNeil.

WALES: David Thomson, William Addams Williams Evans, Samuel Llewelyn Kenrick, Edwin Alfred Cross, William Williams, Dr. Daniel Grey, William Henry Davies, George Frederick Thomson, John Hawley Edwards, John Jones, Alfred Davies.

Goals: John Ferguson (40), James J. Lang (48), William Muir MacKinnon (53), Henry McNeil (70)

7. 03.03.1877
ENGLAND v SCOTLAND 1-3 (0-1)
Kennington Oval, London
Referee: Robert Andrew Ogilvie (England)   Att: 1,200
ENGLAND: Morton Peto Betts, William Lindsay, Lindsay Bury, William Stepney Rawson (Cap), Beaumont Griffith Jarrett, Charles Henry Reynolds Wollaston, Arthur William Cursham, Alfred Lyttelton, Cecil-Vernon Wingfield-Stratford, John Bain, William Mosforth.
SCOTLAND: Alexander McGeoch, Robert W. Neill, Thomas C. Vallance, Charles Campbell (Cap), James Phillips, James Tassie Richmond, William Muir MacKinnon, John C. McGregor, John McDougall, John Smith, John Ferguson.
Goals: Alfred Lyttelton (55) /
John Ferguson (25, 86), James Tassie Richmond (48)

8. 05.03.1877
WALES v SCOTLAND 0-2 (0-0)
The Racecourse, Wrexham
Referee: William A. Dick (Scotland)   Attendance: 4,000
WALES: Thomas Blundell Burnett, William Addams Williams Evans, Samuel Llewelyn Kenrick, John Richard Morgan, Edwin Alfred Cross, William Henry Davies, Alfred Davies, John Henry Price, Alexander Fletcher Jones, John Hughes I, George Frederick Thomson.
SCOTLAND: Alexander McGeoch, Robert W. Neill, Thomas C. Vallance, James Phillips, Charles Campbell (Cap), John Smith, John C. McGregor, John Ferguson, John McDougall, Henry McNeil, John Hunter.
Goals: Charles Campbell (55), William Addams Williams Evans (75 own goal)

9. 02.03.1878
SCOTLAND v ENGLAND 7-2 (4-0)
First Hampden Park, Glasgow
Referee: William A. Dick (Scotland)   Attendance: 10,000
SCOTLAND: Robert W. Gardner, Andrew McIntyre, Thomas C. Vallance, Charles Campbell (Cap), Alexander Kennedy, James Tassie Richmond, John C. McGregor, John McDougall, Thomas Cochrane Highet, William Muir MacKinnon, Henry McNeil.
ENGLAND: Conrad Warner, Edward Lyttelton, John Hunter, Norman Coles Bailey, Beaumont Griffith Jarrett, Arthur William Cursham (Cap), Percy Fairclough, Henry Wace, John George Wylie, George Hubert Hugh Heron, William Mosforth.
Goals: John McDougall (7, 41, 46), John C. McGregor (32), Henry McNeil (39, 70), William Muir MacKinnon (62) /
John George Wylie (65), Arthur William Cursham (75)

10. 23.03.1878
SCOTLAND v WALES 9-0 (6-0)
First Hampden Park, Glasgow
Referee: Robert Gardner (Scotland)   Attendance: 6,000
SCOTLAND: Robert Parlane, James Duncan, Robert W. Neill (Cap), James Phillips, David Davidson, John Ferguson, John Campbell Baird, James J. Lang, James Begg Weir, James A.K. Watson, Peter Campbell.
WALES: Edward Phennah, George Garnet Higham, John Powell, Henry Valentine Edwards, William Williams, George Foulkes Savin, James Davies, Dr. Daniel Grey, Thomas Johnson Britten, John Henry Price, Charles Edwards.
Goals: Peter Campbell (4, 18), James Begg Weir (15, 42), John Campbell Baird (37), John Ferguson (38, 50), James A.K. Watson (#), James J. Lang (#)

11. 05.04.1879
ENGLAND v SCOTLAND 5-4 (1-4)
Kennington Oval, London
Referee: Charles Wollaston (England)   Attendance: 4,500
ENGLAND: Reginald Halsey Birkett, Harold Morse, Edward Christian, Norman Coles Bailey, James Frederick McLeod Prinsep, Arnold Frank Hills, Arthur Copeland Goodyer, Henry Wace (Cap), Francis John Sparks, Edward Charles Bambridge, William Mosforth.
SCOTLAND: Robert Parlane, William S. Somers, Henry McNeil, Thomas C. Vallance, Charles Campbell (Cap), John Campbell McLeod McPherson, Robert Paton, William Wightman Beveridge, John Smith, John McDougall, William Muir MacKinnon.
Goals: William Mosforth (5), Edward Bambridge (48, 83) Arthur Goodyer (60), Norman Coles Bailey (75) /
William Muir MacKinnon (15, 41), John McDougall (23), John Smith (26)

12. 07.04.1879
WALES v SCOTLAND 0-3 (0-1)
The Racecourse, Wrexham
Referee: John W.A. Cooper (Wales)   Attendance: 2,000
WALES: John Davies, Samuel Llewelyn Kenrick, John Richard Morgan, Knyvett Crosse, William Williams, James William Lloyd, George Woosnam, John Hughes I, John Roberts I, William Roberts I, John Vaughan.
SCOTLAND: Robert Parlane, Thomas C. Vallance, William S. Somers, John Campbell McLeod McPherson, David Davidson, Henry McNeil, John McDougall (Cap), Peter Campbell, Robert Paton, William Wightman Beveridge, John Smith.
Goals: Peter Campbell (34), John Smith (60, 70)

13. 13.03.1880
SCOTLAND v ENGLAND 5-4 (3-2)
First Hampden Park, Glasgow

Referee: Donald Hamilton (Scotland)   Attendance: 10,000

SCOTLAND: Archibald Rowan, Alexander McLintock, Robert W. Neill (Cap), Charles Campbell, John Campbell McLeod McPherson, John Smith, Moses McLay McNeil, George Ker, John C. McGregor, John Campbell Baird, John Leck Kay.

ENGLAND: Harry Albemarle Swepstone, Thomas Brindle, Edwin Luntley, Norman Coles Bailey, John Hunter, Charles Henry Reynolds Wollaston (Cap), Richard Segal Bastard, Francis John Sparks, Samuel Weller Widdowson, William Mosforth, Edward Charles Bambridge.

Goals: George Ker (5, 44, 48), John Campbell Baird (39), John Leck Kay (67) / William Mosforth (8), Edward Charles Bambridge (42, 87), Francis John Sparks (89)

14. 27.03.1880
SCOTLAND v WALES 5-1 (2-0)
First Hampden Park, Glasgow

Referee: Alexander Stuart (Scotland)   Attendance: 2,000

SCOTLAND: George Gillespie, William S. Somers, Archibald Lang, David Davidson (Cap), Hugh McIntyre, James Douglas, J. McAdam, Malcolm James Eadie Fraser, Joseph Lindsay, John Campbell, William Wightman Beveridge.

WALES: Harold Hibbott, John Richard Morgan, John Powell, Edward Bowen, Henry Valentine Edwards, William Pierce Owen, William Roberts I, John Roberts I, John Henry Price, Thomas Johnson Britten, John Vaughan.

Goals: David Davidson (38), William Beveridge (40), Joseph Lindsay (#), J. McAdam (#), John Campbell (#) / William Roberts I (#)

15. 12.03.1881
ENGLAND v SCOTLAND 1-6 (0-1)
Kennington Oval, London

Referee: Francis Arthur Marindin (England)   Att: 8,500

ENGLAND: John Purvis Hawtrey, Edgar Field, Claude William Wilson, Norman Coles Bailey (Cap), John Hunter, George Holden, Tot Rostron, Reginald Heber Macauley, Clement Mitchell, Edward Charles Bambridge, John Hargreaves.

SCOTLAND: George Gillespie, Andrew Watson, Thomas C. Vallance, Charles Campbell (Cap), David Davidson, David Hill, William McGuire, George Ker, Joseph Lindsay, Henry McNeil, John Smith.

Goals: Edward Charles Bambridge (64) / John Smith (10, 69, 79), David Hill (53), George Ker (74, 89)

16. 14.03.1881
WALES v SCOTLAND 1-5 (1-4)
The Racecourse, Wrexham

Referee: Samuel Llewelyn Kenrick (Wales)   Att: 1,500

WALES: Robert McMillan, John Richard Morgan, John Roberts II, William Stafford Bell, William Williams, William Pierce Owen, Thomas Lewis, Knyvett Crosse, John Henry Price, William Roberts I, John Vaughan.

SCOTLAND: George Gillespie, Andrew Watson, Thomas C. Vallance, John Campbell McLeod McPherson, David Davidson (Cap), William McGuire, David Hill, George Ker, Joseph Lindsay, Henry McNeil, John Smith.

Goals: Knyvett Crosse (5) / George Ker (7, 44), Henry McNeil (9), William Stafford Bell (10 own goal), John Richard Morgan (52 own goal)

17. 11.03.1882
SCOTLAND v ENGLAND 5-1 (2-1)
First Hampden Park, Glasgow

Referee: John Wallace (Scotland)   Attendance: 10,000

SCOTLAND: George Gillespie, Andrew Watson, Andrew McIntyre, Charles Campbell (Cap), Peter Miller, Malcolm James Eadie Fraser, William Anderson, George Ker, William Harrower, John Leck Kay, Robert McPherson.

ENGLAND: Harry Albemarle Swepstone, Doctor Haydock Greenwood, Alfred Jones, Norman Coles Bailey (Cap), John Hunter, Henry Alfred Cursham, Edward Hagarty Parry, Arthur Brown, Oliver Howard Vaughton, William Mosforth, Edward Charles Bambridge.

Goals: William Harrower (15), George Ker (43, 70), Robert McPherson (46), John Leck Kay (85) / Oliver Howard Vaughton (35)

18. 25.03.1882
SCOTLAND v WALES 5-0 (1-0)
First Hampden Park, Glasgow

Referee: Donald Hamilton (Scotland)   Attendance: 5,000

SCOTLAND: Archibald Rowan (Cap), Andrew Hair Holm, James Duncan, Charles Campbell, Alexander Kennedy, Malcolm James Eadie Fraser, David Hill, George Ker, James McAulay, John Leck Kay, James Tassie Richmond.

WALES: Henry Phoenix, John Richard Morgan, John Powell, Henry Valentine Edwards, William Williams, John Roberts II, William Pierce Owen, Walter Hugh Roberts, John Henry Price, John Roberts I, John Vaughan.

Goals: John Leck Kay (25), George Ker (#), Malcolm James Eadie Fraser (#, #), James McAulay (88)

19. 10.03.1883
ENGLAND v SCOTLAND 2-3 (2-2)
Bramall Lane, Sheffield
Referee: John Sinclair (Ireland)   Attendance: 7,000
ENGLAND: Harry Albemarle Swepstone, Percy John de Paravicini, Alfred Jones, Norman Coles Bailey (Cap), Stuart Macrae, Arthur William Cursham, William Nevill Cobbold, Clement Mitchell, Harry Chester Goodhart, Henry Alfred Cursham, Oliver Whateley.
SCOTLAND: James McAulay, Andrew Hair Holm (Cap), Michael Paton, Peter Miller, John Campbell McLeod McPherson, Malcolm James Eadie Fraser, William Anderson, John Smith, John Inglis, John Leck Kay, William Neilson McKinnon.
Goals: Clement Mitchell (24), William Nevill Cobbold (43) / John Smith (22, 39), Malcolm James Eadie Fraser (86)

20. 12.03.1883
WALES v SCOTLAND 0-3 (0-2)
The Racecourse, Wrexham
Referee: Robert E. Lythgoe (England)   Attendance: 2,000
WALES: Richard Thomas Gough, Frederick William Hughes, John Powell, Edward Bowen, Henry Valentine Edwards, John Jones II, William Pierce Owen, Walter Hugh Roberts, John Henry Price, William Roberts II, John Vaughan.
SCOTLAND: James McAulay, Andrew Hair Holm (Cap), Walter Arnott, Peter Miller, John Campbell McLeod McPherson, Malcolm James Eadie Fraser, William Anderson, John Smith, John Inglis, John Leck Kay, William Neilson McKinnon.
Goals: John Smith (35), Malcolm James Eadie Fraser (38), William Anderson (#)

21. 26.01.1884   Home Championship
IRELAND v SCOTLAND 0-5 (0-2)
Ballynafeigh Park, Belfast
Referee: Thomas Hindle (England)   Attendance: 2,000
NORTHERN IRELAND: R.J. Hunter, M. Wilson, William Crone, John Hastings, Thomas Bryson Molyneux, A.H. Dill, E. Arthur Spiller, John T. Gibb, William J. Morrow, Dr. John Robert Davison, Arthur W. Gaussen.
SCOTLAND: John Inglis II, John Forbes, Walter Arnott (Cap), John Graham, William Fulton, Robert Brown, Samuel Thomson, James Gossland, John Wilson Goudie, William Harrower, J. McAulay.
Goals: William Harrower (12, 86), James Gossland (#, #), John Wilson Goudie (60)

22. 15.03.1884   Home Championship
SCOTLAND v ENGLAND 1-0 (1-0)
Cathkin Park, Glasgow
Referee: John Sinclair (Ireland)   Attendance: 10,000
SCOTLAND: James McAulay, Walter Arnott, John Forbes, Charles Campbell (Cap), John Campbell McLeod McPherson, William Anderson, Francis Watson Shaw, John Smith, Joseph Lindsay, Robert Main Christie, William Neilson McKinnon.
ENGLAND: William Crispin Rose, Alfred Thomas Carrick Dobson, Joseph Beverley, Norman Coles Bailey (Cap), Stuart Macrae, Charles Plumpton Wilson, William Bromley-Davenport, William Gunn, Edward Charles Bambridge, Oliver Howard Vaughton, George Holden.
Goal: John Smith (7)

23. 29.03.1884   Home Championship
SCOTLAND v WALES 4-1 (1-1)
Cathkin Park, Glasgow
Referee: R.M. Sloane (England)   Attendance: 5,000
SCOTLAND: Thomas Turner, Michael Paton (Cap), John Forbes, Alexander Kennedy, James McIntyre, Robert Brown, Francis Watson Shaw, Samuel Thomson, Joseph Lindsay, John Leck Kay, William Neilson McKinnon.
WALES: Elias Owen, Robert Roberts I, Charles Conde, Frederick William Hughes, Thomas Burke, John Jones II, William Pierce Owen, Walter Hugh Roberts, Edward Gough Shaw, John Arthur Eyton-Jones, Robert Albert Jones.
Goals: Joseph Lindsay (22), Francis Watson Shaw (49), John Leck Kay (#, 87) / Robert Roberts I (7)

24. 14.03.1885   Home Championship
SCOTLAND v IRELAND 8-2 (4-0)
First Hampden Park, Glasgow
Referee: William Pierce Dix (England)   Attendance: 6,000
SCOTLAND: William Chalmers, Hugh McHardy, James B. Niven, Robert Robinson Kelso, John Campbell McLeod McPherson (Cap), Alexander Barbour, John Marshall, William Turner, Alexander F. Higgins, Robert Calderwood, W. Lamont.
IRELAND: Anthony W. Henderson, George Hewison, R. Johnston, Robert Muir, William John Houston, William L'Estrange Eames, T. McLean, Joseph Sherrard, John T. Gibb, George McGee, A.H. Dill.
Goals: W. Lamont (10), William Turner (12), Robert Calderwood (15), John Marshall (35), Alexander F. Higgins (51, #, #), Alexander Barbour (53) / John T. Gibb (81, 89)

25. 21.03.1885   Home Championship
ENGLAND v SCOTLAND 1-1 (0-1)

Kennington Oval, London

Referee: John Sinclair (Ireland)   Attendance: 8,000

ENGLAND: William John Herbert Arthur, Percy Melmoth Walters, Arthur Melmoth Walters, Norman Coles Bailey (Cap), James Henry Forrest, Andrew Amos, James Brown, Joseph Morris Lofthouse, Thomas Danks, Edward Charles Bambridge, William Nevill Cobbold.

SCOTLAND: James McAulay, Walter Arnott, Michael Paton, Charles Campbell (Cap), John James Gow, William Anderson, Alexander Hamilton, William Sellar, Joseph Lindsay, David Steel Allan, Robert Calderwood.

Goals: Edward Charles Bambridge (57) / Joseph Lindsay (20).

26. 23.03.1885   Home Championship
WALES v SCOTLAND 1-8 (0-3)

The Racecourse, Wrexham

Referee: R.M. Sloane (England)   Attendance: 2,000

WALES: Dr. Robert Herbert Mills-Roberts, George Thomas, Seth Powell, Thomas Burke, William Tanat Foulkes, Humphrey Jones, James William Lloyd, Job Wilding, Harold Hibbott, George Farmer, Robert Albert Jones.

SCOTLAND: James McAulay, Walter Arnott, Michael Paton (Cap), Robert Robinson Kelso, Leitch Keir, Alexander Hamilton, William Anderson, Joseph Lindsay, Robert Calderwood, Robert Brown, David Steel Allan.

Goals: Robert Albert Jones (54) / Robert Calderwood (8, 88), William Anderson (#, 78), David Steel Allan (#), Joseph Lindsay (56, #, #).

27. 20.03.1886   Home Championship
IRELAND v SCOTLAND 2-7 (2-5)

Ballynafeigh Park, Belfast

Referee: Wolstenholme (Ireland)   Attendance: 3,000

IRELAND: Shaw Gillespie, W. Devine, James Watson, William Crone, Thomas Bryson Molyneux, John Hastings (Cap), John McClatchey, Samuel Johnston I, John T. Gibb, J. Condy, William Turner.

SCOTLAND: James Connor, Andrew Thomson, William McLeod, John Cameron, Leitch Keir, Robert Fleming, John Alexander Lambie (Cap), Charles Winton Heggie, William Turner, James McCrory Gourlay, Michael Dunbar.

Goals: J. Condy (#), Samuel Johnston I (#) / Charles Winton Heggie (4 goals), John Alexander Lambie (#), Michael Dunbar (#), James McCrory Gourlay (#).

28. 27.03.1886   Home Championship
SCOTLAND v ENGLAND 1-1 (0-1)

First Hampden Park, Glasgow

Referee: Alexander Hunter (Wales)   Attendance: 11,000

ENGLAND: William John Herbert Arthur, Arthur Melmoth Walters, Percy Melmoth Walters, Norman Coles Bailey (Cap), Ralph Tyndall Squire, James Henry Forrest, William Nevill Cobbold, Edward Charles Bambridge, Tinsley Lindley, Benjamin Ward Spilsbury, George Brann.

SCOTLAND: James McAulay, Walter Arnott (Cap), Michael Paton, Charles Campbell, John MacDonald, Alexander Hamilton, William Sellar, George Somerville, Joseph Lindsay, Woodville Gray, Ralph Allan Aitken.

Goals: George Somerville (80) / Tinsley Lindley (35)

29. 10.04.1886   Home Championship
SCOTLAND v WALES 4-1 (1-0)

First Hampden Park, Glasgow

Referee: John Sinclair (Ireland)   Attendance: 3,500

SCOTLAND: George Gillespie, James Lundie, William Semple (Cap), Robert Robinson Kelso, Andrew Jackson, John Marshall, Robert McCormick, James McGhee, William Harrower, David Steel Allan, James McCall.

WALES: Albert Malcolm Hersee, Dr. Alfred Owen Davies, Frederick Robert Jones, John Owen Vaughan, William Stafford Bell, Humphrey Jones, Richard Parry Williams, William Roberts III, John Doughty, Herbert Sisson, William Lewis.

Goals: Robert McCormick (30), James McCall (47), David Steel Allan (53), William Harrower (56) / John Owen Vaughan (88)

30. 19.02.1887   Home Championship
SCOTLAND v IRELAND 4-1 (2-1)

First Hampden Park, Glasgow

Referee: Alexander Hunter (Wales)   Attendance: 1,000

SCOTLAND: John Edward Doig, Andrew Whitelaw, Robert Smellie, John Weir, Thomas McMillan, J. Hutton, Thomas James Jenkinson, John Alexander Lambie (Cap), William Wilson Watt, James Lowe, William Johnstone.

IRELAND: Shaw Gillespie, W. Fox, James Watson, T. Moore, Archibald Rosbotham, Robert A. Baxter, John Reid, Olphert M. Stanfield, Frederick Browne, John Peden, John T. Gibb (Cap).

Goals: William Wilson Watt (5), Thomas Jenkinson (43), William Johnstone (55), James Lowe (75) / Frederick Browne (41)

31.   19.03.1887   Home Championship
ENGLAND v SCOTLAND 2-3 (1-1)
Leamington Road, Blackburn
Referee: John Sinclair (Ireland)   Attendance: 12,000
ENGLAND: Robert John Roberts, Arthur Melmoth Walters, Percy Melmoth Walters, Norman Coles Bailey (Cap), George Haworth, James Henry Forrest, Edward Charles Bambridge, William Nevill Cobbold, Joseph Morris Lofthouse, Frederick Dewhurst, Tinsley Lindley.
SCOTLAND: James McAulay (Cap), Walter Arnott, John Forbes, Robert Robinson Kelso, John Robertson Auld, Leitch Keir, John Marshall, William Robertson, William Sellar, James McCall, James Allan.
Goals: Tinsley Lindley (32), Frederick Dewhurst (69) / James McCall (30), Leitch Keir (68), James Allan (70)

32.   21.03.1887   Home Championship
WALES v SCOTLAND 0-2 (0-1)
The Racecourse, Wrexham
Referee: A.B. Hall (England)   Attendance: 2,000
WALES: James Manager, Dr. Alfred Owen Davies, John Powell, Robert Roberts I, James Morris, Thomas Burke, John Bonamy Challen, Richard Owen Jones, William Ernest Pryce-Jones, William Lewis, John Doughty.
SCOTLAND: James McAulay (Cap), Walter Arnott, John Forbes, Robert Robinson Kelso, John Robertson Auld, Leitch Keir, John Marshall, William Robertson, William Sellar, James McCall, James Allan.
Goals: William Robertson (40), James Allan (80)

33.   10.03.1888   Home Championship
SCOTLAND v WALES 5-1 (3-1)
Easter Road Park, Edinburgh
Referee: John Charles Clegg (England)   Attendance: 8,000
SCOTLAND: James Wilson, Andrew Hannah, Robert Smellie (Cap), James Johnstone, James McCrory Gourlay, James McLaren, Alexander Latta, William Groves, William Paul, John "Kitey" McPherson, Neil Munro.
WALES: James Manager, David Jones, John Powell, Thomas Burke, Joseph Davies I, Robert Roberts I, William Ernest Pryce-Jones, Job Wilding, John Doughty, George Alfred Owen, Roger Doughty.
Goals: William Paul (6), Neil Munro (30), Alexander Latta (33, 75), William Groves (65) / John Doughty (41)

34.   17.03.1888   Home Championship
SCOTLAND v ENGLAND 0-5 (0-4)
First Hampden Park, Glasgow
Referee: John Sinclair (Ireland)   Attendance: 10,000
SCOTLAND: John Lindsay, Walter Arnott, Donald Robertson Gow (Cap), James Kelly, Leitch Keir, Robert Robinson Kelso, Alexander Hamilton, William Hall Berry, William Sellar, James McCall, John Alexander Lambie.
ENGLAND: William Robert Moon, Robert Henry Howarth, Percy Melmoth Walters, Henry Allen, George Haworth, Charles Henry Holden-White, George Woodhall, John Goodall, Tinsley Lindley (Cap), Dennis Hodgetts, Frederick Dewhurst.
Goals: Tinsley Lindley (32), Dennis Hodgetts (34), Frederick Dewhurst (40, 49), John Goodall (43)

35.   24.03.1888   Home Championship
IRELAND v SCOTLAND 2-10 (2-7)
Solitude Ground, Belfast
Referee: Robert Parlane (Scotland)   Attendance: 5,000
IRELAND: Ralph Lawther, Robert Wilson, Frederick Browne, James Forsythe, Archibald Rosbotham, Thomas Bryson Molyneux, William Dalton, Olphert M. Stanfield, John Barry, John Lemon, William Turner.
SCOTLAND: John McLeod, Duncan Stewart (Cap), Archibald McCall, Allan Stewart, George Dewar, Andrew Jackson, Neil McCallum, John Robertson Gow, William Alexander Dickson, Thomas Breckenridge, Ralph Allan Aitken.
Goals: William Dalton (#, #) / George Dewar (5), William Dickson (8, 33, 40, 45), Thomas Breckenridge (15), Ralph Allan Aitken (#), Neil McCallum (53), Robert Wilson (77 own goal), Allan Stewart (83)

36.   09.03.1889   Home Championship
SCOTLAND v IRELAND 7-0 (4-0)
Ibrox Park, Glasgow
Referee: William H. Stacey (England)   Attendance: 6,000
SCOTLAND: John Edward Doig, James Adams, Thomas Michael McKeown, Thomas Robertson (Cap), David Calderhead, John Buchanan, Francis Watt, Thomas McInnes, William Groves, R. Boyd, David George Black.
IRELAND: John Clugston, John McVicker, Robert Crone, John Thompson, James Christian, William Crone, Samuel Torrans, Olphert M. Stanfield, John T. Gibb, James M. Wilton, John Peden.
Goals: Francis Watt (7, 10), David George Black (25), William Groves (32, 50, #), Thomas McInnes (88)

10

37. 13.04.1889   Home Championship
ENGLAND v SCOTLAND 2-3 (2-0)
Kennington Oval, London
Referee: John Sinclair (Ireland)   Attendance: 10,000
ENGLAND: William Robert Moon, Arthur Melmoth Walters (Cap), Percy Melmoth Walters, Henry Edward Denison Hammond, Henry Allen, James Henry Forrest, James Brant Brodie, John Goodall, William Isaiah Bassett, David Weir, Tinsley Lindley.
SCOTLAND: James Wilson, Robert Smellie (Cap), Walter Arnott, James Kelly, George Dewar, James McLaren, James Oswald, William Hall Berry, Alexander Latta, John "Kitey" McPherson, Neil Munro.
Goals: William Isaiah Bassett (15), David Weir (17) / Neil Munro (55), James Oswald (82), John McPherson (90)

38. 15.04.1889   Home Championship
WALES v SCOTLAND 0-0
The Racecourse, Wrexham
Referee: John Sinclair (Ireland)   Attendance: 6,000
WALES: Allen Pugh (30 Samuel Gladstone Gillam), Dr. Alfred Owen Davies, David Jones, Robert Roberts I, Joseph Davies I, Humphrey Jones, Joseph Davies II, William Owen, John Doughty, George Alfred Owen, William Lewis.
SCOTLAND: John McLeod, Andrew Thomson (Cap), James Rae, Allan Stewart, Alexander Lochhead, John Robertson Auld, Francis Watt, Henry Campbell, William Paul, William Johnstone, James Hannah.

39. 22.03.1890   Home Championship
SCOTLAND v WALES 5-0 (3-0)
Underwood Park, Paisley
Referee: W. Finlay (Ireland)   Attendance: 7,500
SCOTLAND: George Gillespie (Cap), Andrew Whitelaw, John Winning Murray, Matthew McQueen, Andrew Brown, Hugh Wilson, J. Brown, Francis Watt, William Paul, James Dunlop, Daniel Bruce.
WALES: James Manager, William P. Jones, Samuel Jones I, Peter Griffiths, Humphrey Jones, Robert Roberts I, David Morral Lewis, Oswald Davies, William Owen, Richard Henry Jarrett, William Haighton Turner.
Goals: Hugh Wilson (#), William Paul (36, 43, #, 70)

40. 29.03.1890   Home Championship
IRELAND v SCOTLAND 1-4 (1-1)
Ballynafeigh Park, Belfast
Referee: William H. Stacey (England)   Attendance: 5,000
IRELAND: John Clugston, Robert K. Stewart (Cap), Robert Crone, John Reid, Samuel Spencer, Samuel Cooke, William Dalton, George Gaffikin, Olphert M. Stanfield, Samuel Torrans, John Peden.
SCOTLAND: John McLeod (Cap), R. Hunter, James Rae, J. Russell, Isaac Begbie, David Mitchell, Thomas G. Wylie, Gilbert Rankin, John "Kitey" McPherson, John Bell, David Baird.
Goals: John Peden (#) / Gilbert Rankin (10, #), Thomas G. Wylie (50), John "Kitey" McPherson (#)

41. 05.04.1890   Home Championship
SCOTLAND v ENGLAND 1-1 (1-1)
2nd Hampden Park, Glasgow
Referee: John Reid (Ireland)   Attendance: 26,379
SCOTLAND: James Wilson, Walter Arnott, Thomas Michael McKeown, Thomas Robertson, James Kelly, James McLaren (Cap), William Groves, William Hall Berry, William Johnstone, John "Kitey" McPherson, James McCall.
ENGLAND: William Robert Moon, Arthur Melmoth Walters, Percy Melmoth Walters (Cap), George Haworth, Henry Allen, Alfred Shelton, William Isaiah Bassett, Edward Samuel Currey, Tinsley Lindley, Harry Wood, Henry Butler Daft.
Goals: John "Kitey" McPherson (37) / Harry Wood (17)

42. 21.03.1891   Home Championship
WALES v SCOTLAND 3-4 (2-1)
The Racecourse, Wrexham
Referee: Charles Crump (England)   Attendance: 4,000
WALES: James Manager, Seth Powell, David Jones, Arthur Lea, Humphrey Jones, Charles Frederick Parry, Joseph Davies II, William Owen, William Haighton Turner, John Charles Henry Bowdler, William Lewis.
SCOTLAND: John McCorkindale, Archibald Ritchie, James Hepburn, Matthew McQueen, Andrew Brown, Thomas Robertson (Cap), William Gulliland, Robert Buchanan, James Logan, R. Boyd, Alexander Lowson Keillor.
Goals: John Bowdler (#, #), William Owen (#) / James Logan (#), Robert Buchanan (#), R. Boyd (#, #)

43. 28.03.1891   Home Championship
SCOTLAND v IRELAND 2-1 (1-0)
Celtic Park, Glasgow

Referee: William H. Stacey (England)   Attendance: 8,000

SCOTLAND: George Gillespie (Cap), Donald Currie Sillars, William Paul, T. Hamilton, James W. Cleland, James Campbell, James Low, William Bowie, Robert Clements, Thomas Smith Waddell, J. Fraser.

IRELAND: Joseph Loyal, William Gordon, George Forbes, Alexander Crawford, John Reynolds, Richard Moore, William Dalton, George Gaffikin, Olphert M. Stanfield, David Brisby, Samuel Torrans.

Goals: James Low (6), Thomas Smith Waddell (60) / Olphert M. Stanfield (85)

44. 04.04.1891   Home Championship
ENGLAND v SCOTLAND 2-1 (2-0)
Ewood Park, Blackburn

Referee: William J. Morrow (Ireland)   Attendance: 31,000

ENGLAND: William Robert Moon (Cap), Robert Henry Howarth, Robert Holmes, Albert Smith, John Holt, Alfred Shelton, William Isaiah Bassett, John Goodall, Frederick Geary, Edgar Wallace Chadwick, Alfred Weatherell Milward.

SCOTLAND: James Wilson, Walter Arnott (Cap), Robert Smellie, Isaac Begbie, John McPherson, John Hill, Gilbert Rankin, Francis Watt, William Sellar, William Hall Berry, David Baird.

Goals: John Goodall (20), Edgar Wallace Chadwick (30) / Francis Watt (85)

45. 19.03.1892   Home Championship
IRELAND v SCOTLAND 2-3 (1-2)
Solitude Ground, Belfast

Referee: John Taylor (Wales)   Attendance: 10,500

IRELAND: John Clugston, William Gordon, Robert K. Stewart, Nathaniel McKeown, Samuel Spencer, William Cunningham I, William Dalton, George Gaffikin, James Williamson, Olphert M. Stanfield, Samuel Torrans.

SCOTLAND: Andrew Baird, George Alexander Bowman, John Drummond, Robert W. Marshall, Thomas Robertson (Cap), Peter Dowds, William Gulliland, David Murray McPherson, James Ellis, William Allan Lambie, Alexander Lowson Keillor.

Goals: James Williamson (42), George Gaffikin (86) / Alexander Lowson Keillor (17), William Allan Lambie (28), James Ellis (70)

46. 26.03.1892   Home Championship
SCOTLAND v WALES 6-1 (4-0)
Tynecastle Park, Edinburgh

Referee: John Reid (Ireland)   Attendance: 600

SCOTLAND: Robert Downie, James Adams, James Orr, Isaac Begbie, James Campbell, John Hill (Cap), John Daniel Taylor, William Thomson, James Hamilton, John "Kitey" McPherson, David Baird.

WALES: James Manager, Smart Arridge, Seth Powell, William Hughes, Caesar August Llewelyn Jenkyns, Robert Roberts I, Job Wilding, William Owen, William Lewis, Thomas William Egan, Benjamin Lewis.

Goals: William Thomson (1), James Hamilton (8, 65), John "Kitey" McPherson (15, 44), David Baird (55) / Benjamin Lewis (87)

47. 02.04.1892   Home Championship
SCOTLAND v ENGLAND 1-4 (0-4)
Ibrox Park, Glasgow

Referee: Dr. John Smith (Scotland)   Attendance: 21,000

SCOTLAND: John McLeod, Daniel Doyle, Walter Arnott, James Kelly, William Sellar (Cap), David Mitchell, Donald Currie Sillars, William Taylor, Thomas Smith Waddell, Alexander McMahon, John Bell.

ENGLAND: George Toone, Arthur Tempest Blakiston Dunn (Cap), Robert Holmes, John Holt, John Reynolds, Alfred Shelton, William Isaiah Bassett, John Goodall, John Southworth, Dennis Hodgetts, Edgar Wallace Chadwick.

Goals: John Bell (80) / Edgar Wallace Chadwick (1), John Goodall (20, 26), John Southworth (25)

48. 18.03.1893   Home Championship
WALES v SCOTLAND 0-8 (0-5)
The Racecourse, Wrexham

Referee: William H. Stacey (England)   Attendance: 4,500

WALES: Samuel Jones II, Oliver David Shepston Taylor, Frederick William Jones, George Williams, Edwin Hugh Williams, Edward Morris, William Owen, James Vaughan, John Butler, Benjamin Lewis, Harold Ernest Bowdler.

SCOTLAND: John McLeod, Daniel Doyle, Robert Foyers, Donald Currie Sillars (Cap), Andrew McCreadie, David Stewart, John Daniel Taylor, William Thomson, John Madden, John Barker, William Allan Lambie.

Goals: John Madden (4, 20, 47), John Barker (25, #, #), William Allan Lambie (65), John Madden (89)

49. 25.03.1893   Home Championship
SCOTLAND v IRELAND 6-1 (4-1)

Celtic Park, Glasgow

Referee: John Taylor (Wales)   Attendance: 12,000

SCOTLAND: John Lindsay, James Adams, Robert Smellie, William Maley, James Kelly (Cap), David Mitchell, William Sellar, Thomas Smith Waddell, James Hamilton, Alexander McMahon, John Campbell.

IRELAND: John Clugston, William Gordon, Robert Torrans, Nathaniel McKeown, Samuel Johnston II, Samuel Torrans, James M. Small, George Gaffikin, James Williamson, James M. Wilton, John Peden.

Goals: William Sellar (10, 27), Samuel Torrans (20 own goal), Alexander McMahon (28), James Kelly (#), James Hamilton (#) / George Gaffikin (44)

50. 01.04.1893   Home Championship
ENGLAND v SCOTLAND 5-2 (1-1)

Richmond Athletic Ground, London

Referee: John Charles Clegg (England)   Attendance: 16,000

ENGLAND: Leslie Hewitt Gay, Alban Hugh Harrison, Robert Holmes, John Reynolds, John Holt, George Kinsey, William Isaiah Bassett, Robert Cunliffe Gosling, George Huth Cotterill (Cap), Edgar Wallace Chadwick, Frederick Spiksley.

SCOTLAND: John Lindsay, Walter Arnott, Robert Smellie, William Maley, James Kelly (Cap), David Mitchell, William Sellar, Thomas Smith Waddell, James Hamilton, Alexander McMahon, John Campbell.

Goals: Robert Cunliffe Gosling (15), George Cotterill (65), Frederick Spiksley (75, 80), John Reynolds (86) / William Sellar (20, 47)

51. 24.03.1894   Home Championship
SCOTLAND v WALES 5-2 (2-2)

Rugby Park, Kilmarnock

Referee: Joseph McBride (Ireland)   Attendance: 10,000

SCOTLAND: Andrew Baird, David Crawford, Robert Foyers, Edward McBain, James Kelly (Cap), John Johnstone, Andrew Stewart, Thomas Chambers, David Alexander, Davidson Berry, John Barker.

WALES: Samuel Gladstone Gillam, Oliver David Shepston Taylor, Abel Hughes, George Williams, Thomas Chapman, Thomas Worthington, Hugh Morris, Benjamin Lewis, William Lewis, John Charles Rea, Edwin James.

Goals: Davidson Berry (42), John Barker (44), Thomas Chambers (70), David Alexander (#), John Johnstone (#) / Hugh Morris (#, #)

52. 31.03.1894   Home Championship
IRELAND v SCOTLAND 1-2 (0-2)

Solitude Ground, Belfast

Referee: Edward Phennah (Wales)   Attendance: 6,000

IRELAND: Thomas Scott, Robert K. Stewart, Samuel Torrans, Nathaniel McKeown, John Burnett, Robert G. Milne, William Dalton, George Gaffikin, Olphert M. Stanfield, William Kennedy Gibson, James H. Barron.

SCOTLAND: Francis Barrett, David Crawford, John Drummond, Robert W. Marshall (Cap), William Longair, David Stewart, John Daniel Taylor, James Blessington, David Alexander, Robert Scott, Alexander Lowson Keillor.

Goals: Olphert M. Stanfield (#) / Samuel Torrans (25 own goal), John Daniel Taylor (28)

53. 07.04.1894   Home Championship
SCOTLAND v ENGLAND 2-2 (1-1)

Celtic Park, Glasgow

Referee: John Reid (Ireland)   Attendance: 45,107

SCOTLAND: David Haddow, Donald Currie Sillars, Daniel Doyle (Cap), Isaac Begbie, Andrew McCreadie, David Mitchell, William Gulliland, James Blessington, Alexander McMahon, John "Kitey" McPherson, William Allan Lambie.

ENGLAND: Leslie Hewitt Gay, Thomas Clare, Frederick Raymond Pelly, John Reynolds, John Holt, Ernest Needham, William Isaiah Bassett, Gilbert Oswald Smith, John Goodall (Cap), Edgar Wallace Chadwick, Frederick Spiksley.

Goals: William Allan Lambie (7), Alexander McMahon (75) / John Goodall (35), John Reynolds (85)

54. 23.03.1895   Home Championship
WALES v SCOTLAND 2-2 (1-2)

The Racecourse, Wrexham

Referee: William H. Jope (England)   Attendance: 4,000

WALES: Samuel Jones II, Robert Arthur Lloyd, Charles Frederick Parry, George Williams, Thomas Chapman, John Leonard Jones, Joseph Davies II, Benjamin Lewis, Harry Manager, William Lewis, John Charles Rea.

SCOTLAND: Francis Barrett, Donald Currie Sillars (Cap), Robert Glen, James Simpson, William McColl, Alexander Lowson Keillor, John H. Fyfe, John Murray, John Madden, William Sawers, John Divers.

Goals: William Lewis (#), Thomas Chapman (#) / John Madden (30), John Divers (39)

55. 30.03.1895   Home Championship
SCOTLAND v IRELAND 3-1 (1-1)

Celtic Park, Glasgow

Referee: T.B. Mitchell (England)   Attendance: 15,000

SCOTLAND: Daniel McArthur, John Drummond (Cap), Daniel Doyle, James Simpson, David Kennedy Russell, Neil Gibson, John Daniel Taylor, Thomas Smith Waddell, John "Kitey" McPherson, John Walker, William Allan Lambie.

IRELAND: Thomas Scott, Joseph Ponsonby, Lewis Irwin Scott, Hymie McKie, Thomas E. Alexander, Thomas McClatchey, Thomas Morrison, William Sherrard, Olphert M. Stanfield, William Kennedy Gibson, James H. Barron.

Goals: William Allan Lambie (1), John Walker (#, #) / William Sherrard (#)

56. 06.04.1895   Home Championship
ENGLAND v SCOTLAND 3-0 (3-0)

Goodison Park, Liverpool

Referee: John Reid (Ireland)   Attendance: 42,500

ENGLAND: John William Sutcliffe, James William Crabtree, Lewis Vaughn Lodge, Ernest Needham, John Holt, John Reynolds, Robert Cunliffe Gosling, Stephen Smith, John Goodall (Cap), William Isaiah Bassett, Stephen Bloomer.

SCOTLAND: Daniel McArthur, John Drummond, Daniel Doyle, David Kennedy Russell, James Simpson, Neil Gibson, William Allan Lambie, John "Kitey" McPherson, James Oswald (Cap), Thomas Smith Waddell, William Gulliland.

Goals: Stephen Bloomer (30), Neil Gibson (35 own goal), Stephen Smith (44)

57. 21.03.1896   Home Championship
SCOTLAND v WALES 4-0 (2-0)

Carolina Port, Dundee

Referee: Joseph McBride (Ireland)   Attendance: 11,700

SCOTLAND: Robert MacFarlane, Duncan McLean, Robert Glen, John Gillespie (Cap), Robert G. Neil, William Blair, Willliam Thomson, Daniel John Ferguson Paton, Robert Smyth McColl, Alexander King, Alexander Lowson Keillor.

WALES: James Manager, Charles Frederick Parry, John Samuel Matthias, Joseph P. Rogers, Caesar August Llewelyn Jenkyns, John Leonard Jones, David Henry Pugh, John Garner, Arthur Grenville Morris, John Charles Rea, William Lewis.

Goals: Robert G. Neil (#, #), Alexander Lowson Keillor (#), Daniel John Ferguson Paton (#)

58. 28.03.1896   Home Championship
IRELAND v SCOTLAND 3-3 (3-2)

Solitude Ground, Belfast

Referee: James Cooper (England)   Attendance: 8,000

IRELAND: Thomas Scott, Joseph Ponsonby, Samuel Torrans, Hugh Gordon, Robert G. Milne, James C. Fitzpatrick, Giddy Baird, E. Morrogh, Olphert M. Stanfield, James H. Barron, John Peden.

SCOTLAND: Kenneth Anderson, Peter Meechan, John Drummond, Neil Gibson, James Kelly (Cap), George Hogg, Patrick Murray, James Blessington, Robert Smyth McColl, John Cameron, William Allan Lambie.

Goals: James H. Barron (#, #), Robert G. Milne (43 pen) / Robert Smyth McColl (7, 25), Patrick Murray (78)

59. 04.04.1896   Home Championship
SCOTLAND v ENGLAND 2-1 (2-0)

Celtic Park, Glasgow

Referee: Humphrey Percy Jones (Wales)   Att: 56,500

SCOTLAND: John Edward Doig, John Drummond (Cap), Thomas Brandon, George Hogg, James Cowan, Neil Gibson, Alexander King, William Allan Lambie, Thomas Hyslop, James Blessington, John Bell.

ENGLAND: George Berkeley Raikes, Lewis Vaughn Lodge, William John Oakley, James William Crabtree, Thomas Henry Crawshaw, Arthur George Henfrey, John Goodall, William Isaiah Bassett, Gilbert Oswald Smith (Cap), Harry Wood, Cuthbert James Burnup.

Goals: William Allan Lambie (22), John Bell (33) / William Isaiah Bassett (80)

60. 20.03.1897   Home Championship
WALES v SCOTLAND 2-2 (1-1)

The Racecourse, Wrexham

Referee: Thomas Armitt (England)   Attendance: 5,000

WALES: James Manager, William Roberts Jones, John Samuel Matthias, Sydney Darvell, John Mates, John Leonard Jones, William Henry Meredith, David Henry Pugh, Morgan Maddox Morgan-Owen, John Charles Rea, William Lewis.

SCOTLAND: John Patrick, John L. Ritchie (Cap), David Richmond Gardner, Bernard Breslin, David Kennedy Russell, Alexander Lowson Keillor, John Kennedy, Patrick Murray, James Oswald, J. McMillan, John Walker.

Goals: Morgan Maddox Morgan-Owen (40), David Pugh (#) / John L. Ritchie (11 pen), John Walker (#)

61.   27.03.1897   Home Championship
SCOTLAND v IRELAND 5-1 (4-0)

Ibrox Park, Glasgow

Referee: James Cooper (England)   Attendance: 15,000

SCOTLAND: Matthew Dickie, Duncan McLean, John Drummond (Cap), Neil Gibson, William Urquhart Baird, David Stewart, Thomas Pollock Low, John "Kitey" McPherson, Robert Smyth McColl, Alexander King, William Allan Lambie.

IRELAND: James Thompson, Joseph Ponsonby, Samuel Torrans, John S. Pyper, Robert G. Milne, George McMaster, James Campbell, Olphert M. Stanfield, James Pyper, John Darling, John Peden.

Goals: John "Kitey" McPherson (#, #), Neil Gibson (#), Robert Smyth McColl (#), Alexander King (#) / James Pyper (#)

62.   03.04.1897   Home Championship
ENGLAND v SCOTLAND 1-2 (1-1)

Crystal Palace, London

Referee: Richard Thomas Gough (Wales)   Att: 37,000

ENGLAND: John William Robinson, William John Oakley, Howard Spencer, John Reynolds, Thomas Henry Crawshaw, Ernest Needham, William Charles Athersmith, Stephen Bloomer, Gilbert Oswald Smith (Cap), Edgar Wallace Chadwick, Alfred Weatherell Milward.

SCOTLAND: John Patrick, Nicol Smith, Daniel Doyle, Neil Gibson, James Cowan, Hugh Wilson, John Bell, James Millar, George Horsburgh Allan, Thomas Hyslop, William Allan Lambie (Cap).

Goals: Stephen Bloomer (19) / Thomas Hyslop (27), James Millar (83)

63.   19.03.1898   Home Championship
SCOTLAND v WALES 5-2 (4-1)

Fir Park, Motherwell

Referee: William H. Stacey (England)   Attendance: 3,500

SCOTLAND: W. Watson, Nicol Smith, Matthew McLintock Scott (Cap), William Thomson, Alexander John Christie, Peter Campbell, James Gillespie, James Millar, James McKie, Hugh Morgan, Robert Findlay.

WALES: James Manager, Charles Frederick Parry, David Jones, Richard Jones I, Caesar August Llewelyn Jenkyns, John Leonard Jones, Edwin James, Thomas John Thomas, Morgan Maddox Morgan-Owen, Arthur Grenville Morris, Alfred Ernest Watkins.

Goals: James Gillespie (12, #, #), James McKie (#, 40) / Thomas John Thomas (44), Morgan Morgan-Owen (#)

64.   26.03.1898   Home Championship
IRELAND v SCOTLAND 0-3 (0-2)

Solitude Ground, Belfast

Referee: John Lewis (England)   Attendance: 5,000

IRELAND: Thomas Scott, William Kennedy Gibson, Samuel Torrans, William Anderson, Robert G. Milne, Michael Cochrane, James Campbell, John Thompson Mercer, James Pyper, James McCashin, John Peden.

SCOTLAND: Kenneth Anderson, Robert Robinson Kelso (Cap), Daniel Doyle, William Thomson, David Kennedy Russell, Alexander King, William Graham Stewart, John Campbell, Robert Smyth McColl, John Walker, Thomas Robertson.

Goals: Thomas Robertson (30), Robert Smyth McColl (42), William Graham Stewart (70)

65.   02.04.1898   Home Championship
SCOTLAND v ENGLAND 1-3 (0-2)

Celtic Park, Glasgow

Referee: Thomas Robertson (Scotland)   Attendance: 40,000

SCOTLAND: Kenneth Anderson, John Drummond, Daniel Doyle, Neil Gibson, James Cowan (Cap), John Tait Robertson, John Bell, John Campbell, William Sturrock Maxwell, James Millar, Alexander Smith.

ENGLAND: John William Robinson, William Williams, William John Oakley, Ernest Needham, Charles Wreford-Brown, Frank Forman, Frederick Spiksley, George Frederick Wheldon, Gilbert Oswald Smith (Cap), Stephen Bloomer, William Charles Athersmith.

Goals: James Millar (48) / George Frederick Wheldon (3), Stephen Bloomer (23, 72)

66.   18.03.1899   Home Championship
WALES v SCOTLAND 0-6 (0-1)

The Racecourse, Wrexham

Referee: Charles E. Sutcliffe (England)   Attendance: 12,000

WALES: James Manager, John Samuel Matthias, Horace Elford Blew, George Richards, John Leonard Jones, Edward Hughes, Frederick Charles Kelly, Trevor Owen, Morgan Maddox Morgan-Owen, Ralph Stanley Jones, Arthur Grenville Morris.

SCOTLAND: Daniel McArthur, Nicol Smith (Cap), David Storrier, Neil Gibson, Henry James Hall Marshall, Alexander King, John Campbell, Robert Cumming Hamilton, Robert Smyth McColl, John Bell, Davidson Berry.

Goals: John Campbell (22, #), Robert Smyth McColl (50, #, #), Henry James Hall Marshall (#)

67. 25.03.1899   Home Championship
SCOTLAND v IRELAND 9-1 (5-0)

Celtic Park, Glasgow

Referee: Charles E. Sutcliffe (England)   Attendance: 11,000

SCOTLAND: Matthew Dickie, Nicol Smith, David Storrier (Cap), Neil Gibson, Alexander John Christie, Alexander King, John Campbell, Robert Cumming Hamilton, Robert Smyth McColl, Davidson Berry, John Bell.

IRELAND: James Lewis, Samuel Swan, Thomas A. Foreman, William Anderson, Archibald L. Goodall, John McShane, Dr. George F. Sheehan, James Meldon, James Pyper, James McCashin, Joseph McAllen.

Goals: Robert Smyth McColl (5, #, 47), Alexander Christie (#), Robert Cumming Hamilton (#, #), John Bell (#), John Campbell (#, #) / Archibald L. Goodall (#)

68. 08.04.1899   Home Championship
ENGLAND v SCOTLAND 2-1 (2-0)

Villa Park, Birmingham

Referee: James Torrans (Ireland)   Attendance: 25,590

ENGLAND: John William Robinson, Henry Thickett, James William Crabtree, Frank Forman, Rabbi Howell, Ernest Needham, William Charles Athersmith, Stephen Bloomer, Gilbert Oswald Smith (Cap), James Settle, Frederick Ralph Forman.

SCOTLAND: John Edward Doig, Nicol Smith (Cap), David Storrier, Neil Gibson, Alexander John Christie, John Tait Robertson, John Campbell, Robert Cumming Hamilton, Robert Smyth McColl, Hugh Morgan, John Bell.

Goal: Gilbert Oswald Smith (25), James Settle (40) / Robert Cumming Hamilton (52)

69. 03.02.1900   Home Championship
SCOTLAND v WALES 5-2 (4-1)

Pittodrie Park, Aberdeen

Referee: Charles E. Sutcliffe (England)   Attendance: 12,500

SCOTLAND: Matthew Dickie, Nicol Smith, David Crawford, James Hay Irons, Robert G. Neil, John Tait Robertson, John Bell, David Wilson, Robert Smyth McColl, Robert Cumming Hamilton (Cap), Alexander Smith.

WALES: Frederick John Griffiths, Charles Edward Thomas, Charles Richard Morris, Samuel Meredith, John Leonard Jones, William Clare Harrison, David Henry Pugh, William Thomas Butler, Richard Jones II, Thomas David Parry, Alfred Ernest Watkins.

Goals: John Bell (2), David Wilson (7, 35), Robert Cumming Hamilton (37), Alexander Smith (60) / Thomas David Parry (44), William Thomas Butler (52)

70. 03.03.1900   Home Championship
IRELAND v SCOTLAND 0-3 (0-2)

Solitude Ground, Belfast

Referee: Charles E. Sutcliffe (England)   Attendance: 6,000

IRELAND: James Lewis, John S. Pyper, Michael Cochrane, John McShane, H. Barry, Hugh Maginnis, James Campbell, John Darling, Patrick McAuley, Joseph McAllen, Alfred Kearns.

SCOTLAND: Henry George Rennie, Nicol Smith, Robert Glen, Neil Gibson, Henry James Hall Marshall (Cap), William Orr, William Graham Stewart, Robert Walker, John Campbell, Patrick Callaghan, Alexander Smith.

Goals: John Campbell (8, 83), Alexander Smith (23)

71. 07.04.1900   Home Championship
SCOTLAND v ENGLAND 4-1 (4-1)

Celtic Park, Glasgow

Referee: James Torrans (Ireland)   Attendance: 64,000

ENGLAND: John William Robinson, William John Oakley, James William Crabtree, William Harrison Johnson, Arthur Chadwick, Ernest Needham, William Charles Athersmith, Stephen Bloomer, Gilbert Oswald Smith (Cap), George Plumpton Wilson, John Plant.

SCOTLAND: Henry George Rennie, Nicol Smith, John Drummond, Neil Gibson, Alexander Galloway Raisbeck, John Tait Robertson (Cap), John Bell, Robert Walker, Robert Smyth McColl, John Campbell, Alexander Smith.

Goals: Robert Smyth McColl (1, 25, 44), John Bell (6) / Stephen Bloomer (35)

72. 23.02.1901   Home Championship
SCOTLAND v IRELAND 11-0 (5-0)

Celtic Park, Glasgow

Referee: Richard Thomas Gough (Wales)   Att: 15,000

SCOTLAND: George Chappell McWattie, Nicol Smith, Bernard Battles, David Kennedy Russell, George Anderson, John Tait Robertson, John Campbell, John Campbell, Robert Cumming Hamilton (Cap), Alexander McMahon, Alexander Smith.

IRELAND: Samuel McAlpine, William Kennedy Gibson, Samuel Torrans, Patrick Farrell I, James Connor, Michael Cochrane, James E. Scott, James Smith, James Campbell, Harry O'Reilly, Robert Clarke.

Goals: Alexander McMahon (6, #, #, #), David Kennedy Russell (#), John Campbell (30, #), Robert Cumming Hamilton (#, #, #, #)

73. 02.03.1901   Home Championship
WALES v SCOTLAND 1-1 (0-0)
The Racecourse, Wrexham

Referee: Charles E. Sutcliffe (England)   Attendance: 5,000

WALES: Leigh Richmond Roose, Samuel Meredith, Charles Richard Morris, Maurice Pryce Parry, William James Jones, Edward Hughes, David Henry Pugh, John Owen Jones, Morgan Maddox Morgan-Owen, Thomas David Parry, Ephrahim Williams.

SCOTLAND: George Chappell McWattie, Nicol Smith, Bernard Battles, Neil Gibson, David Kennedy Russell, John Tait Robertson (Cap), Mark Dickson Bell, Robert Walker, Robert Smyth McColl, John Campbell, Alexander Smith.

Goals: Thomas David Parry (70) / John Tait Robertson (74)

74. 30.03.1901   Home Championship
ENGLAND v SCOTLAND 2-2 (1-0)
Crystal Palace, London

Referee: James Torrans (Ireland)   Attendance: 18,520

ENGLAND: John William Sutcliffe, James Iremonger, William John Oakley, Albert Wilkes, Frank Forman, Ernest Needham, Walter Bennett, Stephen Bloomer, Gilbert Oswald Smith (Cap), Reginald Erskine Foster, Frederick Blackburn.

SCOTLAND: Henry George Rennie, Bernard Battles, John Drummond, Andrew Aitken, Alexander Galloway Raisbeck, John Tait Robertson (Cap), Robert Walker, John Campbell, Robert Smyth McColl, Robert Cumming Hamilton, Alexander Smith.

Goals: Frederick Blackburn (36), Stephen Bloomer (80) / John Campbell (48), Robert Cumming Hamilton (75)

75. 01.03.1902   Home Championship
IRELAND v SCOTLAND 1-5 (0-1)
Grosvenor Park, Belfast

Referee: Frederick Bye (England)   Attendance: 15,000

IRELAND: James V. Nolan-Whelan, William Kennedy Gibson, John S. Pyper, John Darling, Archibald L. Goodall, Robert G. Milne, James Campbell, Thomas Morrison, Andrew Gara, Alfred Kearns, Joseph McAllen.

SCOTLAND: Henry George Rennie, Nicol Smith, John Drummond, George Brown Key, Albert Thoroughgood Buick (Cap), John Tait Robertson, William McCartney, Robert Walker, Robert Cumming Hamilton, John Campbell, Alexander Smith.

Goals: Robert G. Milne (89) / Robert Cumming Hamilton (43, 70, 74), Robert Walker (49), Albert Thoroughgood Buick (76)

76. 15.03.1902   Home Championship
SCOTLAND v WALES 5-1 (1-0)
Cappielow Park, Greenock

Referee: Joseph McBride (Ireland)   Attendance: 5,284

SCOTLAND: Henry George Rennie, Henry Allan, John Drummond, Hugh Wilson, Albert Thoroughgood Buick, John Tait Robertson, John Campbell (Cap), Robert Walker, Robert Cumming Hamilton, Alexander McMahon, Alexander Smith.

WALES: Leigh Richmond Roose, Horace Elford Blew, Robert Morris, Maurice Pryce Parry, John Leonard Jones, William James Jones, William Henry Meredith, Llewelyn L. Griffiths, Hugh Morgan-Owen, Richard Morris, Joseph Owens.

Goals: Alexander Smith (#, #, 88), Albert Thoroughgood Buick (#), John Drummond (#) / Hugh Morgan-Owen (#)

77. 03.05.1902   Home Championship
ENGLAND v SCOTLAND 2-2 (0-2)
Villa Park, Birmingham

Referee: James Torrans (Ireland)   Attendance: 15,000

ENGLAND: William George, Robert Crompton, George Molyneux, Albert Wilkes, Frank Forman, Albert Edward Houlker, William Hogg, Stephen Bloomer (Cap), William Edwin Beats, James Settle, John Cox.

SCOTLAND: Henry George Rennie, Nicol Smith, John Drummond, Andrew Aitken (Cap), Alexander Galloway Raisbeck, John Tait Robertson, Robert Bryson Templeton, Robert Walker, Robert Smyth McColl, Ronald Orr, Alexander Smith.

Goals: James Settle (65), Albert Wilkes (67) / Robert Bryson Templeton (3), Ronald Orr (28)

78. 09.03.1903   Home Championship
WALES v SCOTLAND 0-1 (0-1)
Arms Park, Cardiff

Referee: Frederick Thomas Kirkham (England)   Att: 11,000

WALES: Robert Owen Evans, Horace Elford Blew, Charles Richard Morris, Maurice Pryce Parry, Morgan Maddox Morgan-Owen, Thomas Davies II, William Henry Meredith, Walter Martin Watkins, Arthur Grenville Morris, Richard Morris, Robert Atherton.

SCOTLAND: Henry George Rennie, Andrew McCombie, James Watson, Andrew Aitken, Alexander Galloway Raisbeck (Cap), John Tait Robertson, Robert Bryson Templeton, Robert Walker, John Campbell, Finlay Ballantyne Speedie, Alexander Smith.

Goal: Finlay Ballantyne Speedie (25)

79. 21.03.1903   Home Championship
SCOTLAND v IRELAND 0-2 (0-1)
Celtic Park, Glasgow

Referee: Frederick Thomas Kirkham (England)   Att: 17,000

SCOTLAND: Henry George Rennie, Archibald Colin Gray, John Drummond (Cap), John H. Cross, Peter Robertson, William Orr, David Lindsay, Robert Walker, William Porteous, Finlay Ballantyne Speedie, Alexander Smith.

IRELAND: William Scott, Alexander McCartney, Peter Boyle, John Darling, Robert G. Milne, Hugh Maginnis, John Thompson Mercer, James Sheridan, Maurice Joseph Connor, Thomas Shanks, John Henry Kirwan.

Goals: Maurice Joseph Connor (9), John Henry Kirwan (83)

80. 04.04.1903   Home Championship
ENGLAND v SCOTLAND 1-2 (1-0)
Bramall Lane, Sheffield

Referee: William Nunnerley (Wales)   Attendance: 32,000

ENGLAND: Thomas Baddeley, Robert Crompton (Cap), George Molyneux, William Harrison Johnson, Thomas Edward Booth, Albert Edward Houlker, Harry Davis, Percy Humphreys, Vivian John Woodward, Arthur John Capes, John Cox.

SCOTLAND: John Edward Doig, Andrew McCombie, James Watson, Andrew Aitken, Alexander Galloway Raisbeck (Cap), John Tait Robertson, Robert Bryson Templeton, Robert Walker, Robert Cumming Hamilton, Finlay Ballantyne Speedie, Alexander Smith.

Goals: Vivian John Woodward (10) / Finlay Ballantyne Speedie (57), Robert Walker (59)

81. 12.03.1904   Home Championship
SCOTLAND v WALES 1-1 (1-0)
Dens Park, Dundee

Referee: Frederick Thomas Kirkham (England)   Att: 12,000

SCOTLAND: Dr.Leslie Henderson Skene, Thomas Alexander Skinner Jackson, James Sharp (Cap), William Orr, Thomas Parker Sloan, John Tait Robertson, John Walker, Robert Walker, Alexander Bennett, Alexander MacFarlane, George W. Wilson.

WALES: David Davies, Horace Elford Blew, Thomas Davies II, George Richards, Edward Hughes, John Leonard Jones, Arthur Davies, Walter Martin Watkins, Arthur William Green, Richard Morris, Robert Atherton.

Goals: Robert Walker (5) / Robert Atherton (65)

82. 26.03.1904   Home Championship
IRELAND v SCOTLAND 1-1 (0-1)
Dalymount Park, Dublin

Referee: Frederick Thomas Kirkham (England)   Att: 1,000

SCOTLAND: Henry George Rennie, Thomas Alexander Skinner Jackson, John Cameron, George Hunter Henderson, Charles Bellany Thomson, John Tait Robertson (Cap), John Walker, Robert Walker, Robert Cumming Hamilton, Hugh Wilson, Alexander Smith.

IRELAND: William Scott, William R. McCracken, Alexander McCartney, James English McConnell, Robert G. Milne, Hugh Maginnis, James Campbell, James Sheridan, Harry O'Reilly, Harold Alexander Sloan, John Henry Kirwan.

Goals: James Sheridan (74) / Robert Cumming Hamilton (22)

83. 09.04.1904   Home Championship
SCOTLAND v ENGLAND 0-1 (0-0)
Celtic Park, Glasgow

Referee: William Nunnerley (Wales)   Attendance: 40,000

SCOTLAND: Peter McBride, Thomas Alexander Skinner Jackson, James Watson, Andrew Aitken, Alexander Galloway Raisbeck, John Tait Robertson (Cap), Thomas Bruce Niblo, Robert Walker, Alexander Brown, Ronald Orr, Robert Bryson Templeton.

ENGLAND: Thomas Baddeley, Robert Crompton (Cap), Herbert Burgess, Samuel Wolstenholme, Bernard Wilkinson, Alexander Leake, John Rutherford, Stephen Bloomer, Vivian John Woodward, Stanley Schute Harris, Frederick Blackburn.

Goal: Stephen Bloomer (64)

84. 06.03.1905   Home Championship
WALES v SCOTLAND 3-1 (1-0)
The Racecourse, Wrexham

Referee: Frederick Thomas Kirkham (England)   Att: 6,000

WALES: Leigh Richmond Roose, Horace Elford Blew, Charles Richard Morris, George Latham, Edward Hughes, John Hughes II, William Henry Meredith, Arthur Davies, Walter Martin Watkins, Arthur Grenville Morris, Alfred Oliver.

SCOTLAND: Henry George Rennie, Andrew McCombie, Thomas Alexander Skinner Jackson (Cap), Andrew Aitken, Charles Bellany Thomson, John Tait Robertson, Robert Bryson Templeton, Robert Walker, Samuel Watson Kennedy, Thomas Tindal Fitchie, Alexander Smith.

Goals: Walter Watkins (30), Arthur Grenville Morris (47), William Henry Meredith (76) / John Tait Robertson (86)

85. 18.03.1905   Home Championship
SCOTLAND v IRELAND 4-0 (2-0)
Celtic Park, Glasgow
Referee: Frederick Thomas Kirkham (England)   Att: 35,000
SCOTLAND: William Hay Howden, Donald McLeod, William McIntosh, Neil Gibson (Cap), Charles Bellany Thomson, James Hay, James McMenemy, Robert Walker, James Quinn, Peter Somers, George W. Wilson.
IRELAND: William Scott, Alexander McCartney, William R. McCracken, John Darling, James Connor, James English McConnell, John Thompson Mercer, James Maxwell, Neill Murphy, Charles O'Hagan, John Henry Kirwan.
Goals: Charles Bellany Thomson (14 pen, 61 pen), Robert Walker (35), James Quinn (50).

86. 01.04.1905   Home Championship
ENGLAND v SCOTLAND 1-0 (0-0)
Crystal Palace, London
Referee: William Nunnerley (Wales)   Attendance: 27,559
ENGLAND: James Henry Linacre, Howard Spencer (Cap), Herbert Smith, Herod Ruddlesdin, Charles Roberts, Alexander Leake, John Sharp, Stephen Bloomer, Vivian John Woodward, Joseph William Bache, George Arthur Bridgett.
SCOTLAND: John Lyall, Andrew McCombie, James Watson, Andrew Aitken, Charles Bellany Thomson (Cap), Peter McWilliam, Robert Walker, James Howie, Alexander Simpson Young, Peter Somers, George W. Wilson.
Goal: Joseph William Bache (80).

87. 03.03.1906   Home Championship
SCOTLAND v WALES 0-2 (0-0)
Tynecastle Park, Edinburgh
Referee: John Lewis (England)   Attendance: 25,000
SCOTLAND: James Smith Raeside, Donald McLeod, Andrew Richmond, Alexander McNair, Charles Bellany Thomson (Cap), John May, George Stewart, Alexander MacFarlane, James Quinn, Thomas Tindal Fitchie, George W. Wilson.
WALES: Leigh Richmond Roose, Horace Elford Blew, Charles Richard Morris, Edwin Hughes, Morgan Maddox Morgan-Owen, George Latham, William L. Jones, Richard Morris, John "Love" Jones, Richard Jones III, Robert Ernest Evans.
Goals: William L. Jones (50), John "Love" Jones (65)

88. 17.03.1906   Home Championship
IRELAND v SCOTLAND 0-1 (0-0)
Dalymount Park, Dublin
Referee: Frederick Bye (England)   Attendance: 8,000
IRELAND: Frederick W. McKee, George Willis, John Darling, John Wright, Robert G. Milne, Joseph J. Ledwige, Andrew Hunter I, Thomas Stephen Mulholland, Thomas M.R. Waddell, Charles O'Hagan, John Henry Kirwan.
SCOTLAND: Henry George Rennie, Donald McLeod, David Alexander Hill, James S. Young, Charles Bellany Thomson (Cap), John May, Gladstone Hamilton, Robert Walker, James Quinn, Thomas Tindal Fitchie, Alexander Smith.
Goal: Thomas Tindal Fitchie (52).

89. 07.04.1906   Home Championship
SCOTLAND v ENGLAND 2-1 (1-0)
Hampden Park, Glasgow
Referee: William Nunnerley (Wales)   Attendance: 102,741
SCOTLAND: Peter McBride, Donald McLeod, William T. Dunlop, Andrew Aitken, Alexander Galloway Raisbeck (Cap), Peter McWilliam, George Stewart, James Howie, Alexander William Menzies, George Turner Livingstone, Alexander Smith.
ENGLAND: James Ashcroft, Robert Crompton, Herbert Burgess, Benjamin Warren, Colin Campbell McKechnie Veitch, Joseph William Harry Makepeace, Richard Bond, Samuel Hulme Day, Albert Shepherd, Stanley Schute Harris (Cap), James Conlin.
Goals: James Howie (40, 55) / Albert Shepherd (81)

90. 04.03.1907   Home Championship
WALES v SCOTLAND 1-0 (0-0)
The Racecourse, Wrexham
Referee: James Mason (England)   Attendance: 7,715
WALES: Leigh Richmond Roose, Horace Elford Blew, Charles Richard Morris, George Latham, Lloyd Davies, Ioan Haydn Price, William Henry Meredith, William L. Jones, Hugh Morgan-Owen, Arthur Grenville Morris, Gordon Peace Jones.
SCOTLAND: Peter McBride, Thomas Alexander Skinner Jackson, James Sharp, Andrew Aitken, Charles Bellany Thomson (Cap), Peter McWilliam, George Stewart, George Turner Livingstone, Alexander Simpson Young, Thomas Tindal Fitchie, Alexander Smith.
Goal: Arthur Grenville Morris (50)

91. 16.03.1907 Home Championship
SCOTLAND v IRELAND 3-0 (1-0)
Celtic Park, Glasgow
Referee: John Lewis (England)   Attendance: 26,000
SCOTLAND: William Muir, Thomas Alexander Skinner Jackson, William Barbour Agnew, William Key, Charles Bellany Thomson (Cap), Alexander McNair, Alexander Bennett, Robert Walker, Frank O'Rourke, Peter Somers, John Fraser.
IRELAND: William Scott, George Willis, Alexander McCartney, John Wright, James Connor, George McClure, John Blair, James Maxwell, Edward McGuire, Charles O'Hagan, Samuel Young.
Goals: Frank O'Rourke (40), Robert Walker (48), Charles Bellany Thomson (82 pen)

92. 06.04.1907 Home Championship
ENGLAND v SCOTLAND 1-1 (1-1)
St. James´ Park, Newcastle
Referee: Thomas Robertson (Scotland)   Attendance: 35,829
ENGLAND: Samuel Hardy, Robert Crompton (Cap), Jesse Pennington, Benjamin Warren, William John Wedlock, Colin Campbell McKechnie Veitch, John Rutherford, Stephen Bloomer, Vivian John Woodward, James Stewart, Harold Payne Hardman.
SCOTLAND: Peter McBride, Charles Bellany Thomson, James Sharp, Andrew Aitken, Alexander Galloway Raisbeck (Cap), Peter McWilliam, George Stewart, Robert Walker, Andrew Wilson, Walter White, George W. Wilson.
Goals: Stephen Bloomer (42) / Robert Crompton (2 own goal)

93. 07.03.1908 Home Championship
SCOTLAND v WALES 2-1 (0-1)
Dens Park, Dundee
Referee: James Mason (England)   Attendance: 18,000
SCOTLAND: Henry George Rennie, William Barbour Agnew, George Duncan Chaplin, Alexander McNair, Charles Bellany Thomson (Cap), James Hill Galt, Alexander Bennett, Robert Walker, James Hamilton Speirs, Alexander MacFarlane, William Lennie.
WALES: Leigh Richmond Roose, Horace Elford Blew, Charles Richard Morris, Maurice Pryce Parry, Edwin Hughes, Lloyd Davies, William Charles Davies, William L. Jones, William Davies, Arthur William Green, Robert Ernest Evans.
Goals: Alexander Bennett (60), William Lennie (87) / William L. Jones (30)

94. 14.03.1908 Home Championship
IRELAND v SCOTLAND 0-5 (0-2)
Dalymount Park, Dublin
Referee: James Ibbotson (England)   Attendance: 9,000
IRELAND: William Scott, Alexander Craig, Alexander McCartney, Valentine Harris, James Connor, James English McConnell, John Blair, Denis J. Hannon, William Andrews, Charles O'Hagan, Samuel Young.
SCOTLAND: Henry George Rennie, James Mitchell, William Barbour Agnew, John May, Charles Bellany Thomson (Cap), James Hill Galt, Robert Bryson Templeton, Robert Walker, James Quinn, Robert Smyth McColl, William Lennie.
Goals: James Quinn (3, #, 70, 75), James Hill Galt (23)

95. 04.04.1908 Home Championship
SCOTLAND v ENGLAND 1-1 (1-0)
Hampden Park, Glasgow
Referee: James Mason (England)   Attendance: 121,452
SCOTLAND: Peter McBride, Alexander McNair, James Sharp, Andrew Aitken, Charles Bellany Thomson (Cap), John May, James Howie, Robert Walker, Andrew Wilson, Walter White, James Quinn.
ENGLAND: Samuel Hardy, Robert Crompton, Jesse Pennington, Benjamin Warren, William John Wedlock, Evelyn Henry Lintott, John Rutherford, Vivian John Woodward (Cap), George Richard Hilsdon, James Edward Windridge, George Arthur Bridgett.
Goals: Andrew Wilson (27) / James Edward Windridge (75)

96. 01.03.1909 Home Championship
WALES v SCOTLAND 3-2 (3-0)
The Racecourse, Wrexham
Referee: Thomas P. Campbell (England)   Attendance: 6,000
WALES: Leigh Richmond Roose, Horace Elford Blew, Charles Richard Morris, Maurice Pryce Parry, Ernest Peake, Ioan Haydn Price, William Henry Meredith, George Arthur Wynn, William Davies, William L. Jones, Robert Ernest Evans.
SCOTLAND: Peter McBride, Thomas Collins, James Sharp, John May, Charles Bellany Thomson (Cap), Peter McWilliam, Alexander Bennett, John Bryson Hunter, Robert Walker, Peter Somers, Harold McDonald Paul.
Goals: William Davies (25, 39), William L. Jones (29) / Robert Walker (70), Harold McDonald Paul (73)

97. 15.03.1909   Home Championship
SCOTLAND v IRELAND 5-0 (2-0)
Ibrox Park, Glasgow

Referee: James Mason (England)   Attendance: 24,000

SCOTLAND: James Brownlie, James Main, James Watson, William Walker, James Stark (Cap), James Hay, Alexander Bennett, James McMenemy, Alexander Thomson, Alexander MacFarlane, Harold McDonald Paul.

IRELAND: William Scott, Alexander Craig, Alexander McCartney, Valentine Harris, James English McConnell, Harold Alexander Sloan, Andrew Hunter I, William Lacey, William Greer, Charles G. Webb, John Henry Kirwan.

Goals: James McMenemy (15, 77), Alex. MacFarlane (20), Alexander Thomson (48), Harold McDonald Paul (84)

98. 03.04.1909   Home Championship
ENGLAND v SCOTLAND 2-0 (2-0)
Crystal Palace, London

Referee: James Stark (Scotland)   Attendance: 27,000

ENGLAND: Samuel Hardy, Robert Crompton (Cap), Jesse Pennington, Benjamin Warren, William John Wedlock, Evelyn Henry Lintott, Frederick Beaconsfield Pentland, Harold John Fleming, Bertram Clewley Freeman, George Henry Holley, George Wall.

SCOTLAND: James Brownlie, John Cameron, James Watson, Alexander McNair, James Stark (Cap), Peter McWilliam, Alexander Bennett, Robert Walker, James Quinn, George W. Wilson, Harold McDonald Paul.

Goals: George Wall (3, 10)

99. 05.03.1910   Home Championship
SCOTLAND v WALES 1-0 (0-0)
Rugby Park, Kilmarnock

Referee: Herbert S. Bamlett (England)   Attendance: 22,000

SCOTLAND: James Brownlie, George Law, James Mitchell, Alexander McNair, William Loney, James Hay (Cap), Alexander Bennett, James McMenemy, James Quinn, Andrew Devine, George Robertson.

WALES: Leigh Richmond Roose, Jeffrey Woodward Jones, Charles Richard Morris, Edwin Hughes, Ernest Peake, Llewelyn Davies, William Henry Meredith, William Charles Davies, Evan Jones, Arthur Grenville Morris, Robert Ernest Evans.

Goal: Andrew Devine (86)

100. 19.03.1910   Home Championship
IRELAND v SCOTLAND 1-0 (0-0)
Windsor Park, Belfast

Referee: John Thomas Howcroft (England)   Att: 18,000

IRELAND: William Scott, Samuel Burnison, P. McCann, Valentine Harris, James English McConnell, John Darling, William Thomas James Renneville, William Lacey, James M. Murray, John Murphy, Frank W. Thompson.

SCOTLAND: James Brownlie, George Law, James Mitchell, William Walker, William Loney, James Hay (Cap), George William Llyod Sinclair, John Kay McTavish, James Quinn, Alexander Higgins, Robert Bryson Templeton.

Goal: Frank W. Thompson (65)

101. 02.04.1910   Home Championship
SCOTLAND v ENGLAND 2-0 (2-0)
Hampden Park, Glasgow

Referee: James Mason (England)   Attendance: 106,205

SCOTLAND: James Brownlie, George Law, James Hay, Andrew Aitken, Charles Bellany Thomson (Cap), Peter McWilliam, Alexander Bennett, James McMenemy, James Quinn, Alexander Higgins, Robert Bryson Templeton.

ENGLAND: Samuel Hardy, Robert Crompton (Cap), Jesse Pennington, Andrew Ducat, William John Wedlock, Joseph William Harry Makepeace, Richard Bond, William Hibbert, John Parkinson, Harold Thomas Walter Hardinge, George Wall.

Goals: James McMenemy (20), James Quinn (32)

102. 06.03.1911   Home Championship
WALES v SCOTLAND 2-2 (1-1)
Ninian Park, Cardiff

Referee: James Mason (England)   Attendance: 14,000

WALES: Leigh Richmond Roose, Thomas John Hewitt, Charles Richard Morris, Edwin Hughes, Lloyd Davies, Llewelyn Davies, William Henry Meredith, Evan Jones, William Davies, Arthur Grenville Morris, Edward Thomas Vizard.

SCOTLAND: James Brownlie, Donald Cameron Colman, John Walker, Thomas Somerville Tait, Wilfrid Lawson Low, Peter McWilliam (Cap), Alexander Bennett, James McMenemy, William Reid, Alexander MacFarlane, Robert Cumming Hamilton.

Goals: Arthur Grenville Morris (20, 67) / Robert Cumming Hamilton (#, 89)

103. 18.03.1911   Home Championship
SCOTLAND v IRELAND 2-0 (1-0)
Celtic Park, Glasgow
Referee: Herbert S. Bamlett (England)   Attendance: 32,000
SCOTLAND: James Brownlie, Donald Cameron Colman, John Walker, Andrew Aitken (Cap), Charles Bellany Thomson, James Hay, Angus Douglas, James McMenemy, William Reid, Alexander Higgins, Alexander Smith.
IRELAND: William Scott, Samuel Burnison, Patrick McCann, Valentine Harris, James Connor, Henry Vernon Hampton, William Lacey, Denis J. Hannon, John McDonnell, Charles G. Webb, Thomas Walker.
Goals: William Reid (23), James McMenemy (53)

104. 01.04.1911   Home Championship
ENGLAND v SCOTLAND 1-1 (1-0)
Goodison Park, Liverpool
Referee: William Nunnerley (Wales)   Attendance: 38,000
ENGLAND: Reginald Garnet Williamson, Robert Crompton (Cap), Jesse Pennington, Benjamin Warren, William John Wedlock, Kenneth Reginald Gunnery Hunt, John Simpson, James Stewart, George William Webb, Joseph William Bache, Robert Ernest Evans.
SCOTLAND: James Lawrence, Donald Cameron Colman, John Walker, Andrew Aitken, Wilfrid Lawson Low, James Hay (Cap), Alexander Bennett, James McMenemy, William Reid, Alexander Higgins, Alexander Smith.
Goals: James Stewart (20) / Alexander Higgins (88)

105. 02.03.1912   Home Championship
SCOTLAND v WALES 1-0 (0-0)
Tynecastle Park, Edinburgh
Referee: James Mason (England)   Attendance: 32,000
SCOTLAND: James Brownlie, Alexander McNair, John Walker, Robert Mercer, Charles Bellany Thomson (Cap), James Hay, George William Llyod Sinclair, James McMenemy, James Quinn, Robert Walker, George Robertson.
WALES: Robert Owen Evans, Llewelyn Davies, Lloyd Davies, Joseph Thomas Jones, Edwin Hughes, Moses Richard Russell, William Henry Meredith, George Arthur Wynn, Evan Jones, James William Williams, Edward Thomas Vizard.
Goal: James Quinn (87)

106. 16.03.1912   Home Championship
IRELAND v SCOTLAND 1-4 (1-2)
Windsor Park, Belfast
Referee: Herbert S. Bamlett (England)   Attendance: 12,000
IRELAND: John Hanna, George Willis, Alexander Craig, John Darling, Patrick O'Connell, Joseph Moran, John Houston, James McKnight, James Lowry Macauley, Joseph Enright, Samuel Young.
SCOTLAND: James Brownlie, Alexander McNair (Cap), John Walker, James Eadie Gordon, Wilfrid Lawson Low, Alexander Bell, George William Llyod Sinclair, Robert Walker, William Reid, Walter Campbell Allison Aitkenhead, Robert Bryson Templeton.
Goals: James McKnight (42 pen) /
Walter Campbell Allison Aitkenhead (8, 23), William Reid (#), Robert Walker (#)

107. 23.03.1912   Home Championship
SCOTLAND v ENGLAND 1-1 (1-1)
Hampden Park, Glasgow
Referee: James Mason (England)   Attendance: 127,307
SCOTLAND: James Brownlie, Alexander McNair (Cap), John Walker, James Eadie Gordon, Charles Bellany Thomson, James Hay, Robert Bryson Templeton, Robert Walker, David Prophet McLean, Andrew Wilson, James Quinn.
ENGLAND: Reginald Garnet Williamson, Robert Crompton (Cap), Jesse Pennington, James Thomas Brittleton, William John Wedlock, Joseph William Harry Makepeace, John Simpson, Frank Jefferis, Bertram Clewley Freeman, George Henry Holley, George Wall.
Goals: Andrew Wilson (7) / George Henry Holley (13)

108. 03.03.1913   Home Championship
WALES v SCOTLAND 0-0
The Racecourse, Wrexham
Referee: Isaac Baker (England)   Attendance: 8,000
WALES: William Ellis Bailiff, Thomas John Hewitt, Llewelyn Davies, Edwin Hughes, Lloyd Davies, William L. Jones, William Henry Meredith, George Arthur Wynn, Walter Otto Davis, James Roberts II, Edward Thomas Vizard.
SCOTLAND: James Brownlie, Robert Abbie Orrock, John Walker, James Eadie Gordon, Charles Bellany Thomson (Cap), James Campbell, Andrew McAtee, Robert Walker, William Reid, Andrew Wilson, Robert Bryson Templeton.

109. 15.03.1913   Home Championship
IRELAND v SCOTLAND 1-2 (1-2)
Dalymount Park, Dublin

Referee: Arthur Adams (England)   Attendance: 12,000

IRELAND: William Scott, William George McConnell, Peter Warren, William Andrews, Valentine Harris, Henry Vernon Hampton, John Houston, James McKnight, William Gillespie, James Lowry Macauley, Frank W. Thompson.

SCOTLAND: James Brownlie, Donald Cameron Colman (Cap), John Walker, Robert Mercer, Thomas Logan, Peter Nellies, Alexander Bennett, James Eadie Gordon, William Reid, James Anderson Croal, George Robertson.

Goals: James McKnight (42) /
William Reid (16), Alexander Bennett (32)

110. 05.04.1913   Home Championship
ENGLAND v SCOTLAND 1-0 (1-0)
Stamford Bridge, London

Referee: Alexander Skinner Jackson (Scotland)   Att: 52,500

ENGLAND: Samuel Hardy, Robert Crompton (Cap), Jesse Pennington, James Thomas Brittleton, Joseph McCall, William Watson, John Simpson, Harold John Fleming, Joseph Harold Hampton, George Henry Holley, Joseph Charles Hodkinson.

SCOTLAND: James Brownlie, Alexander McNair, John Walker, James Eadie Gordon, Charles Bellany Thomson (Cap), David Wilson, Joseph Donnachie, Robert Walker, William Reid, Andrew Wilson, George Robertson.

Goal: Joseph Harold Hampton (37)

111. 28.02.1914   Home Championship
SCOTLAND v WALES 0-0
Celtic Park, Glasgow

Referee: Harold H. Taylor (England)   Attendance: 10,000

SCOTLAND: James Brownlie, Thomas Kelso, Joseph Dodds, Peter Nellies (Cap), Peter Pursell, Harold A. Anderson, Alexander Pollock Donaldson, James McMenemy, James Greig Reid, James Anderson Croal, J. Browning.

WALES: Edward John Peers, Thomas John Hewitt, William Jennings, Thomas James Matthias, Lloyd Davies, Joseph Thomas Jones, William Henry Meredith, George Arthur Wynn, Walter Otto Davis, William L. Jones, John Hugh Evans.

112. 14.03.1914   Home Championship
IRELAND v SCOTLAND 1-1 (0-0)
Windsor Park, Belfast

Referee: Herbert S. Bamlett (England)   Attendance: 31,000

IRELAND: Frederick W. McKee, William George McConnell, Alexander Craig, Valentine Harris, Patrick O'Connell, Michael Hamill, John Houston, Robert Nixon, Samuel Young, William Lacey, Frank W. Thompson.

SCOTLAND: James Brownlie, Joseph Dodds, Alexander McNair (Cap), James Eadie Gordon, Charles Bellany Thomson, James Hay, Alexander Pollock Donaldson, James McMenemy, William Reid, Andrew Wilson, Joseph Donnachie.

Goals: Samuel Young (89) / Joseph Donnachie (70)

113. 04.04.1914   Home Championship
SCOTLAND v ENGLAND 3-1 (1-1)
Hampden Park, Glasgow

Referee: Herbert S. Bamlett (England)   Attendance: 105,000

SCOTLAND: James Brownlie, Alexander McNair, Joseph Dodds, James Eadie Gordon (Cap), Charles Bellany Thomson, James Hay, Alexander Pollock Donaldson, James McMenemy, William Reid, James Anderson Croal, Joseph Donnachie.

ENGLAND: Samuel Hardy, Robert Crompton (Cap), Jesse Pennington, Albert Sturgess, Joseph McCall, Robert McNeal, Frederick Ingram Walden, Harold John Fleming, Joseph Harold Hampton, Joseph Smith I, Edwin Mosscrop.

Goals: Charles Bellany Thomson (2), James McMenemy (50), William Reid (67) / Harold John Fleming (15)

114. 26.02.1920   Home Championship
WALES v SCOTLAND 1-1 (1-0)
Ninian Park, Cardiff

Referee: James Mason (England)   Attendance: 16,000

WALES: Edward John Peers, Harold Millership, Moses Richard Russell, Thomas James Matthias, Joseph Thomas Jones, William Jennings, William Henry Meredith, Ivor Jones, Stanley Charles Davies, Richard William Richards, John Hugh Evans.

SCOTLAND: Kenneth Campbell, Alexander McNair, David Thomson, James Eadie Gordon, William Cringan (Cap), James McMullan, James Greig Reid, John Anderson Crosbie, Andrew Nesbit Wilson, Thomas Cairns, Alan Lauder Morton.

Goals: John Hugh Evans (5) / Thomas Cairns (78)

115. 13.03.1920   Home Championship
SCOTLAND v IRELAND 3-0 (2-0)

Celtic Park, Glasgow

Referee: James Mason (England)   Attendance: 39,757

SCOTLAND: Kenneth Campbell, Alexander McNair (Cap), James Blair, James Bowie, Wilfrid Lawson Low, James Eadie Gordon, Alexander Pollock Donaldson, James McMenemy, Andrew Nesbit Wilson, Andrew Cunningham, Alan Lauder Morton.

IRELAND: Elisha Scott, Robert B. Manderson, David Rollo, Michael Hamill, William Lacey, William Emerson, Patrick Robinson, Patrick Gallagher, Edward A. Brookes, William Gillespie, John McCandless.

Goals: Andrew Nesbit Wilson (8), Alan Lauder Morton (42), Andrew Cunningham (55)

116. 10.04.1920   Home Championship
ENGLAND v SCOTLAND 5-4 (2-4)

Hillsborough, Sheffield

Referee: Thomas Dougray (Scotland)   Attendance: 35,000

ENGLAND: Samuel Hardy, Ephraim Longworth, Jesse Pennington (Cap), Andrew Ducat, Joseph McCall, Arthur Grimsdell, Charles William Wallace, Robert Kelly, John Gilbert Cock, Frederick Morris, Alfred Edward Quantrill.

SCOTLAND: Kenneth Campbell, Alexander McNair (Cap), James Blair, James Bowie, Wilfrid Lawson Low, James Eadie Gordon, Alexander Pollock Donaldson, Thomas Miller, Andrew Nesbit Wilson, John Paterson, Alexander Troup.

Goals: John Gilbert Cock (9), Alfred Edward Quantrill (15), Robert Kelly (57, 73), Frederick Morris (67) /
Thomas Miller (13, 40), Andrew Nesbit Wilson (21), Alexander Pollock Donaldson (31)

117. 12.02.1921   Home Championship
SCOTLAND v WALES 2-1 (1-1)

Pittodrie, Aberdeen

Referee: James Mason (England)   Attendance: 20,824

SCOTLAND: Kenneth Campbell (Cap), John Marshall, William McStay, Joseph Harris, Charles Ross Pringle, James McMullan, Alexander Archibald, Andrew Cunningham, Andrew Nesbit Wilson, Joseph Cassidy, Alexander Troup.

WALES: Edward John Peers, Harold Millership, Moses Richard Russell, Frederick Charles Keenor, Joseph Thomas Jones, Thomas James Matthias, David R. Williams, David Collier, Francis Hoddinott, Stanley Charles Davies, Edward Thomas Vizard.

Goals: Andrew Nesbit Wilson (10, 46) / David Collier (30)

118. 26.02.1921   Home Championship
IRELAND v SCOTLAND 0-2 (0-1)

Windsor Park, Belfast

Referee: Arthur Ward (England)   Attendance: 35,000

IRELAND: Elisha Scott, James Mulligan, David Rollo, William Lacey, Ernest Edwin Smith, Michael Terence O'Brien, Samuel McGregor, James Ferris, Daniel McKinney, Michael Hamill, Louis J.O Bookman.

SCOTLAND: Kenneth Campbell, John Marshall, William McStay, Joseph Harris, John Alexander Graham, James McMullan, Alexander McNab, Thomas Miller, Andrew Nesbit Wilson (Cap), Joseph Cassidy, Alexander Troup.

Goals: Andrew Nesbit Wilson (11 pen), Joseph Cassidy (89)

119. 09.04.1921   Home Championship
SCOTLAND v ENGLAND 3-0 (1-0)

Hampden Park, Glasgow

Referee: Arthur Ward (England)   Attendance: 85,000

SCOTLAND: John Ewart, John Marshall (Cap), James Blair, Stewart Davidson, George Brewster, James McMullan, Alexander McNab, Thomas Miller, Andrew Nesbit Wilson, Andrew Cunningham, Alan Lauder Morton.

ENGLAND: Harold Gough, Thomas Smart, John Silcock, Bertram Smith, George Wilson, Arthur Grimsdell (Cap), Samuel Chedgzoy, Robert Kelly, Henry Chambers, Herbert Bliss, James Henry Dimmock.

Goals: Andrew Nesbit Wilson (20), Alan Lauder Morton (46), Andrew Cunningham (57)

120. 04.02.1922   Home Championship
WALES v SCOTLAND 2-1 (2-0)

The Racecourse, Wrexham

Referee: Arthur Ward (England)   Attendance: 8,000

WALES: Edward John Peers, Edward Parry, James H. Evans, Herbert P. Evans, Joseph Thomas Jones, Thomas James Matthias, Stanley Charles Davies, Ivor Jones, Leonard S. Davies, Richard William Richards, Edward Thomas Vizard.

SCOTLAND: Kenneth Campbell, John Marshall (Cap), Donald McKinlay, David Ditchburn Meiklejohn, Michael Gilhooley, William Collier, Alexander Archibald, John White, Andrew Nesbit Wilson, Frank Walker, Alan Lauder Morton.

Goals: Leonard S. Davies (7), Stanley Charles Davies (25) / Alexander Archibald (65)

121. 04.03.1922   Home Championship
SCOTLAND v NORTHERN IRELAND 2-1 (0-1)
Celtic Park, Glasgow

Referee: Arthur Ward (England)   Attendance: 36,000

SCOTLAND: Kenneth Campbell, John Marshall, Donald McKinlay, James Hogg, William Cringan, Thomas Allan Muirhead, Alexander Pollock Donaldson, James D. Kinloch, Andrew Nesbit Wilson, Andrew Cunningham (Cap), Alexander Troup.

NORTHERN IRELAND: Francis Collins, William R. McCracken, William McCandless, Robert McCracken, Michael Terence O'Brien, William Emerson, William Lacey, Patrick Gallagher, Robert William Irvine, William Gillespie, David R. Lyner.

Goals: Andrew Nesbit Wilson (60, 83) / William Gillespie (42)

122. 08.04.1922   Home Championship
ENGLAND v SCOTLAND 0-1 (0-0)
Villa Park, Birmingham

Referee: Thomas Dougray (Scotland)   Attendance: 33,646

ENGLAND: Jeremiah Dawson, Thomas Clay, Samuel John Wadsworth, Frank Moss, George Wilson (Cap), Thomas George Bromilow, Richard Ernest York, Robert Kelly, William Ernest Rawlings, William Henry Walker, William Henry Smith.

SCOTLAND: Kenneth Campbell, John Marshall, James Blair (Cap), John Wotherspoon Gilchrist, William Cringan, Neil McBain, Alexander Archibald, John Anderson Crosbie, Andrew Nesbit Wilson, Thomas Cairns, Alan Lauder Morton.

Goal: Andrew Nesbit Wilson (63)

123. 03.03.1923   Home Championship
NORTHERN IRELAND v SCOTLAND 0-1 (0-0)
Windsor Park, Belfast

Referee: Arthur Ward (England)   Attendance: 30,000

NORTHERN IRELAND: Thomas J. Farquharson, William R. McCracken, John Joseph Curran, Samuel Johnstone Irving, George Moorehead, William Emerson, Hamilton McKenzie, Patrick Gallagher, George Hull Reid, William Gillespie, William Moore.

SCOTLAND: William Harper, John Hutton, James Blair (Cap), David Morton Steele, David Morris, Neil McBain, Alexander Archibald, John White, Andrew Nesbit Wilson, Joseph Cassidy, Alan Lauder Morton.

Goal: Andrew Nesbit Wilson (69)

124. 17.03.1923   Home Championship
SCOTLAND v WALES 2-0 (1-0)
Love Street, St.Mirren Park, Paisley

Referee: Isaac Baker (England)   Attendance: 25,000

SCOTLAND: William Harper, John Hutton, James Blair, John S. McNab, William Cringan (Cap), David Morton Steele, Henry McGill Ritchie, Andrew Cunningham, Andrew Nesbit Wilson, Thomas Cairns, Alan Lauder Morton.

WALES: George Godding, Moses Richard Russell, James H. Evans, Thomas James Matthias, Frederick Charles Keenor, Robert John, David R. Williams, Idwal Davies, Stanley Charles Davies, Leonard S. Davies, David Nicholas.

Goals: Andrew Nesbit Wilson (7, 55)

125. 14.04.1923   Home Championship
SCOTLAND v ENGLAND 2-2 (1-2)
Hampden Park, Glasgow

Referee: Arthur Ward (England)   Attendance: 71,000

SCOTLAND: William Harper, John Hutton, James Blair, David Morton Steele, William Cringan (Cap), Thomas Allan Muirhead, Denis Lawson, Andrew Cunningham, Andrew Nesbit Wilson, Thomas Cairns, Alan Lauder Morton.

ENGLAND: Edward Hallows Taylor, Ephraim Longworth, Samuel John Wadsworth, Frederick William Kean, George Wilson (Cap), John Tresadern, Samuel Chedgzoy, Robert Kelly, Victor Martin Watson, Henry Chambers, Frederick Edward Tunstall.

Goals: Andrew Cunningham (28), Andrew Wilson (55) / Robert Kelly (31), Victor Martin Watson (42)

126. 16.02.1924   Home Championship
WALES v SCOTLAND 2-0 (0-0)
Ninian Park, Cardiff

Referee: H.W. Andrews (England)   Attendance: 26,000

WALES: Albert Gray, Moses Richard Russell, John Jenkins, Herbert P. Evans, Frederick Charles Keenor, William Jennings, William Davies, Ivor Jones, Leonard S. Davies, Richard William Richards, Edward Thomas Vizard.

SCOTLAND: William Harper, John Marshall, James Blair (Cap), David Ditchburn Meiklejohn, Neil McBain, Thomas Allan Muirhead, Alexander Archibald, William Fraser Russell, Joseph Cassidy, John McKay, Alan Lauder Morton.

Goals: William Davies (61), Leonard S. Davies (72)

127. 01.03.1924   Home Championship
SCOTLAND v NORTHERN IRELAND   2-0 (0-0)
Celtic Park, Glasgow

Referee: George Noel Watson (England)   Att: 30,000

SCOTLAND: William Harper, John Hutton (Cap), James Hamilton, Peter Kerr, David Morris, James McMullan, James Greig Reid, Andrew Cunningham, Hugh Kilpatrick Gallacher, Thomas Cairns, Alan Lauder Morton.

NORTHERN IRELAND: Thomas J. Farquharson, David Rollo, William McCandless, Samuel Johnstone Irving, Michael Terence O'Brien, Francis Gerald Morgan, Daniel McKinney, Patrick Gallagher, Robert William Irvine, William Gillespie, John McGrillen.

Goals: Andrew Cunningham (85), David Morris (89)

128. 12.04.1924   Home Championship
ENGLAND v SCOTLAND   1-1 (0-1)
Wembley, London

Referee: Thomas Dougray (Scotland)   Attendance: 37,250

ENGLAND: Edward Hallows Taylor, Thomas Smart, Samuel John Wadsworth, Frank Moss (Cap), Charles William Spencer, Percival Henry Barton, William Butler, David Bone Nightingale Jack, Charles Murray Buchan, William Henry Walker, Frederick Edward Tunstall.

SCOTLAND: William Harper, John Smith, Philip McCloy, William Clunas, David Morris, James McMullan (Cap), Alexander Archibald, William Duncan Cowan, Neil L. Harris, Andrew Cunningham, Alan Lauder Morton.

Goals: William Henry Walker (60) / William Duncan Cowan (40)

129. 14.02.1925   Home Championship
SCOTLAND v WALES   3-1 (2-1)
Tynecastle Park, Edinburgh

Referee: Arthur Ward (England)   Attendance: 25,000

SCOTLAND: William Harper, James Nelson, William McStay, David Ditchburn Meiklejohn, David Morris (Cap), Robert Hunter Brown Bennie, Alexander Skinner Jackson, James Dunn, Hugh Kilpatrick Gallacher, Thomas Cairns, Alan Lauder Morton.

WALES: Albert Gray, Moses Richard Russell, John Jenkins, Stanley Charles Davies, Frederick Charles Keenor, William Williams II, William Davies, John Nicholls, Leonard S. Davies, George Beadles, Frederick Cook.

Goals: David Meiklejohn (9), Hugh Gallacher (20, 61) / William Williams II (43)

130. 28.02.1925   Home Championship
NORTHERN IRELAND v SCOTLAND   0-3 (0-3)
Windsor Park, Belfast

Referee: George Noel Watson (England)   Att: 41,000

NORTHERN IRELAND: Thomas J. Farquharson, Robert B. Manderson, William McCandless, James H.A. Chatton, Michael Terence O'Brien, Samuel Johnstone Irving, David Martin, Patrick Gallagher, Edward Carrol, William Gillespie, Joseph Toner.

SCOTLAND: William Harper, James Nelson, William McStay, David Ditchburn Meiklejohn, David Morris (Cap), Robert Hunter Brown Bennie, Alexander Skinner Jackson, James Dunn, Hugh Kilpatrick Gallacher, Thomas Cairns, Alan Lauder Morton.

Goals: David Ditchburn Meiklejohn (4), Hugh Kilpatrick Gallacher (25), James Dunn (35)

131. 04.04.1925   Home Championship
SCOTLAND v ENGLAND   2-0 (1-0)
Hampden Park, Glasgow

Referee: Arthur Ward (England)   Attendance: 92,000

SCOTLAND: William Harper, William McStay, Philip McCloy, David Ditchburn Meiklejohn, David Morris (Cap), James McMullan, Alexander Skinner Jackson, William Fraser Russell, Hugh Kilpatrick Gallacher, Thomas Cairns, Alan Lauder Morton.

ENGLAND: Richard Henry Pym, William Ashurst, Samuel John Wadsworth (Cap), Thomas Patrick Magee, John Edward Townrow, Leonard Graham, Robert Kelly, James Marshall Seed, Frank Roberts, William Henry Walker, Frederick Edward Tunstall.

Goals: Hugh Kilpatrick Gallacher (36, 86)

132. 31.10.1925   Home Championship
WALES v SCOTLAND   0-3 (0-0)
Ninian Park, Cardiff

Referee: E. Pinkstone (England)   Attendance: 18,000

SCOTLAND: William Robb, John Hutton, William McStay, William Clunas, Thomas Townsley (Cap), James McMullan, Alexander Skinner Jackson, John Duncan, Hugh Kilpatrick Gallacher, Alexander Wilson James, Adam McLean.

WALES: Albert Gray, Moses Richard Russell, John Jenkins, Samuel Bennion, Frederick Charles Keenor, James J. Lewis, David R. Williams, William Davies, Stanley Charles Davies, Richard William Richards, Edward Thomas Vizard.

Goals: John Duncan (70), Adam McLean (80), William Clunas (82)

133. 27.02.1926   Home Championship
SCOTLAND v NORTHERN IRELAND 4-0 (2-0)
Ibrox Park, Glasgow

Referee: George Noel Watson (England)   Att: 30,000

SCOTLAND: William Harper, John Hutton, William McStay (Cap), Peter Wilson, John McDougall, Robert Hunter Brown Bennie, Alexander Skinner Jackson, Andrew Cunningham, Hugh Kilpatrick Gallacher, Thomas Bruce McInally, Adam McLean.

NORTHERN IRELAND: Elisha Scott, Robert B. Manderson, Thomas Watson, Samuel Johnstone Irving, Joseph Gowdy, Thomas Sloan, Andrew Bothwell, Alexander Steele, Samuel Curran, William Gillespie, John Mahood.

Goals: Hugh Kilpatrick Gallacher (13, 60, 66), Andrew Cunningham (40)

134. 17.04.1926   Home Championship
ENGLAND v SCOTLAND 0-1 (0-1)
Old Trafford, Manchester

Referee: Thomas Dougray (Scotland)   Attendance: 49,000

ENGLAND: Edward Hallows Taylor, Frederick Roy Goodall, Thomas Mort, Willis Edwards, John Henry Hill, George Henry Green, Richard Ernest York, Sydney Charles Puddefoot, Edward Cashfield Harper, William Henry Walker (Cap), James William Ruffel.

SCOTLAND: William Harper, John Hutton, William McStay (Cap), James Davidson Gibson, William Summers, James McMullan, Alexander Skinner Jackson, Alexander Thomson, Hugh Kilpatrick Gallacher, Andrew Cunningham, Alexander Troup.

Goal: Alexander Skinner Jackson (37)

135. 30.10.1926   Home Championship
SCOTLAND v WALES 3-0 (2-0)
Ibrox Park, Glasgow

Referee: John G. Forshaw (England)   Attendance: 41,000

SCOTLAND: Allan McClory, William McStay (Cap), William Wiseman, James Davidson Gibson, Robert Gillespie, James McMullan, Alexander Skinner Jackson, Andrew Cunningham, Hugh Kilpatrick Gallacher, Thomas Bruce McInally, Adam McLean.

WALES: Albert Gray, Thomas J. Evans, John Jenkins, Samuel Bennion, Frederick Charles Keenor, William Jennings, William Davies, Stanley Charles Davies, John Fowler, Charles Jones, Edward Thomas Vizard.

Goals: Hugh Gallacher (20), Alexander Jackson (33, 73)

136. 26.02.1927   Home Championship
NORTHERN IRELAND v SCOTLAND 0-2 (0-1)
Windsor Park, Belfast

Referee: George Noel Watson (England)   Att: 40,000

NORTHERN IRELAND: Elisha Scott, Andrew McCluggage, William Henry McConnell, Joseph Gowdy, Thomas Sloan, David McMullan, John McGrillen, Patrick Gallagher, Hugh H. Davey, Samuel Johnstone Irving, Joseph Toner.

SCOTLAND: John Diamond Harkness, John Hutton, William McStay (Cap), Thomas Allan Muirhead, James Davidson Gibson, Thomas Craig, Alexander Skinner Jackson, James Dunn, Hugh Kilpatrick Gallacher, James Howieson, Alan Lauder Morton.

Goals: Alan Lauder Morton (44, 88)

137. 02.04.1927   Home Championship
SCOTLAND v ENGLAND 1-2 (0-0)
Hampden Park, Glasgow

Referee: Arthur Ward (England)   Attendance: 111,214

SCOTLAND: John Diamond Harkness, William McStay (Cap), Robert Thomson, Thomas Morrison, James Davidson Gibson, James McMullan, Adam McLean, Andrew Cunningham, Hugh Kilpatrick Gallacher, Robert Low McPhail, Alan Lauder Morton.

ENGLAND: John Henry Brown, Frederick Roy Goodall, Herbert Jones, Willis Edwards, John Henry Hill (Cap), Sidney Macdonald Bishop, Joseph Harold Anthony Hulme, George Brown, William Ralph Dean, Arthur Rigby, Louis Antonio Page.

Goals: Alan Lauder Morton (53) / William Dean (69, 88)

138. 29.10.1927   Home Championship
WALES v SCOTLAND 2-2 (1-2)
The Racecourse, Wrexham

Referee: Arthur H. Kingscott (England)   Attendance: 16,000

WALES: Albert Gray, Moses Richard Russell, Thomas J. Evans, Samuel Bennion, Frederick Charles Keenor, Stanley Charles Davies, William James Hole, Leonard S. Davies, John Fowler, Ernest Curtis, Frederick Cook.

SCOTLAND: William Robb, John Hutton, William McStay, David Ditchburn Meiklejohn, James Davidson Gibson, James McMullan (Cap), Alexander Skinner Jackson, Robert McKay, Hugh Kilpatrick Gallacher, George Stevenson, Alan Lauder Morton.

Goals: Ernest Curtis (44), James Gibson (76 own goal) / Hugh Kilpatrick Gallacher (14), John Hutton (16 pen)

139. 25.02.1928   Home Championship
SCOTLAND v NORTHERN IRELAND 0-1 (0-1)
Firhill Park, Glasgow

Referee: Arthur Ward (England)   Attendance: 55,000

SCOTLAND: Allan McClory, John Hutton, William McStay, Thomas Allan Muirhead (Cap), David Ditchburn Meiklejohn, Thomas Craig, Henry McGill Ritchie, James Dunn, James Edward McGrory, George Stevenson, Alan Lauder Morton.

NORTHERN IRELAND: Elisha Scott, Andrew McCluggage, Robert Hamilton, Samuel Johnstone Irving, George Moorehead, Francis Gerald Morgan, Robert James Chambers, Robert William Irvine, Samuel Curran, James Ferris, John Mahood.

Goal: Robert James Chambers (10)

140. 31.03.1928   Home Championship
ENGLAND v SCOTLAND 1-5 (0-2)
Wembley, London

Referee: William Bell (Scotland)   Attendance: 80,868

ENGLAND: Arthur Edward Hufton, Frederick Roy Goodall (Cap), Herbert Jones, Willis Edwards, Thomas Wilson, Henry Healless, Joseph Harold Anthony Hulme, Robert Kelly, William Ralph Dean, Joseph Bradford, William Henry Smith.

SCOTLAND: John Diamond Harkness, James Nelson, Thomas Law, James Davidson Gibson, Thomas Bradshaw, James McMullan (Cap), Alexander Skinner Jackson, James Dunn, Hugh Kilpatrick Gallacher, Alexander Wilson James, Alan Lauder Morton.

Goals: Robert Kelly (89) / Alexander Jackson (3, 65, 85), Alexander Wilson James (44, 66)

141. 27.10.1928   Home Championship
SCOTLAND v WALES 4-2 (2-1)
Ibrox Park, Glasgow

Referee: Arthur H. Kingscott (England)   Attendance: 55,000

SCOTLAND: John Diamond Harkness, Douglas Herbert Gray, Daniel Blair, Thomas Allan Muirhead, William S. King, James McMullan (Cap), Alexander Skinner Jackson, James Dunn, Hugh Kilpatrick Gallacher, Robert Low McPhail, Alan Lauder Morton.

WALES: Albert Gray, Ernest Morley, William Jennings, Samuel Bennion, Frederick Charles Keenor, David Evans, William James Hole, William Davies, Wilfred L. Lewis, Leonard S. Davies, David R. Williams.

Goals: Hugh Gallacher (25, 42, 49), James Dunn (56) / William Davies (12, 75)

142. 23.02.1929   Home Championship
NORTHERN IRELAND v SCOTLAND 3-7 (2-4)
Windsor Park, Belfast

Referee: Albert Edward Fogg (England)   Att: 35,000

NORTHERN IRELAND: Elisha Scott, Andrew McCluggage, Hugh Flack, Joseph Miller, George Moorehead, Alexander Steele, Robert James Chambers, Richard William Morris Rowley, Joseph Bambrick, Lawrence Cumming, John Mahood.

SCOTLAND: John Diamond Harkness, Douglas Herbert Gray, Daniel Blair, Thomas Allan Muirhead, David Ditchburn Meiklejohn, James McMullan (Cap), Alexander Skinner Jackson, William Stewart Chalmers, Hugh Kilpatrick Gallacher, Alexander Wilson James, Alan Lauder Morton.

Goals: Richard William Morris Rowley (#), Joseph Bambrick (#, #) / Hugh Gallacher (3, 9, 14, 51, 76), Alexander Jackson (36, 82)

143. 13.04.1929   Home Championship
SCOTLAND v ENGLAND 1-0 (0-0)
Hampden Park, Glasgow

Referee: Arthur Joseph (England)   Attendance: 110,512

SCOTLAND: John Diamond Harkness, James Sermagour Crapnell, Joseph Nibloe, John Buchanan, David Ditchburn Meiklejohn, James McMullan (Cap), Alexander Skinner Jackson, Alexander George Cheyne, Hugh Kilpatrick Gallacher, Alexander Wilson James, Alan Lauder Morton.

ENGLAND: John Hacking, Thomas Cooper, Ernest Blenkinsop, Willis Edwards (Cap), James Seddon, Henry Nuttall, John Bruton, George Brown, William Ralph Dean, William Russell Wainscoat, James William Ruffel.

Goal: Alexander George Cheyne (90)

144. 26.05.1929
NORWAY v SCOTLAND 3-7 (2-3)
Brann, Bergen

Referee: Schielderop (Norway)   Attendance: 4,000

NORWAY: Hugo Hoftstad, Haakon Walde, Egil Brenna Lund, T.R. Tollefsen, Alexander Olsen, Kjeld Kjos, Kaare Kongsvik, Oscar Thorstensen, R. Brodahl, Kaare Lie, Sverre Berg-Johannesen.

SCOTLAND: Alexander McLaren, James Sermagour Crapnell, Joseph Nibloe, William Noble Imrie, Allan Craig, Thomas Craig (Cap), James Nisbet, Alexander George Cheyne, David McCrae, Robert Rankin, Robert Howe.

Goals: Kaare Kongsvik (#, #), Sverre Berg-Johannesen (#) / Robert Rankin (6), Thomas Craig (27), Alexander George Cheyne (30, 64, 68), James Nisbet (47, 52)

28

145. 01.06.1929
GERMANY v SCOTLAND 1-1 (0-0)
Deutsches Stadion, Berlin

Referee: Otto Ohlsson (Sweden)   Attendance: 42,000

GERMANY: Heinrich Stuhlfauth (Cap), Franz Schütz, Hans Brunke, Hans Geiger, Hans Gruber, Conrad Heidkamp, Hans Ruch, Hans Sobeck, Josef Pöttinger, Richard Hofmann, Ludwig Hofmann.   Trainer: Prof Dr. Otto Nerz.

SCOTLAND: Alexander McLaren, Douglas Herbert Gray, James Sermagour Crapnell, Hugh Auld Morton, William Noble Imrie, Thomas Craig (Cap), James Nisbet, Alexander George Cheyne, David McCrae, Robert Rankin, James William Fleming.

Goals: Hans Ruch (49) / William Noble Imrie (87)

146. 04.06.1929
HOLLAND v SCOTLAND 0-2 (0-2)
Olympisch, Amsterdam

Referee: John Langenus (Belgium)   Attendance: 24,000

HOLLAND: Ageaus Yme van der Meulen, Adolf Henri van Kol, Sjaak de Bruin, Huib de Leeuw, Maarten Grobbe, Jacobus van der Wildt, Cornelis Wilhelmus Kools, Frans Hombörg, Wilhelmus Tap, Felix Smeets, Gerrit Johan Landaal. Trainer: Robert Glendenning.

SCOTLAND: Alexander McLaren, Douglas Herbert Gray, Joseph Nibloe, Hugh Auld Morton, Allan Craig, Thomas Craig (Cap), James Nisbet, Alexander George Cheyne, James William Fleming, Robert Rankin, Robert Howe.

Goals: James William Fleming (31), Robert Rankin (44 pen)

147. 26.10.1929   Home Championship
WALES v SCOTLAND 2-4 (0-2)
Ninian Park, Cardiff

Referee: William McLean (Northern Ireland)   Att: 25,000

WALES: Albert Gray, Benjamin D. Williams, Arthur Lumberg, Samuel Bennion, Frederick Charles Keenor, Robert John, William Davies, Eugene O'Callaghan, Leonard S. Davies, Charles Jones, Frederick Cook.

SCOTLAND: John Diamond Harkness, Douglas Herbert Gray, Joseph Nibloe, James Davidson Gibson, John Ainslie Johnstone, Thomas Craig, Alexander Skinner Jackson, Thomas Allan Muirhead (Cap), Hugh Kilpatrick Gallacher, Alexander Wilson James, Alan Lauder Morton.

Goals: Eugene O'Callaghan (55), Leonard S. Davies (63) / Hugh Kilpatrick Gallacher (7, 20), Alexander James (74), James Davidson Gibson (77)

148. 22.02.1930   Home Championship
SCOTLAND v NORTHERN IRELAND 3-1 (1-1)
Celtic Park, Glasgow

Referee: Arthur Joseph (England)   Attendance: 30,000

SCOTLAND: Robert Collin Middleton, Douglas Herbert Gray, William Wiseman, James Davidson Gibson, David Ditchburn Meiklejohn (Cap), Thomas Craig, Alexander Skinner Jackson, George Stevenson, Hugh Kilpatrick Gallacher, Alexander Wilson James, Alan Lauder Morton.

NORTHERN IRELAND: Alfred Gardiner, Samuel R. Russell, Robert Hamilton, Robert McDonald, John Jones, Thomas Sloan, Robert James Chambers, Robert William Irvine, Joseph Bambrick, James McCambridge, J. Harold McCaw.

Goals: Hugh Gallacher (32, 61), George Stevenson (70) / J. Harold McCaw (40)

149. 05.04.1930   Home Championship
ENGLAND v SCOTLAND 5-2 (4-0)
Wembley, London

Referee: William McLean (Northern Ireland)   Att: 87,375

ENGLAND: Henry Edward Hibbs, Frederick Roy Goodall, Ernest Blenkinsop, Alfred Henry Strange, Maurice Webster, William Marsden, Samuel Dickinson Crooks, David Bone Nightingale Jack (Cap), Victor Martin Watson, Joseph Bradford, Ellis James Rimmer.

SCOTLAND: John Diamond Harkness, Douglas Herbert Gray, Thomas Law, John Buchanan, David Ditchburn Meiklejohn (Cap), Thomas Craig, Alexander Skinner Jackson, Alexander Wilson James, James William Fleming, George Stevenson, Alan Lauder Morton.

Goals: Victor Martin Watson (12, 28), Ellis Rimmer (30, 54), David Bone Nightingale Jack (33) / James William Fleming (48, 62)

150. 18.05.1930
FRANCE v SCOTLAND 0-2 (0-1)
Yves du Manoir, Colombes, Paris

Referee: Raphaël Van Praag (Belgium)   Attendance: 25,000

FRANCE: Alexis Thépot, Manuel Anatol, Marcel Capelle, Jean Laurent, Maurice Banide, Augustine Chantrel, Marcel Kauffmann, Henri Pavillard (Cap), Marcel Pinel, Edmond Delfour, Pierre Korb.

SCOTLAND: John Thomson, James Nelson, James Sermagour Crapnell (Cap), Peter Wilson, George Walker, Frank Robert Hill, Alexander Skinner Jackson, Alexander George Cheyne, Hugh Kilpatrick Gallacher, George Stevenson, James Connor.

Goals: Hugh Kilpatrick Gallacher (42, 85)

151. 25.10.1930   Home Championship
SCOTLAND v WALES 1-1 (1-1)

Ibrox Park, Glasgow

Referee: C.E. Lines (England)   Attendance: 23,106

SCOTLAND: John Thomson, Douglas Herbert Gray, John Rooney Gilmour, Colin Duncan McNab, Robert Gillespie (Cap), Frank Robert Hill, Daniel McRorie, George Clark Phillips Brown, Bernard Joseph Battles, George Stevenson, Alan Lauder Morton.

WALES: Leonard Evans, Frederick Dewey, Wynne Crompton, William Rogers, Frederick Charles Keenor, Emrys Ellis, William Collins, John Neal, Thomas Bamford, Walter Robbins, William Thomas.

Goals: Bernard Joseph Battles (37) / Thomas Bamford (6)

152. 21.02.1931   Home Championship
NORTHERN IRELAND v SCOTLAND 0-0

Windsor Park, Belfast

Referee: H.E. Hull (England)   Attendance: 20,000

SCOTLAND: John Thomson, James Sermagour Crapnell, Joseph Nibloe, Peter Wilson, George Walker, Frank Robert Hill, John Livingstone Murdoch, Peter Scarff, Benjamin Collard Yorston, Robert Low McPhail, Alan Lauder Morton (Cap).

NORTHERN IRELAND: Alfred Gardiner, John McNinch, Robert P. Fulton, William McCleery, John Jones, Thomas Sloan, Hugh Blair, Edward Falloon, Frederick C. Roberts, John Geary, J. Harold McCaw.

153. 28.03.1931   Home Championship
SCOTLAND v ENGLAND 2-0 (0-0)

Hampden Park, Glasgow

Referee: Alfred James Atwood (Wales)   Att: 129,810

SCOTLAND: John Thomson, Daniel Blair, Joseph Nibloe, Colin Duncan McNab, David Ditchburn Meiklejohn (Cap), John Miller, Alexander Archibald, George Stevenson, James Edward McGrory, Robert Low McPhail, Alan Lauder Morton.

ENGLAND: Henry Edward Hibbs, Frederick Roy Goodall (Cap), Ernest Blenkinsop, Alfred Henry Strange, Herbert Roberts, Austin Fenwick Campbell, Samuel Dickinson Crooks, Gordon Hodgson, William Ralph Dean, Harry Burgess, John Forsyth Crawford.

Goals: George Stevenson (60), James Edward McGrory (62)

154. 16.05.1931
AUSTRIA v SCOTLAND 5-0 (2-0)

Hohe Warte, Wien

Referee: Paul Ruoff (Switzerland)   Attendance: 45,000

AUSTRIA: Rudolf Hiden, Roman Schramseis, Josef Blum, Georg Braun, Josef Smistik, Karl Gall, Karl Zischek, Friedrich Gschweidl, Matthias Sindelar, Anton Schall, Adolf Vogel. Trainer: Hugo Meisl.

SCOTLAND: John Jackson, Daniel Blair (Cap), Joseph Nibloe, Colin Duncan McNab, James McDougall, George Walker, Andrew Robb Love, James Paterson, James Ferrier Easson, James Robertson, Daniel Hamilton Sneddon Liddle.

Goals: Anton Schall (27), Karl Zischek (29), Adolf Vogel (49), Karl Zischek (69), Matthias Sindelar (79)

155. 20.05.1931
ITALY v SCOTLAND 3-0 (2-0)

Nazionale del PNF, Roma

Referee: Dr. Peco J. Bauwens (Germany)   Att: 25,000

ITALY: Gianpiero Combi, Eraldo Monzeglio, Umberto Caligaris (Cap), Attilio Ferraris IV, Fulvio Bernardini, Luigi Bertolini, Raffaele Costantino, Renato Cesarini, Giuseppe Meazza, Giovanni Ferrari, Raimondo Orsi. Trainer: Vittorio Pozzo.

SCOTLAND: John Jackson, Daniel Blair, Joseph Nibloe, Colin Duncan McNab, James McDougall (Cap), John Miller, Andrew Robb Love, James Paterson, William Gillespie Boyd, James Robertson, Daniel Hamilton Sneddon Liddle.

Goals: Raffaele Costantino (6), Giuseppe Meazza (42), Raimondo Orsi (87)

156. 24.05.1931
SWITZERLAND v SCOTLAND 2-3 (1-2)

Charmilles, Genève

Referee: Albino Carraro (Italy)   Attendance: 10,000

SWITZERLAND: Charles Pasche, Severino Minelli, Rudolf Ramseyer, Edmond Loichot, Otto Imhof, Gabriele Gilardoni, Edmond Kramer III, André Syrvet, Albert Büche, André Abegglen III, Max Fauguel.

SCOTLAND: John Jackson, James Sermagour Crapnell (Cap), Joseph Nibloe, Colin Duncan McNab, George Walker, John Miller, Andrew Robb Love, James Paterson, William Gillespie Boyd, James Ferrier Easson, Daniel Hamilton Sneddon Liddle.

Goals: Albert Büche (31), Max Fauguel (66) / James Ferrier Easson (22), William Gillespie Boyd (24), Andrew Robb Love (89)

157. 19.09.1931   Home Championship
SCOTLAND v NORTHERN IRELAND 3-1 (2-1)

Ibrox Park, Glasgow

Referee: Isaac Caswell (England)   Attendance: 40,000

SCOTLAND: Robert Hepburn, Daniel Blair, Robert McAulay, Alexander Massie, David Ditchburn Meiklejohn (Cap), George Clark Phillips Brown, James Crawford, George Stevenson, James Edward McGrory, Robert Low McPhail, James Connor.

NORTHERN IRELAND: Alfred Gardiner, John McNinch, Robert Hamilton, William McCleery, John Jones, William Alexander Gowdy, Hugh Blair, Richard William Morris Rowley, James Dunne, John Geary, Robert James Chambers.

Goals: George Stevenson (5), James Edward McGrory (34), Robert Low McPhail (72) / James Dunne (20)

158. 31.10.1931   Home Championship
WALES v SCOTLAND 2-3 (1-2)

The Racecourse, Wrexham

Referee: Isaac Caswell (England)   Attendance: 10,860

WALES: Albert Gray, Aneurin Richards, Arthur Lumberg, Thomas Edwards, Thomas P. Griffiths, Edward Lawrence, Philip Griffiths, Eugene O'Callaghan, Ernest Glover, Walter Robbins, Ernest Curtis.

SCOTLAND: John Diamond Harkness, Daniel Blair, Robert McAulay, Alexander Massie, David Ditchburn Meiklejohn (Cap), George Clark Phillips Brown, Robert Austin Thomson, George Stevenson, James Edward McGrory, Robert Low McPhail, Alan Lauder Morton.

Goals: Ernest Curtis (15 pen), Eugene O'Callaghan (78) / George Stevenson (25), Robert Austin Thomson (31), James Edward McGrory (55)

159. 09.04.1932   Home Championship
ENGLAND v SCOTLAND 3-0 (1-0)

Wembley, London

Referee: Samuel Thompson (Northern Ireland)   Att: 92,180

ENGLAND: Harold Frederick Pearson, George Edward Shaw, Ernest Blenkinsop (Cap), Alfred Henry Strange, James Peter O'Dowd, Samuel Weaver, Samuel Dickinson Crooks, Robert Barclay, Thomas Waring, Thomas Clark Fisher Johnson, William Eric Houghton.

SCOTLAND: Thomas Hamilton, James Sermagour Crapnell (Cap), Joseph Nibloe, Colin Duncan McNab, Allan Craig, George Clark Phillips Brown, Alexander Archibald, Dr. James Marshall, Neil Hamilton Dewar, Charles Edward Napier, Alan Lauder Morton.

Goals: Thomas Waring (36), Robert Barclay (79), Samuel Dickinson Crooks (88)

160. 08.05.1932
FRANCE v SCOTLAND 1-3 (1-3)

Yves du Manoir, Colombes, Paris

Referee: Albino Carraro (Italy)   Attendance: 8,000

FRANCE: Alexis Thépot (Cap), Manuel Anatol, André Chardar, Émile Scharwath, Joseph Kaucsar, Jean Laurent, Ernest Liberati, Joseph Alcazar, Robert Mercier, René Gérard, Marcel Langiller.

SCOTLAND: John Diamond Harkness, James Sermagour Crapnell, Joseph Nibloe, Alexander Massie, Robert Gillespie (Cap), John Miller, James Crawford, Alexander Thomson, Neil Hamilton Dewar, Robert Low McPhail, Alan Lauder Morton.

Goals: Neil Hamilton Dewar (14, 27, 40)

161. 17.09.1932   Home Championship
NORTHERN IRELAND v SCOTLAND 0-4 (0-2)

Windsor Park, Belfast

Referee: William Harper (England)   Attendance: 40,000

NORTHERN IRELAND: Elisha Scott, William Cook, Robert P. Fulton, Edward Falloon, John Jones, William Alexander Gowdy, Edward Mitchell, Thomas J.M. Priestley, William Millar, Samuel English, James Kelly.

SCOTLAND: Alexander McLaren, Douglas Herbert Gray, James Sermagour Crapnell (Cap), Alexander Massie, John Ainslie Johnstone, William Telfer, James Crawford, George Stevenson, James Edward McGrory, Robert Low McPhail, James Munro King.

Goals: James Munro King (3), Robert Low McPhail (35, 67), James Edward McGrory (75)

162. 26.10.1932   Home Championship
SCOTLAND v WALES 2-5 (0-4)

Tynecastle Park, Edinburgh

Referee: William Harper (England)   Attendance: 31,000

SCOTLAND: Alexander McLaren, Douglas Herbert Gray, Daniel Blair, Hugh Morrison Wales, John Ainslie Johnstone (Cap), John Ross Thomson, James Crawford, Alexander Thomson, Neil Hamilton Dewar, Alexander Wilson James, Douglas Duncan.

WALES: William John, Benjamin D. Williams, Benjamin Ellis, Frederick Charles Keenor, Thomas P. Griffiths, David Richards, Cuthbert Phillips, Eugene O'Callaghan, David Astley, Walter Robbins, David J. Lewis.

Goals: Neil Hamilton Dewar (63), Douglas Duncan (70) / John Ross Thomson (9 own goal), Thomas P. Griffiths (20), Eugene O'Callaghan (25, 46), David Astley (43)

163. 01.04.1933   Home Championship
SCOTLAND v ENGLAND   2-1 (1-1)
Hampden Park, Glasgow

Referee: Samuel Thompson (Northern Ireland)
Attendance: 134,170

SCOTLAND: John Jackson, Andrew Anderson, Peter McGonagle, Peter Wilson, Robert Gillespie (Cap), George Clark Phillips Brown, James Crawford, Dr. James Marshall, James Edward McGrory, Robert Low McPhail, Douglas Duncan.

ENGLAND: Henry Edward Hibbs, Thomas Cooper, Ernest Blenkinsop (Cap), Alfred Henry Strange, Ernest Arthur Hart, Samuel Weaver, Joseph Harold Anthony Hulme, Ronald William Starling, George Samuel Hunt, John Pickering, John Arnold.

Goals: James Edward McGrory (4, 81) /
George Samuel Hunt (30)

164. 16.09.1933   Home Championship
SCOTLAND v NORTHERN IRELAND   1-2 (0-2)
Celtic Park, Glasgow

Referee: Edward Wood (England)   Attendance: 27,135

SCOTLAND: John Diamond Harkness, Andrew Anderson, Peter McGonagle (Cap), Alexander Massie, Alexander Low, William Telfer, James Murray Boyd, Alexander Venters, James Edward McGrory, Robert Low McPhail, James Munro King.

NORTHERN IRELAND: Elisha Scott, Thomas Willighan, Robert P. Fulton, John McMahon, John Jones, William Mitchell, Hugh Blair, Alexander Ernest Stevenson, David Kirker Martin, John Coulter, John Mahood.

Goals: Robert McPhail (60) / David Kirker Martin (8, 13)

165. 04.10.1933   Home Championship
WALES v SCOTLAND   3-2 (2-0)
Ninian Park, Cardiff

Referee: Edward Wood (England)   Attendance: 40,000

WALES: William John, Sidney Lawrence, Benjamin Ellis, James Murphy, Thomas P. Griffiths, David Richards, Cuthbert Phillips, Eugene O'Callaghan, David Astley, Walter Robbins, William Evans.

SCOTLAND: John Diamond Harkness, Andrew Anderson (Cap), Duncan Urquhart, Matthew Busby, John Blair, James Sime McLuckie, Francis Reynolds McGurk, John McMenemy, William McFadyen, James Ferrier Easson, Douglas Duncan.

Goals: William Evans (25), Walter Robbins (35), David Astley (56) /
William McFadyen (76), Douglas Duncan (81)

166. 29.11.1933
SCOTLAND v AUSTRIA   2-2 (1-1)
Hampden Park, Glasgow

Referee: John Langenus (Belgium)   Attendance: 62,000

SCOTLAND: James Kennaway, Andrew Anderson, Peter McGonagle, David Ditchburn Meiklejohn (Cap), Philip Ross Watson, George Clark Phillips Brown, Duncan Henderson Ogilvie, Robert Bruce, William McFadyen, Robert Low McPhail, Douglas Duncan.

AUSTRIA: Peter Platzer, Anton Janda, Karl Sesta, Franz Wagner, Josef Smistik, Walter Nausch, Karl Zischek, Josef Bican, Matthias Sindelar, Anton Schall, Rudolf Viertl.
Trainer: Hugo Meisl.

Goals: David Meiklejohn (7), William McFadyen (49) /
Karl Zischek (39), Anton Schall (52)

167. 14.04.1934   Home Championship
ENGLAND v SCOTLAND   3-0 (1-0)
Wembley, London

Referee: Samuel Thompson (Northern Ireland)   Att: 92,363

ENGLAND: Frank Moss, Thomas Cooper (Cap), Edris Albert Hapgood, Lewis Stoker, Ernest Arthur Hart, Wilfred Copping, Samuel Dickinson Crooks, Horatio Stratton Carter, John William Anslow Bowers, Clifford Sydney Bastin, Eric Frederick George Brook.

SCOTLAND: John Jackson, Andrew Anderson, Peter McGonagle, Alexander Massie (Cap), Thomas M. Smith, John Miller, William Lawrence Cook, Dr. James Marshall, Hugh Kilpatrick Gallacher, George Stevenson, James Connor.

Goals: Clifford Bastin (43), Eric Frederick George Brook (80), John William Anslow Bowers (88)

168. 20.10.1934   Home Championship
NORTHERN IRELAND v SCOTLAND   2-1 (0-1)
Windsor Park, Belfast

Referee: Henry Norman Mee (England)   Att: 39,752

NORTHERN IRELAND: Elisha Scott, John Alexander Mackie, Robert P. Fulton, Walter S. McMillen, John Jones, William Mitchell, Harold Anthony Duggan, William Alexander Gowdy, David Kirker Martin, Alexander Ernest Stevenson, John Coulter.

SCOTLAND: James Dawson, Andrew Anderson, Peter McGonagle, Alexander Massie (Cap), James McMillan Simpson, Andrew Clark Herd, William Lawrence Cook, George Stevenson, James Smith, Patrick Gallacher, James Connor.

Goals: David Kirker Martin (76), John Coulter (89) /
Patrick Gallacher (43)

169. 21.11.1934   Home Championship
SCOTLAND v WALES 3-2 (1-0)
Pittodrie Park, Aberdeen
Referee: Samuel Thompson (Northern Ireland)   Att: 26,334
SCOTLAND: Allan McClory, Andrew Anderson, Peter McGonagle, Alexander Massie, James McMillan Simpson (Cap), George Clark Phillips Brown, William Lawrence Cook, Thomas Walker, David McCulloch, Charles Edward Napier, Douglas Duncan.
WALES: William John, Sidney Lawrence, David Owen Jones, James Murphy, Harry Hanford, David Richards, Idris Morgan Hopkins, Ronald Williams, David Astley, Thomas Mills, Cuthbert Phillips.
Goals: Douglas Duncan (23), Charles Napier (46, 85) / Cuthbert Phillips (73), David Astley (88)

170. 06.04.1935   Home Championship
SCOTLAND v ENGLAND 2-0 (1-0)
Hampden Park, Glasgow
Referee: Samuel Thompson (Northern Ireland)
Attendance: 129,693
SCOTLAND: John Jackson, Andrew Anderson, George Wilfred Cummings, Alexander Massie, James McMillan Simpson (Cap), George Clark Phillips Brown, Charles Edward Napier, Thomas Walker, Hugh Kilpatrick Gallacher, Robert Low McPhail, Douglas Duncan.
ENGLAND: Henry Edward Hibbs, Charles George Male, Edris Albert Hapgood (Cap), Clifford Samuel Britton, John William Barker, Walter John Alsford, Albert Geldard, Clifford Sydney Bastin, Robert Gurney, Raymond William Westwood, Eric Frederick George Brook.
Goals: Douglas Duncan (43, 50)

171. 05.10.1935   Home Championship
WALES v SCOTLAND 1-1 (1-1)
Ninian Park, Cardiff
Referee: Isaac Caswell (England)   Attendance: 35,004
WALES: William John, Sidney Lawrence, Robert John, James Murphy, Thomas P. Griffiths, David Richards, Cuthbert Phillips, Brynmor Jones, Ernest Glover, Leslie Jenkin Jones, Walter Robbins.
SCOTLAND: John Jackson, Andrew Anderson, George Wilfred Cummings, Alexander Massie, James McMillan Simpson (Cap), George Clark Phillips Brown, James Delaney, Thomas Walker, Matthew Armstrong, William Mills, Douglas Duncan.
Goals: Cuthbert Phillips (42) / Douglas Duncan (35)

172. 13.11.1935   Home Championship
SCOTLAND v NORTHERN IRELAND 2-1 (0-0)
Tynecastle Park, Edinburgh
Referee: Henry Nattrass (England)   Attendance: 30,000
SCOTLAND: John Jackson, Andrew Anderson, George Wilfred Cummings, Alexander Massie, James McMillan Simpson (Cap), Alexander Cockburn Hastings, James Delaney, Thomas Walker, Matthew Armstrong, William Mills, Douglas Duncan.
NORTHERN IRELAND: Elisha Scott, William Cook, Robert P. Fulton, Keiller McCullough, John Jones, William Mitchell, Harold Anthony Duggan, Alexander Ernest Stevenson, Joseph Bambrick, Peter Dermont Doherty, James Kelly.
Goals: Thomas Walker (58), Douglas Duncan (89) / James Kelly (49)

173. 04.04.1936   Home Championship
ENGLAND v SCOTLAND 1-1 (1-0)
Wembley, London
Referee: William Hamilton (Northern Ireland)   Att: 93,267
ENGLAND: Edward Sagar, Charles George Male, Edris Albert Hapgood (Cap), William John Crayston, John William Barker, John Bray, Samuel Dickinson Crooks, Robert Barclay, George Henry Camsell, Clifford Sydney Bastin, Eric Frederick George Brook.
SCOTLAND: James Dawson, Andrew Anderson, George Wilfred Cummings, Alexander Massie, James McMillan Simpson (Cap), George Clark Phillips Brown, John Crum, Thomas Walker, David McCulloch, Alexander Venters, Douglas Duncan.
Goals: George Henry Camsell (30) / Thomas Walker (77 pen)

174. 14.10.1936
SCOTLAND v GERMANY 2-0 (0-0)
Ibrox Park, Glasgow
Referee: Henry Nattras (England)   Attendance: 50,000
SCOTLAND: James Dawson, Andrew Anderson, George Wilfred Cummings, Alexander Massie, James McMillan Simpson (Cap), George Clark Phillips Brown, James Delaney, Thomas Walker, Matthew Armstrong, Robert Low McPhail, Douglas Duncan.
GERMANY: Hans Jakob, Reinhold Münzenberg, Andreas Munkert, Paul Janes, Ludwig Goldbrunner, Albin Kitzinger, Franz Elbern, Rudolf Gellesch, Otto Siffling, Fritz Szepan (Cap), Adolf Urban.   Trainer: Josef Herberger.
Goals: James Delaney (67, 83)

175. 31.10.1936   Home Championship
NORTHERN IRELAND v SCOTLAND 1-3 (1-1)

Windsor Park, Belfast

Referee: Thomas Thompson (England)   Attendance: 45,000

NORTHERN IRELAND: Thomas Breen, William Cook, Robert P. Fulton, Walter S. McMillen, John Jones, William Mitchell, Noel Kernaghan, Keiller McCullough, David Kirker Martin, John Coulter, James Kelly.

SCOTLAND: James Dawson, Andrew Anderson, Robert Francis Dudgeon Ancell, Alexander Massie, James McMillan Simpson (Cap), George Clark Phillips Brown, Alexander Dewar Munro, Thomas Walker, David McCulloch, Charles Edward Napier, Douglas Duncan.

Goals: Noel Kernaghan (25) / Charles Edward Napier (27), Alexander Dewar Munro (42), David McCulloch (63)

176. 02.12.1936   Home Championship
SCOTLAND v WALES 1-2 (0-1)

Dens Park, Dundee

Referee: Dr. Arthur W. Barton (England)   Att: 23,858

SCOTLAND: James Dawson, Andrew Anderson, Robert Francis Dudgeon Ancell, Alexander Massie, James McMillan Simpson (Cap), George Clark Phillips Brown, Alexander Dewar Munro, Thomas Walker, David McCulloch, William Mills, Douglas Duncan.

WALES: Albert Gray, Herbert Gwyn Turner, Benjamin Ellis, James Murphy, Thomas P. Griffiths, David Richards, Idris Morgan Hopkins, Brynmor Jones, Ernest Glover, Leslie Jenkin Jones, Seymour Morris.

Goals: Thomas Walker (59) / Ernest Glover (22, 47)

177. 17.04.1937   Home Championship
SCOTLAND v ENGLAND 3-1 (0-1)

Hampden Park, Glasgow

Referee: William McLean (Northern Ireland)   Att: 149,547

SCOTLAND: James Dawson, Andrew Anderson, Andrew Beattie, Alexander Massie, James McMillan Simpson (Cap), George Clark Phillips Brown, James Delaney, Thomas Walker, Francis O'Donnell, Robert Low McPhail, Douglas Duncan.

ENGLAND: Victor Robert Woodley, Charles George Male (Cap), Samuel Barkas, Clifford Samuel Britton, Alfred Young, John Bray, Stanley Matthews, Horatio Stratton Carter, Frederick Charles Steele, Ronald William Starling, Joseph Arthur Johnson.

Goals: Francis O'Donnell (47), Robert Low McPhail (80, 88) / Frederick Charles Steele (40)

178. 09.05.1937
AUSTRIA v SCOTLAND 1-1 (0-0)

Prater, Wien

Referee: John Langenus (Belgium)   Attendance: 60,000

AUSTRIA: Peter Platzer, Karl Sesta, Willibald Schmaus, Karl Adamek, Josef Pekarek, Walter Nausch, Rudolf Geiter, Josef Stroh, Matthias Sindelar, Camillo Jerusalem, Johann Pesser.

SCOTLAND: James Dawson, Andrew Anderson, Andrew Beattie, Alexander Massie, James McMillan Simpson (Cap), Alexander McNab, James Delaney, Thomas Walker, Francis O'Donnell, Charles Edward Napier, Torance Gillick.

Goals: Camillo Jerusalem (76) / Francis O'Donnell (80)

179. 15.05.1937
CZECHOSLOVAKIA v SCOTLAND 1-3 (1-2)

Sparta, Praha

Referee: Dr. Peco J. Bauwens (Germany)   Att: 35,000

CZECHOSLOVAKIA: František Plánička (Cap), Jaroslav Burgr, Josef Čtyřoký, Josef Košťálek, Jaroslav Bouček, Karel Kolský, Vilém Zlatník, František Svoboda, Jiří Sobotka, Vlastimil Kopecký, Antonín Puč.   Trainer: Josef Tesař.

SCOTLAND: James Dawson, Robert Brown Hogg, Andrew Beattie, Charles Morgan Thomson, James McMillan Simpson (Cap), George Clark Phillips Brown, James Delaney, Thomas Walker, Francis O'Donnell, Robert Low McPhail, Torance Gillick.

Goals: Antonín Puč (29) / James McMillan Simpson (14), Robert Low McPhail (32), Torance Gillick (69)

180. 30.10.1937   Home Championship
WALES v SCOTLAND 2-1 (1-0)

Ninian Park, Cardiff

Referee: Charles E. Argent (England)   Attendance: 41,800

WALES: Albert Gray, Herbert Gwyn Turner, William Marshall Hughes, James Murphy, Harry Hanford, David Richards, Cuthbert Phillips, Brynmor Jones, Edwin Perry, Leslie Jenkin Jones, Seymour Morris.

SCOTLAND: James Dawson, Andrew Anderson, George Wilfred Cummings, Alexander Massie, James McMillan Simpson (Cap), George Clark Phillips Brown, Robert Frame Main, Thomas Walker, Francis O'Donnell, Robert Low McPhail, Douglas Duncan.

Goals: Brynmor Jones (26), Seymour Morris (51) / Alexander Massie (72)

181. 10.11.1937   Home Championship
SCOTLAND v NORTHERN IRELAND 1-1 (0-1)

Pittodrie Park, Aberdeen

Referee: Arthur James Jewell (England)   Attendance: 21,878

SCOTLAND: James Dawson, Andrew Anderson, George Wilfred Cummings, Duncan McKenzie, James McMillan Simpson (Cap), Alexander Cockburn Hastings, James Delaney, Thomas Walker, James Smith, Robert Low McPhail, Robert Reid.

NORTHERN IRELAND: Thomas Breen, William Edward Hayes, William Cook, Matthew Doherty, Walter S. McMillen, William Mitchell, John Brown II, James McAlinden, David Kirker Martin, Peter Dermont Doherty, John Coulter.

Goals: James Smith (49) / Peter Dermont Doherty (14)

182. 08.12.1937
SCOTLAND v CZECHOSLOVAKIA 5-0 (3-0)

Hampden Park, Glasgow

Referee: Thomas Thompson (England)   Attendance: 41,000

SCOTLAND: William Waugh, Andrew Anderson (Cap), George Wilfred Cummings, George Robertson, Robert Johnston, George Clark Phillips Brown, Peter Symington Buchanan, Thomas Walker, David McCulloch, Andrew Black, David Kinnear.

CZECHOSLOVAKIA: František Plánička (Cap), Josef Košťálek, Ferdinand Daučík, Antonín Vodička, Jaroslav Bouček, Karel Kolský, Jan Říha, Jiří Sobotka, Josef Zeman, Oldřich Nejedlý, Antonín Puč.   Trainer: Josef Tesař.

Goals: Andrew Black (1), David McCulloch (30, 62), Peter Symington Buchanan (38), David Kinnear (70)

183. 09.04.1938   Home Championship
ENGLAND v SCOTLAND 0-1 (0-1)

Wembley, London

Referee: William Hamilton (Northern Ireland)   Att: 93,267

ENGLAND: Victor Robert Woodley, Bert Sproston, Edris Albert Hapgood (Cap), Charles Kenneth Willingham, Stanley Cullis, Wilfred Copping, Stanley Matthews, George William Hall, Michael Fenton, Joseph Eric Stephenson, Clifford Sydney Bastin.

SCOTLAND: David Scott Cumming, Andrew Anderson, Andrew Beattie, William Shankly, Thomas M. Smith, George Clark Phillips Brown (Cap), John Vance Milne, Thomas Walker, Francis O'Donnell, George Mutch, Robert Reid.

Goal: Thomas Walker (6)

184. 21.05.1938
HOLLAND v SCOTLAND 1-3 (0-0)

Olympisch, Amsterdam

Referee: Charles E. Argent (England)   Attendance: 50,000

HOLLAND: Adriaanus van Male, Bartholomeus Marius Weber, Bernardus Johannes Caldenhove, Bastiaan Jacob Paauwe, Willem Gerardus Anderiesen, Gerardus Henricus van Heel (Cap), Frank Wels, Henricus Josephus van Spaandonck, Leendert Roedolf Johan Vente, Franciscus Christiaan van der Veen, Johannes Lambertus de Harder.
Trainer: Robert Glendenning.

SCOTLAND: James Dawson, Andrew Anderson, James Carabine, Thomas Boyd McKillop, James Dykes, George Clark Phillips Brown (Cap), Alexander Dewar Munro, Thomas Walker, Francis O'Donnell, Andrew Black, Francis Murphy.

Goals: Leendert Roedolf Johan Vente (86) / Andrew Black (52), Francis Murphy (56), Thomas Walker (70)

185. 08.10.1938   Home Championship
NORTHERN IRELAND v SCOTLAND 0-2 (0-1)

Windsor Park, Belfast

Referee: Herbert Mortimer (England)   Attendance: 40,000

NORTHERN IRELAND: Thomas Breen, William Edward Hayes, William Cook, Walter S. McMillen, Matthew Augustine O'Mahoney, Robert James Browne, John Brown II, James McAlinden, David Kirker Martin, Alexander Ernest Stevenson, John Coulter.

SCOTLAND: James Dawson, James Carabine (Cap), Andrew Beattie, William Shankly, James Dykes, George Denholm Paterson, James Delaney, Thomas Walker, John Crum, John Divers, Torance Gillick.

Goals: James Delaney (33), Thomas Walker (48)

186. 09.11.1938   Home Championship
SCOTLAND v WALES 3-2 (1-1)

Tynecastle Park, Edinburgh

Referee: Thomas Thompson (England)   Attendance: 34,810

SCOTLAND: John Bell Brown, Andrew Anderson (Cap), Andrew Beattie, William Shankly, Robert Denholm Baxter, Archibald Miller, James Delaney, Thomas Walker, David McCulloch, Robert Beattie, Torance Gillick.

WALES: William John, William Whatley, William Marshall Hughes, Donald John Dearson, Thomas George Jones, David Richards, Idris Morgan Hopkins, Leslie Jenkin Jones, David Astley, Brynmor Jones, Reginald Horace Cumner.

Goals: Torance Gillick (38), Thomas Walker (83, 84) / David Astley (20), Leslie Jenkin Jones (86)

187. 07.12.1938
SCOTLAND v HUNGARY 3-1 (3-0)
Ibrox Park, Glasgow

Referee: Henry Nattrass (England)   Attendance: 20,000

SCOTLAND: James Dawson, Andrew Anderson (Cap), Andrew Beattie, William Shankly, Robert Denholm Baxter, James Scotland Symon, Alexander McSpadyen, Thomas Walker, David McCulloch, Andrew Black, Torance Gillick.

HUNGARY: Antal Szabó, Lajos Korányi I, Sándor Bíró, Gyula Polgár, József Turay, János Dudás, Pál Titkos, László Cseh II, György Sárosi dr., Géza Toldi, László Gyetvai.
Trainer: Dr. Károly Dietz.

Goals: Thomas Walker (19 pen), Andrew Black (27), Torance Gillick (28) / György Sárosi dr. (72 pen)

188. 15.04.1939   Home Championship
SCOTLAND v ENGLAND 1-2 (1-0)
Hampden Park, Glasgow

Referee: William Hamilton (Northern Ireland)   Att: 149,269

SCOTLAND: James Dawson, James Carabine, George Wilfred Cummings, William Shankly, Robert Denholm Baxter, Alexander McNab, Alexander McSpadyen, Thomas Walker, James Dougall (Cap), Alexander Venters, John Vance Milne.

ENGLAND: Victor Robert Woodley, William Walker Morris, Edris Albert Hapgood (Cap), Charles Kenneth Willingham, Stanley Cullis, Joseph Mercer, Stanley Matthews, George William Hall, Thomas Lawton, Leonard Arthur Goulden, Albert Beasley.

Goals: James Dougall (21) / Albert Beasley (66), Thomas Lawton (88)

189. 23.01.1946
SCOTLAND v BELGIUM 2-2 (0-0)
Hampden Park, Glasgow

Referee: Joseph Jackson (Scotland)   Attendance: 46,000

SCOTLAND: Robert Brown, James McGowan, John Shaw (Cap), James Campbell, Andrew Paton, George Denholm Paterson, Gordon Smith, Archibald Baird, James Delaney, John Deakin, James Walker.

BELGIUM: François Daenen, Robert Paverick, Joseph Pannaye, Antoine Puttaert, Marcel Vercammen, René Devos, Victor Lemberechts, Henri Coppens, Albert De Cleyn, Frédéric Chavès D'Aguilar, François Sermon.
Trainer: François Demol.

Goals: James Delaney (50, 90 pen) / Victor Lemberechts (60), Frédéric Chavès D'Aguilar (73)

190. 15.05.1946
SCOTLAND v SWITZERLAND 3-1 (3-1)
Hampden Park, Glasgow

Referee: P. Stevens (England)   Attendance: 113,000

SCOTLAND: Robert Brown, David Shaw, John Shaw (Cap), William Bowie Campbell, Francis Brennan, John Husband, William Waddell, William Thornton, James Delaney, Thomas Walker, William Beveridge Liddell.

SWITZERLAND: Erwin Ballabio, Rudolf Gyger, Willy Steffen, Franz Rickenbach, Franco Andreoli, Roger Bocquet, Lauro Amadò, Walter Fink, Hans-Peter Friedländer, René Maillard II, Georges Aeby.   Trainer: Karl Rappan.

Goals: William Liddell (25, 28), James Delaney (35) / Georges Aeby (1)

191. 19.10.1946   Home Championship
WALES v SCOTLAND 3-1 (0-0)
The Racecourse, Wrexham

Referee: W.H.E. Evans (England)   Attendance: 29,568

WALES: Cyril Sidlow, Raymond Lambert, William Marshall Hughes, Douglas Frederick Witcomb, Thomas George Jones, William Arthur Ronald Burgess, William Ernest Arthur Jones, Aubrey Powell, Trevor Ford, Brynmor Jones, George Edwards.

SCOTLAND: William Miller, James Findlay Stephen (Cap), David Shaw, Hugh Brown, Francis Brennan, John Husband, William Waddell, Cornelius Dougall, William Thornton, James Alfred Blair, William Beveridge Liddell.

Goals: Brynmor Jones (52), Trevor Ford (78), James Findlay Stephen (87 own goal) / William Waddell (49 pen)

192. 27.11.1946   Home Championship
SCOTLAND v NORTHERN IRELAND 0-0
Hampden Park, Glasgow

Referee: George Reader (England)   Attendance: 98,776

SCOTLAND: Robert Brown, George Lewis Young, David Shaw (Cap), William Bowie Campbell, Francis Brennan, Hugh Long, Gordon Smith, George Hamilton, William Thornton, James Duncanson, William Beveridge Liddell.

NORTHERN IRELAND: Edward Hinton, William Charles Gorman, James McBurney Feeney, Cornelius Joseph Martin, John Joseph Vernon, Peter Desmond Farrell, David Cochrane, John James Carey, David John Walsh, Alexander Ernest Stevenson, Thomas Joseph Eglington.

193. 12.04.1947   Home Championship
ENGLAND v SCOTLAND 1-1 (0-1)
Wembley, London

Referee: Charles de la Salle (France)   Attendance: 98,200

ENGLAND: Frank Victor Swift, Lawrence Scott, George Francis Moutry Hardwick (Cap), William Ambrose Wright, Cornelius "Neil" Franklin, Henry Johnston, Stanley Matthews, Horatio Stratton Carter, Thomas Lawton, Wilfred Mannion, James Mullen.   Manager: Walter Winterbottom.

SCOTLAND: William Miller, George Lewis Young, John Shaw (Cap), Archibald Renwick MacAuley, William Alexander Woodburn, Alexander Rooney Forbes, Gordon Smith, Andrew McLaren, James Delaney, William Steel, Thomas Usher Pearson.

Goals: Horatio Stratton Carter (56) / Andrew McLaren (16)

194. 18.05.1947
BELGIUM v SCOTLAND 2-1 (1-0)
Heysel, Bruxelles

Referee: Valdemar Laursen (Denmark)   Attendance: 51,161

SCOTLAND: William Miller, George Lewis Young, John Shaw (Cap), Hugh Brown, William Alexander Woodburn, Alexander Rooney Forbes, Robert Inglis Campbell, Andrew McLaren, Robert Flavell, William Steel, Thomas Usher Pearson.

BELGIUM: François Daenen, Léon Aernaudts, Joseph Pannaye, Alfons De Buck, Jules Henriet, Fernand Massay, Victor Lemberechts, Henri Coppens, Albert De Cleyn, Léopold Anoul, René Thirifays.   Trainer: William Gormlie (England).

Goals: Léopold Anoul (28, 75) / William Steel (64)

195. 24.05.1947
LUXEMBOURG v SCOTLAND 0-6 (0-2)
Municipal, Luxembourg

Referee: Wouters (Belgium)   Attendance: 4,000

LUXEMBOURG: Bernard Michaux, René Marchetti, François Dumont, Alphonse Feyder, Arnold Kieffer, Remy Wagner, Paul Feller II, Camille Libar (Cap), Nicolas Kettel, Marcel Rewenig, Léon Letsch (82 Fernand Guth).

SCOTLAND: William Miller, George Lewis Young, John Shaw (Cap), Hugh Brown, William Alexander Woodburn, Alexander Rooney Forbes, William MacFarlane, Andrew McLaren, Robert Flavell, William Steel, Robert Inglis Campbell.

Goals: Robert Flavell (6, 69), William Steel (13, 48), Andrew McLaren (60), Alexander Rooney Forbes (86)

196. 04.10.1947   Home Championship
NORTHERN IRELAND v SCOTLAND 2-0 (1-0)
Windsor Park, Belfast

Referee: Thomas Smith (England)   Attendance: 52,000

NORTHERN IRELAND: Edward Hinton, Cornelius Joseph Martin, Thomas Aherne, William Walsh, John Joseph Vernon, Peter Desmond Farrell, David Cochrane, Samuel Smyth, David John Walsh, Alexander Ernest Stevenson, Thomas Joseph Eglington.

SCOTLAND: William Miller, George Lewis Young, John Shaw (Cap), Archibald Renwick MacAuley, William Alexander Woodburn, Alexander Rooney Forbes, James Delaney, James Watson, William Thornton, William Steel, William Beveridge Liddell.

Goals: Samuel Smyth (35, 54)

197. 12.11.1947   Home Championship
SCOTLAND v WALES 1-2 (1-2)
Hampden Park, Glasgow

Referee: Arthur Edward Ellis (England)   Att: 88,000

SCOTLAND: William Miller, John Govan, James Findlay Stephen, Archibald Renwick MacAuley, William Alexander Woodburn (Cap), Alexander Rooney Forbes, Gordon Smith, Andrew McLaren, James Delaney, William Steel, William Beveridge Liddell.

WALES: Cyril Sidlow, Alfred Thomas Sherwood, Walley Barnes, Ivor Verdun Powell, Thomas George Jones, William Arthur Ronald Burgess, David Sidney Thomas, Aubrey Powell, Trevor Ford, George Lowrie, George Edwards.

Goals: Andrew McLaren (10) / Trevor Ford (35), George Lowrie (42)

198. 10.04.1948   Home Championship
SCOTLAND v ENGLAND 0-2 (0-1)
Hampden Park, Glasgow

Referee: David Maxwell (Northern Ireland)   Att: 135,376

SCOTLAND: Ian Henderson Black, John Govan, David Shaw, William Bowie Campbell, George Lewis Young (Cap), Archibald Renwick MacAuley, James Delaney, James Robert Combe, William Thornton, William Steel, William Beveridge Liddell.

ENGLAND: Frank Victor Swift, Lawrence Scott, George Francis Moutry Hardwick (Cap), William Ambrose Wright, Cornelius "Neil" Franklin, Henry Cockburn, Stanley Matthews, Stanley Harding Mortensen, Thomas Lawton, Stanley Clare Pearson, Thomas Finney.   Manager: Walter Winterbottom.

Goals: Thomas Finney (44), Stanley Harding Mortensen (62)

199. 28.04.1948
SCOTLAND v BELGIUM 2-0 (1-0)

Hampden Park, Glasgow

Referee: William Ling (England)   Attendance: 70,000

SCOTLAND: James Clews Cowan, John Govan, David Shaw, William Bowie Campbell, George Lewis Young (Cap), Archibald Renwick MacAuley, Gordon Smith, James Robert Combe, Leslie Hamilton Johnston, Edward Hunter Turnbull, David Millar Duncan.

BELGIUM: François Daenen, Léon Aernaudts, Léopold Anoul, Alfons De Buck, Victor Erroelen, Jules Henriet, Victor Lemberechts, Henri Govard, Joseph Mermans, August Van Steenlant, Albert De Cleyn.
Trainer: William Gormlie (England)

Goals: James Robert Combe (25), David Millar Duncan (59)

200. 17.05.1948
SWITZERLAND v SCOTLAND 2-1 (1-1)

Wankdorf, Bern

Referee: Alois Beranek (Austria)   Attendance: 30,000

SWITZERLAND: Eugenio Corrodi, André Belli, Willy Steffen, Gerhard Lusenti, Oliver Eggimann, Roger Bocquet, Alfred Bickel (46 Jean Tamini), Hans-Peter Friedländer, Lauro Amadò, René Maillard II, Jacques Fatton.
Trainer: Karl Rappan.

SCOTLAND: James Clews Cowan, John Govan, David Shaw, William Bowie Campbell, George Lewis Young (Cap), Archibald Renwick MacAuley, Gordon Smith, James Robert Combe, Leslie Hamilton Johnston, Edward Hunter Turnbull, David Millar Duncan.

Goals: René Maillard II (45), Jacques Fatton (78) /
Leslie Hamilton Johnston (19)

201. 23.05.1948
FRANCE v SCOTLAND 3-0 (0-0)

Yves du Manoir, Colombes, Paris

Referee: Karel van der Meer (Holland)   Attendance: 46,032

FRANCE: Julien Darui (Cap), Guy Huguet, Jean Grégoire, Roger Marche, Antoine Cuissard, Jean Prouff, Jean Baratte, Larbi Ben Barek, Georges Sésia, Émile Bongiorni, Pierre Flamion.

SCOTLAND: James Clews Cowan, John Govan, David Shaw, William Bowie Campbell, George Lewis Young (Cap), Archibald Renwick MacAuley, Edward Rutherford, William Steel, Gordon Smith, Charles John Cox, David Millar Duncan.

Goals: Émile Bongiorni (55), Pierre Flamion (60), Jean Baratte (79)

202. 23.10.1948   Home Championship
WALES v SCOTLAND 1-3 (1-3)

Ninian Park, Cardiff

Referee: David Maxwell (Northern Ireland)   Att: 59,911

WALES: Cyril Sidlow, Alfred Thomas Sherwood, Walley Barnes, Roy Paul, Frederick Stansfield, William Arthur Ronald Burgess, David Sidney Thomas, William Henry Lucas, Trevor Ford, Brynmor Jones, William Ernest Arthur Jones.

SCOTLAND: James Clews Cowan, Hugh Howie, David Shaw, Robert Evans, George Lewis Young (Cap), William Yates Redpath, William Waddell, James Mason, Lawrence Reilly, William Steel, John Carmichael Kelly.

Goals: Brynmor Jones (22) /
Hugh Howie (15), William Waddell (20, 30)

203. 17.11.1948   Home Championship
SCOTLAND v NORTHERN IRELAND 3-2 (1-2)

Hampden Park, Glasgow

Referee: W.H.E. Evans (England)   Attendance: 93,182

SCOTLAND: Robert Brown, John Govan, David Shaw, Robert Evans, George Lewis Young (Cap), William Yates Redpath, William Waddell, James Mason, William Houliston, William Steel, John Carmichael Kelly.

NORTHERN IRELAND: William Smyth, John James Carey, Thomas Roderick Keane, James Joseph McCabe, John Joseph Vernon, William Walsh, David Cochrane, Samuel Smyth, David John Walsh, Peter Dermont Doherty, John Francis O'Driscoll.

Goals: William Houliston (27, 89), James Mason (72) /
David John Walsh (1, 4)

204. 09.04.1949   Home Championship
ENGLAND v SCOTLAND 1-3 (0-1)

Wembley, London

Referee: Mervyn Griffiths (Wales)   Attendance: 98,188

ENGLAND: Frank Victor Swift, John Aston, John Robert Howe, William Ambrose Wright (Cap), Cornelius "Neil" Franklin, Henry Cockburn, Stanley Matthews, Stanley Harding Mortensen, John Edward Thompson Milburn, Stanley Clare Pearson, Thomas Finney.   Manager: Walter Winterbottom.

SCOTLAND: James Clews Cowan, George Lewis Young (Cap), Samuel Richmond Cox, Robert Evans, William Alexander Woodburn, George Graham Aitken, William Waddell, James Mason, William Houliston, William Steel, Lawrence Reilly.

Goals: John Milburn (75) /
James Mason (28), William Steel (52), Lawrence Reilly (61)

205. 27.04.1949
SCOTLAND v FRANCE 2-0 (1-0)
Hampden Park, Glasgow
Referee: William Ling (England)   Attendance: 125,631
SCOTLAND: James Clews Cowan, George Lewis Young (Cap), Samuel Richmond Cox, Robert Evans, William Alexander Woodburn, George Graham Aitken, William Waddell, William Thornton, William Houliston, William Steel, Lawrence Reilly.
FRANCE: René Vignal, Marcel Salva, Roger Mindonnet, Roger Marche, Robert Jonquet, Louis Hon, Antoine Cuissard, Albert Batteux (Cap), Roger Gabet, Jean Baratte, Pierre Flamion.
Goals: William Steel (37, 80)

206. 01.10.1949   Home Championship, 4th World Cup Qualifiers
NORTHERN IRELAND v SCOTLAND 2-8 (0-5)
Windsor Park, Belfast
Referee: R.E. Mortimer (England)   Attendance: 50,000
NORTHERN IRELAND: Patrick M. Kelly II, Gerard Columba Bowler, Alfred McMichael, Robert Denis Blanchflower, John Joseph Vernon, Raymond Osborn Ferris, David Cochrane, Samuel Smyth, Robert Anderson Brennan, Edward Crossan, John McKenna.
SCOTLAND: James Clews Cowan, George Lewis Young (Cap), Samuel Richmond Cox, Robert Evans, William Alexander Woodburn, George Graham Aitken, William Waddell, James Mason, Henry Miller Morris, William Steel, Lawrence Reilly.
Goals: Samuel Smyth (50, 59) /
Henry Miller Morris (2, 70, 89), William Waddell (5, 42 pen), William Steel (25), Lawrence Reilly (26), James Mason (80)

207. 09.11.1949   Home Championship, 4th World Cup Qualifiers
SCOTLAND v WALES 2-0 (1-0)
Hampden Park, Glasgow
Referee: S.E.Law (England)   Attendance: 73,781
SCOTLAND: James Clews Cowan, George Lewis Young (Cap), Samuel Richmond Cox, Robert Evans, William Alexander Woodburn, George Graham Aitken, William Beveridge Liddell, John McPhail, Alexander Bryce Linwood, William Steel, Lawrence Reilly.
WALES: Keith B. Jones, Walley Barnes, Alfred Thomas Sherwood, Ivor Verdun Powell, Thomas George Jones, William Arthur Ronald Burgess, William Malwyn Griffiths, Roy Paul, Trevor Ford, Royston James Clarke, George Edwards.
Goals: John McPhail (25), Alexander Bryce Linwood (78)

208. 15.04.1950   Home Championship, 4th World Cup Qualifiers
SCOTLAND v ENGLAND 0-1 (0-0)
Hampden Park, Glasgow
Referee: Reginald A. Leafe (England)   Attendance: 133,300
SCOTLAND: James Clews Cowan, George Lewis Young (Cap), Samuel Richmond Cox, John Miller McColl, William Alexander Woodburn, Alexander Rooney Forbes, William Waddell, William Moir, William Russell Logan Bauld, William Steel, William Beveridge Liddell.
ENGLAND: Bert Frederick Williams, Alfred Ernest Ramsey, John Aston, William Ambrose Wright (Cap), Cornelius "Neil" Franklin, James William Dickinson, Thomas Finney, Wilfred Mannion, Stanley Harding Mortensen, Roy Thomas Frank Bentley, Robert Langton.   Manager: Walter Winterbottom.
Goal: Roy Thomas Frank Bentley (64)

209. 26.04.1950
SCOTLAND v SWITZERLAND 3-1 (3-1)
Hampden Park, Glasgow
Referee: George Reader (England)   Attendance: 123,751
SCOTLAND: James Clews Cowan, George Lewis Young (Cap), Samuel Richmond Cox, Robert Evans, Robert Dougan, George Graham Aitken, Robert Inglis Campbell, Allan Duncan Brown, William Russell Logan Bauld, William Steel, Lawrence Reilly.
SWITZERLAND: Georges Stuber, Rudolf Gyger, Willy Steffen, André Neury, Oliver Eggimann, Roger Bocquet, Alfred Bickel, Charles Antenen, Jean Tamini, René Bader, Jacques Fatton.   Selection Commission: Gaston Tschirren, Franco Andreoli & Severino Minelli.
Goals: William Bauld (9), Robert Inglis Campbell (38), Allan Duncan Brown (44) / Charles Antenen (20)

210. 21.05.1950
PORTUGAL v SCOTLAND 2-2 (2-2)
Nacional, Lisboa
Referee: Ramón Azon (Spain)   Attendance: 68,000
PORTUGAL: Ernesto Nogueira de Oliveira, Octávio dos Santos Barrosa (Cap), Ângelo Ferreira Carvalho, Carlos Augusto Ribeiro Canário, Félix Assunção Antunes, Serafim Pereira Baptista, Mário Fernando Ribeiro Pacheco Nobre, Manuel Vasques, Henrique Ben David, José António Barreto Travaços, Albano Narciso Pereira.
Trainer: Salvador do Carmo.
SCOTLAND: James Clews Cowan, George Lewis Young (Cap), Samuel Richmond Cox, Robert Evans, William Alexander Woodburn, Alexander Rooney Forbes, Robert Inglis Campbell, Allan Duncan Brown, William Russell Logan Bauld, William Steel, William Beveridge Liddell.
Goals: José António Barreto Travaços (9), Albano Narciso Pereira (29) /
William Russell Logan Bauld (20), Allan Duncan Brown (23)

211. 27.05.1950
FRANCE v SCOTLAND 0-1 (0-0)
Yves du Manoir, Colombes, Paris

Referee: Julian Arque (Spain)   Attendance: 35,568

FRANCE: Abderrahman Ibrir, Guy Huguet, Roger Lamy, Roger Marche, Jean Grégoire, Antoine Cuissard, André Strappe, Jean Grumellon, Henri Baillot, Jean Baratte (Cap), Geoges Dard.

SCOTLAND: James Clews Cowan, George Lewis Young (Cap), Samuel Richmond Cox, John Miller McColl, William Alexander Woodburn, Alexander Rooney Forbes, Robert Inglis Campbell, Allan Duncan Brown, Lawrence Reilly, William Steel, William Beveridge Liddell.

Goal: Allan Duncan Brown (69)

212. 21.10.1950   Home Championship
WALES v SCOTLAND 1-3 (0-1)
Ninian Park, Cardiff

Referee: Arthur Edward Ellis (England)   Att: 50,000

WALES: Brinley John Parry, Walley Barnes, Alfred Thomas Sherwood, Ivor Verdun Powell, Roy Paul, William Arthur Ronald Burgess, Harold Williams, Brynley William Allen, Trevor Ford, Aubrey Powell, Royston James Clarke.

SCOTLAND: James Clews Cowan, George Lewis Young (Cap), William McNaught, John Miller McColl, William Alexander Woodburn, Alexander Rooney Forbes, Robert Young Collins, John McPhail, Lawrence Reilly, William Steel, William Beveridge Liddell.

Goals: Aubrey Powell (68) /
Lawrence Reilly (23, 65), William Beveridge Liddell (72)

213. 01.11.1950   Home Championship
SCOTLAND v NORTHERN IRELAND 6-1 (2-1)
Hampden Park, Glasgow

Referee: Benjamin Mervyn Griffiths (Wales)   Att: 83,142

SCOTLAND: James Clews Cowan, George Lewis Young (Cap), William McNaught, John Miller McColl, William Alexander Woodburn, Alexander Rooney Forbes, Robert Young Collins, James Mason, John McPhail, William Steel, William Beveridge Liddell.

NORTHERN IRELAND: Hugh Redmond Kelly, Charles Gallogly, Alfred McMichael, Robert Denis Blanchflower, John Joseph Vernon, Wilbur W. Cush, John Peter Campbell, J. Kevin McGarry, Edward James McMorran, Peter Dermont Doherty, John McKenna.

Goals: John McPhail (8, 13), William Steel (53, 57, 66, 79) /
J. Kevin McGarry (43)

214. 13.12.1950
SCOTLAND v AUSTRIA 0-1 (0-1)
Hampden Park, Glasgow

Referee: William H. Ling (England)   Attendance: 68,000

SCOTLAND: James Clews Cowan, George Lewis Young (Cap), William McNaught, Robert Evans, William Alexander Woodburn, Alexander Rooney Forbes, Robert Young Collins, Edward Hunter Turnbull, John McPhail, William Steel, William Beveridge Liddell.

AUSTRIA: Walter Zeman, Rudolf Röckl, Ernst Happel, Gerhard Hanappi, Ernst Ocwirk, Leopold Gernhardt, Ernst Melchior, Karl Decker, Theodor Wagner, Ernst Stojaspal, Lukas Aurednik.   Trainer: Walter Nausch.

Goal: Ernst Melchior (26)

215. 14.04.1951   Home Championship
ENGLAND v SCOTLAND 2-3 (1-1)
Wembley, London

Referee: George Mitchell (Scotland)   Attendance: 98,000

ENGLAND: Bert Frederick Williams, Alfred Ernest Ramsey, William Eckersley, Henry Johnston, John Froggatt, William Ambrose Wright (Cap), Stanley Matthews, Wilfred Mannion, Stanley Harding Mortensen, Harold William Hassall, Thomas Finney.   Manager: Walter Winterbottom.

SCOTLAND: James Clews Cowan, George Lewis Young (Cap), Samuel Richmond Cox, Robert Evans, William Alexander Woodburn, William Yates Redpath, William Waddell, Robert Johnstone, Lawrence Reilly, William Steel, William Beveridge Liddell.

Goals: Harold William Hassall (26), Thomas Finney (63) /
Robert Johnstone (33), Lawrence Reilly (47),
William Beveridge Liddell (53)

216. 12.05.1951
SCOTLAND v DENMARK 3-1 (1-1)
Hampden Park, Glasgow

Referee: W.H.E. Evans (England)   Attendance: 75,000

SCOTLAND: James Clews Cowan, George Lewis Young (Cap), Samuel Richmond Cox, James Scoular, William Alexander Woodburn, William Yates Redpath, William Waddell, Robert Johnstone, Lawrence Reilly, William Steel, Robert Carmichael Mitchell.

DENMARK: Eigil Nielsen, Dan Ohland-Andersen, Poul Petersen, Erik Hansen, Edvin Hansen, Steen Blicher, James Rønvang, Jørgen W. Hansen, Jens Torstensen, Knud Lundberg (Cap), Jens Peder Hansen.

Goals: William Steel (33), Lawrence Reilly (59), Robert Carmichael Mitchell (86) / Jørgen W. Hansen (6)

217. 16.05.1951
SCOTLAND v FRANCE 1-0 (0-0)

Hampden Park, Glasgow

Referee: Herbert Mortimer (England)   Attendance: 75,394

SCOTLAND: James Clews Cowan, George Lewis Young (Cap), Samuel Richmond Cox, James Scoular, William Alexander Woodburn, William Yates Redpath, William Waddell, Robert Johnstone, Lawrence Reilly, William Steel, Robert Carmichael Mitchell.

FRANCE: Stéphane Dakoski, Guy Huguet, Robert Jonquet, Roger Marche (Cap), Antoine Bonifaci, Antoine Cuissard, André Strappe, Édouard Kargu, René Alpsteg, Jean Baratte, Edmond Haan.

Goal: Lawrence Reilly (78)

218. 20.05.1951
BELGIUM v SCOTLAND 0-5 (0-2)

Heysel, Bruxelles

Referee: Louis Fauquemberghe (France)   Att: 55,135

BELGIUM: Henri Meert, Arsène Vaillant, Léopold Anoul, Jan Van der Auwera, Louis Carré, Victor Mees, Victor Lemberechts, Frédéric Chavès D'Aguilar, Rik Coppens, Joseph Mermans, François Sermon.
Trainer: William Gormlie (England)

SCOTLAND: James Clews Cowan, George Lewis Young (Cap), Samuel Richmond Cox, John Miller McColl, William Alexander Woodburn, William Yates Redpath, William Waddell, James Mason, George Hamilton, William Steel, Lawrence Reilly.

Goals: George Hamilton (8, 58, 65), James Mason (17), William Waddell (81)

219. 27.05.1951
AUSTRIA v SCOTLAND 4-0 (1-0)

Prater, Wien

Referee: Jean Lutz (Switzerland)   Attendance: 65,000

AUSTRIA: Walter Zeman, Rudolf Röckl, Ernst Happel, Gerhard Hanappi, Ernst Ocwirk, Leopold Gernhardt, Ernst Melchior, Johann Riegler, Theodor Wagner, Erich Probst, Alfred Körner II.   Trainer: Walter Nausch.

SCOTLAND: James Clews Cowan, George Lewis Young (Cap), Samuel Richmond Cox, James Scoular, William Alexander Woodburn, William Yates Redpath, William Waddell, James Mason, George Hamilton, William Steel, Lawrence Reilly.

Goals: Gerhard Hanappi (42, 57), Theodor Wagner (70, 87)

220. 06.10.1951   Home Championship
NORTHERN IRELAND v SCOTLAND 0-3 (0-2)

Windsor Park, Belfast

Referee: W.H.E. Evans (England)   Attendance: 56,946

NORTHERN IRELAND: William Uprichard, William George Leonard Graham, Alfred McMichael, William Dickson, John Joseph Vernon, Raymond Osborn Ferris, William Laurence Bingham, James McIlroy, Edward James McMorran, Robert Peacock, Charles P. Tully.

SCOTLAND: James Clews Cowan, George Lewis Young (Cap), Samuel Richmond Cox, Robert Evans, William Alexander Woodburn, William Yates Redpath, William Waddell, Robert Johnstone, Lawrence Reilly, Thomas Bingham Orr, William Beveridge Liddell.

Goals: Thomas Bingham Orr (32), Robert Johnstone (44, 62)

221. 14.11.1951   Home Championship
SCOTLAND v WALES 0-1 (0-0)

Hampden Park, Glasgow

Referee: Patrick Morris (Northern Ireland)   Att: 71,272

SCOTLAND: James Clews Cowan, George Lewis Young (Cap), Samuel Richmond Cox, Thomas Henderson Docherty, William Alexander Woodburn, Alexander Rooney Forbes, William Waddell, Thomas Bingham Orr, Lawrence Reilly, William Steel, William Beveridge Liddell.

WALES: William Warren Shortt, Walley Barnes, Alfred Thomas Sherwood, Roy Paul, William Raymond Daniel, William Arthur Ronald Burgess, William Isaiah Foulkes, William Morris, Trevor Ford, Ivor John Allchurch, Royston James Clarke.

Goal: Ivor John Allchurch (89)

222. 05.04.1952   Home Championship
SCOTLAND v ENGLAND 1-2 (0-2)

Hampden Park, Glasgow

Referee: Patrick Morris (Northern Ireland)   Att: 133,991

SCOTLAND: Robert Brown, George Lewis Young (Cap), William McNaught, James Scoular, William Alexander Woodburn, William Yates Redpath, Gordon Smith, Robert Johnstone, Lawrence Reilly, John Livingstone McMillan, William Beveridge Liddell.

ENGLAND: Gilbert Harold Merrick, Alfred Ernest Ramsey, Thomas Garrett, William Ambrose Wright (Cap), John Froggatt, James William Dickinson, Thomas Finney, Ivan Arthur Broadis, Nathaniel Lofthouse, Stanley Clare Pearson, John Frederick Rowley.   Manager: Walter Winterbottom.

Goals: Lawrence Reilly (77) / Stanley Clare Pearson (9, 44)

223. 30.04.1952
SCOTLAND v UNITED STATES 6-0 (4-0)

Hampden Park, Glasgow

Referee: Douglas Gerrard (Scotland)   Attendance: 107,765

SCOTLAND: James Clews Cowan, George Lewis Young (Cap), Samuel Richmond Cox, James Scoular, William Alexander Woodburn, Hugh Thomas Kelly, Gordon Smith, John Livingstone McMillan, Lawrence Reilly, Allan Duncan Brown, William Beveridge Liddell.

UNITED STATES: Frank Borghi, Harry Joseph Keough, John O'Connell, William Sheppell, Charles Martin Colombo, Walter Alfred Bahr (Cap), Lloyd Monsen, Edward Netto Souza, Richard Roberts, John Benevides Souza, Bernard McLaughlin. Trainer: John Wood.

Goals: Lawrence Reilly (9, 10, 34), John Livingstone McMillan (29, 89), John O'Connell (60 own goal)

224. 25.05.1952
DENMARK v SCOTLAND 1-2 (0-0)

Idrætsparken, København

Referee: Sten Ahlner (Sweden)   Attendance: 39,000

DENMARK: Kaj Jørgensen, Poul Petersen, Svend Nielsen, Erik Terkelsen, Christen Brøgger, Steen Blicher, Carl Holm, Poul Rasmussen, Jens Torstensen, Knud Lundberg (Cap), Holger Seebach.

SCOTLAND: James Clews Cowan, George Lewis Young (Cap), Samuel Richmond Cox, James Scoular, Andrew Paton, Alexander Rooney Forbes, Lawrence Reilly, John Livingstone McMillan, William Thornton, Allan Duncan Brown, William Beveridge Liddell.

Goals: Poul Rasmussen (63) / William Thornton (49), Lawrence Reilly (71)

225. 30.05.1952
SWEDEN v SCOTLAND 3-1 (2-1)

Råsunda, Stockholm

Referee: Karel van der Meer (Holland)   Attendance: 32,122

SWEDEN: Karl Svensson, Lennart Samuelsson, Erik Nilsson (Cap), Holger Hansson, Bengt Gustavsson, Gösta Lindh, Sylve Bengtsson, Gösta Löfgren, Lars Eriksson, Yngve Brodd, Gösta Sandberg.   Trainer: Rudolf Kock.

SCOTLAND: James Clews Cowan, George Lewis Young (Cap), Samuel Richmond Cox, James Scoular, Andrew Paton, Alexander Rooney Forbes, Lawrence Reilly, Wilson Humphries, William Thornton, Allan Duncan Brown, William Beveridge Liddell.

Goals: Gösta Sandberg (2), Gösta Löfgren (3), Sylve Bengtsson (71) / William Beveridge Liddell (6)

226. 18.10.1952   Home Championship
WALES v SCOTLAND 1-2 (1-1)

Ninian Park, Cardiff

Referee: Alfred Bond (England)   Attendance: 60,261

WALES: William Warren Shortt, Arthur Richard Lever, Alfred Thomas Sherwood, Roy Paul, William Raymond Daniel, William Arthur Ronald Burgess, William Isaiah Foulkes, Ellis Reginald Davies, Trevor Ford, Ivor John Allchurch, Royston James Clarke.

SCOTLAND: George Neil Farm, George Lewis Young (Cap), Samuel Richmond Cox, James Scoular, Francis Brennan, George Graham Aitken, Thomas Wright, Allan Duncan Brown, Lawrence Reilly, William Steel, William Beveridge Liddell.

Goals: Trevor Ford (23) / Allan Duncan Brown (32), William Beveridge Liddell (69)

227. 05.11.1952   Home Championship
SCOTLAND v NORTHERN IRELAND 1-1 (0-0)

Hampden Park, Glasgow

Referee: Robert E. Smith (Wales)   Attendance: 65,057

SCOTLAND: George Neil Farm, George Lewis Young (Cap), Samuel Richmond Cox, James Scoular, Francis Brennan, George Graham Aitken, Thomas Wright, James Tullis Logie, Lawrence Reilly, William Steel, William Beveridge Liddell.

NORTHERN IRELAND: William Uprichard, William George Leonard Graham, Alfred McMichael, Robert Denis Blanchflower, William Dickson, Francis Joseph McCourt, William Laurence Bingham, Samuel Donal D'Arcy, Edward James McMorran, James McIlroy, Charles P. Tully.

Goals: Lawrence Reilly (90) / Samuel Donal D'Arcy (80)

228. 18.04.1953   Home Championship
ENGLAND v SCOTLAND 2-2 (1-0)

Wembley, London

Referee: Thomas Mitchell (Northern Ireland)   Att: 97,000

ENGLAND: Gilbert Harold Merrick, Alfred Ernest Ramsey, Lionel Smith, William Ambrose Wright (Cap), Malcolm Williamson Barrass, James William Dickinson, Thomas Finney, Ivan Arthur Broadis, Nathaniel Lofthouse, Redfern Froggatt, John Froggatt.   Manager: Walter Winterbottom.

SCOTLAND: George Neil Farm, George Lewis Young (Cap), Samuel Richmond Cox, Thomas Henderson Docherty, Francis Brennan, Douglas Cowie, Thomas Wright, Robert Johnstone, Lawrence Reilly, William Steel, William Beveridge Liddell.

Goals: Ivan Arthur Broadis (18, 70) / Lawrence Reilly (54, 89)

229. 06.05.1953
SCOTLAND v SWEDEN 1-2 (1-1)
Hampden Park, Glasgow

Referee: William Ling (England)   Attendance: 83,800

SCOTLAND: George Neil Farm, George Lewis Young (Cap), John Little, Robert Evans, Douglas Cowie, Thomas Henderson Docherty, John Gillespie Henderson, Robert Johnstone, Lawrence Reilly, William Steel, Thomas Ring.

SWEDEN: Karl Svensson, Lennart Samuelsson, Orvar Bergmark, Sven-Ove Svensson, Bengt Gustavsson (Cap), Gösta Lindh, Sylve Bengtsson, Gösta Löfgren, Lars Eriksson, Hans Andersson-Tvilling, Gösta Sandberg.   Trainer: Rudolf Kock.

Goals: Robert Johnstone (41) /
Gösta Löfgren (34), Lars Eriksson (53)

230. 03.10.1953   Home Championship,
5th World Cup Qualifiers
NORTHERN IRELAND v SCOTLAND 1-3 (0-0)
Hampden Park, Glasgow

Referee: Arthur Edward Ellis (Wales)   Attendance: 58,248

NORTHERN IRELAND: William Smyth, William Edward Cunningham, Alfred McMichael, Robert Denis Blanchflower, James Joseph McCabe, Wilbur W. Cush, William Laurence Bingham, James McIlroy, William J. Simpson, Charles P. Tully, Norman Lockhart.

SCOTLAND: George Neil Farm, George Lewis Young (Cap), Samuel Richmond Cox, Robert Evans, Francis Brennan, Douglas Cowie, William Waddell, Charles Fleming, John McPhail, James Watson, John Gillespie Henderson.

Goals: Norman Lockhart (72 pen) /
Charles Fleming (47, 69), John Gillespie Henderson (89)

231. 04.11.1953   Home Championship,
5th World Cup Qualifiers
SCOTLAND v WALES 3-3 (2-0)
Hampden Park, Glasgow

Referee: Thomas Mitchell (Northern Ireland)   Att: 71,387

SCOTLAND: George Neil Farm, George Lewis Young (Cap), Samuel Richmond Cox, Robert Evans, William Douglas Telfer, Douglas Cowie, John Archibald MacKenzie, Robert Johnstone, Lawrence Reilly, Allan Duncan Brown, William Beveridge Liddell.

WALES: Ronald Gilbert Howells, Walley Barnes, Alfred Thomas Sherwood, Roy Paul, William Raymond Daniel, William Arthur Ronald Burgess, William Isaiah Foulkes, Ellis Reginald Davies, William John Charles, Ivor John Allchurch, Royston James Clarke.

Goals: Allan Duncan Brown (19), Robert Johnstone (42), Lawrence Reilly (58) /
William John Charles (49, 88), Ivor John Allchurch (73)

232. 03.04.1954   Home Championship,
5th World Cup Qualifiers
SCOTLAND v ENGLAND 2-4 (1-1)
Hampden Park, Glasgow

Referee: Thomas Mitchell (Northern Ireland)   Att: 134,544

SCOTLAND: George Neil Farm, Michael Haughney, Samuel Richmond Cox (Cap), Robert Evans, Francis Brennan, George Graham Aitken, John Archibald MacKenzie, Robert Johnstone, John Gillespie Henderson, Allan Duncan Brown, William Esplin Ormond.   Manager: Andrew Beattie.

ENGLAND: Gilbert Harold Merrick, Ronald Staniforth, Roger William Byrne, William Ambrose Wright (Cap), Henry Alfred Clarke, James William Dickinson, Thomas Finney, Ivan Arthur Broadis, Ronald Allen, John Nicholls, James Mullen.   Manager: Walter Winterbottom.

Goals: Allan Duncan Brown (7), William Ormond (89) /
Ivan Broadis (14), John Nicholls (51), Ronald Allen (68), James Mullen (83)

233. 05.05.1954
SCOTLAND v NORWAY 1-0 (1-0)
Hampden Park, Glasgow

Referee: John Harold Clough (England)   Att: 25,897

SCOTLAND: Frederick Martin, William Carruthers Cunningham, John Rae Aird, Thomas Henderson Docherty (Cap), James Anderson Davidson, Robert Evans, Robert Johnstone, George Hamilton, Patrick McCabe Buckley, Allan Duncan Brown, William Esplin Ormond.
Manager: Andrew Beattie

NORWAY: Asbjørn Hammer, Oddvar Hansen, Harry Boye Karlsen, Thorleif Olsen, Thor Hernes, Arne Natland, Willy Fossli, Gunnar Thoresen, Arne Kotte, Hans Nordahl, Gunnar Dybwad.   Trainer: Willibald Hahn (Austria)

Goal: George Hamilton (34)

234. 19.05.1954
NORWAY v SCOTLAND 1-1 (0-0)
Ullevaal, Oslo

Referee: John Erik Andersson (Sweden)   Att: 25,000

NORWAY: Asbjørn Hammer, Oddvar Hansen, Harry Boye Karlsen, Thorleif Olsen, Thorbjørn Svenssen, Thor Hernes (58 Arne Natland), Ragnar Hvidsten, Gunnar Thoresen, Arne Kotte, Gunnar Arnesen, Harry Kure.
Trainer: Willibald Hahn (Austria)

SCOTLAND: Frederick Martin, William Carruthers Cunningham, John Rae Aird, Thomas Henderson Docherty (Cap), James Anderson Davidson, Douglas Cowie, John Archibald MacKenzie, George Hamilton, John Gillespie Henderson, Allan Duncan Brown, Neil Mochan.   Manager: Andrew Beattie.

Goals: Harry Kure (88) / John Archibald MacKenzie (56)

235. 25.05.1954
FINLAND v SCOTLAND 1-2 (0-1)
Olympiastadion, Helsinki
Referee: Sten Ahlner (Sweden)   Attendance: 21,685
FINLAND: Mauno Rintanen (Cap) (48 Aarre Klinga), Åke Lindman, Ibert Henriksson, Turkka Sundbäck, Lauri Lehtinen, Aimo Sommarberg, Pertti Vanhanen, Matti Hiltunen, Rainer Forss, Olavi Lahtinen, Börje Nygård. Trainer: Aatos Lehtonen.
SCOTLAND: John Anderson, Alexander Wilson, William Carruthers Cunningham (Cap), Robert Evans, Douglas Cowie, David Cochrane Mathers, John Archibald MacKenzie, Robert Johnstone, Allan Duncan Brown, William Fernie, William Esplin Ormond.   Manager: Andrew Beattie.

Goals: Olavi Lahtinen (85) /
William Esplin Ormond (10), Robert Johnstone (47)

236. 16.06.1954   5th World Cup, 1st Round
AUSTRIA v SCOTLAND 1-0 (1-0)
Hardturm, Zürich
Referee: Laurent Franken (Belgium)   Attendance: 25,000
AUSTRIA: Kurt Schmied, Gerhard Hanappi, Leopold Barschandt, Ernst Ocwirk, Ernst Happel, Karl Koller, Robert Körner I, Dr. Walter Schleger, Robert Dienst, Erich Probst, Alfred Körner II.   Trainer: Walter Nausch.
SCOTLAND: Frederick Martin, William Carruthers Cunningham (Cap), John Rae Aird, Thomas Henderson Docherty, James Anderson Davidson, Douglas Cowie, John Archibald MacKenzie, William Fernie, Neil Mochan, Allan Duncan Brown, William Esplin Ormond.
Manager: Andrew Beattie.

Goal: Erich Probst (32)

237. 19.06.1954   5th World Cup, 1st Round
URUGUAY v SCOTLAND 7-0 (2-0)
St.Jakob, Basel
Referee: Vincenzo Orlandini (Italy)   Attendance: 34,000
URUGUAY: Roque Gastón Máspoli, José Emilio Santamaría, William Ruben Martínez, Víctor Pablo Rodríguez Andrade, Obdulio Jacinto Varela (Cap), Luis Alberto Cruz, Julio César Abbadie, Javier Ambrois, Oscar Omar Míguez, Juan Alberto Schiaffino, Carlos Ariel Borges.   Trainer: Juan López.
SCOTLAND: Frederick Martin, William Carruthers Cunningham (Cap), John Rae Aird, Thomas Henderson Docherty, James Anderson Davidson, Douglas Cowie, John Archibald MacKenzie, William Fernie, Neil Mochan, Allan Duncan Brown, William Esplin Ormond.
Manager: Andrew Beattie.

Goals: Carlos Ariel Borges (17, 48, 58),
Oscar Omar Míguez (31, 82), Julio César Abbadie (55, 84)

238. 16.10.1954   Home Championship
WALES v SCOTLAND 0-1 (0-0)
Ninian Park, Cardiff
Referee: William Ling (England)   Attendance: 53,000
WALES: Alfred John Kelsey, Walley Barnes, Alfred Thomas Sherwood, Roy Paul, William John Charles, David Lloyd Bowen, William George Reed, Derek Robert Tapscott, Trevor Ford, Ivor John Allchurch, Royston James Clarke.
SCOTLAND: William Alexander Fraser, George Lewis Young (Cap), William Carruthers Cunningham, Thomas Henderson Docherty, James Anderson Davidson, Douglas Cowie, William Waddell, Henry Yorston, Patrick McCabe Buckley, William Fernie, Thomas Ring.

Goal: Patrick McCabe Buckley (70)

239. 03.11.1954   Home Championship
SCOTLAND v NORTHERN IRELAND 2-2 (1-2)
Hampden Park, Glasgow
Referee: Alfred Bond (England)   Attendance: 46,200
SCOTLAND: William Alexander Fraser, George Lewis Young (Cap), William McNaught, Robert Evans, James Anderson Davidson, Douglas Cowie, William Waddell, Robert Johnstone, Patrick McCabe Buckley, William Fernie, Thomas Ring.
NORTHERN IRELAND: William Uprichard, William George Leonard Graham, William Edward Cunningham, Robert Denis Blanchflower, William Terence McCavana, Robert Peacock, William Laurence Bingham, John Blanchflower, William John McAdams, James McIlroy, Peter James McParland.

Goals: James Davidson (22), Robert Johnstone (74) /
William Laurence Bingham (24), William John McAdams (44)

240. 08.12.1954
SCOTLAND v HUNGARY 2-4 (1-3)
Hampden Park, Glasgow
Referee: Leopold Sylvain Horn (Holland)   Att: 113,146
SCOTLAND: Frederick Martin, William Carruthers Cunningham (Cap), Harold Haddock, Thomas Henderson Docherty, James Anderson Davidson, John Cumming, John Archibald MacKenzie, Robert Johnstone, Lawrence Reilly, James Wardhaug, Thomas Ring.
HUNGARY: Lajos Faragó, Jenő Buzánszky, Gyula Lóránt, Mihály Lantos, József Bozsik, Ferenc Szojka, Károly Sándor, Sándor Kocsis, Nándor Hidegkuti, Ferenc Puskás, Máté Fenyvesi.   Trainer: Gusztáv Sebes.

Goals: Thomas Ring (36), Robert Johnstone (46) /
József Bozsik (20), Nándor Hidegkuti (26), Károly Sándor (43), Sándor Kocsis (90)

241. 02.04.1955   Home Championship
ENGLAND v SCOTLAND 7-2 (4-1)

Wembley, London

Referee: Benjamin Mervyn Griffiths (Wales)   Att: 96,847

ENGLAND: Bert Frederick Williams, James Meadows, Roger William Byrne, Kenneth Armstrong, William Ambrose Wright (Cap), Duncan Edwards, Stanley Matthews, Donald George Revie, Nathaniel Lofthouse, Dennis James Wilshaw, Frank Blunstone.   Manager: Walter Winterbottom.

SCOTLAND: Frederick Martin, William Carruthers Cunningham (Cap), Harold Haddock, Thomas Henderson Docherty, James Anderson Davidson, John Cumming, John Archibald MacKenzie, Robert Johnstone, Lawrence Reilly, John Livingstone McMillan, Thomas Ring.

Goals: Dennis James Wilshaw (1, 70, 73, 80), Nathaniel Lofthouse (7, 27), Donald George Revie (25) / Lawrence Reilly (15), Thomas Henderson Docherty (85)

242. 04.05.1955
SCOTLAND v PORTUGAL 3-0 (2-0)

Hampden Park, Glasgow

Referee: Juan Gardeazábal Garay (Spain)   Att: 20,858

SCOTLAND: Thomas Younger, Alexander Hershaw Parker, Harold Haddock, Robert Evans, George Lewis Young (Cap), John Cumming, Gordon Smith, Archibald Clark Robertson, Lawrence Reilly, Thomas Gemmell, William Beveridge Liddell.

PORTUGAL: Carlos António de Carmo Costa Gomes, Manuel António Caldeira, Ângelo Ferreira Carvalho, Fernando Augusto Amoral Caiado, Manuel Passos Fernandes (Cap), Emídio da Silva Graça, José Carvalho Santos Pinto Águas, Lucas Sebastião da Fonseca "Matateu", Mário Esteves Coluna, José António Barreto Travaços, João Batista Martins.   Trainer: Tavares da Silva.

Goals: Thomas Gemmell (7), William Beveridge Liddell (36), Lawrence Reilly (86)

243. 15.05.1955
YUGOSLAVIA v SCOTLAND 2-2 (2-2)

JNA, Beograd

Referee: Vincenzo Orlandini (Italy)   Attendance: 20,000

YUGOSLAVIA: Vladimir Beara (65 Branko Kralj), Bruno Belin, Milan Zeković, Zlatko Čajkovski, Suad Švraka, Vujadin Boškov, Todor Veselinović, Miloš Milutinović, Bernard Vukas, Stjepan Bobek (Cap), Branko Zebec.   Trainer: Aleksandar Tirnanić.

SCOTLAND: Thomas Younger, Alexander Hershaw Parker, Harold Haddock, Robert Evans, George Lewis Young (Cap), John Cumming, Gordon Smith, Robert Young Collins, Lawrence Reilly, Thomas Gemmell, William Beveridge Liddell.

Goals: Todor Veselinović (13), Bernard Vukas (38) / Lawrence Reilly (30), Gordon Smith (40)

244. 19.05.1955
AUSTRIA v SCOTLAND 1-4 (0-2)

Prater, Wien

Referee: Giorgio Bernardi (Italy)   Attendance: 65,000

AUSTRIA: Kurt Schmied, Paul Halla, Leopold Barschandt, Gerhard Hanappi, Rudolf Röckl, Ernst Ocwirk, Karl Hofbauer, Theodor Wagner, Richard Brousek (42 Robert Dienst), Erich Probst, Dr. Walter Schleger.   Trainer: Karl Geyer.

SCOTLAND: Thomas Younger, Alexander Hershaw Parker, Andrew Kerr, Thomas Henderson Docherty, Robert Evans, Douglas Cowie, Gordon Smith (Cap), Robert Young Collins, Lawrence Reilly, Archibald Clark Robertson, William Beveridge Liddell.

Goals: Ernst Ocwirk (87) / Archibald Clark Robertson (1), Gordon Smith (44), William Beveridge Liddell (70), Lawrence Reilly (89)

245. 29.05.1955
HUNGARY v SCOTLAND 3-1 (0-1)

Népstadion, Budapest

Referee: Friedrich Seipelt (Austria)   Attendance: 100,000

HUNGARY: Imre Danka (46 Lajos Faragó), Jenő Buzánszky, Pál Várhidi, Mihály Lantos, József Bozsik, Ferenc Szojka, Károly Sándor (44 Péter Palotás), Sándor Kocsis, Nándor Hidegkuti, Ferenc Puskás, Máté Fenyvesi.   Trainer: Gusztáv Sebes.

SCOTLAND: Thomas Younger, Andrew Kerr, Harold Haddock, Thomas Henderson Docherty, Robert Evans, Douglas Cowie, Gordon Smith (Cap), Robert Young Collins, Lawrence Reilly, Archibald Clark Robertson, William Beveridge Liddell.

Goals: Nándor Hidegkuti (51), Sándor Kocsis (58), Máté Fenyvesi (69) / Gordon Smith (42)

246. 08.10.1955   Home Championship
NORTHERN IRELAND v SCOTLAND 2-1 (2-0)

Windsor Park, Belfast

Referee: John H. Kelly (England)   Attendance: 48,000

SCOTLAND: Thomas Younger, Alexander Hershaw Parker, Joseph McDonald, Robert Evans, George Lewis Young (Cap), Archibald Glen, Gordon Smith, Robert Young Collins, Lawrence Reilly, Robert Johnstone, William Beveridge Liddell.

NORTHERN IRELAND: William Uprichard, William George Leonard Graham, William Edward Cunningham, Robert Denis Blanchflower, William Terence McCavana, Robert Peacock, William Laurence Bingham, John Blanchflower, Francis Coyle, James McIlroy, Peter James McParland.

Goals: John Blanchflower (7), William Bingham (16) / Lawrence Reilly (62)

45

247. 09.11.1955   Home Championship
SCOTLAND v WALES 2-0 (2-0)
Hampden Park, Glasgow

Referee: Reginald J. Leafe (England)   Attendance: 53,887

SCOTLAND: Thomas Younger, Alexander Hershaw Parker, Joseph McDonald, Robert Evans, George Lewis Young (Cap), Douglas Cowie, Gordon Smith, Robert Johnstone, Lawrence Reilly, Robert Young Collins, John Gillespie Henderson.

WALES: Alfred John Kelsey, Stuart Grenville Williams, Alfred Thomas Sherwood, Melvyn Charles, William John Charles, Roy Paul, Derek Robert Tapscott, Noel Kinsey, Trevor Ford, Ivor John Allchurch, Clifford William Jones. Manager: Walley Barnes.

Goals: Robert Johnstone (14, 25)

248. 14.04.1956   Home Championship
SCOTLAND v ENGLAND 1-1 (0-0)
Hampden Park, Glasgow

Referee: Leo Callaghan (Wales)   Attendance: 132,817

SCOTLAND: Thomas Younger, Alexander Hershaw Parker, John Davidson Hewie, Robert Evans, George Lewis Young (Cap), Archibald Glen, Graham Leggat, Robert Johnstone, Lawrence Reilly, John Livingstone McMillan, Gordon Smith.

ENGLAND: Reginald Derrick Matthews, Jeffrey James Hall, Roger William Byrne, James William Dickinson, William Ambrose Wright (Cap), Duncan Edwards, Thomas Finney, Thomas Taylor, Nathaniel Lofthouse, John Norman Haynes, William Perry.   Manager: Walter Winterbottom.

Goals: Graham Leggat (60) / John Norman Haynes (89)

249. 02.05.1956
SCOTLAND v AUSTRIA 1-1 (1-1)
Hampden Park, Glasgow

Referee: Johannes Bronkhorst (Holland)   Att: 80,509

SCOTLAND: Thomas Younger, Alexander Hershaw Parker, John Davidson Hewie, Robert Evans, George Lewis Young (Cap), Douglas Cowie, John Archibald MacKenzie, Alfred Conn, Lawrence Reilly, Hugh Baird, Michael Joseph Cullen.

AUSTRIA: Bruno Engelmeier, Paul Halla, Leopold Barschandt, Ernst Ocwirk, Walter Kollmann, Karl Koller, Herbert Grohs, Theodor Wagner, Gerhard Hanappi, Alfred Körner II, Walter Haummer.   Trainer: Josef Argauer.

Goals: Alfred Conn (12) / Theodor Wagner (13)

250. 20.10.1956   Home Championship
WALES v SCOTLAND 2-2 (2-2)
Ninian Park, Cardiff

Referee: Robert Mann (England)   Attendance: 60,000

WALES: Alfred John Kelsey, Alfred Thomas Sherwood, Melvyn Hopkins, Alan Charles Harrington, William Raymond Daniel, Derrick Sullivan, Terence Cameron Medwin, William John Charles, Trevor Ford, Ivor John Allchurch, Clifford William Jones.   Manager: James Patrick Murphy.

SCOTLAND: Thomas Younger, Alexander Hershaw Parker, John Davidson Hewie, John Miller McColl, George Lewis Young (Cap), Douglas Cowie, Graham Leggat, John Knight Mudie, Lawrence Reilly, Robert Young Collins, William Fernie.

Goals: Trevor Ford (7), Terence Cameron Medwin (32) / William Fernie (22), Lawrence Reilly (36)

251. 07.11.1956   Home Championship
SCOTLAND v NORTHERN IRELAND 1-0 (1-0)
Hampden Park, Glasgow

Referee: Reginald J. Leafe (England)   Attendance: 62,035

SCOTLAND: Thomas Younger, Alexander Hershaw Parker, John Davidson Hewie, John Miller McColl, George Lewis Young (Cap), Douglas Cowie, Alexander Silcock Scott, John Knight Mudie, Lawrence Reilly, James Wardhaug, William Fernie.

NORTHERN IRELAND: Harold Gregg, William Edward Cunningham, Alfred McMichael, Robert Denis Blanchflower, John Blanchflower, Thomas Casey, William Laurence Bingham, James McIlroy, Robert James Shields, Thomas A. Dickson, Peter James McParland.

Goal: Alexander Silcock Scott (25)

252. 21.11.1956
SCOTLAND v YUGOSLAVIA 2-0 (1-0)
Hampden Park, Glasgow

Referee: Pieter Paulus Roomer (Holland)   Att: 55,521

SCOTLAND: Thomas Younger, Alexander Hershaw Parker, John Davidson Hewie, John Miller McColl, George Lewis Young (Cap), Thomas Henderson Docherty, Alexander Silcock Scott, John Knight Mudie, Lawrence Reilly, Samuel Baird, William Fernie.

YUGOSLAVIA: Vladimir Beara, Bruno Belin, Branko Stanković (Cap), Lazar Tasić, Ivan Horvat, Vujadin Boškov, Aleksandar Petaković, Miloš Milutinović, Tihomir Ognjanov, Bernard Vukas, Branko Zebec.   Trainer: Aleksandar Tirnanić.

Goals: John Knight Mudie (36), Samuel Baird (55)

253. 06.04.1957   Home Championship
ENGLAND v SCOTLAND 2-1 (0-1)
Wembley, London
Referee: Pieter Paulus Roomer (Holland)   Att: 97,520
ENGLAND: Alan Hodgkinson, Jeffrey James Hall, Roger William Byrne, Ronald Clayton, William Ambrose Wright (Cap), Duncan Edwards, Stanley Matthews, Thomas Thompson, Thomas Finney, Derek Tennyson Kevan, Colin Grainger.   Manager: Walter Winterbottom.
SCOTLAND: Thomas Younger, Eric Caldow, John Davidson Hewie, John Miller McColl, George Lewis Young (Cap), Thomas Henderson Docherty, Robert Young Collins, William Fernie, Lawrence Reilly, John Knight Mudie, Thomas Ring.
Goals: Derek Tennyson Kevan (63), Duncan Edwards (80) / Thomas Ring (1)

254. 08.05.1957   6th World Cup Qualifiers
SCOTLAND v SPAIN 4-2 (2-1)
Hampden Park, Glasgow
Referee: Albert Dusch (West Germany)   Attendance: 88,890
SCOTLAND: Thomas Younger, Eric Caldow, John Davidson Hewie, John Miller McColl, George Lewis Young (Cap), Thomas Henderson Docherty, Gordon Smith, Robert Young Collins, John Knight Mudie, Samuel Baird, Thomas Ring.
SPAIN: Antonio Ramallets Simón, Fernando Olivella Pons, Marcelino Vaquero González "Campanal II", Jesús Garay Vecino (Cap), Martín Vergés Massa, José María Zárraga Martín, Miguel González Pérez, Ladislao Kubala, Alfredo Di Stéfano Lahule, Luis Suárez Miramónte, Francisco Gento López.   Trainer: Manuel Meana Vallina.
Goals: John Knight Mudie (22, 70, 79), John Hewie (41 pen) / Ladislao Kubala (29), Luis Suárez Miramónte (50)

255. 19.05.1957   6th World Cup Qualifiers
SWITZERLAND v SCOTLAND 1-2 (1-1)
St.Jakob, Basel
Referee: Friedrich Seipelt (Austria)   Attendance: 48,000
SWITZERLAND: Eugène Parlier, Willy Kernen, Harry Koch, André Grobéty, Ivo Frosio, Heinz Schneiter, Charles Antenen, Eugen Meier, Roger Vonlanthen II, Robert Ballaman, Fernando Riva IV.   Trainer: Jacques Spagnoli.
SCOTLAND: Thomas Younger, Eric Caldow, John Davidson Hewie, John Miller McColl, George Lewis Young (Cap), Thomas Henderson Docherty, Gordon Smith, Robert Young Collins, John Knight Mudie, Samuel Baird, Thomas Ring.
Goals: Roger Vonlanthen II (12) / John Knight Mudie (33), Robert Young Collins (71)

256. 22.05.1957
WEST GERMANY v SCOTLAND 1-3 (0-2)
Neckarstadion, Stuttgart
Referee: Gottfried Dienst (Switzerland)   Attendance: 80,000
GERMANY: Hans Tilkowski, Willi Gerdau, Erich Juskowiak, Georg Stollenwerk, Heinz Wewers, Horst Szymaniak, Helmut Rahn (Cap), Willi Schröder, Alfred Kelbassa, Alfred Schmidt, Gerhard Siedl.   Trainer: Josef Herberger.
SCOTLAND: Thomas Younger, Eric Caldow, John Davidson Hewie, John Miller McColl, Robert Evans, Thomas Henderson Docherty (Cap), Alexander Silcock Scott, Robert Young Collins, John Knight Mudie, Samuel Baird, Thomas Ring.
Goals: Gerhard Siedl (70) / Robert Young Collins (20, 54), John Knight Mudie (33)

257. 26.05.1957   6th World Cup Qualifiers
SPAIN v SCOTLAND 4-1 (2-0)
"Santiago Bernabéu", Madrid
Referee: Reginald J. Leafe (England)   Attendance: 90,000
SPAIN: Antonio Ramallets Simón, Juan Carlos Díaz Quincoces, Jesús Garay Vecino, Joan Segarra Iracheta, Martín Vergés Massa, Enric Gensana Merciés, Estanislao Basora Brunet (Cap), Ladislao Kubala, Alfredo Di Stéfano Lahule, Enrique Mateos Mancebo, Francisco Gento López.   Trainer: Manuel Meana Vallina.
SCOTLAND: Thomas Younger, Eric Caldow, John Davidson Hewie, David Craig MacKay, Robert Evans, Thomas Henderson Docherty (Cap), Gordon Smith, Robert Young Collins, John Knight Mudie, Samuel Baird, Thomas Ring.
Goals: Estanislao Basora Brunet (27, 63), Ladislao Kubala (34), Enrique Mateos Mancebo (70) / Gordon Smith (79)

258. 05.10.1957   Home Championship
NORTHERN IRELAND v SCOTLAND 1-1 (0-0)
Windsor Park, Belfast
Referee: Leo Callaghan (Wales)   Attendance: 50,000
NORTHERN IRELAND: William Uprichard, William Edward Cunningham, Alfred McMichael, Robert Denis Blanchflower, John Blanchflower, Robert Peacock, William Laurence Bingham, William J. Simpson, William John McAdams, James McIlroy, Peter James McParland.
SCOTLAND: Thomas Younger, Alexander Hershaw Parker, Eric Caldow, John Miller McColl, Robert Evans, Thomas Henderson Docherty (Cap), Graham Leggat, Robert Young Collins, John Knight Mudie, Samuel Baird, Thomas Ring.
Goals: William J. Simpson (47) / Graham Leggat (58)

259. 06.11.1957   6th World Cup Qualifiers
SCOTLAND v SWITZERLAND 3-2 (1-1)
Hampden Park, Glasgow
Referee: Reginald J. Leafe (England)   Attendance: 58,811
SCOTLAND: Thomas Younger, Alexander Hershaw Parker, Eric Caldow, William Fernie, Robert Evans, Thomas Henderson Docherty (Cap), Alexander Silcock Scott, Robert Young Collins, John Knight Mudie, Archibald Clark Robertson, Thomas Ring.
SWITZERLAND: Eugène Parlier, Willy Kernen, Fritz Morf, André Grobéty, Harry Koch, Heinz Schneiter, Francesco Chiesa, Robert Ballaman, Eugen Meier, Roger Vonlanthen II, Fernando Riva IV.   Trainer: Jacques Spagnoli.
Goals: Archibald Robertson (29), John Knight Mudie (52), Alexander Silcock Scott (70) /
Fernando Riva IV (35), Roger Vonlanthen II (80)

260. 13.11.1957   Home Championship
SCOTLAND v WALES 1-1 (1-0)
Hampden Park, Glasgow
Referee: John Harold Clough (England)   Att: 42,918
SCOTLAND: Thomas Younger, Alexander Hershaw Parker, Eric Caldow, Thomas Henderson Docherty (Cap), Robert Evans, William Fernie, Alexander Silcock Scott, Robert Young Collins, James Ian Gardiner, John Knight Mudie, Thomas Ewing.
WALES: Alfred John Kelsey, Stuart Grenville Williams, Melvyn Hopkins, Alan Charles Harrington, Melvyn Charles, David Lloyd Bowen, Leonard Allchurch, William Charles Harris, Terence Cameron Medwin, Thomas Royston Vernon, Clifford William Jones.   Manager: James Patrick Murphy.
Goals: Robert Young Collins (14) /
Terence Cameron Medwin (76)

261. 19.04.1958   Home Championship
SCOTLAND v ENGLAND 0-4 (0-2)
Hampden Park, Glasgow
Referee: Albert Dusch (West Germany)   Att: 127,874
SCOTLAND: Thomas Younger, Alexander Hershaw Parker, Harold Haddock, John Miller McColl, Robert Evans, Thomas Henderson Docherty (Cap), George Herd, James Murray, John Knight Mudie, James Forrest, Thomas Ewing. Manager: Dawson Walker.
ENGLAND: Edward Hopkinson, Donald Howe, Ernest James Langley, Ronald Clayton, William Ambrose Wright (Cap), William John Slater, Bryan Douglas, Robert Charlton, Derek Tennyson Kevan, John Norman Haynes, Thomas Finney.   Manager: Walter Winterbottom.
Goals: Bryan Douglas (20), Derek Tennyson Kevan (33, 75), Robert Charlton (67)

262. 07.05.1958
SCOTLAND v HUNGARY 1-1 (1-0)
Hampden Park, Glasgow
Referee: John Harold Clough (England)   Att: 54,900
SCOTLAND: Thomas Younger (Cap), Eric Caldow, John Davidson Hewie, Edward Hunter Turnbull, Robert Evans, Douglas Cowie, Graham Leggat, James Murray, John Knight Mudie, Robert Young Collins, James John Stuart Imlach. Manager: Dawson Walker.
HUNGARY: Gyula Grosics, Sándor Mátrai, Ferenc Sipos, László Sárosi, József Bozsik, Pál Berendi, László Budai II, Ferenc Machos, Lajos Tichy, Dezső Bundzsák, Máté Fenyvesi. Trainer: Lajos Baróti.
Goals: John Knight Mudie (14) / Máté Fenyvesi (54)

263. 01.06.1958
POLAND v SCOTLAND 1-2 (0-1)
Dziesięciolecia, Warszawa
Referee: Jenő Szrankó (Hungary)   Attendance: 75,000
POLAND: Edward Szymkowiak, Henryk Szczepański, Roman Korynt, Jerzy Woźniak, Witold Majewski, Edmund Zientara, Marian Nowara, Marian Norkowski, Henryk Kempny, Gerard Cieślik (Cap), Roman Lentner.   Trainers: Henryk Reyman, Feliks Dyrda & Stanisław Szymaniak.
SCOTLAND: Thomas Younger (Cap), Eric Caldow, John Davidson Hewie, Edward Hunter Turnbull, Robert Evans, Douglas Cowie, Graham Leggat, James Murray, John Knight Mudie, Robert Young Collins, James John Stuart Imlach. Manager: Dawson Walker.
Goals: Gerard Cieślik (84) / Robert Young Collins (21, 53)

264. 08.06.1958   6th World Cup, 1st Round
YUGOSLAVIA v SCOTLAND 1-1 (1-0)
Arosvallen, Västerås
Referee: Paul Wyssling (Switzerland)   Attendance: 9,591
YUGOSLAVIA: Vladimir Beara, Tomislav Crnković, Vasilije Šijaković, Dobrosav Krstić, Branko Zebec (Cap), Vujadin Boškov, Aleksandar Petaković, Todor Veselinović, Miloš Milutinović, Dragoslav Šekularac, Zdravko Rajkov. Trainer: Aleksandar Tirnanić.
SCOTLAND: Thomas Younger (Cap), Eric Caldow, John Davidson Hewie, Edward Hunter Turnbull, Robert Evans, Douglas Cowie, Graham Leggat, James Murray, John Knight Mudie, Robert Young Collins, James John Stuart Imlach. Manager: Dawson Walker.
Goals: Aleksandar Petaković (6) / James Murray (51)

265. 11.06.1958 6th World Cup, 1st Round
PARAGUAY v SCOTLAND 3-2 (2-1)
Idrottsparken, Norrköping
Referee: Vincenzo Orlandini (Italy)   Attendance: 11,665
PARAGUAY: Samuel Aguilar, Edelmiro Arévalos, Juan Vicente Lezcano, Eligio Echagüe, Salvador Villalba, Ignacio Achucarro, Juan Bautista Agüero (Cap), José del Rosario Parodi, Jorgelino Romero, Cayetano Ré Ramírez, Florencio Amarilla.   Trainer: Aurelio González.
SCOTLAND: Thomas Younger (Cap), Alexander Hershaw Parker, Eric Caldow, Edward Hunter Turnbull, Robert Evans, Douglas Cowie, Graham Leggat, Robert Young Collins, John Knight Mudie, Archibald Clark Robertson, William Fernie.   Manager: Dawson Walker.
Goals: Juan Bautista Agüero (4), Cayetano Ré Ramírez (44), José del Rosario Parodi (74) /
John Knight Mudie (23), Robert Young Collins (76)

266. 15.06.1958 6th World Cup, 1st Round
FRANCE v SCOTLAND 2-1 (2-0)
Eyravallen, Örebro
Referee: Juan Regis Brozzi (Argentina)   Attendance: 13,554
FRANCE: Claude Abbes, Raymond Kaelbel, Robert Jonquet (Cap), André Lerond, Armand Penverne, Jean-Jacques Marcel, Maryan Wisnieski, Just Fontaine, Raymond Kopa, Roger Piantoni, Jean Vincent.   Trainer: Albert Batteux.
SCOTLAND: William Dallas Fyfe Brown, Eric Caldow, John Davidson Hewie, Edward Hunter Turnbull, Robert Evans (Cap), David Craig MacKay, Robert Young Collins, James Murray, John Knight Mudie, Samuel Baird, James John Stuart Imlach.   Manager: Dawson Walker.
Goals: Raymond Kopa (4), Just Fontaine (85) /
Samuel Baird (58)

267. 18.10.1958 Home Championship
WALES v SCOTLAND 0-3 (0-1)
Ninian Park, Cardiff
Referee: Reginald J. Leafe (England)   Attendance: 59,162
WALES: Alfred John Kelsey, Stuart Grenville Williams, Melvyn Hopkins, Derrick Sullivan, Melvyn Charles, David Lloyd Bowen, Leonard Allchurch, Thomas Royston Vernon, Terence Cameron Medwin, Ivor John Allchurch, Philip Abraham Woosnam.   Manager: James Patrick Murphy.
SCOTLAND: William Dallas Fyfe Brown, John Grant, Eric Caldow, David Craig MacKay (Cap), William Toner, Thomas Henderson Docherty, Graham Leggat, Robert Young Collins, David George Herd, Denis Law, John Gillespie Henderson.   Manager: Alexander Matthew Busby.
Goals: Graham Leggat (30), Denis Law (70),
Robert Young Collins (82)

268. 05.11.1958 Home Championship
SCOTLAND v NORTHERN IRELAND 2-2 (0-0)
Hampden Park, Glasgow
Referee: John Harold Clough (England)   Att: 72,732
SCOTLAND: William Dallas Fyfe Brown, John Grant, Eric Caldow, David Craig MacKay (Cap), William Toner, Thomas Henderson Docherty, Graham Leggat, Robert Young Collins, David George Herd, Denis Law, John Gillespie Henderson.   Manager: Alexander Matthew Busby.
NORTHERN IRELAND: William Uprichard, Richard Matthewson Keith, Alfred McMichael, Robert Denis Blanchflower, William Edward Cunningham, Robert Peacock, William Laurence Bingham, Wilbur W. Cush, William J. Simpson, James McIlroy, Peter James McParland.
Goals: David George Herd (51), Robert Young Collins (54) /
Eric Caldow (72 own goal), James McIlroy (76)

269. 11.04.1959 Home Championship
ENGLAND v SCOTLAND 1-0 (0-0)
Wembley, London
Referee: Joaquim de Campos (Portugal)   Att: 98,329
SCOTLAND: William Dallas Fyfe Brown, Duncan Mackay, Eric Caldow, Thomas Henderson Docherty, Robert Evans (Cap), David Craig MacKay, Graham Leggat, Robert Young Collins, David George Herd, John Hart Dick, William Esplin Ormond.   Manager: Andrew Beattie.
ENGLAND: Edward Hopkinson, Donald Howe, Graham Laurence Shaw, Ronald Clayton, William Ambrose Wright (Cap), Ronald Flowers, Bryan Douglas, Peter Frank Broadbent, Robert Charlton, John Norman Haynes, Albert Douglas Holden.   Manager: Walter Winterbottom.
Goal: Robert Charlton (59)

270. 06.05.1959
SCOTLAND v WEST GERMANY 3-2 (3-2)
Hampden Park, Glasgow
Referee: Arthur Edward Ellis (England)   Att: 103,415
SCOTLAND: George Neil Farm, Duncan Mackay, Eric Caldow, David Craig MacKay, Robert Evans (Cap), Robert Johnston McCann, Graham Leggat, John Anderson White, Ian St. John, Robert Young Collins, Andrew Best Weir.   Manager: Andrew Beattie.
GERMANY: Günter Sawitzki, Erich Juskowiak, Karl-Heinz Schnellinger, Helmut Benthaus, Herbert Erhardt, Horst Szymaniak, Helmut Rahn (Cap), Rolf Geiger, Uwe Seeler, Alfred Schmidt, Hans Schäfer.   Trainer: Josef Herberger.
Goals: John Anderson White (1), Andrew Best Weir (6), Graham Leggat (23) /
Uwe Seeler (14), Erich Juskowiak (36 pen)

271. 27.05.1959
HOLLAND v SCOTLAND 1-2 (1-0)

Olympisch, Amsterdam

Referee: Joaquim Fernandes Campos (Portugal)   Attendance: 55,000

HOLLAND: Frans de Munck, Roelof Wiersma, Johannes Hendrikus Kraay, Jan Martin Gerardus Notermans, Cornelius van der Hart (Cap), Jean Anna Klaassens, Pieter van der Kuil, Cornelis Bernardus Rijvers, Leonard Canjels, Cornelis van der Gijp, Coenraad Moulijn.   Trainer: Elek Schwartz (Hungary)

SCOTLAND: George Neil Farm, Duncan Mackay, Eric Caldow, John Eric Smith, Robert Evans (Cap), John Davidson Hewie, Graham Leggat, Robert Young Collins, John Anderson White, Denis Law, Robert Auld.   Manager: Andrew Beattie.

Goals: Cornelis van der Gijp (18) / Robert Young Collins (61), Graham Leggat (65)

272. 03.06.1959
PORTUGAL v SCOTLAND 1-0 (1-0)

"José Alvalade", Lisboa

Referee: Daniel Zariquiegui (Spain)   Attendance: 30,000

PORTUGAL: Acúrsio Alves Carrelo, Virgílio Marques Mendes (Cap), Ângelo Gaspar Martins, Fernando Mamede Mendes, Raul António Leandro de Figueiredo, Vincente Lucas "Vicente", Carlos Domingos Duarte, Mário Esteves Coluna, Lucas Sebastião da Fonseca "Matateu", Augusto Francisco Rocha, Hernâni Ferreira da Silva.
Trainer: José Maria Antunes.

SCOTLAND: George Neil Farm, Duncan Mackay, Eric Caldow, John Eric Smith, Robert Evans (Cap), John Davidson Hewie, Alexander Silcock Scott, Robert Young Collins, John Anderson White, Denis Law, Robert Auld.
Manager: Andrew Beattie.

Goal: Lucas Sebastião da Fonseca "Matateu" (25)

273. 03.10.1959   Home Championship
NORTHERN IRELAND v SCOTLAND 0-4 (0-3)

Windsor Park, Belfast

Referee: Reginald J. Leafe (England)   Attendance: 59,000

NORTHERN IRELAND: Harold Gregg, Richard Matthewson Keith, Alfred McMichael, Robert Denis Blanchflower, William Edward Cunningham, Robert Peacock, William Laurence Bingham, Wilbur W. Cush, Alexander Derek Dougan, James McIlroy, Peter James McParland.

SCOTLAND: William Dallas Fyfe Brown, Eric Caldow, John Davidson Hewie, David Craig MacKay, Robert Evans (Cap), Robert Johnston McCann, Graham Leggat, John Anderson White, Ian St. John, Denis Law, George Mulhall.   Manager: Andrew Beattie.

Goals: Graham Leggat (25), John Davidson Hewie (34 pen), John Anderson White (41), George Mulhall (54)

274. 04.11.1959   Home Championship
SCOTLAND v WALES 1-1 (0-1)

Hampden Park, Cardiff

Referee: Kevin Howley (England)   Attendance: 55,813

SCOTLAND: William Dallas Fyfe Brown, Eric Caldow, John Davidson Hewie, David Craig MacKay, Robert Evans (Cap), Robert Johnston McCann, Graham Leggat, John Anderson White, Ian St. John, Denis Law, Robert Auld.
Manager: Andrew Beattie.

WALES: Alfred John Kelsey, Stuart Grenville Williams, Melvyn Hopkins, Derrick Sullivan, William John Charles, Colin Walter Baker, Terence Cameron Medwin, Philip Abraham Woosnam, Graham Moore, Ivor John Allchurch, Clifford William Jones.   Manager: James Patrick Murphy.

Goals: Graham Leggat (46) / William John Charles (8)

275. 09.04.1960   Home Championship
SCOTLAND v ENGLAND 1-1 (1-0)

Hampden Park, Glasgow

Referee: Jenő Szrankó (Hungary)   Attendance: 129,193

SCOTLAND: Francis Haffey, Duncan Mackay, Eric Caldow, John Cumming, Robert Evans (Cap), Robert Johnston McCann, Graham Leggat, Alexander Young, Ian St. John, Denis Law, Andrew Best Weir.   Manager: Andrew Beattie.

ENGLAND: Ronald Derrick Springettt, James Christopher Armfield, Ramon Wilson, Ronald Clayton (Cap), William John Slater, Ronald Flowers, John Michael Connelly, Peter Frank Broadbent, Joseph Henry Baker, Raymond Alan Parry, Robert Charlton.   Manager: Walter Winterbottom.

Goals: Graham Leggat (16) / Robert Charlton (50 pen)

276. 04.05.1960
SCOTLAND v POLAND 2-3 (1-2)

Hampden Park, Glasgow

Referee: Arthur Holland (England)   Attendance: 26,643

SCOTLAND: William Dallas Fyfe Brown, Duncan Mackay, John Davidson Hewie, David Craig MacKay, Robert Evans (Cap), John Cumming, Graham Leggat, John Anderson White, Ian St. John, Denis Law, Andrew Best Weir.
Manager: Andrew Beattie.

POLAND: Tomasz Stefaniszyn (77 Edward Szymkowiak), Henryk Szczepański, Henryk Grzybowski, Fryderyk Monica, Adam Michel, Edmund Zientara (Cap), Jan Kowalski, Lucjan Brychczy, Stanisław Hachorek, Ernest Pol, Krzysztof Baszkiewicz.   Trainer: Czesław Krug.

Goals: Denis Law (23), Ian St. John (46) / Krzysztof Baszkiewicz (12), Lucjan Brychczy (29), Ernest Pol (60)

277. 29.05.1960
AUSTRIA v SCOTLAND 4-1 (3-0)
Prater, Wien
Referee: Albert Dusch (West Germany)   Attendance: 60,000
AUSTRIA: Walter Zeman, Erich Hasenkopf, Franz Swoboda, Walter Skocik, Walter Glechner, Karl Koller, Rudolf Flögel, Gerhard Hanappi, Erich Hof, Josef Hamerl, Karl Skerlan. Trainer: Karl Decker.
SCOTLAND: William Dallas Fyfe Brown, Duncan Mackay, Eric Caldow, David Craig MacKay, Robert Evans (Cap), John Cumming, Graham Leggat, John Anderson White, Ian St. John, Denis Law (12 Alexander Young), Andrew Best Weir. Manager: Andrew Beattie.
Goals: Gerhard Hanappi (28, 32), Erich Hof (44, 62) / David Craig MacKay (76)

278. 05.06.1960
HUNGARY v SCOTLAND 3-3 (1-1)
Népstadion, Budapest
Referee: Arthur Edward Ellis (England)   Att: 85,000
SCOTLAND: William Dallas Fyfe Brown, Duncan Mackay, Eric Caldow, John Cumming, Robert Evans (Cap), David Craig MacKay, Graham Leggat, George Herd, Alexander Young, William Hunter, Andrew Best Weir. Manager: Andrew Beattie.
HUNGARY: Gyula Grosics, Sándor Mátrai, Ferenc Sipos, Jenő Dalnoki, Dezső Bundzsák, Antal Kotász, Károly Sándor, János Göröcs, Flórián Albert, Lajos Tichy, Máté Fenyvesi. Trainer: Lajos Baróti.
Goals: William Hunter (34), George Herd (62), Alexander Young (66) /
Károly Sándor (20), János Göröcs (72), Lajos Tichy (90)

279. 08.06.1960
TURKEY v SCOTLAND 4-2 (3-1)
19 Mayis, Ankara
Referee: Erich Steiner (Austria)   Attendance: 22,500
TURKEY: Turgay Şeren, Naci Erdem, Basri Dirimlili, Suat Mamat, Ergun Ercins, Kaya Köstepen, Lefter Küçükandonyadis, Can Bartu, Metin Oktay, Şenol Birol, Birol Pekel.   Trainer: Ignác Molnár (Hungary)
SCOTLAND: William Dallas Fyfe Brown, Duncan Mackay, Eric Caldow, David Craig MacKay, Robert Evans (Cap), John Cumming, John Anderson White, George Herd, Alexander Young, William Hunter, Andrew Best Weir. Manager: Andrew Beattie.
Goals: Metin Oktay (9), Lefter Küçükandonyadis (33, 35), Şenol Birol (61) / Eric Caldow (12 pen), Alexander Young (72)

280. 22.10.1960   Home Championship
WALES v SCOTLAND 2-0 (1-0)
Ninian Park, Cardiff
Referee: Arthur Holland (England)   Attendance: 55,000
WALES: Alfred John Kelsey, Alan Charles Harrington, Graham Evan Williams, Victor Herbert Crowe, Melvyn Tudor George Nurse, Colin Walter Baker, Terence Cameron Medwin, Philip Abraham Woosnam, Kenneth Leek, Thomas Royston Vernon, Clifford William Jones.
Manager: James Patrick Murphy.
SCOTLAND: Lawrence Grant Leslie, Duncan Mackay, Eric Caldow (Cap), James Gabriel, John Martis, David Craig MacKay, George Herd, John Anderson White, Alexander Young, William Hunter, David Wilson.
Goals: Clifford Jones (43), Thomas Royston Vernon (72)

281. 09.11.1960   Home Championship
SCOTLAND v NORTHERN IRELAND 5-2 (2-0)
Hampden Park, Glasgow
Referee: Kevin Howley (England)   Attendance: 34,564
SCOTLAND: Lawrence Grant Leslie, Duncan Mackay, Eric Caldow (Cap), David Craig MacKay, John Boyd Plenderleith, James Curran Baxter, George Herd, Denis Law, Alexander Young, Ralph Laidlaw Brand, David Wilson.
Manager: John Miller McColl.
NORTHERN IRELAND: Harold Gregg, Richard Matthewson Keith, Alexander Russell, Robert Denis Blanchflower, John T. Forde, Robert Peacock, William Laurence Bingham, Walter Bruce, William John McAdams, James Joseph Nicholson, Peter James McParland.
Goals: Denis Law (8), Eric Caldow (43 pen), Alexander Young (78), Ralph Laidlaw Brand (81, 90) / Robert Blanchflower (48 pen), Peter James McParland (84)

282. 15.04.1961   Home Championship
ENGLAND v SCOTLAND 9-3 (3-0)
Wembley, London
Referee: Marcel Lequesne (France)   Attendance: 97,350
ENGLAND: Ronald Derrick Springettt, James Christopher Armfield, Michael McNeil, Robert William Robson, Peter Swan, Ronald Flowers, Bryan Douglas, James Peter Greaves, Robert Alfred Smith, John Norman Haynes (Cap), Robert Charlton.   Manager: Walter Winterbottom.
SCOTLAND: Francis Haffey, Robert Shearer, Eric Caldow (Cap), David Craig MacKay, William McNeill, Robert Johnston McCann, John Murdoch MacLeod, Denis Law, Ian St. John, Patrick Quinn, David Wilson.   Manager: John Miller McColl.
Goals: Robert Robson (8), James Greaves (20, 29, 83), Bryan Douglas (55), Robert Alfred Smith (74, 85), John Norman Haynes (80, 82) / David Craig MacKay (49), David Wilson (53), Patrick Quinn (75)

283. 03.05.1961   7th World Cup Qualifiers
SCOTLAND v REPUBLIC OF IRELAND 4-1 (2-0)
Hampden Park, Glasgow

Referee: Maurice Guigue (France)   Attendance: 46,696

SCOTLAND: Lawrence Grant Leslie, Robert Shearer, Eric Caldow (Cap), Patrick Timothy Crerand, William McNeill, James Curran Baxter, John Murdoch MacLeod, Patrick Quinn, David George Herd, Ralph Laidlaw Brand, David Wilson.   Manager: John Miller McColl.

REPUBLIC OF IRELAND: Noel Michael Dwyer, John Brendan McNally, Noel Euchuria Cornelius Cantwell (Cap), Matthew Andrew McEvoy, Charles John Hurley, Patrick Saward, John Michael Giles, Ambrose Gerald Fogarty, Dermot Patrick Curtis, George Patrick Cummins, Joseph Haverty.

Goals: Ralph Laidlaw Brand (14, 40), David Herd (59, 85) / Joseph Haverty (52)

284. 07.05.1961   7th World Cup Qualifiers
REPUBLIC OF IRELAND v SCOTLAND 0-3 (0-2)
Dalymount Park, Dublin

Referee: Gaston Grandain (Belgium)   Attendance: 45,000

REPUBLIC OF IRELAND: Noel Michael Dwyer, James Philip Vincent Kelly, Noel Euchuria Cornelius Cantwell (Cap), Matthew Andrew McEvoy, Charles John Hurley, Michael Kevin Meagan, Fionan Fagan, John Michael Giles, Peter Joseph Fitzgerald, George Patrick Cummins, Joseph Haverty.

SCOTLAND: Lawrence Grant Leslie, Robert Shearer, Eric Caldow (Cap), Patrick Timothy Crerand, William McNeill, James Curran Baxter, John Murdoch MacLeod, Patrick Quinn, Alexander Young, Ralph Laidlaw Brand, David Wilson.   Manager: John Miller McColl.

Goals: Alexander Young (4, 16), Ralph Laidlaw Brand (86)

285. 14.05.1961   7th World Cup Qualifiers
CZECHOSLOVAKIA v SCOTLAND 4-0 (3-0)
Tehelné pole, Bratislava

Referee: Erich Steiner (Austria)   Attendance: 50,000

CZECHOSLOVAKIA: Viliam Schrojf, František Šafránek, Ján Popluhár, Jiří Tichý, Svatopluk Pluskal, Josef Masopust (Cap), Tomáš Pospíchal, Adolf Scherer, Josef Kadraba, Andrej Kvašňák, Václav Mašek.   Trainer: Rudolf Vytlačil.

SCOTLAND: Lawrence Grant Leslie, Robert Shearer, Eric Caldow (Cap), Patrick Timothy Crerand, William McNeill, James Curran Baxter, John Murdoch MacLeod, John Livingstone McMillan, David George Herd, Ralph Laidlaw Brand, David Wilson.   Manager: John Miller McColl.

Sent off: Andrej Kvašňák (35)

Goals: Tomáš Pospíchal (8), Andrej Kvašňák (14 pen), Josef Kadraba (40), Tomáš Pospíchal (85)

286. 26.09.1961   7th World Cup Qualifiers
SCOTLAND v CZECHOSLOVAKIA 3-2 (1-1)
Hampden Park, Glasgow

Referee: Leif Gulliksen (Norway)   Attendance: 51,590

SCOTLAND: William Dallas Fyfe Brown, Duncan Mackay, Eric Caldow (Cap), Patrick Timothy Crerand, William McNeill, James Curran Baxter, Alexander Silcock Scott, John Anderson White, Ian St. John, Denis Law, David Wilson.   Manager: John Miller McColl.

CZECHOSLOVAKIA: Viliam Schrojf, Jozef Bomba, Ján Popluhár, Ladislav Novák (Cap), Titus Buberník, Josef Masopust, Tomáš Pospíchal, Adolf Scherer, Josef Kadraba, Andrej Kvašňák, Václav Mašek.   Trainer: Rudolf Vytlačil.

Goals: Ian St. John (21), Denis Law (62, 83) / Andrej Kvašňák (6), Adolf Scherer (51)

287. 07.10.1961   Home Championship
NORTHERN IRELAND v SCOTLAND 1-6 (1-3)
Windsor Park, Belfast

Referee: James Finney (England)   Attendance: 41,000

NORTHERN IRELAND: Harold Gregg, Edward James Magill, Alexander Russell, Robert Denis Blanchflower, William John Terence Neill, Robert Peacock, Samuel J. Wilson, James McIlroy, William Ian Lawther, Matthew James Hill, James Christopher McLaughlin.

SCOTLAND: William Dallas Fyfe Brown, Duncan Mackay, Eric Caldow (Cap), Patrick Timothy Crerand, William McNeill, James Curran Baxter, Alexander Silcock Scott, John Anderson White, Ian St. John, Ralph Laidlaw Brand, David Wilson.   Manager: John Miller McColl.

Goals: James Christopher McLaughlin (17) / David Wilson (14), Alexander Silcock Scott (34, 53, 79), Ralph Laidlaw Brand (38, 69)

288. 08.11.1961   Home Championship
SCOTLAND v WALES 2-0 (1-0)
Hampden Park, Glasgow

Referee: Arthur Holland (England)   Attendance: 74,329

SCOTLAND: William Dallas Fyfe Brown, Alexander William Hamilton, Eric Caldow (Cap), Patrick Timothy Crerand, John Francombe Ure, James Curran Baxter, Alexander Silcock Scott, John Anderson White, Ian St. John, Ralph Laidlaw Brand, David Wilson.   Manager: John Miller McColl.

WALES: Alfred John Kelsey, Alan Charles Harrington, Stuart Grenville Williams, Victor Herbert Crowe, Melvyn Charles, Colin Walter Baker, Leonard Allchurch, Philip Abraham Woosnam, Kenneth Leek, Ivor John Allchurch, Clifford William Jones.   Manager: James Patrick Murphy.

Goals: Ian St. John (22, 50)

289. 29.11.1961   7th World Cup Qualifiers Play-Off
CZECHOSLOVAKIA
v SCOTLAND   4-2 (0-1, 2-2) (AET)
Heysel, Bruxelles (Belgium)

Referee: Gérard Versyp (Belgium)   Attendance: 7,000

CZECHOSLOVAKIA: Viliam Schrojf, Jiří Hledík, Ján Popluhár, Jiří Tichý (Cap), Svatopluk Pluskal, Josef Masopust, Tomáš Pospíchal, Adolf Scherer, Andrej Kvašňák, Rudolf Kučera, Josef Jelínek II.   Trainer: Rudolf Vytlačil.

SCOTLAND: Edward Devlin Connachan, Alexander William Hamilton, Eric Caldow (Cap), Patrick Timothy Crerand, John Francombe Ure, James Curran Baxter, Ralph Laidlaw Brand, John Anderson White, Ian St. John, Denis Law, Hugh Robertson.   Manager: John Miller McColl.

Goals: Jiří Hledík (70), Adolf Scherer (80), Tomáš Pospíchal (96), Andrej Kvašňák (101) / Ian St. John (35, 71)

290. 14.04.1962   Home Championship
SCOTLAND v ENGLAND   2-0 (1-0)
Hampden Park, Glasgow

Referee: Leopold Sylvain Horn (Holland)   Att: 132,431

SCOTLAND: William Dallas Fyfe Brown, Alexander William Hamilton, Eric Caldow (Cap), Patrick Timothy Crerand, William McNeill, James Curran Baxter, Alexander Silcock Scott, John Anderson White, Ian St. John, Denis Law, David Wilson.   Manager: John Miller McColl.

ENGLAND: Ronald Derrick Springettt, James Christopher Armfield, Ramon Wilson, Stanley Anderson, Peter Swan, Ronald Flowers, Bryan Douglas, James Peter Greaves, Robert Alfred Smith, John Norman Haynes (Cap), Robert Charlton.   Manager: Walter Winterbottom.

Goals: David Wilson (13), Eric Caldow (88 pen)

291. 02.05.1962
SCOTLAND v URUGUAY   2-3 (0-2)
Hampden Park, Glasgow

Referee: Arthur Holland (England)   Attendance: 67,181

SCOTLAND: Edward Devlin Connachan (46 William Ritchie), Alexander William Hamilton, Eric Caldow (Cap), Patrick Timothy Crerand (75 Duncan Mackay), William McNeill, James Curran Baxter, Alexander Silcock Scott, Patrick Quinn, Ian St. John, Ralph Laidlaw Brand, David Wilson.   Manager: John Miller McColl.

URUGUAY: Roberto Eduardo Sosa, Horácio Florentín Troche, Ruben Soria, Edgardo Nilson González, Néstor Gonçalves, Pedro Ramón Cubilla, Ronald Arturo Langón, Julio César Cortés, José Francisco Sacía, Vladas Douksas, Luis Alberto Cubilla.   Trainer: Juan Carlos Corazzo.

Goals: James Curran Baxter (81), Ralph Laidlaw Brand (88) / José Francisco Sacía (33), Luis Alberto Cubilla (44, 48)

292. 20.10.1962   Home Championship
WALES v SCOTLAND   2-3 (1-1)
Ninian Park, Cardiff

Referee: Kenneth Dagnall (England)   Attendance: 58,000

WALES: Anthony Horace Millington, Stuart Grenville Williams, Melvyn Hopkins, William Terence Hennessey, William John Charles, Peter Malcolm Lucas, Barrie Spencer Jones, Ivor John Allchurch, Melvyn Charles, Thomas Royston Vernon, Clifford William Jones.   Manager: James Patrick Murphy.

SCOTLAND: William Dallas Fyfe Brown, Alexander William Hamilton, Eric Caldow (Cap), Patrick Timothy Crerand, John Francombe Ure, James Curran Baxter, William Henderson, John Anderson White, Ian St. John, Denis Law, David Wilson.   Manager: John Miller McColl.

Goals: Ivor Allchurch (40), William John Charles (88) / Eric Caldow (19 pen), Denis Law (63), William Henderson (79)

293. 07.11.1962   Home Championship
SCOTLAND v NORTHERN IRELAND   5-1 (1-1)
Hampden Park, Glasgow

Referee: James Finney (England)   Attendance: 58,734

SCOTLAND: William Dallas Fyfe Brown, Alexander William Hamilton, Eric Caldow (Cap), Patrick Timothy Crerand, John Francombe Ure, James Curran Baxter, William Henderson, John Anderson White, Ian St. John, Denis Law, George Mulhall.   Manager: John Miller McColl.

NORTHERN IRELAND: Robert James Irvine, Edward James Magill, Alexander Russell, Robert Denis Blanchflower, Samuel Hatton, James Joseph Nicholson, William Humphries, Samuel Thomas McMillan, Alexander Derek Dougan, James McIlroy, William Laurence Bingham.   Manager: Robert Peacock.

Goals: Denis Law (40, 64, 77, 87), William Henderson (79) / William Laurence Bingham (8)

294. 06.04.1963   Home Championship
ENGLAND v SCOTLAND   1-2 (0-2)
Wembley, London

Referee: Leopold Sylvain Horn (Holland)   Att: 98,606

ENGLAND: Gordon Banks, James Christopher Armfield (Cap), Gerald Byrne, Robert Frederick Moore, Maurice Norman, Ronald Flowers, Bryan Douglas, James Peter Greaves, Robert Alfred Smith, James Melia, Robert Charlton.   Manager: Alfred Ernest Ramsey.

SCOTLAND: William Dallas Fyfe Brown, Alexander William Hamilton, Eric Caldow (Cap), David Craig MacKay, John Francombe Ure, James Curran Baxter, William Henderson, John Anderson White, Ian St. John, Denis Law, David Wilson.   Manager: John Miller McColl.

Goals: Bryan Douglas (79) / James Curran Baxter (29, 31 pen)

295. 08.05.1963
SCOTLAND v AUSTRIA 4-1 (3-0) *

Hampden Park, Glasgow

Referee: James Finney (England)   Attendance: 94,596

SCOTLAND: William Dallas Fyfe Brown, Alexander William Hamilton, David Duff Holt, David Craig MacKay (Cap), John Francombe Ure, James Curran Baxter, William Henderson, David Wedderburn Gibson, James Millar, Denis Law, David Wilson.   Manager: John Miller McColl.

AUSTRIA: Gernot Fraydl, Ferdinand Kolarik, Erich Hasenkopf, Alfred Gager, Walter Glechner, Karl Koller, Anton Linhart, Erich Hof, Horst Nemec, Ernst Fiala, Friedrich Rafreider.   Trainer: Karl Decker.

Goals: David Wilson (16, 26), Denis Law (33, 71) / Anton Linhart (77)

* The match was abandoned after 79 minutes

296. 04.06.1963
NORWAY v SCOTLAND 4-3 (1-2)

Brann, Bergen

Referee: H. Oskarsson (Iceland)   Attendance: 23,000

NORWAY: Sverre Andersen II, Erik Hagen, Edgar Stakset, Roar Johansen, Finn Thorsen, Arild Gulden, Roald Jensen, Arne Pedersen, John Krogh, Olav Nilsen, Erik Johansen.   Trainer: Ragnar Nikolay Larsen.

SCOTLAND: Adam Smith Blacklaw, Alexander William Hamilton, David Duff Holt, David Craig MacKay (Cap) (78 Francis McLintock), John Francombe Ure, James Curran Baxter, William Henderson, David Wedderburn Gibson, Ian St. John, Denis Law, David Wilson.   Manager: John Miller McColl.

Goals: Olav Nilsen (5), Erik Johansen (60), Arne Pedersen (81), John Krogh (83) / Denis Law (14, 22, 76)

297. 09.06.1963
REPUBLIC OF IRELAND v SCOTLAND 1-0 (1-0)

Dalymount Park, Dublin

Referee: Kevin Howley (England)   Attendance: 30,000

REPUBLIC OF IRELAND: Alan James Alexander Kelly, Anthony Peter Dunne, Thomas Joseph Traynor, Matthew Andrew McEvoy, Charles John Hurley, Michael McGrath, John Michael Giles, Patrick Turner, Noel Euchuria Cornelius Cantwell (Cap), Noel Peyton (44 Ambrose Gerald Fogarty), Joseph Haverty.

SCOTLAND: Thomas Johnstone Lawrence, Alexander William Hamilton, David Duff Holt, Francis McLintock, William McNeill, James Curran Baxter, William Henderson, David Wedderburn Gibson, James Millar, Denis Law (Cap), David Wilson (44 Ian St. John).   Manager: John Miller McColl.

Goal: Noel Euchuria Cornelius Cantwell (6)

298. 13.06.1963
SPAIN v SCOTLAND 2-6 (2-4)

"Santiago Bernabéu", Madrid

Referee: Giulio Campanati (Italy)   Attendance: 40,000

SPAIN: José Vicente Traín (46 Carmelo Cedrún Ochandategui), Feliciano Ruiz Muñoz Rivilla (Cap), José Mingorance Chimeno (32 Ignacio Zoco Esparza), Severino Reija Vásquez, Luis María Aguirre Vidaurrázaga "Koldo Aguirre", Jesús Glaría Roldán, Amancio Amaro Varela, Adelardo Rodríguez Sánchez, José Fidalgo Veloso, Vicente Guillot Fabián, Carlos Lapetra Coarasa.   Trainer: José Luis Villalonga.

SCOTLAND: Adam Smith Blacklaw, William McNeill, David Duff Holt, Francis McLintock, John Francombe Ure, James Curran Baxter, William Henderson, David Wedderburn Gibson, Ian St. John, Denis Law (Cap), David Wilson.   Manager: John Miller McColl.

Goals: Adelardo Sánchez (8), José Fidalgo Veloso (43) / Denis Law (16), David Gibson (17), Francis McLintock (20), David Wilson (33), William Henderson (51), Ian St. John (83)

299. 12.10.1963   Home Championship
NORTHERN IRELAND v SCOTLAND 2-1 (1-0)

Windsor Park, Belfast

Referee: John Keith Taylor (England)   Attendance: 39,000

NORTHERN IRELAND: Harold Gregg, Edward James Magill, John Parke, Martin Harvey, William John Terence Neill, William James McCullough, William Laurence Bingham, William Humphries, Samuel J. Wilson, John Andrew Crossan, Matthew James Hill.   Manager: Robert Peacock.

SCOTLAND: William Dallas Fyfe Brown, Alexander William Hamilton, David Provan, Patrick Timothy Crerand, John Francombe Ure, David Craig MacKay (Cap), William Henderson, John Anderson White, Ian St. John, David Wedderburn Gibson, George Mulhall.   Manager: John Miller McColl.

Goals: William Bingham (25), Samuel J. Wilson (63) / Ian St. John (49)

300. 07.11.1963
SCOTLAND v NORWAY 6-1 (2-1)

Hampden Park, Glasgow

Referee: Kevin Howley (England)   Attendance: 35,416

SCOTLAND: William Dallas Fyfe Brown, Alexander William Hamilton, David Provan, David Craig MacKay (Cap), John Francombe Ure, James Curran Baxter (46 James Gabriel), Alexander Silcock Scott, John Anderson White, Alan John Gilzean, Denis Law, William Henderson.
Manager: John Miller McColl.

NORWAY: Sverre Andersen II (78 Kjell Kaspersen), Erik Hagen, Edgar Stakset, Roar Johansen, Finn Thorsen, Arild Gulden, Roald Jensen, Arne Pedersen, Per Kristoffersen, Olav Nilsen, Erik Johansen.   Trainer: Ragnar Nikolay Larsen.

Goals: Denis Law (19, 44, 59, 82), David MacKay (74, 76) / Per Kristoffersen (8)

301. 20.11.1963   Home Championship
SCOTLAND v WALES 2-1 (1-0)

Hampden Park, Glasgow

Referee: William Clements (England)   Attendance: 51,167

SCOTLAND: William Dallas Fyfe Brown, Alexander William Hamilton, James Kennedy, David Craig MacKay (Cap), William McNeill, James Curran Baxter, William Henderson, John Anderson White, Alan John Gilzean, Denis Law, Alexander Silcock Scott.   Manager: John Miller McColl.

WALES: Gareth Sprake, Stuart Grenville Williams, Graham Evan Williams, William Terence Hennessey, Harold Michael England, Melvyn Tudor George Nurse, Barrie Spencer Jones, Graham Moore, William John Charles, Thomas Royston Vernon, Clifford William Jones.
Manager: James Patrick Murphy.

Goals: John Anderson White (44), Denis Law (47) / Barrie Spencer Jones (57)

302. 11.04.1964   Home Championship
SCOTLAND v ENGLAND 1-0 (0-0)

Hampden Park, Glasgow

Referee: Leopold Sylvain Horn (Holland)   Att: 133,245

SCOTLAND: Robert Campbell Forsyth, Alexander William Hamilton, James Kennedy, John Greig, William McNeill (Cap), James Curran Baxter, William Henderson, John Anderson White, Alan John Gilzean, Denis Law, David Wilson.
Manager: John Miller McColl.

ENGLAND: Gordon Banks, James Christopher Armfield (Cap), Ramon Wilson, Gordon Milne, Maurice Norman, Robert Frederick Moore, Terence Lionel Paine, Roger Hunt, John Joseph Byrne, George Edward Eastham, Robert Charlton.
Manager: Alfred Ernest Ramsey.

Goal: Alan John Gilzean (72)

303. 12.05.1964
WEST GERMANY v SCOTLAND 2-2 (2-0)

Niedersachsen, Hannover

Referee: Tonny Kolbech Poulsen (Denmark)   Att: 75,000

GERMANY: Hans Tilkowski, Hans Nowak, Rudolf Steiner, Horst Szymaniak, Willi Giesemann, Wolfgang Weber, Reinhard Libuda, Alfred Schmidt (25 Stefan Reisch), Uwe Seeler (Cap), Rolf Geiger, Gert Dörfel.   Trainer: Josef Herberger.

SCOTLAND: James Fergus Cruickshank, Alexander William Hamilton (40 David Duff Holt), James Kennedy, John Greig, William McNeill (Cap), James Curran Baxter, William Henderson, John Anderson White, Alan John Gilzean, Denis Law, David Wilson.   Manager: John Miller McColl.

Goals: Uwe Seeler (32, 33) / Alan John Gilzean (70, 84)

304. 03.10.1964   Home Championship
WALES v SCOTLAND 3-2 (1-2)

Ninian Park, Cardiff

Referee: Kevin Howley (England)   Attendance: 37,093

WALES: Gareth Sprake, Stuart Grenville Williams, Graham Evan Williams, Barrington Gerard Hole, William John Charles, William Terence Hennessey, Clifford William Jones, Kenneth Leek, Ronald Wyn Davies, Ivor John Allchurch, Ronald Raymond Rees.   Manager: David Lloyd Bowen.

SCOTLAND: Robert Campbell Forsyth, Alexander William Hamilton, James Kennedy, John Greig, Ronald Yeats, James Curran Baxter, James Connolly Johnstone, David Wedderburn Gibson, Stephen Chalmers, Denis Law (Cap), James Gillen Robertson.   Manager: John Miller McColl.

Goals: Ronald Wyn Davies (6), Kenneth Leek (87, 89) / Stephen Chalmers (28), David Wedderburn Gibson (29)

305. 21.10.1964   8th World Cup Qualifiers
SCOTLAND v FINLAND 3-1 (3-0)

Hampden Park, Glasgow

Referee: Joseph Hannet (Belgium)   Attendance: 54,442

SCOTLAND: Robert Campbell Forsyth, Alexander William Hamilton, James Kennedy, John Greig, John McGrory, James Curran Baxter, James Connolly Johnstone, David Wedderburn Gibson, Stephen Chalmers, Denis Law (Cap), Alexander Silcock Scott.   Manager: John Miller McColl.

FINLAND: Martti Halme, Pertti Mäkipää, Tirno Kautonen, Stig Holmqvist (Cap), Aarno Rinne, Veijo Valtonen, Harri Järvi, Juhani Peltonen, Arto Tolsa, Simo Syrjävaara, Martti Hyvärinen.   Trainer: Kaarlo Olavi Laaksonen.

Goals: Denis Law (2), Stephen Chalmers (38), David Wedderburn Gibson (42) / Juhani Peltonen (70)

306. 25.11.1964   Home Championship
SCOTLAND v NORTHERN IRELAND 3-2 (3-2)
Hampden Park, Glasgow

Referee: Geoffrey Powell (Wales)   Attendance: 48,752

SCOTLAND: Robert Campbell Forsyth, Alexander William Hamilton, James Kennedy, John Greig, John McGrory, Francis McLintock, William Semple Brown Wallace, Denis Law, Alan John Gilzean, James Curran Baxter (Cap), David Wilson. Manager: John Miller McColl.

NORTHERN IRELAND: Patrick Anthony Jennings, Edward James Magill, Alexander Russell, Martin Harvey, William John Terence Neill, John Parke, George Best, William Humphries, William John Irvine, John Andrew Crossan, Robert Munn Braithwaite.   Manager: Robert Peacock.

Goals: David Wilson (10, 31), Alan John Gilzean (17) / George Best (9), William John Irvine (19)

307. 10.04.1965   Home Championship
ENGLAND v SCOTLAND 2-2 (2-1)
Wembley, London

Referee: István Zsolt (Hungary)   Attendance: 98,199

ENGLAND: Gordon Banks, George Reginald Cohen, Ramon Wilson, Norbert Peter Stiles, John "Jack" Charlton, Robert Frederick Moore (Cap), Peter Thompson, James Peter Greaves, Barry John Bridges, John Joseph Byrne, Robert Charlton. Manager: Alfred Ernest Ramsey.

SCOTLAND: William Dallas Fyfe Brown, Alexander William Hamilton, Edward Graham McCreadie, Patrick Timothy Crerand, William McNeill (Cap), John Greig, William Henderson, Robert Young Collins, Ian St. John, Denis Law, David Wilson.   Manager: John Miller McColl.

Goals: Robert Charlton (25), James Peter Greaves (35) / Denis Law (41), Ian St. John (59)

308. 08.05.1965
SCOTLAND v SPAIN 0-0
Hampden Park, Glasgow

Referee: Kevin Howley (England)   Attendance: 60,146

SCOTLAND: William Dallas Fyfe Brown, Alexander William Hamilton, Edward Graham McCreadie, William John Bremner, William McNeill (Cap), John Greig, William Henderson, Robert Young Collins, Denis Law, Alan John Gilzean, John Hughes.   Manager: John Miller McColl.

SPAIN: José Ángel Iribar Cortajarena, Feliciano Ruiz Muñoz Rivilla, Fernando Olivella Pons (Cap), Severino Reija Vásquez, Ignacio Zoco Esparza, Jesús Glaría Roldán, José Armando Ufarte Ventoso "Luego Ufarte", José Luis Aragonés Suárez, Marcelino Martínez Cao, Luis María Aguirre Vidaurrázaga "Koldo Aguirre", Carlos Lapetra Coarasa. Trainer: José Luis Villalonga.

309. 23.05.1965   8th World Cup Qualifiers
POLAND v SCOTLAND 1-1 (0-0)
Śląski, Chorzów

Referee: Sergey Alimov (Soviet Union)   Attendance: 67,462

POLAND: Edward Szymkowiak, Henryk Szczepański (Cap), Jacek Gmoch, Stanisław Oślizło, Roman Bazan, Antoni Nieroba, Ryszard Grzegorczyk, Jan Banaś, Jan Liberda, Ernest Pol, Roman Lentner.   Trainers: Wiesław Motoczyński, Ryszard Koncewicz & Karol Krawczyk.

SCOTLAND: William Dallas Fyfe Brown, Alexander William Hamilton, Edward Graham McCreadie, John Greig, William McNeill (Cap), Patrick Timothy Crerand, William Henderson, Robert Young Collins, Neil Martin, Denis Law, John Hughes.   Manager: John Stein.

Goals: Roman Lentner (52) / Denis Law (76)

310. 27.05.1965   8th World Cup Qualifiers
FINLAND v SCOTLAND 1-2 (1-1)
Olympiastadion, Helsinki

Referee: Erwin Vetter (East Germany)   Attendance: 20,162

FINLAND: Lars Näsman, Pertti Mäkipää, Timo Kautonen, Stig Holmqvist, Aarno Rinne, Olli Heinonen (Cap), Markku Kumpulampi, Juhani Peltonen, Martti Hyvärinen, Rauno Ruotsalainen, Semi Nuoranen. Trainer: Kaarlo Olavi Laaksonen.

SCOTLAND: William Dallas Fyfe Brown, Alexander William Hamilton, Edward Graham McCreadie, Patrick Timothy Crerand, William McNeill (Cap), John Greig, William Henderson, Denis Law, Neil Martin, William Murdoch Hamilton, David Wilson.   Manager: John Stein.

Goals: Martti Hyvärinen (5) / David Wilson (37), John Greig (50)

311. 02.10.1965   Home Championship
NORTHERN IRELAND v SCOTLAND 3-2 (1-1)
Windsor Park, Belfast

Referee: John Keith Taylor (England)   Attendance: 53,000

NORTHERN IRELAND: Patrick Anthony Jennings, Edward James Magill, Alexander Russell, Martin Harvey, William John Terence Neill, James Joseph Nicholson, James McIlroy, John Andrew Crossan, William John Irvine, Alexander Derek Dougan, George Best.   Manager: Robert Peacock.

SCOTLAND: William Dallas Fyfe Brown, Alexander William Hamilton, Edward Graham McCreadie, David Craig MacKay, William McNeill (Cap), John Greig, William Henderson, Denis Law, Alan John Gilzean, James Curran Baxter, John Hughes.   Manager: John Stein.

Goals: Alexander Derek Dougan (42), John Crossan (59), William John Irvine (89) / Alan John Gilzean (17, 81)

312. 13.10.1965   8th World Cup Qualifiers
SCOTLAND v POLAND 1-2 (1-0)
Hampden Park, Glasgow

Referee: Hans Carlsson (Sweden)   Attendance: 107,508

SCOTLAND: William Dallas Fyfe Brown, Alexander William Hamilton, Edward Graham McCreadie, Patrick Timothy Crerand, William McNeill (Cap), John Greig, William Henderson, William John Bremner, Alan John Gilzean, Denis Law, William McClure Johnston.   Manager: John Stein.

POLAND: Konrad Kornek, Henryk Szczepański (Cap), Jacek Gmoch, Stanisław Oślizło, Zygmunt Anczok, Antoni Nieroba, Zygfryd Szołtysik, Jerzy Sadek, Ernest Pol, Jan Liberda, Eugeniusz Faber.   Trainers: Wiesław Motoczyński, Ryszard Koncewicz & Karol Krawczyk.

Goals: William McNeill (14) /
Ernest Pol (85), Jerzy Sadek (87)

313. 09.11.1965   8th World Cup Qualifiers
SCOTLAND v ITALY 1-0 (0-0)
Celtic Park, Glasgow

Referee: Rudolf Kreitlein (West Germany)   Att: 100,393

SCOTLAND: William Dallas Fyfe Brown, John Greig, David Provan, Robert White Murdoch, Ronald McKinnon, James Curran Baxter (Cap), William Henderson, William John Bremner, Alan John Gilzean, Neil Martin, John Hughes.   Manager: John Stein.

ITALY: William Negri, Tarcisio Burgnich, Giacinto Facchetti, Aristide Guarneri, Sandro Salvadore (Cap), Roberto Rosato, Giovanni Lodetti, Giacomo Bulgarelli, Alessandro Mazzola, Gianni Rivera, Paolo Barison.   Trainer: Edmondo Fabbri.

Goal: John Greig (88)

314. 24.11.1965   Home Championship
SCOTLAND v WALES 4-1 (3-1)
Hampden Park, Glasgow

Referee: James Finney (England)   Attendance: 49,888

SCOTLAND: Robert Ferguson, John Greig, Edward Graham McCreadie, Robert White Murdoch, Ronald McKinnon, James Curran Baxter (Cap), William Henderson, Charles Cooke, James Forrest, Alan John Gilzean, William McClure Johnston.   Manager: John Stein.

WALES: David Michael Hollins, Peter Joseph Rodrigues, Colin Robert Green, William Terence Hennessey, Harold Michael England, Barrington Gerard Hole, Ronald Raymond Rees, Thomas Royston Vernon, Ronald Wyn Davies, Ivor John Allchurch, Gilbert Ivor Reece.   Manager: David Lloyd Bowen.

Goals: Robert Murdoch (10, 29), William Henderson (13), John Greig (86) / Ivor John Allchurch (12)

315. 07.12.1965   8th World Cup Qualifiers
ITALY v SCOTLAND 3-0 (1-0)
San Paolo, Napoli

Referee: István Zsolt (Hungary)   Attendance: 68,873

ITALY: Enrico Albertosi, Tarcisio Burgnich, Giacinto Facchetti, Roberto Rosato, Sandro Salvadore (Cap), Giovanni Lodetti, Bruno Mora, Giacomo Bulgarelli, Alessandro Mazzola, Gianni Rivera, Ezio Pascutti.   Trainer: Edmondo Fabbri.

SCOTLAND: Adam Smith Blacklaw, David Provan, Edward Graham McCreadie, Robert White Murdoch, Ronald McKinnon, John Greig (Cap), James Forrest, William John Bremner, Ronald Yeats, Charles Cooke, John Hughes.   Manager: John Stein.

Goals: Ezio Pascutti (38), Giacinto Facchetti (73), Bruno Mora (89)

316. 02.04.1966   Home Championship
SCOTLAND v ENGLAND 3-4 (1-2)
Hampden Park, Glasgow

Referee: Henri Faucheux (France)   Attendance: 123,052

SCOTLAND: Robert Ferguson, John Greig (Cap), Thomas Gemmell, Robert White Murdoch, Ronald McKinnon, James Curran Baxter, James Connolly Johnstone, Denis Law, William Semple Brown Wallace, William John Bremner, William McClure Johnston.   Manager: John Prentice.

ENGLAND: Gordon Banks, George Reginald Cohen, Keith Robert Newton, Norbert Peter Stiles, John "Jack" Charlton, Robert Frederick Moore (Cap), Alan James Ball, Roger Hunt, Robert Charlton, Geoffrey Charles Hurst, John Michael Connelly.   Manager: Alfred Ernest Ramsey.

Goals: Denis Law (42), James Johnstone (57, 82) /
Geoffrey Charles Hurst (18), Roger Hunt (34, 47), Robert Charlton (73)

317. 11.05.1966
SCOTLAND v HOLLAND 0-3 (0-1)
Hampden Park, Glasgow

Referee: Kevin Howley (England)   Attendance: 16,513

SCOTLAND: Robert Ferguson, John Greig (Cap), David Provan, Patrick Gordon Stanton, Ronald McKinnon, David Bruce Smith, William Henderson, Andrew Penman, James Scott, William Semple Brown Wallace, William McClure Johnston.   Manager: John Prentice.

HOLLAND: Eduard Laurens Pieters Graafland, Frederik Arnoldus Flinkevleugel, Emil Franciscus Cornelis Pijs, Daniël Christiaan Schrijvers (Cap), Cornelius Pleun Veldhoen, Wilhelmus Maria Dullens, Bernardus Muller, Jesaia Swart, Wilhelmus Martinus Leonardus Johannes van der Kuylen, Klaas Nuninga, Petrus Johannes Keizer.
Trainer: Georg Kessler.

Goals: Klaas Nuninga (14), Wilhelmus Martinus Leonardus Johannes van der Kuylen (52, 84)

318. 18.06.1966
SCOTLAND v PORTUGAL 0-1 (0-0)
Hampden Park, Glasgow
Referee: George McCabe (England)   Attendance: 23,321
SCOTLAND: Robert Ferguson, William John Bell, Edward Graham McCreadie, John Greig (Cap), John McGrory, William John Bremner, Alexander Silcock Scott, Charles Cooke, Alexander Young (46 Stephen Chalmers), James Curran Baxter, John Evans Wright Sinclair.   Manager: John Prentice.
PORTUGAL: José Pereira, João Pedro Morais, José Alexandre da Silva Baptista, Vincente Lucas "Vicente", Hilário Rosário da Conceição, Jaime da Silva Graça, Mário Esteves Coluna (Cap), José Augusto Pinto de Almeida (80 Fernando Peres da Silva), Eusébio da Silva Ferreira, José Augusto da Costa Sénica Torres, António Simões da Costa.
Trainer: Otto Martins Glória (Brazil)
Goal: José Augusto da Costa Sénica Torres (72)

319. 25.06.1966
SCOTLAND v BRAZIL 1-1 (1-1)
Hampden Park, Glasgow
Referee: James Finney (England)   Attendance: 74,933
SCOTLAND: Robert Ferguson, John Greig (Cap), William John Bell, William John Bremner, Ronald McKinnon, John Clark, Alexander Silcock Scott, Charles Cooke, Stephen Chalmers, James Curran Baxter, Peter Barr Cormack.   Manager: John Prentice.
BRAZIL: Gilmar dos Santos Neves "Gilmar I", José Maria Fidélis dos Santos, Hideraldo Luiz Bellini, Orlando Peçanha de Carvalho, Paulo Henrique Souza de Oliveira, José Eli de Miranda "Zito", Gérson de Oliveira Nunes "Gérson I", Jair Ventura Filho "Jairzinho", Servílio de Jesus Filho (46 Wálter Machado da Silva), Édson Arantes do Nascimento "Pelé", Amarildo Tavares da Silveira.   Trainer: Vicente Feola.
Goals: Stephen Chalmers (1) / Servílio de Jesus Filho (16)

320. 22.10.1966   Home Championship,
3rd European Championships Qualifiers
WALES v SCOTLAND 1-1 (0-0)
Ninian Park, Cardiff
Referee: Kenneth Dagnall (England)   Attendance: 33,269
WALES: Gareth Sprake, Peter Joseph Rodrigues, Graham Evan Williams, William Terence Hennessey, Harold Michael England, Barrington Gerard Hole, Gilbert Ivor Reece, Ronald Wyn Davies, Ronald Tudor Davies, Clifford William Jones, Alan Leslie Jarvis.   Manager: David Lloyd Bowen.
SCOTLAND: Robert Ferguson, John Greig (Cap), Thomas Gemmell, William John Bremner, Ronald McKinnon, John Clark, James Connolly Johnstone, Denis Law, Joseph McBride, James Curran Baxter, William Henderson.
Manager: Malcolm MacDonald.
Goals: Ronald Tudor Davies (77) / Denis Law (86)

321. 16.11.1966   Home Championship,
3rd European Championships Qualifiers
SCOTLAND v NORTHERN IRELAND 2-1 (2-1)
Hampden Park, Glasgow
Referee: John Keith Taylor (England)   Attendance: 45,281
SCOTLAND: Robert Ferguson, John Greig (Cap), Thomas Gemmell, William John Bremner, Ronald McKinnon, John Clark, William Henderson, Robert White Murdoch, Joseph McBride, Stephen Chalmers, Robert Lennox.
Manager: Malcolm MacDonald.
NORTHERN IRELAND: Patrick Anthony Jennings, John Parke, Alexander Russell, Martin Harvey, William John Terence Neill, James Joseph Nicholson, Samuel J. Wilson, John Andrew Crossan, William John Irvine, Alexander Derek Dougan, David Clements.   Manager: Robert Peacock.
Goals: Robert White Murdoch (14), Robert Lennox (35) / James Joseph Nicholson (9)

322. 15.04.1967   Home Championship,
3rd European Championships Qualifiers
ENGLAND v SCOTLAND 2-3 (0-1)
Wembley, London
Referee: Gerhard Schulenburg (West Germany)   Att: 99,063
ENGLAND: Gordon Banks, George Reginald Cohen, Ramon Wilson, Norbert Peter Stiles, John "Jack" Charlton, Robert Frederick Moore (Cap), Alan James Ball, James Peter Greaves, Robert Charlton, Geoffrey Charles Hurst, Martin Stanford Peters.   Manager: Alfred Ernest Ramsey.
SCOTLAND: Ronald Campbell Simpson, Thomas Gemmell, Edward Graham McCreadie, John Greig (Cap), Ronald McKinnon, William John Bremner, James McCalliog, Denis Law, William Semple Brown Wallace, James Curran Baxter, Robert Lennox.   Manager: Robert Brown.
Goals: John Charlton (84), Geoffrey Charles Hurst (88) / Denis Law (27), Robert Lennox (78), James McCalliog (87)

323. 10.05.1967
SCOTLAND v SOVIET UNION 0-2 (0-2)
Hampden Park, Glasgow
Referee: Laurens van Ravens (Holland)   Attendance: 53,497
SCOTLAND: Ronald Campbell Simpson, Thomas Gemmell, Edward Graham McCreadie, John Clark, William McNeill, James Curran Baxter (Cap), James Connolly Johnstone, Francis McLintock, James McCalliog, Denis Law (46 William Semple Brown Wallace), Robert Lennox.
Manager: Robert Brown.
SOVIET UNION: Lev Yashin, Valentin Afonin, Albert Shesternev (Cap), Murtaz Khurtzilava, Vasiliy Danilov, Valeriy Voronin, Igor Chislenko, József Sabo, Fedor Medvid, Eduard Streltsov, Eduard Malofeev.   Trainer: Mikhail Yakushin.
Goals: Thomas Gemmell (17 own goal), Fedor Medvid (41)

324. 21.10.1967   Home Championship,
3rd European Championships Qualifiers
NORTHERN IRELAND v SCOTLAND 1-0 (0-0)

Windsor Park, Belfast

Referee: James Finney (England)   Attendance: 55,000

NORTHERN IRELAND: Patrick Anthony Jennings, William McKeag, John Parke, Arthur Stewart, William John Terence Neill, David Clements, William Gibson Campbell, John Andrew Crossan, Alexander Derek Dougan, James Joseph Nicholson, George Best.
Manager: William Laurence Bingham.

SCOTLAND: Ronald Campbell Simpson, Thomas Gemmell, Edward Graham McCreadie, John Greig (Cap), Ronald McKinnon, John Francombe Ure, William Semple Brown Wallace, Robert White Murdoch, James McCalliog, Denis Law, William Morgan.   Manager: Robert Brown.

Goal: David Clements (68)

325. 22.11.1967   Home Championship,
3rd European Championships Qualifiers
SCOTLAND v WALES 3-2 (1-1)

Hampden Park, Glasgow

Referee: James Finney (England)   Attendance: 57,472

SCOTLAND: Robert Brown Clark, James Philip Craig, Edward Graham McCreadie, John Greig (Cap), Ronald McKinnon, James Curran Baxter, James Connolly Johnstone, William John Bremner, Alan John Gilzean, William McClure Johnston, Robert Lennox.   Manager: Robert Brown.

WALES: Gareth Sprake, Peter Joseph Rodrigues, Colin Robert Green, William Terence Hennessey, Edward Glyn James, Barrington Gerard Hole, Ronald Raymond Rees, Ronald Wyn Davies, Ronald Tudor Davies, William Alan Durban, Clifford William Jones.   Manager: David Lloyd Bowen.

Goals: Alan John Gilzean (15, 65), Ronald McKinnon (78) / Ronald Tudor Davies (18), William Alan Durban (57)

326. 24.02.1968   Home Championship,
3rd European Championships Qualifiers
SCOTLAND v ENGLAND 1-1 (1-1)

Hampden Park, Glasgow

Referee: Laurens van Ravens (Holland)   Att: 134,000

SCOTLAND: Ronald Campbell Simpson, Thomas Gemmell, Edward Graham McCreadie, William McNeill, Ronald McKinnon, John Greig (Cap), Charles Cooke, William John Bremner, John Hughes, William McClure Johnston, Robert Lennox.   Manager: Robert Brown.

ENGLAND: Gordon Banks, Keith Robert Newton, Ramon Wilson, Alan Patrick Mullery, Brian Leslie Labone, Robert Frederick Moore (Cap), Alan James Ball, Geoffrey Charles Hurst, Michael George Summerbee, Robert Charlton, Martin Stanford Peters.   Manager: Alfred Ernest Ramsey.

Goals: John Hughes (39) / Martin Stanford Peters (20)

327. 30.05.1968
HOLLAND v SCOTLAND 0-0

Olympisch, Amsterdam

Referee: Karl Riegg (West Germany)   Attendance: 19,000

HOLLAND: Jan van Beveren, Pieter Dirk Gerrit Romeijn, Marinus David Israël, Johannes Antonius Eijkenbroek (Cap), Hendrik Warnas, Wilhelmus Marinus Anthonius Jansen, Hendrik Groot, Johannes Teunis Klijnjan, Wilhelmus Martinus Leonardus Johannes van der Kuylen, Willem van Hanegem, Robert Pieter Rensenbrink.
Trainer: Georg Kessler.

SCOTLAND: Robert Brown Clark, Douglas Michael Fraser, Edward Graham McCreadie, Robert Moncur, Ronald McKinnon, David Bruce Smith, William Henderson, Robert Hope (12 James Smith), George Tomlinson McLean, John Greig (Cap), Charles Cooke.   Manager: Robert Brown.

328. 16.10.1968
DENMARK v SCOTLAND 0-1 (0-0)

Idrætsparken, København

Referee: Hans Carlsson (Sweden)   Attendance: 11,900

DENMARK: Knud Engedal, Jan Larsen, Niels Yde, Leif Sørensen, Henning Munk Jensen, Børge Enemark (Cap), Flemming Mortensen, Finn Wiberg, Bent Jensen, Ole Steffensen, Ulrik Le Fevre.

SCOTLAND: James Herriot, Thomas Gemmell, Edward Graham McCreadie, William John Bremner (Cap), Ronald McKinnon, John Greig, Thomas McLean, James McCalliog (87 Peter Barr Cormack), Colin Anderson Stein, Robert Hope, Robert Lennox.   Manager: Robert Brown.

Goal: Robert Lennox (70)

329. 06.11.1968   9th World Cup Qualifiers
SCOTLAND v AUSTRIA 2-1 (1-1)

Hampden Park, Glasgow

Referee: Curt Liedberg (Sweden)   Attendance: 80,856

SCOTLAND: Ronald Campbell Simpson, Thomas Gemmell, Edward Graham McCreadie, William John Bremner (Cap), Ronald McKinnon, John Greig, James Connolly Johnstone, Charles Cooke, John Hughes, Denis Law (75 Alan John Gilzean), Robert Lennox.   Manager: Robert Brown.

AUSTRIA: Gerald Fuchsbichler, Walter Gebhardt, Gerhard Sturmberger, Johann Eigenstiller, Peter Pumm, Franz Hasil, August Starek, Johann Ettmayer, Helmut Mätzler, Helmut Siber, Helmut Redl (46 Helmut Köglberger).
Trainer: Leopold Stastny.

Goals: Denis Law (7), William John Bremner (75) / August Starek (3)

330. 11.12.1968   9th World Cup Qualifiers
CYPRUS v SCOTLAND 0-5 (0-5)

GSP, Nicosia

Referee: Paul Bonnet (Malta)   Attendance: 5,895

CYPRUS: Makis Alkiviadis, Panicos Iakovou, Lakis Theodorou, Stefanis Michael, Kyriakos Koureas, Costas Panayiotou, Panicos Efthymiadis, Panicos Krystallis (Yiannakis Xypolytas), Melis Asprou, Andreas Christodoulou (Markos Markou), Andreas Stylianou.
Trainer: Pambos Avraamides.

SCOTLAND: James Herriot, Douglas Michael Fraser, Edward Graham McCreadie, William John Bremner (Cap), Ronald McKinnon (46 William McNeill), John Greig, Thomas McLean, Robert White Murdoch, Colin Anderson Stein, Alan John Gilzean, Charles Cooke (80 Robert Lennox).
Manager: Robert Brown.

Goals: Alan Gilzean (3, 30), Robert White Murdoch (23), Colin Anderson Stein (40, 43).

331. 16.04.1969   9th World Cup Qualifiers
SCOTLAND v WEST GERMANY 1-1 (0-1)

Hampden Park, Glasgow

Referee: Juan Garay Gardeazábal (Spain)   Att: 95,491

SCOTLAND: Thomas Johnstone Lawrence, Thomas Gemmell, Edward Graham McCreadie, Robert White Murdoch, Ronald McKinnon, John Greig, James Connolly Johnstone, William John Bremner (Cap), Denis Law, Alan John Gilzean, Robert Lennox (63 Charles Cooke).
Manager: Robert Brown.

GERMANY: Horst Wolter (46 Josef Maier), Karl-Heinz Schnellinger, Hans-Hubert Vogts, Franz Beckenbauer, Willi Schulz (Cap), Bernd Patzke, Bernd Dörfel, Helmut Haller, Gerhard Müller, Wolfgang Overath (79 Max Lorenz), Siegfried Held.   Trainer: Helmut Schön.

Goals: Robert White Murdoch (88) / Gerhard Müller (39)

332. 03.05.1969   Home Championship
WALES v SCOTLAND 3-5 (2-2)

The Racecourse, Wrexham

Referee: James Finney (England)   Attendance: 18,765

WALES: Gareth Sprake, Stephen Clifford Derrett (78 Ronald Raymond Rees), Colin Robert Green, Alwyn Derek Burton, David Powell, Graham Moore, William Alan Durban, John Benjamin Toshack, Ronald Tudor Davies, Ronald Wyn Davies, Barrie Spencer Jones.   Manager: David Lloyd Bowen.

SCOTLAND: Thomas Johnstone Lawrence (46 James Herriot), Thomas Gemmell, Edward Graham McCreadie, William John Bremner (Cap), William McNeill, John Greig, Thomas McLean, Robert White Murdoch, Colin Anderson Stein, Alan John Gilzean, Charles Cooke.
Manager: Robert Brown.

Goals: Ronald Tudor Davies (29, 57), John Toshack (44) / William McNeill (12), Colin Anderson Stein (16), Alan John Gilzean (55), William John Bremner (72), Thomas McLean (87).

333. 06.05.1969   Home Championship
SCOTLAND v NORTHERN IRELAND 1-1 (0-1)

Hampden Park, Glasgow

Referee: David W. Smith (England)   Attendance: 7,483

SCOTLAND: James Herriot, Thomas Gemmell, Edward Graham McCreadie, William John Bremner (Cap), John Greig, Patrick Gordon Stanton, William Henderson, Robert White Murdoch, Colin Anderson Stein, Denis Law, Charles Cooke (75 William McClure Johnston).   Manager: Robert Brown.

NORTHERN IRELAND: Patrick Anthony Jennings, David James Craig, Alexander Russell, Samuel John Todd, William John Terence Neill, James Joseph Nicholson, George Best, Alexander S. McMordie, Alexander Derek Dougan, Thomas A. Jackson, David Clements.
Manager: William Laurence Bingham.

Goals: Colin Anderson Stein (53) / Alexander McMordie (11)

334. 10.05.1969   Home Championship
ENGLAND v SCOTLAND 4-1 (2-1)

Wembley, London

Referee: Robert Héliès (France)   Attendance: 89,902

ENGLAND: Gordon Banks, Keith Robert Newton, Terence Cooper, Alan Patrick Mullery, Brian Leslie Labone, Robert Frederick Moore (Cap), Francis Henry Lee, Alan James Ball, Robert Charlton, Geoffrey Charles Hurst, Martin Stanford Peters.   Manager: Alfred Ernest Ramsey.

SCOTLAND: James Herriot, Thomas Gemmell, Edward Graham McCreadie, Robert White Murdoch, William McNeill, John Greig, William Henderson, William John Bremner (Cap), Colin Anderson Stein, Alan John Gilzean (57 William Semple Brown Wallace), Edwin Gray.   Manager: Robert Brown.

Goals: Martin Stanford Peters (16, 64), Geoffrey Hurst (20, 60 pen) / Colin Anderson Stein (43)

335. 17.05.1969   9th World Cup Qualifiers
SCOTLAND v CYPRUS 8-0 (3-0)
Hampden Park, Glasgow

Referee: Peter P. Coates (Republic of Ireland)   Att: 39,095

SCOTLAND: James Herriot, Thomas Gemmell, Edward Graham McCreadie, William John Bremner (Cap), William McNeill, John Greig, William Henderson, Charles Cooke, Colin Anderson Stein, Alan John Gilzean, Edwin Gray. Manager: Robert Brown.

CYPRUS: Makis Alkiviadis, Yiannis Mertakkas, Savvakis Constantinou (Costas Constantas), Georgiou Sotirakis (46 Dimos Kavazis), Kyriakos Koureas, Stefanis Michael, Panicos Efthymiadis, Markos Markou, Panicos Krystallis, Melis Asprou, Andreas Stylianou.   Trainer: Pambos Avraamides.

Goals: Edwin Gray (15), William McNeill (20), Colin Anderson Stein (28, 49, 59, 67), William Henderson (70), Thomas Gemmell (76 pen)

336. 21.09.1969
REPUBLIC OF IRELAND v SCOTLAND 1-1 (1-1)
Dalymount Park, Dublin

Referee: Norman Burtenshaw (England)   Att: 27,000

REPUBLIC OF IRELAND: Alan James Alexander Kelly, James Seamus Anthony Brennan, Michael Kevin Meagan (Cap), Alfred Finucane, Patrick Martin Mulligan, James Patrick Conway, Edward Eamonn Rogers, John Michael Giles, Daniel Joseph Givens, Alfred Hale, Raymond Christopher Patrick Treacy.   Trainer: Michael Kevin Meagan.

SCOTLAND: Ernest McGarr (24 James Herriot), John Greig, Thomas Gemmell (46 William Thomas Callaghan), Patrick Gordon Stanton, Ronald McKinnon, Robert Moncur, William Henderson, William John Bremner (Cap), Colin Anderson Stein, Peter Barr Cormack, John Hughes. Manager: Robert Brown.

Goals: Daniel Joseph Givens (27) / Colin Anderson Stein (8)

337. 22.10.1969   9th World Cup Qualifiers
WEST GERMANY v SCOTLAND 3-2 (1-1)
Volkspark, Hamburg

Referee: Gilbert Droz (Switzerland)   Attendance: 72,000

GERMANY: Josef Maier, Horst-Dieter Höttges, Hans-Hubert Vogts, Franz Beckenbauer, Willi Schulz, Klaus Fichtel, Reinhard Libuda, Uwe Seeler (Cap), Gerhard Müller, Wolfgang Overath, Helmut Haller.   Trainer: Helmut Schön.

SCOTLAND: James Herriot, John Greig, Thomas Gemmell, William John Bremner (Cap), Ronald McKinnon, William McNeill, James Connolly Johnstone, Peter Barr Cormack, Alan John Gilzean, Colin Anderson Stein, Edwin Gray. Manager: Robert Brown.

Goals: Klaus Fichtel (37), Gerhard Müller (58), Reinhard Libuda (80) / James Connolly Johnstone (3), Alan John Gilzean (64)

338. 05.11.1969   9th World Cup Qualifiers
AUSTRIA v SCOTLAND 2-0 (1-0)
Prater, Wien

Referee: Karlo Kruashvili (Soviet Union)   Att: 10,091

AUSTRIA: Wilhelm Harreither, Helmut Wallner, Gerhard Sturmberger, Johann Schmidradner, Erich Fak, Johann Geyer, Norbert Hof, Johann Ettmayer, Thomas Parits, Robert Kaiser (66 Josef Hickersberger), Helmut Redl.   Trainer: Leopold Stastny.

SCOTLAND: Ernest McGarr, John Greig, Francis Burns, Robert White Murdoch, Ronald McKinnon, Patrick Gordon Stanton, Charles Cooke (72 Colin Anderson Stein), William John Bremner (Cap), Alan John Gilzean, Hugh Patrick Curran (54 Peter Patrick Lorimer), Edwin Gray. Manager: Robert Brown.

Goals: Helmut Redl (15, 52)

339. 18.04.1970   Home Championship
NORTHERN IRELAND v SCOTLAND 0-1 (0-0)
Windsor Park, Belfast

Referee: Eric T. Jennings (England)   Attendance: 31,000

NORTHERN IRELAND: Patrick Anthony Jennings, David James Craig, David Clements, Samuel John Todd (46 William James O'Kane), William John Terence Neill (Cap), James Joseph Nicholson, William Gibson Campbell (75 Desmond Dickson), Robert John Lutton, Alexander Derek Dougan, Alexander S. McMordie, George Best.
Manager: William Laurence Bingham.

SCOTLAND: Robert Brown Clark, David Hay, William Dickson, Francis McLintock (Cap), Ronald McKinnon, Robert Moncur, Thomas McLean, William McInnany Carr, John O'Hare, Alan John Gilzean (70 Colin Anderson Stein), William McClure Johnston.   Manager: Robert Brown.

Goal: John O'Hare (58)

340. 22.04.1970   Home Championship
SCOTLAND v WALES 0-0
Hampden Park, Glasgow

Referee: David W. Smith (England)   Attendance: 30,434

SCOTLAND: James Fergus Cruickshank, William Thomas Callaghan, William Dickson, John Greig (Cap), Ronald McKinnon, Robert Moncur, Thomas McLean (70 Robert Lennox), David Hay, John O'Hare, Colin Anderson Stein, William McInnany Carr.   Manager: Robert Brown.

WALES: Anthony Horace Millington, Peter Joseph Rodrigues, Roderick John Thomas, William Terence Hennessey, Harold Michael England, David Powell, Ryszard Lech Krzywicki, William Alan Durban, Ronald Tudor Davies, Graham Moore, Ronald Raymond Rees.   Manager: David Lloyd Bowen.

341. 25.04.1970   Home Championship
SCOTLAND v ENGLAND   0-0
Hampden Park, Glasgow

Referee: Gerhard Schulenburg (W. Germany)   Att: 137,438

SCOTLAND: James Fergus Cruickshank, Thomas Gemmell, William Dickson, John Greig (Cap), Ronald McKinnon, Robert Moncur (82 Alan John Gilzean), James Connolly Johnstone, David Hay, Colin Anderson Stein, John O'Hare, William McInnany Carr.   Manager: Robert Brown.

ENGLAND: Gordon Banks, Keith Robert Newton, Emlyn Walter Hughes, Norbert Peter Stiles, Brian Leslie Labone, Robert Frederick Moore (Cap), Peter Thompson (58 Alan Patrick Mullery), Alan James Ball, Jeffrey Astle, Geoffrey Charles Hurst, Martin Stanford Peters.   Manager: Alfred Ernest Ramsey.

342. 11.11.1970   4th European Champs. Qualifiers
SCOTLAND v DENMARK   1-0 (1-0)
Hampden Park, Glasgow

Referee: Erich Linemayr (Austria)   Attendance: 24,618

SCOTLAND: James Fergus Cruickshank, David Hay (77 William Pullar Jardine), John Greig, Patrick Gordon Stanton, Ronald McKinnon, Robert Moncur (Cap), James Connolly Johnstone, William McInnany Carr, Colin Anderson Stein, John O'Hare (75 Peter Barr Cormack), William McClure Johnston.   Manager: Robert Brown.

DENMARK: Kaj Paulsen, Torben Nielsen, Povl Henning Frederiksen, Erik Sandvad, Flemming Pedersen, Jens Jørgen Hansen (Cap), Bent Outzen, Kristen Nygaard, Morten Olsen (25 Poul-Erik Thygesen), Keld Pedersen, Benny Nielsen.   Trainer: Rudolf Strittich (Austria)

Goal: John O'Hare (14)

343. 03.02.1971   4th European Champs. Qualifiers
BELGIUM v SCOTLAND   3-0 (1-0)
Sclessin, Liège

Referee: Antonio Sbardella (Italy)   Attendance: 13,931

BELGIUM: Christian Piot, Georges Heylens, Nicolas Dewalque, Jean Plaskie, Jean Thissen, Wilfried Van Moer, Erwin Vandendaele, Léon Semmeling, Henri Depireux, Paul Van Himst, André De Nul.   Trainer: Raymond Goethals.

SCOTLAND: James Fergus Cruickshank, David Hay, Thomas Gemmell, John Greig, Ronald McKinnon, Patrick Gordon Stanton (46 Anthony Green), Robert Moncur (Cap), Archibald Gemmill, Charles Cooke, Colin Anderson Stein (46 James Forrest), John O'Hare.   Manager: Robert Brown.

Goal: Ronald McKinnon (34 own goal), Paul Van Himst (55, 83 pen)

344. 21.04.1971   4th European Champs Qualifiers
PORTUGAL v SCOTLAND   2-0 (1-0)
da Luz, Lisboa

Referee: Michel Kitabdjian (France)   Attendance: 35,463

PORTUGAL: Vítor Manuel Alfonso Damas de Oliveira, Amândio José Malta da Silva, Humberto Manuel de Jesus Coelho, José Carlos da Silva (Cap), Adolfo António da Cruz Calisto, Rui Gouveia Pinto Rodrigues, Fernando Peres da Silva, António Simões da Costa, Tamagnini Manuel Gomes Baptista "Nené" (84 Fernando Pascoal Neves "Pavão"), Vítor Manuel Ferreira Baptista (76 Artur Jorge Braga Melo Teixeira), Eusébio da Silva Ferreira.   Trainer: José Gomes da Silva.

SCOTLAND: Robert Brown Clark, David Hay, James Andrew Brogan, Patrick Gordon Stanton (75 Anthony Green), Ronald McKinnon, Robert Moncur (Cap), William Henderson, David Thomson Robb, Peter Barr Cormack, James McCalliog (63 Andrew Jarvie), Alan John Gilzean.   Manager: Robert Brown.

Goals: Patrick Gordon Stanton (25 own goal), Eusébio da Silva Ferreira (81)

345. 15.05.1971   Home Championship
WALES v SCOTLAND   0-0
Ninian Park, Cardiff

Referee: John Keith Taylor (England)   Attendance: 19,068

WALES: Gareth Sprake, Peter Joseph Rodrigues, Roderick John Thomas, Edward Glyn James, John Griffith Roberts, Terence Charles Yorath, Leighton Phillips, William Alan Durban, Ronald Tudor Davies, John Benjamin Toshack, Gilbert Ivor Reece.   Manager: David Lloyd Bowen.

SCOTLAND: Robert Brown Clark, David Hay, James Andrew Brogan, William John Bremner (72 John Greig), Francis McLintock, Robert Moncur (Cap), Peter Patrick Lorimer, Peter Barr Cormack, Edwin Gray, David Thomson Robb, John O'Hare.   Manager: Robert Brown.

346. 18.05.1971   Home Championship
SCOTLAND v NORTHERN IRELAND   0-1 (0-1)
Hampden Park, Glasgow

Referee: Clive Thomas (Wales)   Attendance: 31,643

SCOTLAND: Robert Brown Clark, David Hay, James Andrew Brogan, John Greig, Francis McLintock (71 Francis Michael Munro), Robert Moncur (Cap), Peter Patrick Lorimer, Anthony Green, Edwin Gray, Hugh Patrick Curran, John O'Hare (46 Andrew Jarvie).   Manager: Robert Brown.

NORTHERN IRELAND: Patrick Anthony Jennings, Patrick James Rice, Samuel Nelson, William James O'Kane, Alan Hunter, James Joseph Nicholson, Bryan Hamilton, Alexander S. McMordie (67 David James Craig), Alexander Derek Dougan (Cap), David Clements, George Best.   Manager: William Laurence Bingham.

Goal: John Greig (14 own goal)

347. 22.05.1971   Home Championship
ENGLAND v SCOTLAND 3-1 (3-1)
Wembley, London

Referee: Jef Dorpmans (Holland)   Attendance: 91,469

ENGLAND: Gordon Banks, Christopher Lawler, Terence Cooper, Peter Edwin Storey, Roy Leslie McFarland, Robert Frederick Moore (Cap), Francis Henry Lee (73 Allan John Clarke), Alan James Ball, Martin Harcourt Chivers, Geoffrey Charles Hurst, Martin Stanford Peters.
Manager: Alfred Ernest Ramsey.

SCOTLAND: Robert Brown Clark, John Greig, James Andrew Brogan, William John Bremner, Francis McLintock, Robert Moncur (Cap), James Connolly Johnstone, Anthony Green (82 Andrew Jarvie), Peter Barr Cormack, David Thomson Robb, Hugh Patrick Curran (46 Francis Michael Munro).
Manager: Robert Brown.

Goals: Martin Stanford Peters (9), Martin Chivers (30, 40) / Hugh Patrick Curran (11)

348. 09.06.1971   4th European Champs. Qualifiers
DENMARK v SCOTLAND 1-0 (1-0)
Idrætsparken, København

Referee: Wolfgang Riedel (East Germany)   Att: 37,682

DENMARK: Erik Lykke Sørensen, Torben Nielsen, Mogens Berg, Preben Arentoft, Jørgen Rasmussen, Kresten Bjerre (Cap), Finn Laudrup (75 Bent Outzen), Ole Bjørnmose, Ulrik Le Fevre, Benny Nielsen (85 Keld Pedersen), Jørgen Kristensen. Trainer: Rudolf Strittich (Austria).

SCOTLAND: Robert Brown Clark, Francis Michael Munro, William Dickson, Patrick Gordon Stanton, Ronald McKinnon, Robert Moncur (Cap), Thomas McLean, Thomas Forsyth (46 David Thomson Robb), James Forrest (70 John Scott), Hugh Patrick Curran, Colin Anderson Stein.
Manager: Robert Brown.

Goal: Finn Laudrup (42)

349. 14.06.1971
SOVIET UNION v SCOTLAND 1-0 (1-0)
"Lenin", Moskva

Referee: Ferdinand Marschall (Austria)   Attendance: 20,000

SOVIET UNION: Evgeniy Rudakov, Yuriy Istomin, Albert Shesternev (Cap), Viktor Matvienko, Vladimir Kaplichniy, Viktor Kolotov, Anatoliy Konikov, Givi Nodia (70 Nikolay Dolgov), Vladimir Fedotov, Vitaliy Shevchenko, Gennadiy Evryuzhikhin (46 Vitaliy Khmelnitskiy).
Trainer: Vladimir Nikolaev.

SCOTLAND: Robert Brown Clark, John Jack Brownlie, William Dickson, Francis Michael Munro, Ronald McKinnon, Patrick Gordon Stanton (Cap), Robert P. Watson, David Thomson Robb, John Scott, James Forrest, Colin Anderson Stein (71 Hugh Patrick Curran).   Manager: Robert Brown.

Goal: Gennadiy Evryuzhikhin (25)

350. 13.10.1971   4th European Champs. Qualifiers
SCOTLAND v PORTUGAL 2-1 (1-0)
Hampden Park, Glasgow

Referee: Bruno Piotrowicz (Poland)   Attendance: 58,612

SCOTLAND: Robert Primrose Wilson, William Pullar Jardine, David Hay, Patrick Gordon Stanton, Edmond Peter Skiruing Colquhoun (60 Martin McLean Buchan), James Connolly Johnstone, William John Bremner (Cap), George Graham, Alexander Wilson James Cropley, Archibald Gemmill, John O'Hare.
Manager: Thomas Henderson Docherty.

PORTUGAL: Vítor Manuel Alfonso Damas de Oliveira, Amândio José Malta da Silva, Francisco António Galinho Caló (66 Fernando Peres da Silva), Rui Gouveia Pinto Rodrigues, Adolfo António da Cruz Calisto, Jaime da Silva Graça, José Rolando Andrade Gonçalves, Tamagnini Manuel Gomes Baptista "Nené", Vítor Manuel Ferreira Baptista, Eusébio da Silva Ferreira (Cap) (46 Artur Jorge Braga Melo Teixeira), António Simões da Costa.   Trainer: José Gomes da Silva.

Goals: John O'Hare (23), Archibald Gemmill (58) / Rui Gouveia Pinto Rodrigues (57)

351. 10.11.1971   4th European Champs. Qualifiers
SCOTLAND v BELGIUM 1-0 (1-0)
Pittodrie, Aberdeen

Referee: Einar Boström (Sweden)   Attendance: 36,500

SCOTLAND: Robert Brown Clark, William Pullar Jardine, David Hay, Patrick Gordon Stanton, Martin McLean Buchan, James Connolly Johnstone (79 John Angus McDonald Hansen), William John Bremner (Cap), Alexander Wilson James Cropley (48 Kenneth Mathieson Dalglish), Edwin Gray, Stephen Murray, John O'Hare.
Manager: Thomas Henderson Docherty.

BELGIUM: Christian Piot, Georges Heylens, Nicolas Dewalque, André Stassart, Leonardus Dolmans, Wilfried Van Moer (57 Maurice Martens), Erwin Vandendaele, Wilfried Puis (69 Raoul Lambert), Léon Semmeling, Johan Devrindt, Paul Van Himst.   Trainer: Raymond Goethals.

Goal: John O'Hare (6)

352. 01.12.1971
HOLLAND v SCOTLAND 2-1 (1-0)
Olympisch, Amsterdam
Referee: Ferdinand Biwersi (West Germany)   Att: 18,000
HOLLAND: Pieter Schrijvers, Johannes Gerardus Nicolaas Venneker, Bernardus Adriaan Hulshoff, Marinus David Israël, Rudolf Jozef Krol, Johannes Jacobus Neeskens, Willem van Hanegem, Hendrikus Wilhelmus Jan Gerardus Wery (46 Wilhelmus Marinus Anthonius Jansen), Theodorus Hermanus Johannes Maria Pahlplatz, Johannes Hendrik Cruijff (Cap), Petrus Johannes Keizer (46 Gerardus Domenicus Hyacinthus Maria Mühren).
Trainer: František Fadrhonc (Czechoslovakia).
SCOTLAND: Robert Primrose Wilson, William Pullar Jardine, David Hay, Patrick Gordon Stanton, Edmond Peter Skiruing Colquhoun, James Connolly Johnstone (56 John O'Hare), William John Bremner (Cap), Archibald Gemmill, Edwin Gray (84 Peter Barr Cormack), George Graham, Kenneth Mathieson Dalglish.
Manager: Thomas Henderson Docherty.
Goals: Johannes Hendrik Cruijff (5), Bernardus Hulshoff (88) / George Graham (58).

353. 26.04.1972
SCOTLAND v PERU 2-0 (0-0)
Hampden Park, Glasgow
Referee: Patrick Partridge (England)   Attendance: 21,001
SCOTLAND: Alistair Robert Hunter, John Jack Brownlie, William Donachie, Robert Moncur, Edmond Peter Skiruing Colquhoun, William Morgan, William McInnany Carr, Richard Asa Hartford, Archibald Gemmill, John O'Hare, Denis Law (Cap). Manager: Thomas Henderson Docherty.
PERU: Manuel Uribe, Rodolfo Manzo Audante, José Manuel Velásquez Castillo, Héctor Eduardo Chumpitaz González, Antonio Trigueros, Ramón Mifflin, Alfredo Quesada, Juan José Muñante López, Percy Rojas Montero (46 Hugo Alejandro Sotil Yerén), Teófilo Juan Cubillas Arizaga, Juan Orbegoso.
Trainer: Lajos Baróti (Hungary).
Goals: John O'Hare (47), Denis Law (65).

354. 20.05.1972   Home Championship
SCOTLAND v NORTHERN IRELAND 2-0 (0-0)
Hampden Park, Glasgow
Referee: Clive Thomas (Wales)   Attendance: 39,710
SCOTLAND: Robert Brown Clark, John Jack Brownlie, William Donachie, Robert Moncur, William McNeill, James Connolly Johnstone (61 Peter Patrick Lorimer), William John Bremner (Cap), George Graham, Archibald Gemmill, John O'Hare, Denis Law.   Manager: Thomas Henderson Docherty.
NORTHERN IRELAND: Patrick Anthony Jennings, Patrick James Rice, Samuel Nelson, William John Terence Neill, Alan Hunter, David Clements (83 David James Craig), Daniel Hegan, Alexander S. McMordie (68 Samuel Baxter McIlroy), Alexander Derek Dougan, William John Irvine, Thomas A. Jackson. Manager: Terence Neill.
Goals: Denis Law (86), Peter Patrick Lorimer (89).

355. 24.05.1972   Home Championship
SCOTLAND v WALES 1-0 (0-0)
Hampden Park, Glasgow
Referee: James Lawther (Northern Ireland)   Att: 21,332
SCOTLAND: Robert Brown Clark, Patrick Gordon Stanton, Martin McLean Buchan, Robert Moncur, William McNeill, Peter Patrick Lorimer, William John Bremner (Cap), Anthony Green, Archibald Gemmill (35 Richard Asa Hartford), John O'Hare (56 Luigi Macari), Denis Law.
Manager: Thomas Henderson Docherty.
WALES: Gareth Sprake, Malcolm Edward Page, Roderick John Thomas, William Terence Hennessey (74 Leighton James), Harold Michael England, Terence Charles Yorath, William Alan Durban, Ronald Wyn Davies, Gilbert Ivor Reece, Ronald Tudor Davies, Leighton Phillips.
Manager: David Lloyd Bowen.
Goal: Peter Patrick Lorimer (72).

356. 27.05.1972   Home Championship
SCOTLAND v ENGLAND 0-1 (0-1)
Hampden Park, Glasgow
Referee: Sergio Gonella (Italy)   Attendance: 119,325
SCOTLAND: Robert Brown Clark, John Jack Brownlie, William Donachie (74 Anthony Green), Robert Moncur, William McNeill, Peter Patrick Lorimer, William John Bremner (Cap), Archibald Gemmill (49 James Connolly Johnstone), Richard Asa Hartford, Luigi Macari, Denis Law. Manager: Thomas Henderson Docherty.
ENGLAND: Gordon Banks, Paul Edward Madeley, Emlyn Walter Hughes, Peter Edwin Storey, Roy Leslie McFarland, Robert Frederick Moore (Cap), Alan James Ball, Colin Bell, Martin Harcourt Chivers, Rodney William Marsh (84 Malcolm Ian Macdonald), Norman Hunter.
Manager: Alfred Ernest Ramsey.
Goal: Alan James Ball (28).

357. 29.06.1972   Brazil Independence Cup
YUGOSLAVIA v SCOTLAND 2-2 (0-1)
Mineiro, Belo Horizonte

Referee: Angel Norberto Coerezza (Argentina)   Att: 4,000

YUGOSLAVIA: Rizah Mešković, Petar Krivokuća, Miroslav Bošković (38 Slobodan Santrač), Miroslav Pavlović, Josip Katalinski, Blagoje Paunović (46 Jure Jerković), Danilo Popivoda, Branko Oblak, Dušan Bajević, Jovan Aćimović, Dragan Džajić (Cap).   Trainer: Vujadin Boškov.

SCOTLAND: Alistair Robert Hunter, Alexander Forsyth (46 John Angus McDonald Hansen), William Donachie, Martin McLean Buchan, Edmond Peter Skiruing Colquhoun, William Morgan, William John Bremner (Cap), George Graham, Richard Asa Hartford, Luigi Macari, Denis Law (76 James Bone).   Manager: Thomas Henderson Docherty.

Goals: Dušan Bajević (60), Jure Jerković (86) / Luigi Macari (40, 64)

358. 02.07.1972   Brazil Independence Cup
CZECHOSLOVAKIA v SCOTLAND 0-0
Beira Rio, Porto Alegre

Referee: Armando Marques (Brazil)   Attendance: 15,000

CZECHOSLOVAKIA: Ivo Viktor (Cap), Karel Dobiaš, Ľudovít Zlocha, Vladimír Hagara, Jan Pivarník, Ján Medviď, Ladislav Kuna, Jaroslav Pollák, Vladimír Ternény (70 Anton Hrušecký), Jozef Adamec, Dušan Kabát (60 Ján Čapkovič). Trainers: Ladislav Novák & Ladislav Kačáni.

SCOTLAND: Robert Brown Clark, Alexander Forsyth, William Donachie, Martin McLean Buchan, Edmond Peter Skiruing Colquhoun, William Morgan, William John Bremner (Cap), George Graham, Richard Asa Hartford, Luigi Macari, Denis Law (78 Colin Anderson Stein).
Manager: Thomas Henderson Docherty.

359. 05.07.1972   Brazil Independence Cup
BRAZIL v SCOTLAND 1-0 (0-0)
Maracanã, Rio de Janeiro

Referee: Abraham Klein (Israel)   Attendance: 130,000

BRAZIL: Émerson Leão, José Maria Rodrigues Alves "Zé Maria I", Hércules Brito Ruas, Vantuir Galdino Gomes, Marco Antônio Feliciano, Clodoaldo Tavares Santana, Gérson de Oliveira Nunes "Gérson I", Roberto Rivelino, Jair Ventura Filho "Jairzinho", Eduardo Gonçalves de Andrade "Tostão", João Leiva Campos Filho "Leivinha" (63 Dario José dos Santos). Trainer: Mário Jorge Lobo Zagallo.

SCOTLAND: Robert Brown Clark, Alexander Forsyth, William Donachie, Martin McLean Buchan, Edmond Peter Skiruing Colquhoun, William Morgan, William John Bremner (Cap), George Graham, Richard Asa Hartford, Luigi Macari, Denis Law.   Manager: Thomas Henderson Docherty.

Goal: Jair Ventura Filho "Jairzinho" (80)

360. 18.10.1972   10th World Cup Qualifiers
DENMARK v SCOTLAND 1-4 (1-2)
Idrætsparken, København

Referee: Tofik Bakhramov (Soviet Union)   Att: 31,200

DENMARK: Mogens Therkildsen, Torben Nielsen, Henning Munk Jensen, Per Røntved (Cap), Flemming Ahlberg, John Steen Olsen, Jack Hansen (58 Bent Jensen), Ole Bjørnmose, Finn Laudrup, Eigil Nielsen, Henning Jensen.
Trainer: Rudolf Strittich (Austria).

SCOTLAND: Robert Brown Clark, John Jack Brownlie, Alexander Forsyth, Martin McLean Buchan, Edmond Peter Skiruing Colquhoun, Peter Patrick Lorimer, William John Bremner (Cap), George Graham, William Morgan, Luigi Macari (88 Kenneth Mathieson Dalglish), James Bone (65 Joseph Montgomery Harper).
Manager: Thomas Henderson Docherty.

Goals: Finn Laudrup (29) /
Luigi Macari (17), James Bone (19), Joseph Harper (80), William Morgan (83)

361. 15.11.1972   10th World Cup Qualifiers
SCOTLAND v DENMARK 2-0 (1-0)
Hampden Park, Glasgow

Referee: Charles George Rainier Corver (Holland)
Attendance: 47,109

SCOTLAND: David Harvey, John Jack Brownlie, William Donachie, Martin McLean Buchan, Edmond Peter Skiruing Colquhoun, Peter Patrick Lorimer, William John Bremner (Cap), George Graham, William Morgan, Kenneth Mathieson Dalglish (75 William McInnany Carr), Joseph Montgomery Harper.   Manager: Thomas Henderson Docherty.

DENMARK: Mogens Therkildsen (46 Heinz Hildebrandt), Flemming Ahlberg, Henning Munk Jensen, Per Røntved, Johnny Hansen, Allan Michaelsen, John Steen Olsen, Kresten Bjerre (Cap), Jørgen Kristensen (73 Finn Laudrup), Bent Jensen, Ulrik Le Fevre.   Trainer: Rudolf Strittich (Austria).

Goals: Kenneth Dalglish (2), Peter Patrick Lorimer (48)

362. 14.02.1973
SCOTLAND v ENGLAND 0-5 (0-3)
Hampden Park, Glasgow

Referee: Robert Charles Paul Wurtz (France)   Att: 48,470

SCOTLAND: Robert Brown Clark, Alexander Forsyth, William Donachie, Martin McLean Buchan, Edmond Peter Skiruing Colquhoun, Peter Patrick Lorimer, William John Bremner (Cap), George Graham, William Morgan (19 Colin Anderson Stein), Luigi Macari, Kenneth Mathieson Dalglish. Manager: William Esplin Ormond.

ENGLAND: Peter Leslie Shilton, Peter Edwin Storey, Emlyn Walter Hughes, Colin Bell, Paul Edward Madeley, Robert Frederick Moore (Cap), Alan James Ball, Michael Roger Channon, Martin Harcourt Chivers, Allan John Clarke, Martin Stanford Peters.   Manager: Alfred Ernest Ramsey.

Goals: Peter Lorimer (6 own goal), Allan Clarke (12, 85), Michael Roger Channon (15), Martin Harcourt Chivers (76)

363. 12.05.1973   Home Championship
WALES v SCOTLAND 0-2 (0-1)
The Racecourse, Wrexham

Referee: James Lawther (Northern Ireland)   Att: 18,682

WALES: Gareth Sprake, Peter Joseph Rodrigues, Roderick John Thomas, Trevor Hockey, Harold Michael England, John Griffith Roberts, Brian Clifford Evans (78 Peter Anthony O'Sullivan), John Francis Mahoney, John Benjamin Toshack, Terence Charles Yorath (69 Ronald Wyn Davies), Leighton James.   Manager: David Lloyd Bowen.

SCOTLAND: Peter McCloy, Daniel Fergus McGrain, William Donachie, James Allan Holton, Derek Joseph Johnstone, Patrick Gordon Stanton (Cap), George Graham, David Hay, William Morgan, Kenneth Mathieson Dalglish (84 Luigi Macari), Derek James Parlane (80 Colin Anderson Stein). Manager: William Esplin Ormond.

Goals: George Graham (18, 80)

364. 16.05.1973   Home Championship
SCOTLAND v NORTHERN IRELAND 1-2 (0-2)
Hampden Park, Glasgow

Referee: Kenneth H. Burns (England)   Attendance: 39,018

SCOTLAND: Peter McCloy, Daniel Fergus McGrain, William Donachie, James Allan Holton, Derek Joseph Johnstone, Patrick Gordon Stanton (Cap) (50 William John Bremner), George Graham (77 Luigi Macari), David Hay, William Morgan, Kenneth Mathieson Dalglish, Colin Anderson Stein. Manager: William Esplin Ormond.

NORTHERN IRELAND: Patrick Anthony Jennings, Patrick James Rice, David James Craig, William John Terence Neill (Cap), Alan Hunter, David Clements, Bryan Hamilton, Thomas A. Jackson, Samuel John Morgan, Martin Hugh Michael O'Neill, Trevor Anderson (65 Robert John Lutton). Manager: Terence Neill

Goals: Kenneth Mathieson Dalglish (89) / Martin Hugh Michael O'Neill (3), Trevor Anderson (17)

365. 19.05.1973   Home Championship
ENGLAND v SCOTLAND 1-0 (0-0)
Wembley, London

Referee: Kurt Tschenscher (West Germany)   Att: 95,950

ENGLAND: Peter Leslie Shilton, Peter Edwin Storey, Emlyn Walter Hughes, Colin Bell, Roy Leslie McFarland, Robert Frederick Moore (Cap), Alan James Ball, Michael Roger Channon, Martin Harcourt Chivers, Allan John Clarke, Martin Stanford Peters.   Manager: Alfred Ernest Ramsey.

SCOTLAND: Alistair Robert Hunter, William Pullar Jardine, Daniel Fergus McGrain, James Allan Holton, Derek Joseph Johnstone, Peter Patrick Lorimer (80 Colin Anderson Stein), William John Bremner (Cap), David Hay, William Morgan, Luigi Macari (74 Joseph Jordan), Kenneth Mathieson Dalglish. Manager: William Esplin Ormond.

Goal: Martin Stanford Peters (55)

366. 22.06.1973
SWITZERLAND v SCOTLAND 1-0 (0-0)
Wankdorf, Bern

Referee: Achille Verbecke (France)   Attendance: 10,000

SWITZERLAND: Erich Burgener, Walter Mundschin, Jean-Yves Valentini, Peter Ramseier (46 Ueli Wegmann), René Hasler, Karl Odermatt, Jakob Kuhn, Rolf Blättler (25 René-Pierre Quentin), Walter Balmer, Fernand Luisier, Otto Demarmels.   Trainer: René Hüssy.

SCOTLAND: Peter McCloy, William Pullar Jardine, Daniel Fergus McGrain, James Allan Holton, Derek Joseph Johnstone, John Connelly (46 Joseph Jordan), William John Bremner (Cap), David Hay, William Morgan, Kenneth Mathieson Dalglish, Derek James Parlane. Manager: William Esplin Ormond.

Goal: Walter Mundschin (62)

367. 30.06.1973
SCOTLAND v BRAZIL 0-1 (0-1)
Hampden Park, Glasgow

Referee: Kenneth H. Burns (England)   Attendance: 78,181

SCOTLAND: Peter McCloy, William Pullar Jardine, Daniel Fergus McGrain, James Allan Holton, Derek Joseph Johnstone, David Hay, William John Bremner (Cap), William Morgan, Kenneth Mathieson Dalglish (70 George Graham), Joseph Jordan, Derek James Parlane. Manager: William Esplin Ormond.

BRAZIL: Émerson Leão, José Maria Rodrigues Alves "Zé Maria I", Luís Edmundo Pereira, Wilson da Silva Piazza, Marco Antônio Feliciano, Clodoaldo Tavares Santana, Roberto Rivelino, Valdomiro Vaz Franco, Jair Ventura Filho "Jairzinho", Paulo César Lima, Dirceu José Guimarães. Trainer: Mário Jorge Lobo Zagallo.

Goal: Derek Joseph Johnstone (33 own goal)

66

368. 26.09.1973   10th World Cup Qualifiers
SCOTLAND v CZECHOSLOVAKIA 2-1 (1-1)

Hampden Park, Glasgow

Referee: Henry Öberg (Norway)   Attendance: 95,786

SCOTLAND: Alistair Robert Hunter, William Pullar Jardine, Daniel Fergus McGrain, David Hay, James Allan Holton, Thomas Hutchison, William John Bremner (Cap), George Connelly, William Morgan, Kenneth Mathieson Dalglish (63 Joseph Jordan), Denis Law.
Manager: William Esplin Ormond.

CZECHOSLOVAKIA: Ivo Viktor, Jan Pivarník, Václav Samek, Ľudovít Zlocha, Jaroslav Bendl, Přemysl Bičovský, Antonín Panenka (78 Ján Čapkovič), Ladislav Kuna (Cap) (21 Karel Dobiaš), Jozef Adamec, Zdeněk Nehoda, Pavel Stratil.
Trainer: Václav Ježek.

Goals: James Allan Holton (40), Joseph Jordan (75) / Zdeněk Nehoda (33)

369. 17.10.1973   10th World Cup Qualifiers
CZECHOSLOVAKIA v SCOTLAND 1-0 (1-0)

Tehelné pole, Bratislava

Referee: Ferdinand Biwersi (West Germany)   Att: 13,668

CZECHOSLOVAKIA: Ivo Viktor (Cap), Jan Pivarník, Václav Samek, Karel Dvořák, Vladimír Hagara, Přemysl Bičovský, Jaroslav Pollák, Miroslav Gajdůšek, František Veselý (61 Jiří Klement), Zdeněk Nehoda, Ján Čapkovič (78 Antonín Panenka).   Trainer: Václav Ježek.

SCOTLAND: David Harvey, William Pullar Jardine, Daniel Fergus McGrain, Thomas Forsyth, John Henderson Blackley, Thomas Hutchison, David Hay (Cap), William Morgan, Kenneth Mathieson Dalglish, Joseph Jordan, Denis Law (58 Donald Ford).   Manager: William Esplin Ormond.

Goal: Zdeněk Nehoda (15 pen)

370. 14.11.1973
SCOTLAND v WEST GERMANY 1-1 (1-0)

Hampden Park, Glasgow

Referee: John Keith Taylor (England)   Attendance: 58,235

SCOTLAND: David Harvey, William Pullar Jardine, Daniel Fergus McGrain, George Connelly, James Allan Holton, Thomas Hutchison, William John Bremner (Cap), James Smith (81 Peter Patrick Lorimer), William Morgan, Kenneth Mathieson Dalglish, Denis Law (87 Joseph Jordan).
Manager: William Esplin Ormond.

GERMANY: Wolfgang Kleff (46 Josef Maier), Hans-Hubert Vogts, Wolfgang Weber, Franz Beckenbauer (Cap), Horst-Dieter Höttges, Ulrich Hoeneß, Günter Netzer, Herbert Wimmer (75 Bernhard Cullmann), Jürgen Grabowski, Siegfried Held (75 Heinz Flohe), Erwin Kremers (46 Josef Heynckes).   Trainer: Helmut Schön.

Goals: James Allan Holton (7) / Ulrich Hoeneß (80)

371. 27.03.1974
WEST GERMANY v SCOTLAND 2-1 (2-0)

Wald, Frankfurt/Main

Referee: Paul Schiller (Austria)   Attendance: 62,000

GERMANY: Josef Maier, Hans-Hubert Vogts, Georg Schwarzenbeck, Franz Beckenbauer (Cap), Paul Breitner, Bernhard Cullmann, Ulrich Hoeneß, Herbert Wimmer, Jürgen Grabowski, Gerhard Müller, Dieter Herzog.
Trainer: Helmut Schön.

SCOTLAND: Thomas Sandlands Allan, William Pullar Jardine, Eric Peter Schaedler, Martin McLean Buchan, Kenneth Burns (59 Robert Sharp Robinson), Thomas Hutchison, Patrick Gordon Stanton, David Hay (Cap), William Morgan, Kenneth Mathieson Dalglish, Denis Law (59 Donald Ford).   Manager: William Esplin Ormond.

Goals: Paul Breitner (33 pen), Jürgen Grabowski (35) / Kenneth Mathieson Dalglish (77)

372. 11.05.1974   Home Championship
SCOTLAND v NORTHERN IRELAND 0-1 (0-1)

Hampden Park, Glasgow

Referee: Iorwerth Price-Jones (Wales)   Attendance: 53,775

SCOTLAND: David Harvey, William Pullar Jardine, William Donachie (46 James Smith), Martin McLean Buchan, James Allan Holton, Thomas Hutchison, William John Bremner (Cap), David Hay, William Morgan, Kenneth Mathieson Dalglish, Denis Law (65 Joseph Jordan).
Manager: William Esplin Ormond.

NORTHERN IRELAND: Patrick Anthony Jennings, Patrick James Rice, Samuel Nelson, William James O'Kane, Alan Hunter, David Clements (Cap), Bryan Hamilton (48 Thomas A. Jackson), Thomas Cassidy, Samuel John Morgan, Samuel Baxter McIlroy, Roland Christopher McGrath.
Manager: Terence Neill

Goal: Thomas Cassidy (40)

373. 14.05.1974   Home Championship
SCOTLAND v WALES 2-0 (2-0)

Hampden Park, Glasgow

Referee: Malcolm H. Wright (Northern Ireland)   Att: 41,969

SCOTLAND: David Harvey, William Pullar Jardine, David Hay, Martin McLean Buchan (76 Daniel Fergus McGrain), James Allan Holton, James Connolly Johnstone, William John Bremner (Cap), Donald Ford, Thomas Hutchison (6 James Smith), Kenneth Mathieson Dalglish, Joseph Jordan.
Manager: William Esplin Ormond.

WALES: Gareth Sprake, Roderick John Thomas, Malcolm Edward Page, John Francis Mahoney, John Griffith Roberts, David Frazer Roberts, Gilbert Ivor Reece (46 David Paul Smallman), Anthony Keith Villars, Terence Charles Yorath, Leslie Cartwright, Leighton James.
Manager: David Lloyd Bowen.

Goals: Kenneth Dalglish (24), William Jardine (44 pen)

374. 18.05.1974   Home Championship
SCOTLAND v ENGLAND 2-0 (2-0)
Hampden Park, Glasgow
Referee: Leonardus van der Kroft (Holland)   Att: 94,487
SCOTLAND: David Harvey, William Pullar Jardine, Daniel Fergus McGrain, John Henderson Blackley, James Allan Holton, James Connolly Johnstone, William John Bremner (Cap), David Hay, Peter Patrick Lorimer, Kenneth Mathieson Dalglish, Joseph Jordan.   Manager: William Esplin Ormond.
ENGLAND: Peter Leslie Shilton, David John Nish, Michael Pejic, Emlyn Walter Hughes (Cap), Norman Hunter (46 David Victor Watson), Colin Todd, Michael Roger Channon, Colin Bell, Frank Stewart Worthington (70 Malcolm Ian Macdonald), Keith Weller, Martin Stanford Peters.   Manager: Joseph Mercer.
Goals: Joseph Jordan (5), Colin Todd (31 own goal)

375. 01.06.1974
BELGIUM v SCOTLAND 2-1 (1-1)
Klokke, Brügge
Referee: Klaus Ohmsen (West Germany)   Att: 7,769
BELGIUM: Christian Piot, Gilbert Van Binst, Nicolas Dewalque (40 Jean Thissen), Erwin Vandendaele, Maurice Martens, Wilfried Van Moer, Jan Verheyen, Paul Van Himst, Ivo Van Herp, Raoul Lambert, Roger Henrotay (68 Julien Cools).   Trainer: Raymond Goethals.
SCOTLAND: David Harvey, William Pullar Jardine, Daniel Fergus McGrain, John Henderson Blackley, Gordon McQueen, James Connolly Johnstone (69 William Morgan), William John Bremner (Cap), David Hay, Peter Patrick Lorimer, Kenneth Mathieson Dalglish (80 Thomas Hutchison), Joseph Jordan.   Manager: William Esplin Ormond.
Goals: Roger Henrotay (22), Raoul Lambert (78 pen) / James Connolly Johnstone (41)

376. 06.06.1974
NORWAY v SCOTLAND 1-2 (1-0)
Ullevaal, Oslo
Referee: Arne Axelsson (Sweden)   Attendance: 18,432
NORWAY: Geir Karlsen, Øystein Wormdal, Jan Birkelund, Tore Kordahl, Svein Grøndalen, Harald Berg (70 Stein Thunberg), Tor Egil Johansen, Svein Kvia, Helge Skuseth, Tom Lund, Harry Hestad.   Trainer: George Frederick Curtis (England).
SCOTLAND: Thomas Sandlands Allan, William Pullar Jardine, Daniel Fergus McGrain, Martin McLean Buchan, James Allan Holton, James Connolly Johnstone (70 Kenneth Mathieson Dalglish), William John Bremner (Cap), David Hay, Peter Patrick Lorimer, Thomas Hutchison, Joseph Jordan.   Manager: William Esplin Ormond.
Goals: Tom Lund (19) /
Joseph Jordan (74), Kenneth Mathieson Dalglish (86)

377. 14.06.1974   10th World Cup, 1st Round
ZAIRE v SCOTLAND 0-2 (0-2)
Westfalen, Dortmund
Referee: Gerhard Schulenburg (West Germany)   Att: 25,800
ZAIRE: Mwamba Kazadi, Ilunga Mwepu, Mwanza Mukombo, Tshimen Buhanga, Boba Lobilo, Massamba Kilasu, Mulamba N'Daye, Mantantu Kidumu (Cap) (76 Mafu Kibonge), Mabwene Mana, Maku Mayanga (65 Uba Kembo Kembo), Etepe Kakoko.   Trainer: Blagoje Vidinić (Yugoslavia).
SCOTLAND: David Harvey, William Pullar Jardine, Daniel Fergus McGrain, John Henderson Blackley, James Allan Holton, Peter Patrick Lorimer, William John Bremner (Cap), David Hay, Kenneth Mathieson Dalglish (75 Thomas Hutchison), Joseph Jordan, Denis Law.   Manager: William Esplin Ormond.
Goals: Peter Patrick Lorimer (26), Joseph Jordan (33)

378. 18.06.1974   10th World Cup, 1st Round
BRAZIL v SCOTLAND 0-0
Waldstadion, Frankfurt/Main
Referee: Arie van Gemert (Holland)   Attendance: 62,000
BRAZIL: Émerson Leão, Manoel Resende de Matos Cabral "Nelinho", Luís Edmundo Pereira, Mário Perez Ulibarri "Marinho Perez", Francisco das Chagas Marinho, Wilson da Silva Piazza (Cap), Roberto Rivelino, Jair Ventura Filho "Jairzinho", João Leiva Campos Filho "Leivinha" (66 Paulo César Carpegiani), Mirandinha I, Paulo César Lima.   Trainer: Mário Jorge Lobo Zagallo.
SCOTLAND: David Harvey, William Pullar Jardine, Daniel Fergus McGrain, Martin McLean Buchan, James Allan Holton, Peter Patrick Lorimer, William John Bremner (Cap), David Hay, William Morgan, Kenneth Mathieson Dalglish, Joseph Jordan.   Manager: William Esplin Ormond.

379. 22.06.1974   10th World Cup, 1st Round
YUGOSLAVIA v SCOTLAND 1-1 (0-0)
Wald, Frankfurt/Main
Referee: Alfonso Archundia González (Mexico)   Att: 54,000
YUGOSLAVIA: Enver Marić, Ivan Buljan, Enver Hadžiabdić, Branko Oblak, Josip Katalinski, Vladislav Bogićević, Ilija Petković, Ivan Šurjak, Dušan Bajević (72 Stanislav Karasi), Jovan Aćimović, Dragan Džajić (Cap).
Selection committee: Miljan Miljanić, Milan Ribar, Sulejman Rebac, Tomislav Ivić & Milovan Ćirić.
SCOTLAND: David Harvey, William Pullar Jardine, Daniel Fergus McGrain, Martin McLean Buchan, James Allan Holton, Peter Patrick Lorimer, William John Bremner (Cap), David Hay, William Morgan, Kenneth Mathieson Dalglish (65 Thomas Hutchison), Joseph Jordan.   Manager: William Esplin Ormond.
Goal: Stanislav Karasi (83) / Joseph Jordan (89)

380. 30.10.1974
SCOTLAND v EAST GERMANY 3-0 (2-0)
Hampden Park, Glasgow

Referee: John Keith Taylor (England)   Attendance: 39,445

SCOTLAND: David Harvey, William Pullar Jardine (Cap), Alexander Forsyth, Martin McLean Buchan, James Allan Holton (12 Kenneth Burns), James Connolly Johnstone, Graeme James Souness, Thomas Hutchison, John Kelty Deans, Kenneth Mathieson Dalglish (86 Derek Joseph Johnstone), Joseph Jordan.   Manager: William Esplin Ormond.

EAST GERMANY: Jürgen Croy, Bernd Bransch (Cap) (38 Manfred Zapf), Gerd Kische, Konrad Weise, Siegmar Wätzlich, Lothar Kurbjuweit (56 Harald Irmscher), Reinhard Häfner, Reinhard Lauck (73 Joachim Streich), Hans-Jürgen Kreische, Jürgen Sparwasser, Martin Hoffmann.
Trainer: Georg Buschner.

Goals: Thomas Hutchison (34 pen), Kenneth Burns (36), Kenneth Mathieson Dalglish (75)

381. 20.11.1974   5th European Champs. Qualifiers
SCOTLAND v SPAIN 1-2 (1-1)
Hampden Park, Glasgow

Referee: Erich Linemayr (Austria)   Attendance: 94,331

SCOTLAND: David Harvey, William Pullar Jardine, Alexander Forsyth, Kenneth Burns, Gordon McQueen, James Connolly Johnstone, William John Bremner (Cap), Graeme James Souness, Thomas Hutchison (65 Kenneth Mathieson Dalglish), John Kelty Deans (65 Peter Patrick Lorimer), Joseph Jordan.   Manager: William Esplin Ormond.

SPAIN: José Ángel Iribar Cortajarena, Francisco Ángel Castellanos Céspedes, Gregorio de Benito Rubio, José Luis Capón González, Miguel Bernardo Bianquetti "Migueli" (67 Juan Carlos Cruz Sol Oria), Enrique Alvarez Costas, Roberto Juan Martínez Martínez, Ángel María Villar Llona, Enrique Castro González "Quini", Francisco Javier Planas Abad, Carlos Rexach Cerdá (Cap).   Trainer: Ladislao Kubala.

Goals: William John Bremner (11) / Enrique Castro González "Quini" (36, 60)

382. 05.02.1975   5th European Champs. Qualifiers
SPAIN v SCOTLAND 1-1 (0-1)
"Luis Casanova", Valencia

Referee: Alfred Delcourt (Belgium)   Attendance: 40,952

SPAIN: José Ángel Iribar Cortajarena, Juan Carlos Cruz Sol Oria, Gregorio de Benito Rubio, José Antonio Camacho Alfaro, Enrique Alvarez Costas (67 Miguel Bernardo Bianquetti "Migueli"), José Claramunt Torres (Cap), Enrique Castro González "Quini", Ángel María Villar Llona, José Eulogio Gárate Ormaechea (62 Alfredo Megido Sánchez), Juan Manuel Asensi Ripoll, Carlos Rexach Cerdá.
Trainer: Ladislao Kubala.

SCOTLAND: David Harvey, William Pullar Jardine, Daniel Fergus McGrain, Martin McLean Buchan, Gordon McQueen, Charles Cooke, Kenneth Burns (79 Paul Wilson), William John Bremner (Cap), Thomas Hutchison, Kenneth Mathieson Dalglish, Joseph Jordan (66 Derek James Parlane).   Manager: William Esplin Ormond.

Goals: Alfredo Megido Sánchez (66 pen) / Joseph Jordan (2)

383. 16.04.1975
SWEDEN v SCOTLAND 1-1 (1-0)
Ullevi, Göteborg

Referee: Svein Inge Thime (Norway)   Attendance: 15,574

SWEDEN: Göran Hagberg, Björn Andersson, Kent Karlsson, Björn Nordqvist (46 Roy Andersson), Jörgen Augustsson, Eine Fredriksson, Conny Torstensson, Thomas Ahlström (65 Thomas Nordahl), Ralf Edström (46 Anders Linderoth), Jan Mattsson, Thomas Sjöberg.   Trainer: Georg Ericsson.

SCOTLAND: Stewart J. Kennedy, William Pullar Jardine (Cap), Daniel Fergus McGrain, Francis Michael Munro, Colin MacDonald Jackson, Robert Sharp Robinson, Graeme James Souness (54 William Hughes), Kenneth Mathieson Dalglish, Luigi Macari (54 Derek Joseph Johnstone), Derek James Parlane, Edward John MacDougall.
Manager: William Esplin Ormond.

Goals: Thomas Sjöberg (44) / Edward John MacDougall (86)

384. 13.05.1975
SCOTLAND v PORTUGAL 1-0 (1-0)
Hampden Park, Glasgow

Referee: Robert Matthewson (England)   Att: 34,307

SCOTLAND: Stewart J. Kennedy, William Pullar Jardine (Cap), Daniel Fergus McGrain, Martin McLean Buchan (27 Colin MacDonald Jackson), Gordon McQueen, Charles Cooke (77 Luigi Macari), Bruce David Rioch (77 Arthur Duncan), Kenneth Mathieson Dalglish, Thomas Hutchison, Derek James Parlane, Edward John MacDougall.
Manager: William Esplin Ormond.

PORTUGAL: Vítor Manuel Alfonso Damas de Oliveira, Artur Manuel Soares Correia, Humberto Manuel de Jesus Coelho (Cap), Carlos Alexandre Fortes Alhinho, António Monteiro Teixeira Barros, Octávio Joaquim Coelho Machado, João António Ferreira Resende Alves (46 Vítor Manuel Pereira), Samuel Ferreira Fraguito (66 Minervino José Lopes Pietra), António José da Conceiçao Oliveira "Toni", Tamagnini Manuel Gomes Baptista "Nené" (46 Fernando Mendes Soares Gomes), Mário Jorge Moinhos de Matos (46 Romeu Fernando Fernandes da Silva).   Trainer: José Maria Pedroto.

Goal: Artur Manuel Soares Correia (43 own goal)

385. 17.05.1975   Home Championship
WALES v SCOTLAND 2-2 (2-0)
Ninian Park, Cardiff
Referee: Malcolm H. Wright (Northern Ireland)   Att: 23,509
WALES: William David Davies, Roderick John Thomas, Malcolm Edward Page, Terence Charles Yorath, John Griffith Roberts, Leighton Phillips, John Francis Mahoney, Brian Flynn, Gilbert Ivor Reece, John Benjamin Toshack, Leighton James.   Manager: Michael Smith.

SCOTLAND: Stewart J. Kennedy, William Pullar Jardine (Cap), Daniel Fergus McGrain, Colin MacDonald Jackson (77 Francis Michael Munro), Gordon McQueen, Bruce David Rioch, Luigi Macari, Arthur Duncan, Kenneth Mathieson Dalglish, Derek James Parlane, Edward John MacDougall.   Manager: William Esplin Ormond.

Goals: John Benjamin Toshack (28), Brian Flynn (35) / Colin MacDonald Jackson (54), Bruce David Rioch (62)

386. 20.05.1975   Home Championship
SCOTLAND v NORTHERN IRELAND 3-0 (2-0)
Hampden Park, Glasgow
Referee: Patrick Partridge (England)   Attendance: 64,696
SCOTLAND: Stewart J. Kennedy, William Pullar Jardine (Cap) (89 Alexander Forsyth), Daniel Fergus McGrain, Francis Michael Munro, Gordon McQueen, Robert Sharp Robinson (76 Alfred James Conn), Bruce David Rioch, Kenneth Mathieson Dalglish, Arthur Duncan, Derek James Parlane, Edward John MacDougall.
Manager: William Esplin Ormond.

NORTHERN IRELAND: Patrick Anthony Jennings, Patrick James Rice, William James O'Kane, Christopher James Nicholl, Alan Hunter (83 Ronald Victor Blair), David Clements, Thomas Finney, Martin Hugh Michael O'Neill (87 Trevor Anderson), Derek William Spence, Samuel Baxter McIlroy, Thomas A. Jackson.   Manager: David Clements.

Goals: Edward John MacDougall (15), Kenneth Dalglish (21), Derek James Parlane (80)

387. 24.05.1975   Home Championship
ENGLAND v SCOTLAND 5-1 (3-1)
Wembley, London
Referee: Rudolf Glöckner (East Germany)   Att: 98,241
ENGLAND: Raymond Neal Clemence, Steven Whitworth, Kevin Thomas Beattie, Colin Bell, David Victor Watson, Colin Todd, Alan James Ball (Cap), Michael Roger Channon, David Edward Johnson, Gerald Charles James Francis, Kevin Joseph Keegan (85 David Thomas).   Manager: Donald Revie.

SCOTLAND: Stewart J. Kennedy, William Pullar Jardine (Cap), Daniel Fergus McGrain, Francis Michael Munro, Gordon McQueen, Alfred James Conn, Bruce David Rioch, Kenneth Mathieson Dalglish, Arthur Duncan (61 Thomas Hutchison), Derek James Parlane, Edward John MacDougall (71 Luigi Macari).   Manager: William Esplin Ormond.

Goals: Gerald Francis (6, 65), Kevin Beattie (8), Colin Bell (40), David Johnson (75) / Bruce Rioch (41 pen)

388. 01.06.1975   5th European Champs Qualifiers
ROMANIA v SCOTLAND 1-1 (1-0)
"23 August", Bucureşti
Referee: Ertugrul Dilek (Turkey)   Attendance: 52,203
ROMANIA: Răducanu Necula, Florin Cheran, Gabriel Sandu, Alexandru Sătmăreanu II, Teodor Anghelini, Ion Dumitru, Cornel Dinu (Cap), Dudu Georgescu (37 Ilie Balaci), Zoltan Crişan, Nicolae Dobrin (80 Attila Kun II), Mircea Lucescu.   Trainer: Valentin Stănescu.

SCOTLAND: James Grady Brown, Daniel Fergus McGrain, Alexander Forsyth, Francis Michael Munro, Gordon McQueen (Cap), William Fergus Miller, Bruce David Rioch (67 Thomas Hutchison), Kenneth Mathieson Dalglish, Arthur Duncan, Luigi Macari (67 Robert Sharp Robinson), Derek James Parlane.   Manager: William Esplin Ormond.

Goals: Dudu Georgescu (21) / Gordon McQueen (89)

389. 03.09.1975   5th European Champs. Qualifiers
DENMARK v SCOTLAND 0-1 (0-0)
Idrætsparken, København
Referee: Robert Schaut (Belgium)   Attendance: 40,300
DENMARK: Birger Jensen, Flemming Mortensen, Henning Munk Jensen, Lars Larsen, Niels Tune Hansen, Ove Flindt Bjerg, Ole Bjørnmose, Benny Nielsen, Allan Rodenkam Simonsen, Henning Jensen, Ulrik Le Fevre (Cap).   Trainer: Rudolf Strittich (Austria).

SCOTLAND: David Harvey, Daniel Fergus McGrain, Alexander Forsyth, Martin McLean Buchan, Gordon McQueen, Peter Patrick Lorimer, William John Bremner (Cap), Bruce David Rioch, Thomas Hutchison (71 Arthur Duncan), Kenneth Mathieson Dalglish, Joseph Montgomery Harper.   Manager: William Esplin Ormond.

Goal: Joseph Montgomery Harper (51)

390. 29.10.1975   5th European Champs. Qualifiers
SCOTLAND v DENMARK 3-1 (0-1)
Hampden Park, Glasgow

Referee: Rolf Nyhus (Norway)   Attendance: 48,021

SCOTLAND: David Harvey, Daniel Fergus McGrain, Stewart Mackie Houston, John Greig (Cap), Colin MacDonald Jackson, Peter Patrick Lorimer, Richard Asa Hartford, Bruce David Rioch, Archibald Gemmill, Kenneth Mathieson Dalglish, Edward John MacDougall (85 Derek James Parlane). Manager: William Esplin Ormond.

DENMARK: Benno Larsen, John Andersen, Henning Munk Jensen (Cap), Lars Larsen, Johnny Hansen, Heino Hansen, Niels Tune Hansen (68 Frank Nielsen), Niels Sørensen, Kristen Nygaard, Lars Bastrup, Jens Kolding. Trainer: Rudolf Strittich (Austria).

Goals: Kenneth Dalglish (48), Bruce David Rioch (54), Edward John MacDougall (61) / Lars Bastrup (20)

391. 17.12.1975   5th European Champs. Qualifiers
SCOTLAND v ROMANIA 1-1 (1-0)
Hampden Park, Glasgow

Referee: Adolf Prokop (East Germany)   Attendance: 11,375

SCOTLAND: James Fergus Cruickshank, John Jack Brownlie, William Donachie, Martin McLean Buchan (Cap), Colin MacDonald Jackson, John Doyle (73 Peter Patrick Lorimer), Richard Asa Hartford, Bruce David Rioch, Archibald Gemmill, Kenneth Mathieson Dalglish (73 Edward John MacDougall), Andrew Mullen Gray.   Manager: William Esplin Ormond.

ROMANIA: Răducanu Necula, Florin Cheran, Gabriel Sandu, Alexandru Sătmăreanu II, Teodor Anghelini, Mihai Romilă II (58 Iuliu Hajnal), Cornel Dinu (Cap), Ladislau Bölöni, Mircea Lucescu (60 Zoltan Crişan), Dudu Georgescu, Anghel Iordănescu.   Trainer: Cornel Drăguşin.

Goals: Bruce David Rioch (39) / Zoltan Crişan (73)

392. 07.04.1976
SCOTLAND v SWITZERLAND 1-0 (1-0)
Hampden Park, Glasgow

Referee: Patrick Partridge (England)   Attendance: 15,531

SCOTLAND: Alan Roderick Rough, Daniel Fergus McGrain, Francis Tierney Gray, Thomas Forsyth (Cap), John Henderson Blackley, Thomas Brooks Craig, Alexander MacDonald, Kenneth Mathieson Dalglish (64 Desmond George Bremner), William H. Pettigrew (46 Robert Munro McKean), Andrew Mullen Gray, Derek Joseph Johnstone. Manager: William Esplin Ormond.

SWITZERLAND: Erich Burgener, Gilbert Guyot, Jörg Stohler, Lucio Bizzini, Pius Fischbach, René Hasler (53 Claude Andrey), René Botteron, Rudolf Elsener (64 Marc Schnyder), Kurt Müller, Peter Risi, Daniel Jeandupeux. Trainer: René Hüssy.

Goal: William H. Pettigrew (2)

393. 06.05.1976   Home Championship
SCOTLAND v WALES 3-1 (2-0)
Hampden Park, Glasgow

Referee: Malcolm H. Wright (Northern Ireland)   Att: 35,000

SCOTLAND: Alan Roderick Rough, Daniel Fergus McGrain, William Donachie, Thomas Forsyth, Colin MacDonald Jackson, Archibald Gemmill (Cap), Donald Sanderson Masson, Bruce David Rioch, Edwin Gray, William H. Pettigrew, Joseph Jordan.   Manager: William Esplin Ormond.

WALES: Brian William Lloyd, David Edward Jones, Joseph Patrick Jones, David Frazer Roberts, John Griffith Roberts, Terence Charles Yorath, Arfon Trevor Griffiths, Carl Stephen Harris (46 Leslie Cartwright), Alan Thomas Curtis, Peter Anthony O'Sullivan, Leighton James. Manager: Michael Smith.

Goals: William H. Pettigrew (38), Bruce David Rioch (44), Edwin Gray (69) / Arfon Trevor Griffiths (61 pen)

394. 08.05.1976   Home Championship
SCOTLAND v NORTHERN IRELAND 3-0 (1-0)
Hampden Park, Glasgow

Referee: Thomas Reynolds (Wales)   Attendance: 49,897

SCOTLAND: Alan Roderick Rough, Daniel Fergus McGrain, William Donachie, Thomas Forsyth, Colin MacDonald Jackson, Archibald Gemmill (Cap), Donald Sanderson Masson, Bruce David Rioch (56 Richard Asa Hartford), Kenneth Mathieson Dalglish, William H. Pettigrew (66 Derek Joseph Johnstone), Joseph Jordan. Manager: William Esplin Ormond.

NORTHERN IRELAND: Patrick Anthony Jennings, Peter William Scott, Christopher James Nicholl, Alan Hunter, Patrick James Rice, Bryan Hamilton, Thomas Cassidy, Patrick Gerald Sharp Sharkey (61 David McCreery), Samuel Baxter McIlroy, Samuel John Morgan (85 Derek William Spence), Thomas Finney.   Manager: David Clements.

Goals: Archibald Gemmill (23), Donald Masson (47), Kenneth Mathieson Dalglish (52)

395. 15.05.1976   Home Championship
SCOTLAND v ENGLAND 2-1 (1-1)
Hampden Park, Glasgow
Referee: Károly Palotai (Hungary)   Attendance: 85,165
SCOTLAND: Alan Roderick Rough, Daniel Fergus McGrain, William Donachie, Thomas Forsyth, Colin MacDonald Jackson, Archibald Gemmill (Cap), Donald Sanderson Masson, Bruce David Rioch, Edwin Gray (79 Derek Joseph Johnstone), Kenneth Mathieson Dalglish, Joseph Jordan. Manager: William Esplin Ormond.
ENGLAND: Raymond Neal Clemence, Colin Todd, Michael Dennis Mills, Philip Brian Thompson, Roy Leslie McFarland (70 Michael Doyle), Raymond Kennedy, Kevin Joseph Keegan, Gerald Charles James Francis (Cap), Stuart James Pearson (46 Trevor John Cherry), Michael Roger Channon, Peter John Taylor.   Manager: Donald Revie.
Goals: Donald Masson (18), Kenneth Dalglish (49) / Michael Roger Channon (11)

396. 08.09.1976
SCOTLAND v FINLAND 6-0 (4-0)
Hampden Park, Glasgow
Referee: Gordon Kew (England)   Attendance: 16,338
SCOTLAND: Alan Roderick Rough (46 David Harvey), Daniel Fergus McGrain, William Donachie, Thomas Forsyth, Martin McLean Buchan, Archibald Gemmill (Cap), Donald Sanderson Masson, Bruce David Rioch, Edwin Gray, Kenneth Mathieson Dalglish, Andrew Mullen Gray. Manager: William Esplin Ormond.
FINLAND: Pertti Alaja (46 Göran Enckelman), Teppo Heikkinen (75 Matti Ahonen), Erkki Vihtilä, Ari Mäkynen, Esko Ranta, Pertti Jantunen, Jouko Suomalainen, Miikka Toivola, Olavi Rissanen, Juha Dahllund, Matti Paatelainen (Cap) (37 Jyrki Nieminen).   Trainer: Aulis Rytkönen.
Goals: Bruce David Rioch (7), Donald Masson (16 pen), Kenneth Dalglish (23), Andrew Gray (44, 80), Edwin Gray (68)

397. 13.10.1976   11th World Cup Qualifiers
CZECHOSLOVAKIA v SCOTLAND 2-0 (0-0)
Sparta, Praha
Referee: Alberto Michelotti (Italy)   Attendance: 38,000
CZECHOSLOVAKIA: Alexander Vencel, Pavel Biroš, Anton Ondruš (Cap), Jozef Čapkovič (68 Ladislav Jurkemik), Koloman Gögh (13 Ján Kozák), Jaroslav Pollák, Karel Dobiaš, Antonín Panenka, Marián Masný, Zdeněk Nehoda, Ladislav Petráš.   Trainer: Václav Ježek.

SCOTLAND: Alan Roderick Rough, Daniel Fergus McGrain, William Donachie, Martin McLean Buchan, Gordon McQueen, Archibald Gemmill (Cap), Donald Sanderson Masson (68 Richard Asa Hartford), Bruce David Rioch, Kenneth Mathieson Dalglish (56 Kenneth Burns), Joseph Jordan, Andrew Mullen Gray. Manager: William Esplin Ormond.
Sent off: Anton Ondruš (76)
Goals: Antonín Panenka (48), Ladislav Petráš (50)

398. 17.11.1976   11th World Cup Qualifiers
SCOTLAND v WALES 1-0 (1-0)
Hampden Park, Glasgow
Referee: Ferdinand Biwersi (West Germany)   Att: 63,233
SCOTLAND: Alan Roderick Rough, Daniel Fergus McGrain, William Donachie, John Henderson Blackley, Gordon McQueen, Archibald Gemmill (Cap), Kenneth Burns, Bruce David Rioch (67 Richard Asa Hartford), Edwin Gray (84 William H. Pettigrew), Kenneth Mathieson Dalglish, Joseph Jordan.   Manager: William Esplin Ormond.
WALES: William David Davies, Malcolm Edward Page, Joseph Patrick Jones, Leighton Phillips, Ian Peter Evans, Arfon Trevor Griffiths, Michael Reginald Thomas, Brian Flynn, Terence Charles Yorath, John Benjamin Toshack, Leighton James (76 Alan Thomas Curtis).   Manager: Michael Smith.
Goal: Ian Evans (15 own goal)

399. 27.04.1977
SCOTLAND v SWEDEN 3-1 (1-0)
Hampden Park, Glasgow
Referee: John Keith Taylor (England)   Attendance: 22,659
SCOTLAND: Alan Roderick Rough, Daniel Fergus McGrain, William Donachie, Thomas Forsyth, John Henderson Blackley (76 David Narey), Ronald Michael Glavin (58 William Pullar Jardine), Kenneth Burns (76 Joseph Craig), Richard Asa Hartford, William McClure Johnston, Kenneth Mathieson Dalglish (Cap), William H. Pettigrew.
Manager: William Esplin Ormond.
SWEDEN: Ronnie Carl Hellström, Magnus Andersson, Roy Andersson, Björn Nordqvist, Björn Andersson, Bo Börjesson (65 Anders Ljungberg), Conny Torstensson (55 Hans Borg), Lennart Larsson, Thomas Sjöberg, Benny Wendt, Sigvard Johansson (71 Olle Nordin).   Trainer: Georg Ericsson.
Goals: Ronnie Hellström (30 own goal), Kenneth Mathieson Dalglish (56), Joseph Craig (79) / Benny Wendt (50)

400. 28.05.1977   Home Championship
WALES v SCOTLAND 0-0
The Racecourse, Wrexham

Referee: Malcolm Moffatt (Northern Ireland)   Att: 14,469

WALES: William David Davies, Roderick John Thomas, Joseph Patrick Jones, Leighton Phillips, Ian Peter Evans, John Francis Mahoney, Peter Anthony Sayer, Brian Flynn, Terence Charles Yorath, Nicholas Simon Deacy, Leighton James (67 Michael Reginald Thomas).   Manager: Michael Smith.

SCOTLAND: Alan Roderick Rough, Daniel Fergus McGrain, William Donachie, Thomas Forsyth, Gordon McQueen, Archibald Gemmill, Donald Sanderson Masson, Bruce David Rioch (Cap) (65 William McClure Johnston), Richard Asa Hartford, Kenneth Mathieson Dalglish, Derek James Parlane (74 Kenneth Burns).   Manager: Alistair MacLeod.

401. 01.06.1977   Home Championship
SCOTLAND v NORTHERN IRELAND 3-0 (1-0)
Hampden Park, Glasgow

Referee: William John Gow (Wales)   Attendance: 44,699

SCOTLAND: Alan Roderick Rough, Daniel Fergus McGrain, William Donachie, Thomas Forsyth, Gordon McQueen, Donald Sanderson Masson, Bruce David Rioch (Cap), Richard Asa Hartford, William McClure Johnston (86 Archibald Gemmill), Kenneth Mathieson Dalglish, Joseph Jordan (69 Luigi Macari).   Manager: Alistair MacLeod.

NORTHERN IRELAND: Patrick Anthony Jennings, James Michael Nicholl, Patrick James Rice, Thomas A. Jackson, Alan Hunter, Bryan Hamilton, Roland Christopher McGrath, Samuel Baxter McIlroy, Martin Hugh Michael O'Neill (56 Derek William Spence), David McCreery, Trevor Anderson. Manager: Robert Dennis Blanchflower.

Goals: Kenneth Dalglish (34, 79), Gordon McQueen (61)

402. 04.06.1977   Home Championship
ENGLAND v SCOTLAND 1-2 (0-1)
Wembley, London

Referee: Károly Palotai (Hungary)   Attendance: 98,103

ENGLAND: Raymond Neal Clemence, Philip George Neal, Michael Dennis Mills, Brian Greenhoff (57 Trevor John Cherry), David Victor Watson, Emlyn Walter Hughes (Cap), Trevor John Francis, Michael Roger Channon, Stuart James Pearson, Brian Ernest Talbot, Raymond Kennedy (67 Dennis Tueart).   Manager: Donald Revie.

SCOTLAND: Alan Roderick Rough, Daniel Fergus McGrain, William Donachie, Thomas Forsyth, Gordon McQueen, Donald Sanderson Masson (83 Archibald Gemmill), Bruce David Rioch (Cap), Richard Asa Hartford, William McClure Johnston, Kenneth Mathieson Dalglish, Joseph Jordan (43 Luigi Macari).   Manager: Alistair MacLeod.

Goals: Michael Roger Channon (87 pen) / Gordon McQueen (43), Kenneth Mathieson Dalglish (61)

403. 15.06.1977
CHILE v SCOTLAND 2-4 (0-3)
Nacional, Santiago

Referee: Juan Amrosio Silvagno Cavanna (Chile)
Attendance: 60,000

CHILE: Adolfo Nef Sanhueza, Juan Salvador Machuca Valdéz, Alberto Fernando Ralph Quintano, Elías Ricardo Figueroa Brander, Enzo Sergio Escobar Olivares, Waldo Quiróz, Eddio Inostroza, Héctor Pinto, Juan Soto Quintana (37 Julio Crisosto), Rogelio Farías Salvador (79 Gustavo Segundo Moscoso Huencho), Leonardo Véliz Díaz.
Trainer: Luis Santibáñez.

SCOTLAND: Alan Roderick Rough (46 James Garvin Stewart), Daniel Fergus McGrain, William Donachie, Martin McLean Buchan, Thomas Forsyth, Donald Sanderson Masson, Bruce David Rioch (Cap) (46 Archibald Gemmill), Richard Asa Hartford (80 William Pullar Jardine), William McClure Johnston, Kenneth Mathieson Dalglish, Luigi Macari.
Manager: Alistair MacLeod.

Goals: Julio Crisosto (48, 72) / Kenneth Dalglish (19), Luigi Macari (30, 57), Richard Asa Hartford (37)

404. 18.06.1977
ARGENTINA v SCOTLAND 1-1 (0-0)
Alberto Armando "La Bombonera", Buenos Aires

Referee: Romualdo Arppi Filho (Brazil)   Att: 57,000

ARGENTINA: Héctor Rodolfo Baley, Vicente Alberto Pernía, Daniel Pedro Killer, Daniel Alberto Passarella, Jorge Omar Carrascosa (Cap), Osvaldo César Ardiles, Américo Rubén Gallego, Omar Rubén Larrosa (70 Oscar Víctor Trossero), Pedro Alexis González (59 Alberto César Tarantini), Leopoldo Jacinto Luque, René Orlando Houseman.
Trainer: César Luis Menotti.

SCOTLAND: Alan Roderick Rough, Daniel Fergus McGrain, William Donachie, Martin McLean Buchan (Cap), Thomas Forsyth, Donald Sanderson Masson, Archibald Gemmill, Richard Asa Hartford, William McClure Johnston, Kenneth Mathieson Dalglish, Luigi Macari.
Manager: Alistair MacLeod.

Sent off: Vicente Alberto Pernía (56)

Goals: Daniel Alberto Passarella (80 pen) / Donald Sanderson Masson (77 pen)

405. 23.06.1977
BRAZIL v SCOTLAND 2-0 (0-0)

Maracanã, Rio de Janeiro

Referee: Oscar Scolfaro (Brazil)   Attendance: 60,763

BRAZIL: Émerson Leão, José Maria Rodrigues Alves "Zé Maria I", Luís Edmundo Pereira, Édino Nazareth Filho "Edinho", Francisco das Chagas Marinho, Antônio Carlos Cerezo "Toninho Cerezo", Paulo Isidoro de Jesus, Roberto Rivelino, Gilberto Alves "Gil" (46 Arthur Antunes Coimbra "Zico"), José Reinaldo da Lima "Reinaldo I", Paulo César Lima.   Trainer: Cláudio de Morais "Coutinho".

SCOTLAND: Alan Roderick Rough, Daniel Fergus McGrain, William Donachie, Martin McLean Buchan, Thomas Forsyth, Donald Sanderson Masson, Bruce David Rioch (Cap), Archibald Gemmill, Richard Asa Hartford, William McClure Johnston (61 William Pullar Jardine), Kenneth Mathieson Dalglish.   Manager: Alistair MacLeod.

Goals: Arthur Antunes Coimbra "Zico" (70), Antônio Carlos Cerezo "Toninho Cerezo" (75)

406. 07.09.1977
EAST GERMANY v SCOTLAND 1-0 (0-0)

Weltjugend, Ost-Berlin

Referee: Martin Horbas (Czechoslovakia)   Att: 50,000

EAST GERMANY: Jürgen Croy, Hans-Jürgen Dörner (Cap), Gerd Kische, Konrad Weise, Gerd Weber, Reinhard Häfner, Hartmut Schade, Lutz Lindemann, Gert Heidler, Jürgen Sparwasser (46 Peter Kotte), Joachim Streich (46 Martin Hoffmann).   Trainer: Georg Buschner.

SCOTLAND: David Steel Stewart, Daniel Fergus McGrain, William Donachie, Martin McLean Buchan, Gordon McQueen, Donald Sanderson Masson (Cap), Richard Asa Hartford (65 Archibald Gemmill), Luigi Macari, William McClure Johnston (59 Arthur Graham), Kenneth Mathieson Dalglish, Joseph Jordan.   Manager: Alistair MacLeod.

407. 21.09.1977   11th World Cup Qualifiers
SCOTLAND v CZECHOSLOVAKIA 3-1 (2-0)

Hampden Park, Glasgow

Referee: Francis Jean Joseph Elisa Rion (Belgium)   Attendance: 85,000

SCOTLAND: Alan Roderick Rough, William Pullar Jardine, Daniel Fergus McGrain, Thomas Forsyth, Gordon McQueen, Donald Sanderson Masson, Bruce David Rioch (Cap), Richard Asa Hartford, William McClure Johnston, Kenneth Mathieson Dalglish, Joseph Jordan.   Manager: Alistair MacLeod.

CZECHOSLOVAKIA: Pavol Michalík, Miroslav Paurik, Jozef Čapkovič, Karel Dvořák, Koloman Gögh, Karel Dobiaš (69 Peter Gallis), Jaroslav Pollák (Cap), Jozef Móder (46 Ľubomír Knapp), Miroslav Gajdůšek, Marián Masný, Zdeněk Nehoda.   Trainer: Václav Ježek.

Goals: Joseph Jordan (19), Richard Asa Hartford (35), Kenneth Mathieson Dalglish (54) / Miroslav Gajdůšek (82)

408. 12.10.1977   11th World Cup Qualifiers
WALES v SCOTLAND 0-2 (0-0)

Anfield, Liverpool

Referee: Robert Charles Paul Wurtz (France)   Att: 50,850

WALES: William David Davies, Roderick John Thomas, Joseph Patrick Jones, David Edward Jones, Leighton Phillips, John Francis Mahoney, Peter Anthony Sayer (75 Nicholas Simon Deacy), Brian Flynn, Terence Charles Yorath, John Benjamin Toshack, Michael Reginald Thomas.   Manager: Michael Smith.

SCOTLAND: Alan Roderick Rough, William Pullar Jardine (57 Martin McLean Buchan), William Donachie, Thomas Forsyth, Gordon McQueen, Donald Sanderson Masson (Cap), Richard Asa Hartford, Luigi Macari, William McClure Johnston, Kenneth Mathieson Dalglish, Joseph Jordan.   Manager: Alistair MacLeod.

Goals: Donald Sanderson Masson (79 pen), Kenneth Mathieson Dalglish (87)

409. 22.02.1978
SCOTLAND v BULGARIA 2-1 (1-1)

Hampden Park, Glasgow

Referee: Patrick Partridge (England)   Attendance: 56,000

SCOTLAND: James Anton Blyth, Stuart Robert Kennedy, William Donachie, William Fergus Miller, Gordon McQueen, Archibald Gemmill (Cap), Graeme James Souness, Richard Asa Hartford, Luigi Macari, Kenneth Mathieson Dalglish (65 Ian Andrew Wallace), Joseph Jordan (65 Derek Joseph Johnstone).   Manager: Alistair MacLeod.

BULGARIA: Stefan Staikov, Plamen Nikolov, Dimitar Enchev, Georgi Bonev, Ivan Iliev, Kancho Kasherov, Aleksandar Ivanov, Georgi Slavkov (72 Ivan Tishanski), Andrei Jeliazkov (Cap), Stoicho Mladenov, Radoslav Zdravkov.   Trainer: Tsvetan Ilchev.

Goals: Archibald Gemmill (41 pen), Ian Andrew Wallace (85) / Stoicho Mladenov (9)

410. 13.05.1978   Home Championship
SCOTLAND v NORTHERN IRELAND 1-1 (1-1)

Hampden Park, Glasgow

Referee: William John Gow (Wales)   Attendance: 64,433

SCOTLAND: Alan Roderick Rough, William Pullar Jardine, Martin McLean Buchan (37 Kenneth Burns), Thomas Forsyth, Gordon McQueen, Donald Sanderson Masson, Bruce David Rioch (Cap), Archibald Gemmill, John Neilson Robertson, Joseph Jordan (46 Kenneth Mathieson Dalglish), Derek Joseph Johnstone.   Manager: Alistair MacLeod.

NORTHERN IRELAND: James Archibald Platt, Bryan Hamilton, Peter William Scott, Christopher James Nicholl, James Michael Nicholl, Samuel Baxter McIlroy, David McCreery, Martin Hugh Michael O'Neill, Trevor Anderson (63 William Robert Hamilton), Gerard Joseph Armstrong, Roland Christopher McGrath (77 George Terence Cochrane).   Manager: Robert Dennis Blanchflower.

Goals: Derek Joseph Johnstone (36) / Martin O'Neill (26)

411. 17.05.1978   Home Championship
SCOTLAND v WALES 1-1 (1-0)

Hampden Park, Glasgow

Referee: Malcolm H. Wright (Northern Ireland)   Att: 70,241

SCOTLAND: James Anton Blyth, Stuart Robert Kennedy, William Donachie, Kenneth Burns, Gordon McQueen (32 Thomas Forsyth), Archibald Gemmill (Cap), Graeme James Souness, Richard Asa Hartford, William McClure Johnston (85 John Neilson Robertson), Kenneth Mathieson Dalglish, Derek Joseph Johnstone.   Manager: Alistair MacLeod.

WALES: William David Davies, Malcolm Edward Page (76 Nicholas Simon Deacy), Joseph Patrick Jones, David Frazer Roberts, Leighton Phillips, Terence Charles Yorath, John Francis Mahoney, Brian Flynn, Carl Stephen Harris, Alan Thomas Curtis, Philip John Dwyer.   Manager: M. Smith.

Goals: Derek Johnstone (12) / W. Donachie (89 own goal)

412. 20.05.1978   Home Championship
SCOTLAND v ENGLAND 0-1 (0-0)

Hampden Park, Glasgow

Referee: Georges Konrath (France)   Attendance: 88,319

SCOTLAND: Alan Roderick Rough, Stuart Robert Kennedy, William Donachie, Thomas Forsyth, Kenneth Burns, Donald Sandison Masson (74 Archibald Gemmill), Bruce David Rioch (Cap) (74 Graeme James Souness), Richard Asa Hartford, William McClure Johnston, Kenneth Mathieson Dalglish, Joseph Jordan.   Manager: Alistair MacLeod

ENGLAND: Raymond Neal Clemence, Philip George Neal, Michael Dennis Mills, Anthony William Currie, David Victor Watson, Emlyn Walter Hughes (Cap) (73 Brian Greenhoff), Raymond Colin Wilkins, Steven James Coppell, Paul Mariner (76 Trevor David Brooking), Trevor John Francis, Peter Simon Barnes.   Manager: Ronald Greenwood

Goal: Steven James Coppell (83)

413. 03.06.1978   11th World Cup, 1st Round
PERU v SCOTLAND 3-1 (1-1)

Chateau Carreras, Cordoba

Referee: Ulf Eriksson (Sweden)   Attendance: 37,792

PERU: Ramón Quiroga Arancibia, Jaime Eduardo Duarte Huerta, Rodolfo Manzo Audante, Héctor Eduardo Chumpitaz González (Cap), Rubén Toribio Díaz Rivas, José Manuel Velásquez Castillo, César Augusto Cueto Villa (82 Percy Rojas Montero), Teófilo Juan Cubillas Arizaga, Juan José Muñante López, Guillermo La Rosa Laguna (62 Hugo Alejandro Sotil Yerén), Juan Carlos Oblitas Saba.   Trainer: Marcos Calderón.

SCOTLAND: Alan Roderick Rough, Stuart Robert Kennedy, Martin McLean Buchan, Thomas Forsyth, Kenneth Burns, Donald Sanderson Masson (70 Archibald Gemmill), Bruce David Rioch (Cap) (70 Luigi Macari), Richard Asa Hartford, William McClure Johnston, Kenneth Mathieson Dalglish, Joseph Jordan.   Manager: Alistair MacLeod.

Goals: César Augusto Cueto Villa (42), Teófilo Juan Cubillas Arizaga (71, 77) / Joseph Jordan (15)

414. 07.06.1978   11th World Cup, 1st Round
IRAN v SCOTLAND 1-1 (0-1)

Chateau Carreras, Cordoba

Referee: Youssouf N'Diaye (Senegal)   Attendance: 7,938

SCOTLAND: Alan Roderick Rough, William Pullar Jardine, William Donachie, Martin McLean Buchan (57 Thomas Forsyth), Kenneth Burns, Archibald Gemmill (Cap), Luigi Macari, Richard Asa Hartford, John Neilson Robertson, Kenneth Mathieson Dalglish (73 Joseph Montgomery Harper), Joseph Jordan.   Manager: Alistair MacLeod.

IRAN: Nasser Hejazi, Hassan Nazari, Nasrollah Abdollahi, Hossein Kazerani, Andranik Eskandarian, Mohammed Sadeghi, Ali Parvin (Cap), Ebrahim Ghassempour, Iraj Danaifar (80 Hassan Nayeb-Agha), Ghafoor D'jahani, Hossein Faraki (83 Hassan Rowshan).   Manager: Heshmat Mohajerani.

Goal: Iraj Danaifar (60) / Andranik Eskandarian (43 own goal)

415. 11.06.1978   11th World Cup, 1st Round
HOLLAND v SCOTLAND 2-3 (1-1)
"San Martín", Mendoza
Referee: Erich Linemayr (Austria)   Attendance: 35,130
HOLLAND: Jan Jongbloed, Willem Johannes Laurens Suurbier, Rudolf Jozef Krol (Cap), Wilhelmus Gerardus Rijsbergen (44 Pieter Wildschut), Jan Poortvliet, Wilhelmus Antonius van de Kerkhof, Johannes Jacobus Neeskens (10 Johannes Boskamp), Wilhelmus Marinus Anthonius Jansen, Reinier Lambertus van de Kerkhof, John Nicolaas Rep, Robert Pieter Rensenbrink.   Trainer: Ernst Happel (Austria).
SCOTLAND: Alan Roderick Rough, Stuart Robert Kennedy, William Donachie, Martin McLean Buchan, Thomas Forsyth, Archibald Gemmill, Bruce David Rioch (Cap), Graeme James Souness, Richard Asa Hartford, Kenneth Mathieson Dalglish, Joseph Jordan.   Manager: Alistair MacLeod.
Goals: Robert Rensenbrink (34 pen), John Nicolaas Rep (71) / Kenneth Dalglish (44), Archibald Gemmill (46 pen, 68)

416. 20.09.1978   6th European Champs. Qualifiers
AUSTRIA v SCOTLAND 3-2 (1-0)
Prater, Wien
Referee: Alberto Michelotti (Italy)   Attendance: 62,281
AUSTRIA: Erwin Fuchsbichler, Robert Sara, Erich Obermayer, Bruno Pezzey, Heinrich Strasser, Herbert Prohaska (87 Franz Oberacher), Heribert Weber, Kurt Jara, Walter Schachner, Wilhelm Kreuz, Johann Krankl.   Trainer: Karl Stotz.
SCOTLAND: Alan Roderick Rough, Stuart Robert Kennedy, William Donachie, Martin McLean Buchan, Gordon McQueen, Archibald Gemmill (Cap), Graeme James Souness, Richard Asa Hartford, Kenneth Mathieson Dalglish, Joseph Jordan (61 Arthur Graham), Andrew Mullen Gray.   Manager: Alistair MacLeod.
Goals: Bruno Pezzey (27), Walter Schachner (48), Wilhelm Kreuz (64) / Gordon McQueen (65), Andy Gray (77)

417. 25.10.1978   6th European Champs. Qualifiers
SCOTLAND v NORWAY 3-2 (1-1)
Hampden Park, Glasgow
Referee: Vojtech Christov (Czechoslovakia)   Att: 65,372
SCOTLAND: James Garvin Stewart, William Donachie, Francis Tierney Gray, Martin McLean Buchan, Gordon McQueen, Archibald Gemmill (Cap), Graeme James Souness, Richard Asa Hartford, Arthur Graham, Kenneth Mathieson Dalglish, Andrew Mullen Gray.   Manager: John Stein.
NORWAY: Tom Rüsz Jacobsen, Trond Pedersen (80 Helge Karlsen), Jan Birkelund, Tore Kordahl, Svein Grøndalen, Einar Jan Aas, Tor Egil Johansen, Tom Jacobsen (37 Jan Hansen), Hallvar Thoresen, Svein Mathisen, Arne Larsen Økland.   Trainer: Tor Røste Fossen.
Goals: Kenneth Dalglish (5, 82), Archibald Gemmill (87 pen) / Einar Jan Aas (3), Arne Larsen Økland (64)

418. 29.11.1978   6th European Champs. Qualifiers
PORTUGAL v SCOTLAND 1-0 (1-0)
da Luz, Lisboa
Referee: Ernst Dörflinger (Switzerland)   Attendance: 70,000
PORTUGAL: Manuel Galrinho Bento, Artur Manuel Soares Correia, Humberto Manuel de Jesus Coelho (Cap), Carlos Alexandre Fortes Alhinho, Alberto Gomes Fonseca Júnior, Minervino José Lopes Pietra, António Luís Alves Ribeiro Oliveira (82 Eurico Monteiro Gomes), João António Ferreira Resende Alves, José Alberto Costa (46 Shéu Han), Tamagnini Manuel Gomes Baptista "Nené", Fernando Mendes Soares Gomes.   Trainer: Mário Wilson.
SCOTLAND: Alan Roderick Rough, Stuart Robert Kennedy, Francis Tierney Gray (65 William Donachie), David Narey, Gordon McQueen, Martin McLean Buchan, Archibald Gemmill (Cap), Richard Asa Hartford, John Neilson Robertson, Kenneth Mathieson Dalglish, Joseph Jordan (78 Ian Andrew Wallace).   Manager: John Stein.
Goal: Alberto Gomes Fonseca Júnior (29)

419. 19.05.1979   Home Championship
WALES v SCOTLAND 3-0 (2-0)
Ninian Park, Cardiff
Referee: Patrick Partridge (England)   Attendance: 20,371
WALES: William David Davies, William Byron Stevenson, Joseph Patrick Jones, Leighton Phillips, Philip John Dwyer, John Francis Mahoney, Terence Charles Yorath (89 Peter Nicholas), Brian Flynn, Robert Mark James, John Benjamin Toshack, Alan Thomas Curtis.   Manager: Michael Smith.
SCOTLAND: Alan Roderick Rough, George Elder Burley, Francis Tierney Gray, Alan David Hansen, Paul Anthony Hegarty, John Wark, Richard Asa Hartford, Graeme James Souness, Arthur Graham, Kenneth Mathieson Dalglish (Cap), Ian Andrew Wallace (55 Joseph Jordan).   Manager: John Stein.
Goals: John Benjamin Toshack (28, 35, 75)

420. 22.05.1979   Home Championship
SCOTLAND v NORTHERN IRELAND 1-0 (0-0)
Hampden Park, Glasgow
Referee: Clive Thomas (Wales)   Attendance: 28,524
SCOTLAND: George Wood, George Elder Burley, Francis Tierney Gray, Paul Anthony Hegarty, Gordon McQueen, John Wark (46 David Narey), Graeme James Souness, Richard Asa Hartford, Arthur Graham (89 Francis Peter McGarvey), Kenneth Mathieson Dalglish (Cap), Joseph Jordan.   Manager: John Stein.
NORTHERN IRELAND: Patrick Anthony Jennings, Patrick James Rice, Samuel Nelson, James Michael Nicholl, Alan Hunter, Victor Moreland (62 Peter William Scott), Bryan Hamilton, Samuel Baxter McIlroy, Gerard Joseph Armstrong, Thomas Sloan, Derek William Spence (77 William Thomas Caskey).   Manager: Robert Dennis Blanchflower.
Goal: Arthur Graham (76)

421. 26.05.1979   Home Championship
ENGLAND v SCOTLAND 3-1 (1-1)
Wembley, London
Referee: António José da Silva Garrido (Portugal)
Attendance: 100,000
ENGLAND: Raymond Neal Clemence, Philip George Neal, Michael Dennis Mills, Philip Brian Thompson, David Victor Watson, Raymond Colin Wilkins, Kevin Joseph Keegan (Cap), Steven James Coppell, Robert Dennis Latchford, Trevor David Brooking, Peter Simon Barnes.
Manager: Ronald Greenwood.
SCOTLAND: George Wood, George Elder Burley, Francis Tierney Gray, Paul Anthony Hegarty, Gordon McQueen, John Wark, Graeme James Souness, Richard Asa Hartford, Arthur Graham, Kenneth Mathieson Dalglish (Cap), Joseph Jordan.
Manager: John Stein.
Goals: Peter Simon Barnes (44), Steven James Coppell (64), Kevin Joseph Keegan (70) / John Wark (20)

422. 02.06.1979
SCOTLAND v ARGENTINA 1-3 (0-1)
Hampden Park, Glasgow
Referee: Patrick Partridge (England)   Attendance: 61,918
SCOTLAND: Alan Roderick Rough (46 George Wood), George Elder Burley, Alexander Fordyce Munro, Alan David Hansen, Paul Anthony Hegarty, David Narey, John Wark, Richard Asa Hartford (70 Francis Tierney Gray), Arthur Graham, Kenneth Mathieson Dalglish (Cap), Francis Peter McGarvey. Manager: John Stein.
ARGENTINA: Ubaldo Matildo Fillol, Jorge Mario Olguín, Hugo Eduardo Villaverde (21 Enzo Héctor Trossero), Daniel Alberto Passarella (Cap), Alberto César Tarantini, Juan Alberto Barbas, Américo Rubén Gallego, Diego Armando Maradona, René Orlando Houseman (56 Norberto Daniel Outes), Leopoldo Jacinto Luque, José Daniel Valencia.
Trainer: César Luis Menotti.
Goals: Arthur Graham (85) / Leopoldo Jacinto Luque (33, 61), Diego Maradona (70)

423. 07.06.1979   6th European Champs. Qualifiers
NORWAY v SCOTLAND 0-4 (0-3)
Ullevaal, Oslo
Referee: Ib Nielsen (Denmark)   Attendance: 17,269
NORWAY: Tom Rüsz Jacobsen, Helge Karlsen, Tore Kordahl, Svein Grøndalen, Trond Pedersen (67 Jan Hansen), Einar Jan Aas, Roger Albertsen, Stein Thunberg (75 Torbjørn Svendsen), Hallvar Thoresen, Svein Mathisen, Arne Larsen Økland.
Trainer: Tor Røste Fossen.
SCOTLAND: Alan Roderick Rough, George Elder Burley (46 Paul Anthony Hegarty (70 John Wark)), Alexander Fordyce Munro, Kenneth Burns, Gordon McQueen, Arthur Graham, Archibald Gemmill (Cap), Richard Asa Hartford, John Neilson Robertson, Kenneth Mathieson Dalglish, Joseph Jordan.
Manager: John Stein.
Goals: Joseph Jordan (32), Kenneth Mathieson Dalglish (39), John Neilson Robertson (43), Gordon McQueen (55)

424. 12.09.1979
SCOTLAND v PERU 1-1 (1-0)
Hampden Park, Glasgow
Referee: George Courtney (England)   Attendance: 41,035
SCOTLAND: Alan Roderick Rough, William Pullar Jardine (Cap), Alexander Fordyce Munro, Kenneth Burns, Gordon McQueen, David Cooper (71 Arthur Graham), John Wark (71 Robert Sime Aitken), Graeme James Souness, Richard Asa Hartford, John Neilson Robertson, Kenneth Mathieson Dalglish. Manager: John Stein.
PERU: Eusebio Alfredo Acasuzo Colán, Alejandro Hugo Gastulo Ramírez, Jorge Andrés Olaechea Quijandria, Héctor Eduardo Chumpitaz González, Rubén Toribio Díaz Rivas, José Manuel Velásquez Castillo, Germán Carlos Leguía Dragó, César Augusto Cueto Villa, Roberto Mosquera Zúñiga, Guillermo La Rosa Laguna, Ernesto Labarthe (73 Freddy Ravello). Trainer: José Chiarella.
Goals: Asa Hartford (4) / Germán Carlos Leguía Dragó (85)

425. 17.10.1979   6th European Champs. Qualifiers
SCOTLAND v AUSTRIA 1-1 (0-1)
Hampden Park, Glasgow
Referee: Károly Palotai (Hungary)   Attendance: 67,895
SCOTLAND: Alan Roderick Rough, William Pullar Jardine, Alexander Fordyce Munro, Kenneth Burns, Gordon McQueen, Arthur Graham (61 David Cooper), John Wark, Graeme James Souness, Archibald Gemmill (Cap), John Neilson Robertson, Kenneth Mathieson Dalglish.   Manager: John Stein.
AUSTRIA: Friedrich Koncilia, Robert Sara, Heribert Weber, Bruno Pezzey, Hans-Dieter Mirnegg, Roland Hattenberger, Wilhelm Kreuz, Kurt Jara, Walter Schachner (80 Gerhard Steinkogler), Herbert Prohaska, Johann Krankl (89 Reinhold Hintermaier).   Trainer: Karl Stotz.
Goals: Archibald Gemmill (75) / Johann Krankl (40)

426. 21.11.1979   6th European Champs. Qualifiers
BELGIUM v SCOTLAND 2-0 (1-0)

Heysel, Bruxelles

Referee: Elzar Azim Zade (Soviet Union)   Att: 14,289

BELGIUM: Theo Custers, Eric Gerets, Luc Millecamps, Walter Meeuws, Michel Renquin, Julien Cools, Wilfried Van Moer (66 René Verheyen), René Vandereycken, François Vander Elst, Jan Ceulemans, Edouard Voordeckers.   Trainer: Guy Thys.

SCOTLAND: Alan Roderick Rough, William Pullar Jardine (Cap), Alexander Fordyce Munro (61 Francis Tierney Gray), Alan David Hansen, William Fergus Miller, John Wark, Graeme James Souness, Richard Asa Hartford, John Neilson Robertson, Kenneth Mathieson Dalglish, Joseph Jordan (61 David Alexander Provan).   Manager: John Stein.

Goals: François Vander Elst (6), Edouard Voordeckers (47)

427. 19.12.1979   6th European Champs Qualifiers
SCOTLAND v BELGIUM 1-3 (0-3)

Hampden Park, Glasgow

Referee: Heinz Aldinger (West Germany)   Att: 25,389

SCOTLAND: Alan Roderick Rough, William Pullar Jardine (Cap), Daniel Fergus McGrain, Kenneth Burns, Gordon McQueen, Eamonn John Peter Bannon (46 David Alexander Provan), Robert Sime Aitken, John Wark, John Neilson Robertson, Kenneth Mathieson Dalglish, Derek Joseph Johnstone.   Manager: John Stein.

BELGIUM: Theo Custers, Eric Gerets, Luc Millecamps, Walter Meeuws, Maurice Martens, Julien Cools, Wilfried Van Moer (49 Gérard Plessers), René Vandereycken, François Vander Elst, Erwin Vandenbergh (73 Guy Dardenne), Jan Ceulemans.   Trainer: Guy Thys.

Goals: John Neilson Robertson (55) / Erwin Vandenbergh (18), François Vander Elst (23, 30)

428. 26.03.1980   6th European Champs. Qualifiers
SCOTLAND v PORTUGAL 4-1 (2-0)

Hampden Park, Glasgow

Referee: Robert Charles Paul Wurtz (France)   Att: 20,233

SCOTLAND: Alan Roderick Rough, George Elder Burley, Daniel Fergus McGrain, Alan David Hansen, Alexander McLeish, David Narey, Graeme James Souness, Archibald Gemmill (Cap), John Neilson Robertson (75 David Alexander Provan), Kenneth Mathieson Dalglish (48 Steven Archibald), Andrew Mullen Gray.   Manager: John Stein.

PORTUGAL: Manuel Galrinho Bento, Adelino de Jesus Teixeira, Humberto Manuel de Jesus Coelho (Cap), Carlos António Fonseca Simões, Alberto Gomes Fonseca Júnior, António Manuel Frasco Vieira (77 Carlos Manuel Correia dos Santos), Eurico Monteiro Gomes (35 Shéu Han), José Alberto Costa, Tamagnini Manuel Gomes Baptista "Nené", Fernando Mendes Soares Gomes, Rui Manuel Trindade Jordão.   Trainer: Mário Wilson.

Goals: Kenneth Dalglish (6), Andrew Mullen Gray (26), Steven Archibald (68), Archibald Gemmill (84 pen) / Fernando Mendes Soares Gomes (74)

429. 16.05.1980   Home Championship
NORTHERN IRELAND v SCOTLAND 1-0 (1-0)

Windsor Park, Belfast

Referee: Clive Thomas (Wales)   Attendance: 18,000

NORTHERN IRELAND: James Archibald Platt, James Michael Nicholl, Malachy Martin Donaghy, Christopher James Nicholl, John Patrick O'Neill, Thomas Cassidy (70 David McCreery), Samuel Baxter McIlroy, William Robert Hamilton (52 John McClelland), Gerard Joseph Armstrong, Thomas Finney, Noel Brotherston.
Manager: William Laurence Bingham.

SCOTLAND: William Thomson, George Elder Burley, Daniel Fergus McGrain, David Narey, Alexander McLeish, Gordon David Strachan, Graeme James Souness (59 Joseph Jordan), Archibald Gemmill (Cap), Peter Russell Weir (59 David Alexander Provan), Kenneth Mathieson Dalglish, Steven Archibald.   Manager: John Stein.

Goal: William Robert Hamilton (36)

430. 21.05.1980   Home Championship
SCOTLAND v WALES 1-0 (1-0)

Hampden Park, Glasgow

Referee: Hugh Wilson (Northern Ireland)   Att: 31,359

SCOTLAND: Alan Roderick Rough, Daniel Fergus McGrain, Alexander Fordyce Munro, Paul Anthony Hegarty, Alexander McLeish, William Fergus Miller, Gordon David Strachan, Archibald Gemmill (Cap), Peter Russell Weir (84 Robert Sime Aitken), Kenneth Mathieson Dalglish, Joseph Jordan.   Manager: John Stein.

WALES: William David Davies, Peter Nicholas, Joseph Patrick Jones, Keith Pontin (46 Leighton Phillips), Paul Terence Price, Terence Charles Yorath, David Charles Giles, Brian Flynn, Ian Patrick Walsh (15 Ian James Rush), Leighton James, Michael Reginald Thomas.   Manager: Harold Michael England.

Goal: William Fergus Miller (26)

431. 24.05.1980   Home Championship
SCOTLAND v ENGLAND 0-2 (0-1)
Hampden Park, Glasgow
Referee: Antonio José da Silva Garrido (Portugal)   Attendance: 85,000
SCOTLAND: Alan Roderick Rough, Daniel Fergus McGrain, Alexander Fordyce Munro (62 George Elder Burley), Paul Anthony Hegarty, Alexander McLeish, William Fergus Miller, Gordon David Strachan, Robert Sime Aitken (53 Andrew Mullen Gray), Archibald Gemmill (Cap), Kenneth Mathieson Dalglish, Joseph Jordan.   Manager: John Stein.
ENGLAND: Raymond Neal Clemence, Trevor John Cherry, Kenneth Graham Sansom, Philip Brian Thompson (Cap), David Victor Watson, Raymond Colin Wilkins, Steven James Coppell, Terence McDermott, David Edward Johnson, Paul Mariner (71 Emlyn Walter Hughes), Trevor David Brooking.   Manager: Ronald Greenwood.
Goals: Trevor David Brooking (8), Steven James Coppell (75)

432. 28.05.1980
POLAND v SCOTLAND 1-0 (0-0)
Warta, Poznań
Referee: Ivan Yosifov (Bulgaria)   Attendance: 25,000
POLAND: Piotr Mowlik, Marek Dziuba (Cap) (66 Włodzimierz Ciołek), Paweł Janas, Władysław Żmuda, Hieronim Barczak, Leszek Lipka, Zbigniew Boniek, Adam Nawałka, Grzegorz Lato, Kazimierz Kmiecik, Andrzej Pałasz (46 Stanisław Terlecki).   Trainer: Ryszard Kulesza.
SCOTLAND: Alan Roderick Rough, George Elder Burley (80 Alistair John Dawson), Daniel Fergus McGrain (Cap), William Fergus Miller, Alexander McLeish, David Narey, Gordon David Strachan, Robert Sime Aitken, Kenneth Mathieson Dalglish (56 Peter Russell Weir), Steven Archibald, Joseph Jordan (46 Alan Bernard Brazil).   Manager: John Stein.
Goal: Zbigniew Boniek (69)

433. 31.05.1980
HUNGARY v SCOTLAND 3-1 (1-0)
Népstadion, Budapest
Referee: Jakob Baumann (Switzerland)   Attendance: 10,000
HUNGARY: Ferenc Mészáros, Sándor Paróczai (63 Gábor Szántó), László Bálint, Imre Garaba, József Tóth, József Pásztor, Zoltán Kereki, Tibor Nyilasi, Ferenc Csongrádi, László Kiss (68 Márton Esterházy), András Törőcsik.
Trainer: Kálmán Mészöly.
SCOTLAND: Alan Roderick Rough, Daniel Fergus McGrain, Alistair John Dawson, William Fergus Miller, Alexander McLeish, David Narey, Archibald Gemmill (Cap), Kenneth Mathieson Dalglish, Peter Russell Weir, Alan Bernard Brazil (46 Gordon David Strachan), Steven Archibald.   Manager: John Stein.
Goals: András Törőcsik (6, 69), Zoltán Kereki (76) / Steven Archibald (67)

434. 10.09.1980   12th World Cup Qualifiers
SWEDEN v SCOTLAND 0-1 (0-0)
Råsunda, Stockholm
Referee: Franz Wöhrer (Austria)   Attendance: 39,831
SWEDEN: Ronnie Carl Hellström, Johnny Gustafsson, Hans Borg, Per Olof Bild, Håkan Arvidsson, Ingemar Erlandsson (80 Peter Nilsson), Sten-Ove Ramberg, Mats Nordgren, Thomas Nilsson, Thomas Sjöberg, Billy Ohlsson.
Trainer: Lars Arnesson.
SCOTLAND: Alan Roderick Rough, Daniel Fergus McGrain, Francis Tierney Gray, William Fergus Miller, Alexander McLeish, Alan David Hansen, Gordon David Strachan, Archibald Gemmill (Cap), John Neilson Robertson, Kenneth Mathieson Dalglish (80 Steven Archibald), Andrew Mullen Gray.   Manager: John Stein.
Goal: Gordon David Strachan (72)

435. 15.10.1980   12th World Cup Qualifiers
SCOTLAND v PORTUGAL 0-0
Hampden Park, Glasgow
Referee: Jan Redelfs (West Germany)   Attendance: 60,765
SCOTLAND: Alan Roderick Rough, Daniel Fergus McGrain, Francis Tierney Gray, William Fergus Miller, Alan David Hansen, Gordon David Strachan, Graeme James Souness, Archibald Gemmill (Cap), John Neilson Robertson, Kenneth Mathieson Dalglish, Andrew Mullen Gray.
Manager: John Stein.
PORTUGAL: Manuel Galrinho Bento (Cap), Gabriel Azevedo Mendes, Carlos António Fonseca Simões, João Gonçalves Laranjeira, Minervino José Lopes Pietra, Carlos Manuel Correia dos Santos, Eurico Monteiro Gomes, José Alberto Costa, Fernando Albino de Sousa Chalana (59 Shéu Han), Manuel José Tavares Fernandes, Rui Manuel Trindade Jordão (63 Tamagnini Manuel Gomes Baptista "Nené").
Trainer: Júlio Cernadas Pereira "Juca".

436. 25.02.1981   12th World Cup Qualifiers
ISRAEL v SCOTLAND 0-1 (0-0)
National, Ramat-Gan, Tel-Aviv
Referee: Otto Anderco (Romania)   Attendance: 35,000
ISRAEL: Yossi Mizrahi, Gadi Machnes, Haim Bar, Avi Cohen I, Yaacov Cohen, Nissim Cohen, Yaacov Ekhoiz, Itzhak Shum, Moshe Sinai, Gideon Damti, Beni Tabak.
Trainer: Jack Mansell (England).
SCOTLAND: Alan Roderick Rough, Daniel Fergus McGrain, Francis Tierney Gray, Kenneth Burns, Alexander McLeish, John Wark (46 William Fergus Miller), Graeme James Souness, Archibald Gemmill (Cap), John Neilson Robertson, Kenneth Mathieson Dalglish (69 Andrew Mullen Gray), Steven Archibald.   Manager: John Stein.
Goal: Kenneth Mathieson Dalglish (54)

437. 25.03.1981   12th World Cup Qualifiers
SCOTLAND v NORTHERN IRELAND 1-1 (0-0)
Hampden Park, Glasgow

Referee: Klaus Scheurell (East Germany)   Att: 78,444

SCOTLAND: Alan Roderick Rough (80 William Thomson), Daniel Fergus McGrain, Francis Tierney Gray, William Fergus Miller, Alexander McLeish, John Wark, Kenneth Burns (77 Richard Asa Hartford), Archibald Gemmill (Cap), John Neilson Robertson, Steven Archibald, Andrew Mullen Gray.   Manager: John Stein.

NORTHERN IRELAND: Patrick Anthony Jennings, James Michael Nicholl, Samuel Nelson, John McClelland, Christopher James Nicholl, John Patrick O'Neill, George Terence Cochrane, David McCreery, William Robert Hamilton (78 Derek William Spence), Gerard Joseph Armstrong, Samuel Baxter McIlroy.   Manager: William Laurence Bingham.

Goals: John Wark (75) / William Robert Hamilton (70)

438. 28.04.1981   12th World Cup Qualifiers
SCOTLAND v ISRAEL 3-1 (2-0)
Hampden Park, Glasgow

Referee: Guðmundur Haraldsson (Iceland)   Att: 61,489

SCOTLAND: Alan Roderick Rough, Daniel Fergus McGrain (Cap), Francis Tierney Gray, Alan David Hansen, Alexander McLeish, David Alexander Provan, Graeme James Souness, Richard Asa Hartford, John Neilson Robertson, Steven Archibald, Joseph Jordan.   Manager: John Stein.

ISRAEL: Yossi Mizrahi, Gadi Machnes, Haim Bar, Itzhak Shum, Yaacov Cohen, Cobi Zeituni, Yaacov Ekhoiz, Avi Cohen I, Moshe Sinai, Gideon Damti, Beni Tabak.   Trainer: Jack Mansell.

Goals: John Neilson Robertson (21 pen, 30 pen), David Alexander Provan (53) / Moshe Sinai (57)

439. 16.05.1981   Home Championship
WALES v SCOTLAND 2-0 (2-0)
Vetch Field, Swansea

Referee: Oliver Donnelly (Northern Ireland)   Att: 18,985

WALES: William David Davies, Joseph Patrick Jones (71 Terence David John Boyle), Peter Nicholas, Kevin Ratcliffe, Paul Terence Price, Leighton Phillips, Carl Stephen Harris, Brian Flynn, Ian Patrick Walsh (76 Jeremy Melvyn Charles), Leighton James, Michael Reginald Thomas.   Manager: Harold Michael England.

SCOTLAND: Alan Roderick Rough, Raymond Strean McDonald Stewart, Francis Tierney Gray (46 Daniel Fergus McGrain), David Narey, Gordon McQueen, William Fergus Miller, David Alexander Provan, Kenneth Burns, Richard Asa Hartford (Cap), Arthur Graham (85 Paul Whitehead Sturrock), Joseph Jordan.   Manager: John Stein.

Goal: Ian Patrick Walsh (17, 20)

440. 19.05.1981   Home Championship
SCOTLAND v NORTHERN IRELAND 2-0 (1-0)
Hampden Park, Glasgow

Referee: Patrick Partridge (England)   Attendance: 22,248

SCOTLAND: William Thomson, Daniel Fergus McGrain (Cap), Francis Tierney Gray, William Fergus Miller, Alexander McLeish, Raymond Strean McDonald Stewart, Thomas Burns, Richard Asa Hartford, John Neilson Robertson, Paul Whitehead Sturrock, Steven Archibald.   Manager: John Stein.

NORTHERN IRELAND: Patrick Anthony Jennings, James Michael Nicholl, Samuel Nelson (70 Malachy Martin Donaghy), John McClelland, Christopher James Nicholl, John Patrick O'Neill, George Terence Cochrane, Martin Hugh Michael O'Neill, Gerard Joseph Armstrong, Samuel Baxter McIlroy, William Robert Hamilton.   Manager: William Laurence Bingham.

Goals: Raymond Stewart (5), Steven Archibald (49)

441. 23.05.1981   Home Championship
ENGLAND v SCOTLAND 0-1 (0-0)
Wembley, London

Referee: Robert Charles Paul Wurtz (France)   Att: 90,000

ENGLAND: Joseph Thomas Corrigan, Vivian Alexander Anderson, Kenneth Graham Samson, Raymond Colin Wilkins, David Victor Watson (Cap) (46 Alvin Edward Martin), Bryan Robson, Steven James Coppell, Glenn Hoddle, Peter Withe, Graham Rix, Anthony Stewart Woodcock (46 Trevor John Francis).   Manager: Ronald Greenwood.

SCOTLAND: Alan Roderick Rough, Daniel Fergus McGrain (Cap), Francis Tierney Gray, William Fergus Miller, Alexander McLeish, David Alexander Provan (80 Paul Whitehead Sturrock), Raymond Strean McDonald Stewart, Richard Asa Hartford (27 David Narey), John Neilson Robertson, Steven Archibald, Joseph Jordan.   Manager: John Stein.

Goal: John Neilson Robertson (64 pen)

442. 09.09.1981   12th World Cup Qualifiers
SCOTLAND v SWEDEN 2-0 (1-0)
Hampden Park, Glasgow

Referee: André Daina (Switzerland)   Attendance: 81,511

SCOTLAND: Alan Roderick Rough, Daniel Fergus McGrain (Cap), Francis Tierney Gray, Alan David Hansen, Alexander McLeish, David Alexander Provan, John Wark, Richard Asa Hartford, John Neilson Robertson, Kenneth Mathieson Dalglish (70 Andrew Mullen Gray), Joseph Jordan.   Manager: John Stein.

SWEDEN: Thomas Ravelli, Stig Fredriksson (46 Greger Hallén), Glenn Ingvar Hysén, Bo Börjesson, Andreas Ravelli, Ingemar Erlandsson, Hans Borg, Karl-Gunnar Björklund, Thomas Larsson, Jan Svensson (Tommy Holmgren), Thomas Sjöberg.   Trainer: Lars Arnesson.

Goals: Joseph Jordan (20), John Neilson Robertson (83 pen)

443. 14.10.1981   12th World Cup Qualifiers
NORTHERN IRELAND v SCOTLAND 0-0
Windsor Park, Belfast

Referee: Valeriy Butenko (Soviet Union)   Att: 22,248

NORTHERN IRELAND: Patrick Anthony Jennings, James Michael Nicholl, Christopher James Nicholl, John Patrick O'Neill, Malachy Martin Donaghy, Martin Hugh Michael O'Neill, Samuel Baxter McIlroy, David McCreery, Gerard Joseph Armstrong, William Robert Hamilton, Noel Brotherston.   Manager: William Laurence Bingham.

SCOTLAND: Alan Roderick Rough, Raymond Strean McDonald Stewart, Francis Tierney Gray, William Fergus Miller, Alan David Hansen, Gordon David Strachan, Graeme James Souness (76 Andrew Mullen Gray), Richard Asa Hartford (Cap), John Neilson Robertson, Kenneth Mathieson Dalglish, Steven Archibald.   Manager: John Stein.

444. 18.11.1981   12th World Cup Qualifiers
PORTUGAL v SCOTLAND 2-1 (1-1)
da Luz, Lisboa

Referee: Charles George Rainier Corver (Holland)
Attendance: 25,000

PORTUGAL: Manuel Galrinho Bento (Cap), Carlos António Fonseca Simões, Gregório Francisco Penteado Freixo (50 António Augusto da Silva Veloso), Eurico Monteiro Gomes, Adelino de Jesus Teixeira, Eduardo José Gomes Camassels Mendes "Dito", Jaime Fernandes Magalhães (46 Diamantino Manuel Fernandes Miranda), Romeu Fernando Fernandes da Silva, António Luís Alves Ribeiro Oliveira, Manuel José Tavares Fernandes, José Alberto Costa.
Trainer: Júlio Cernadas Pereira "Juca".

SCOTLAND: William Thomson, Raymond Strean McDonald Stewart, Francis Tierney Gray (42 Stuart Robert Kennedy), William Fergus Miller, Alan David Hansen, David Alexander Provan, Graeme James Souness, Richard Asa Hartford (Cap), Gordon David Strachan, Paul Whitehead Sturrock, Steven Archibald (65 Kenneth Mathieson Dalglish).
Manager: John Stein.

Goals: Manuel José Tavares Fernandes (33, 56) / Paul Whitehead Sturrock (9).

445. 24.02.1982
SPAIN v SCOTLAND 3-0 (1-0)
"Luis Casanova", Valencia

Referee: Albert Rudolf Thomas (Holland)   Att: 30,000

SPAIN: Luis Miguel Arkonada Echarre (Cap), José Antonio Camacho Alfaro, Miguel Tendillo Belenguer, José Ramón Alexanco Ventosa, Rafael Gordillo Vázquez, Miguel Ángel Alonso Oyarbide "Periko Alonso", Víctor Muñoz Manrique (54 Ricardo Gallego Redondo), José Vicente Sánchez Felip, Enrique Saura Gil, Jesús María Satrústegui Azpiroz (46 Enrique Castro González "Quini"), Roberto López Ufarte.
Trainer: José Emilio Santamaría Iglesias.

SCOTLAND: Alan Roderick Rough, Daniel Fergus McGrain (Cap), Francis Tierney Gray, Alan David Hansen, Alexander McLeish, Gordon David Strachan (54 Steven Archibald), Graeme James Souness, Richard Asa Hartford, John Wark, Kenneth Mathieson Dalglish, Alan Bernard Brazil.
Manager: John Stein.

Goals: Víctor Muñoz Manrique (23), Enrique Castro González "Quini" (83 pen), Ricardo Gallego Redondo (86).

446. 23.03.1982
SCOTLAND v HOLLAND 2-1 (2-1)
Hampden Park, Glasgow

Referee: George Courtney (England)   Attendance: 71,848

SCOTLAND: Alan Roderick Rough, Daniel Fergus McGrain (Cap), Francis Tierney Gray, Allan James Evans, William Fergus Miller, David Narey, James Bett, Kenneth Mathieson Dalglish (46 Alan Bernard Brazil), John Wark, Steven Archibald (46 Thomas Burns), Joseph Jordan (62 Gordon David Strachan).   Manager: John Stein.

HOLLAND: Johannes Franciscus van Breukelen, Michael Antonius Bernardus van de Korput, Rudolf Jozef Krol (Cap), Ronald Spelbos, Hugo Hermanus Hovenkamp, Johannes Wilhelmus Peters, Johannes Antonius Bernardus Metgod, Franklin Edmundo Rijkaard, Arnoldus Johannes Hyacinthus Mühren, Willem Cornelis Nicolaas Kieft, Simon Melkianus Tahamata.   Trainer: Cornelis Bernardus Rijvers.

Goals: Francis Tierney Gray (13 pen), Kenneth Dalglish (21) / Willem Cornelis Nicolaas Kieft (31).

81

447. 28.04.1982   Home Championship
NORTHERN IRELAND v SCOTLAND 1-1 (0-1)
Windsor Park, Belfast

Referee: John Hunting (England)   Attendance: 20,000
NORTHERN IRELAND: James Archibald Platt, Malachy Martin Donaghy, Samuel Nelson, John Patrick O'Neill, John McClelland, James Cleary, Noel Brotherston, Martin Hugh Michael O'Neill, Robert McFaul Campbell, Samuel Baxter McIlroy, Patrick Joseph Healy.
Manager: William Laurence Bingham.

SCOTLAND: George Wood, Daniel Fergus McGrain (Cap), Arthur Richard Albiston, Allan James Evans, Alexander McLeish (75 Alan David Hansen), David Alexander Provan, John Wark, Richard Asa Hartford, John Neilson Robertson (80 Paul Whitehead Sturrock), Kenneth Mathieson Dalglish, Alan Bernard Brazil.   Manager: John Stein.

Goals: Samuel Baxter McIlroy (55) / John Wark (32)

448. 24.05.1982   Home Championship
SCOTLAND v WALES 1-0 (1-0)
Hampden Park, Glasgow

Ref: Frederick McKnight (Northern Ireland)   Att: 25,284
SCOTLAND: Alan Roderick Rough, Raymond Strean McDonald Stewart (72 George Elder Burley), Francis Tierney Gray, David Narey, Alan David Hansen, Thomas Burns, Graeme James Souness (Cap), Richard Asa Hartford, Kenneth Mathieson Dalglish, Alan Bernard Brazil, Joseph Jordan (72 Paul Whitehead Sturrock).   Manager: John Stein.

WALES: William David Davies, Christopher Marustik, Joseph Patrick Jones, Peter Nicholas, Nigel Charles Ashley Stevenson, William Byron Stevenson, Alan Thomas Curtis (75 Ian Patrick Walsh), Robert Mark James, Brian Flynn (75 Michael Reginald Thomas), Ian James Rush, Leighton James.
Manager: Harold Michael England.

Goal: Richard Asa Hartford (7)

449. 29.05.1982   Home Championship
SCOTLAND v ENGLAND 0-1 (0-1)
Hampden Park, Glasgow

Referee: Jan Redelfs (West Germany)   Attendance: 80,529
SCOTLAND: Alan Roderick Rough, George Elder Burley, Daniel Fergus McGrain (Cap), Allan James Evans, Alan David Hansen, David Narey, Graeme James Souness, Richard Asa Hartford (46 John Neilson Robertson), Kenneth Mathieson Dalglish, Alan Bernard Brazil, Joseph Jordan (63 Paul Whitehead Sturrock).   Manager: John Stein.

ENGLAND: Peter Leslie Shilton, Michael Dennis Mills, Kenneth Graham Sansom, Philip Brian Thompson, Terence Ian Butcher, Bryan Robson, Kevin Joseph Keegan (Cap) (56 Terence McDermott), Steven James Coppell, Paul Mariner (46 Trevor John Francis), Trevor David Brooking, Raymond Colin Wilkins.   Manager: Ronald Greenwood.

Goal: Paul Mariner (13)

450. 15.06.1982   12th World Cup, 1st Round
NEW ZEALAND v SCOTLAND 2-5 (0-3)
La Rosaleda, Malaga

Referee: David Stanley Socha (United States)
Attendance: 20,000
NEW ZEALAND: Frank van Hattum, John Hill, Robert Almond (65 Ricki Lloyd Herbert), Adrian Coroon Elrick, Samuel Malcomson (77 Duncan Cole), Keith McKay, Allan Roderick Boath, Kenneth Cresswell, Steve Paul Sumner, Wynton Alan Whai Rufer, Steve Wooddin.
Trainer: John Adshead (England).

SCOTLAND: Alan Roderick Rough, Daniel Fergus McGrain (Cap), Francis Tierney Gray, Allan James Evans, Alan David Hansen, Gordon David Strachan (83 David Narey), Graeme James Souness, John Wark, John Neilson Robertson, Kenneth Mathieson Dalglish, Alan Bernard Brazil (53 Steven Archibald).   Manager: John Stein.

Goals: Steve Paul Sumner (54), Steve Woodin (65) / Kenneth Mathieson Dalglish (18), John Wark (29, 32), John Neilson Robertson (73), Steven Archibald (80)

451. 18.06.1982   12th World Cup, 1st Round
BRAZIL v SCOTLAND 4-1 (1-1)
"Benito Villamarín", Sevilla

Referee: Luis Paulino Siles Calderón (Costa Rica)
Attendance: 47,379
BRAZIL: Valdir de Arruda Peres, José Leandro de Souza Ferreira "Leandro I", José Oscar Bernardi, Luiz Carlos Ferreira "Luisinho", Leovegildo Lins Gama Júnior "Júnior I", Paulo Roberto Falcão, Sócrates Brasileiro Sampaio Vieira de Oliveira (Cap), Arthur Antunes Coimbra "Zico", Antônio Carlos Cerezo "Toninho Cerezo", Sérgio Bernardino "Serginho I" (81 Paulo Isidoro de Jesus), Éder Aleixo de Assis.
Trainer: Telê Santana da Silva.

SCOTLAND: Alan Roderick Rough, David Narey, Francis Tierney Gray, William Fergus Miller, Alan David Hansen, Gordon David Strachan (65 Kenneth Mathieson Dalglish), Graeme James Souness (Cap), Richard Asa Hartford (69 Alexander McLeish), John Neilson Robertson, John Wark, Steven Archibald.   Manager: John Stein.

Goals: Arthur Antunes Coimbra "Zico" (33), José Oscar Bernardi (48), Éder Aleixo de Assis (63), Paulo Roberto Falcão (87) / David Narey (18)

452. 22.06.1982   12th World Cup, 1st Round
SOVIET UNION v SCOTLAND 2-2 (0-1)
La Rosaleda, Malaga

Referee: Nicolae Rainea (Romania)   Attendance: 45,000

SOVIET UNION: Rinat Dasaev, Tengiz Sulakvelidze, Sergey Baltacha, Aleksandr Chivadze (Cap), Anatoliy Demyanenko, Andrey Bal, Sergey Borovskiy, Vladimir Bessonov, Ramaz Shengeliya (89 Sergey Andreev), Yuriy Gavrilov, Oleg Blokhin. Trainer: Konstantin Beskov.

SCOTLAND: Alan Roderick Rough, David Narey, Francis Tierney Gray, William Fergus Miller, Alan David Hansen, Gordon David Strachan (71 Daniel Fergus McGrain), Graeme James Souness (Cap), John Wark, John Neilson Robertson, Steven Archibald, Joseph Jordan (71 Alan Bernard Brazil). Manager: John Stein.

Goals: Aleksandr Chivadze (59), Ramaz Shengeliya (85) / Joseph Jordan (15), Graeme James Souness (88)

453. 13.10.1982   7th European Champs. Qualifiers
SCOTLAND v EAST GERMANY 2-0 (0-0)
Hampden Park, Glasgow

Referee: Georges Konrath (France)   Attendance: 40,355

SCOTLAND: James Leighton, David Narey, Francis Tierney Gray, William Fergus Miller, Alan David Hansen, Gordon David Strachan, Graeme James Souness (Cap), John Wark, John Neilson Robertson, Alan Bernard Brazil (71 Paul Whitehead Sturrock), Steven Archibald. Manager: John Stein.

EAST GERMANY: Bodo Rudwaleit, Norbert Trieloff, Ronald Kreer, Dirk Stahmann, Rüdiger Schnuphase (Cap), Frank Baum, Reinhard Häfner (72 Matthias Liebers), Hans-Jürgen Dörner (72 Jürgen Pommerenke), Hans-Uwe Pilz, Joachim Streich, Hans-Jürgen Riediger.   Trainer: Rudolf Krause.

Goals: John Wark (53), Paul Whitehead Sturrock (75)

454. 17.11.1982   7th European Champs. Qualifiers
SWITZERLAND v SCOTLAND 2-0 (0-0)
Wankdorf, Bern

Referee: Vojtech Christov (Czechoslovakia)   Att: 26,000

SWITZERLAND: Erich Burgener, Heinz Lüdi, André Egli, Alain Geiger, Roger Wehrli, Michel Decastel (61 Umberto Barberis), Heinz Hermann, Lucien Favre, Raimondo Ponte, Claudio Sulser, Rudolf Elsener (85 Hanspeter Zwicker). Trainer: Paul Wolfisberg.

SCOTLAND: James Leighton, David Narey, Francis Tierney Gray, William Fergus Miller, Alan David Hansen, Gordon David Strachan, Graeme James Souness (Cap), John Wark, John Neilson Robertson, Paul Whitehead Sturrock (46 Steven Archibald), Alan Bernard Brazil.   Manager: John Stein.

Goals: Claudio Sulser (49), André Egli (60)

455. 15.12.1982   7th European Champs. Qualifiers
BELGIUM v SCOTLAND 3-2 (2-2)
Heysel, Bruxelles

Ref: Antonio José Da Silva Garrido (Portugal)   Att: 48,877

BELGIUM: Jean-Marie Pfaff, Eric Gerets, Walter Meeuws, Joseph Daerden, Marc Baecke, Guy Vandersmissen, Ludo Coeck, Jan Ceulemans, Frank Vercauteren (63 René Verheyen), Erwin Vandenbergh (87 Maurits De Schrijver), François Vander Elst.   Trainer: Guy Thys.

SCOTLAND: James Leighton, David Narey, Francis Tierney Gray, Alan David Hansen, Alexander McLeish, Gordon David Strachan (77 Thomas Burns), Graeme James Souness (Cap), Robert Sime Aitken, James Bett (77 Paul Whitehead Sturrock), Kenneth Mathieson Dalglish, Steven Archibald. Manager: John Stein.

Goals: Erwin Vandenbergh (25), F. Vander Elst (39, 63) / Kenneth Mathieson Dalglish (13, 36)

456. 30.03.1983   7th European Champs. Qualifiers
SCOTLAND v SWITZERLAND 2-2 (0-1)
Hampden Park, Glasgow

Referee: Charles George Rainier Corver (Holland)
Attendance: 36,923

SCOTLAND: James Leighton, Richard Charles Gough, Francis Tierney Gray, William Fergus Miller, Alan David Hansen (46 Alexander McLeish), Gordon David Strachan, Graeme James Souness (Cap), John Wark, Peter Russell Weir, Kenneth Mathieson Dalglish, Charles Nicholas. Manager: John Stein.

SWITZERLAND: Erich Burgener, Heinz Lüdi, André Egli, Alain Geiger, Roger Wehrli, Michel Decastel, Lucien Favre, Heinz Hermann (69 Hanspeter Zwicker), Claudio Sulser (84 Charles In-Albon), Raimondo Ponte, Rudolf Elsener. Trainer: Paul Wolfisberg.

Goals: John Wark (70), Charles Nicholas (76) / André Egli (15), Heinz Hermann (58)

457. 24.05.1983   Home Championship
SCOTLAND v NORTHERN IRELAND 0-0
Hampden Park, Glasgow

Referee: Keith Hackett (England)   Attendance: 16,238

SCOTLAND: William Thomson, Richard Charles Gough, Alistair John Dawson, David Narey, Paul Anthony Hegarty (Cap), Thomas Burns, Neil Simpson (65 Gordon David Strachan), John Wark, Eamonn John Peter Bannon, Andrew Mullen Gray, Charles Nicholas.   Manager: John Stein.

NORTHERN IRELAND: Patrick Anthony Jennings, James Michael Nicholl, Malachy Martin Donaghy, John Patrick O'Neill (46 Christopher James Nicholl), John McClelland, Martin Hugh Michael O'Neill (Cap), Gerald Mullan, Samuel Baxter McIlroy, Gerard Joseph Armstrong, William Robert Hamilton (89 Noel Brotherston), Ian Edwin Stewart. Manager: William Laurence Bingham.

458. 28.05.1983   Home Championship
WALES v SCOTLAND 0-2 (0-1)
Ninian Park, Cardiff
Referee: Malcolm Moffatt (Northern Ireland)   Att: 14,100
WALES: Neville Southall, Joseph Patrick Jones, Neil John Slatter, Kevin Ratcliffe, Paul Terence Price, Peter Nicholas, Brian Flynn (57 Stephen Robert Lowndes), Kenneth Francis Jackett, Jeremy Melvyn Charles, Michael Reginald Thomas, Gordon John Davies.   Manager: Harold Michael England.
SCOTLAND: James Leighton, Richard Charles Gough, Francis Tierney Gray, David Narey, Alexander McLeish, Gordon David Strachan, William Fergus Miller, Graeme James Souness (Cap), Eamonn John Peter Bannon, Andrew Mullen Gray, Alan Bernard Brazil.   Manager: John Stein.
Goals: Andrew Mullen Gray (11), Alan Bernard Brazil (67)

459. 01.06.1983   Home Championship
ENGLAND v SCOTLAND 2-0 (1-0)
Wembley, London
Referee: Erik Fredriksson (Sweden)   Attendance: 84,000
ENGLAND: Peter Leslie Shilton (Cap), Philip George Neal, Kenneth Graham Sansom, Samuel Lee, Graham Paul Roberts, Terence Ian Butcher, Bryan Robson (25 Gary Vincent Mabbutt), Trevor John Francis, Peter Withe (46 Luther Loide Blissett), Glenn Hoddle, Gordon Sidney Cowans.   Manager: Robert William Robson.
SCOTLAND: James Leighton, Richard Charles Gough, Francis Tierney Gray, David Narey, Alexander McLeish, Gordon David Strachan, William Fergus Miller, Graeme James Souness (Cap), Eamonn John Peter Bannon (53 Alan Bernard Brazil), Andrew Mullen Gray, Charles Nicholas (67 John Wark).   Manager: John Stein.
Goals: Bryan Robson (12), Gordon Sidney Cowans (52)

460. 12.06.1983
CANADA v SCOTLAND 0-2 (0-1)
Empire, Vancouver
Referee: Philip Clarke (Canada)   Attendance: 14,942
CANADA: Matire Lettieri, Robert Iarusci, Robert Lenarduzzi, Ian Bridge, Bruce Wilson, Gerard Gray, Randy Ragan, Peter Roe (46 John Connor), Mike Sweeney, Edward McNally (46 Terence Felix), Dale William Mitchell.
Trainer: Anthony Keith Waiters.
SCOTLAND: William Thomson, Richard Charles Gough, Alistair John Dawson, David Narey, Alexander McLeish, Gordon David Strachan (70 Graeme James Souness), William Fergus Miller (Cap), Thomas Burns, Eamonn John Peter Bannon, Paul Whitehead Sturrock, Charles Nicholas (37 Mark Edward McGhee).   Manager: John Stein.
Goals: Gordon Strachan (36 pen), Mark McGhee (75)

461. 16.06.1983
CANADA v SCOTLAND 0-3 (0-1)
Commonwealth, Edmonton
Referee: Rolando B. Fusco (Canada)   Attendance: 12,258
CANADA: Matire Lettieri, Robert Iarusci, Robert Lenarduzzi, Ian Bridge, Bruce Wilson, Gerard Gray (46 Terence Felix), Randy Ragan, Peter Roe, Mike Sweeney, Edward McNally, Dale William Mitchell.   Trainer: Anthony Keith Waiters.
SCOTLAND: James Leighton, Richard Charles Gough, Francis Tierney Gray, David Narey, Alexander McLeish, Gordon David Strachan (46 Robert Sime Aitken), William Fergus Miller, Graeme James Souness (Cap), Paul Whitehead Sturrock, Mark Edward McGhee (54 Andrew Mullen Gray), Charles Nicholas.   Manager: John Stein.
Goals: Charles Nicholas (20), Richard Charles Gough (50), Graeme James Souness (89)

462. 19.06.1983
CANADA v SCOTLAND 0-2 (0-2)
Varsity, Toronto
Referee: Antonio Evangelista (Canada)   Attendance: 15,500
CANADA: Christopher Turner, Paul Lee (46 Craig Martin), Ian Bridge (46 Edward McNally), Terence Moore, Bruce Wilson, Gerard Gray, Peter Roe, John Connor, Colin Fyfe Miller, Terence Felix, Dale William Mitchell.
Trainer: Anthony Keith Waiters.
SCOTLAND: James Leighton, Richard Charles Gough, Alistair John Dawson, David Narey (65 Thomas Burns), Alexander McLeish, William Fergus Miller, Graeme James Souness (Cap), Robert Sime Aitken, Paul Whitehead Sturrock, Andrew Mullen Gray (46 Gordon David Strachan), Charles Nicholas.   Manager: John Stein.
Goals: Andrew Mullen Gray (17, 32)

463. 21.09.1983
SCOTLAND v URUGUAY 2-0 (1-0)
Hampden Park, Glasgow
Referee: David Richardson (England)   Attendance: 20,545
SCOTLAND: James Leighton, Richard Charles Gough, Arthur Richard Albiston, William Fergus Miller, Alexander McLeish, John Wark, Paul Michael Lyons McStay (77 Neil Simpson), Graeme James Souness (Cap), John Neilson Robertson, Kenneth Mathieson Dalglish, Francis Peter McGarvey (17 David Dodds).   Manager: John Stein.
URUGUAY: Rodolfo Sergio Rodríguez, Víctor Hugo Diogo, Washington González, Nelson Daniel Gutiérrez, Eduardo Mario Acevedo, Nelson Agresta, Venancio Ariel Ramos (70 Néstor Montelongo), Mario Daniel Saralegui, Alberto Raúl Santelli (70 Carlos Alberto Aguilera), Jorge Walter Barrios, Luis Alberto Acosta (Alfredo De los Santos).
Trainer: Omar Borrás.
Goals: John Neilson Robertson (24 pen), David Dodds (55)

464. 12.10.1983   7th European Champs. Qualifiers
SCOTLAND v BELGIUM 1-1 (0-1)
Hampden Park, Glasgow

Referee: Enzo Barbaresco (Italy)   Attendance: 23,475

SCOTLAND: James Leighton, Richard Charles Gough, Arthur Richard Albiston, William Fergus Miller (Cap), Alexander McLeish, John Wark (80 Robert Sime Aitken), Paul Michael Lyons McStay, James Bett, John Neilson Robertson, Kenneth Mathieson Dalglish, Charles Nicholas (74 Francis Peter McGarvey).   Manager: John Stein.

BELGIUM: Jean-Marie Pfaff, Eric Gerets, Luc Millecamps, Walter Meeuws (76 Michel De Wolf), Michel Wintacq, François Vander Elst, Ludo Coeck, Jan Ceulemans, Frank Vercauteren, Nicolaas Pieter Claesen, Edouard Voordeckers. Trainer: Guy Thys.

Goals: Charles Nicholas (49) / Frank Vercauteren (31)

465. 16.11.1983   7th European Champs. Qualifiers
EAST GERMANY v SCOTLAND 2-1 (2-0)
Kurt Wabbel, Halle

Referee: Franz Wöhrer (Austria)   Attendance: 18,000

EAST GERMANY: Bodo Rudwaleit, Dirk Stahmann, Ronald Kreer, Rainer Troppa, Uwe Zötzsche, Hans-Uwe Pilz, Rainer Ernst (87 Jürgen Raab), Christian Backs, Wolfgang Steinbach, Joachim Streich (Cap), Hans Richter.   Trainer: Bernd Stange.

SCOTLAND: William Thomson, Richard Charles Gough, Arthur Richard Albiston, William Fergus Miller (Cap), Alexander McLeish, Gordon David Strachan, John Wark, Paul Michael Lyons McStay (60 Francis Peter McGarvey), Eamonn John Peter Bannon, Kenneth Mathieson Dalglish, Steven Archibald.   Manager: John Stein.

Goal: Eamonn John Peter Bannon (78)

466. 13.12.1983   Home Championship
NORTHERN IRELAND v SCOTLAND 2-0 (1-0)
Windsor Park, Belfast

Referee: Neil Midgley (England)   Attendance: 12,000

NORTHERN IRELAND: Patrick Anthony Jennings, James Michael Nicholl, Malachy Martin Donaghy, John McClelland, Gerard McElhinney, Paul Christopher Ramsey, George Terence Cochrane (86 John Patrick O'Neill), Samuel Baxter McIlroy (Cap), William Robert Hamilton, Norman Whiteside, Ian Edwin Stewart.   Manager: William Laurence Bingham.

SCOTLAND: James Leighton, Richard Charles Gough, Douglas Rougvie, Robert Sime Aitken, Alexander McLeish, Gordon David Strachan, Paul Michael Lyons McStay, Graeme James Souness (Cap), Peter Russell Weir, David Dodds, Francis Peter McGarvey (60 Mark Edward McGhee).   Manager: John Stein.

Goals: Norman Whiteside (17), Samuel Baxter McIlroy (56)

467. 28.02.1984   Home Championship
SCOTLAND v WALES 2-1 (1-0)
Hampden Park, Glasgow

Referee: Jack Poucher (Northern Ireland)   Att: 21,542

SCOTLAND: James Leighton, Richard Charles Gough, Arthur Richard Albiston, William Fergus Miller, Alexander McLeish, Paul Michael Lyons McStay (64 Robert Sime Aitken), Graeme James Souness (Cap), James Bett, David Cooper, Paul Whitehead Sturrock, Francis Peter McGarvey (46 Maurice Johnston).   Manager: John Stein.

WALES: Neville Southall, Jeffrey Hopkins, Kevin Ratcliffe, Joseph Patrick Jones, Jeremy Melvyn Charles, Brian Flynn, Kenneth Francis Jackett, Alan Thomas Curtis (84 Paul Terence Price), Ian James Rush (64 Gordon John Davies), Michael Reginald Thomas, Robert Mark James.
Manager: Harold Michael England.

Goals: David Cooper (37 pen), Maurice Johnston (78) / Robert Mark James (47)

468. 26.05.1984   Home Championship
SCOTLAND v ENGLAND 1-1 (1-1)
Hampden Park, Glasgow

Referee: Paolo Casarin (Italy)   Attendance: 73,064

SCOTLAND: James Leighton, Richard Charles Gough, Arthur Richard Albiston, William Fergus Miller (Cap), Alexander McLeish, Gordon David Strachan (62 Paul Michael Lyons McStay), James Bett, John Wark, David Cooper, Steven Archibald, Mark Edward McGhee (62 Maurice Johnston).   Manager: John Stein.

ENGLAND: Peter Leslie Shilton, Michael Duxburyy, Kenneth Graham Sansom, Raymond Colin Wilkins, Graham Paul Roberts, Terence William Fenwick, Mark Valentine Chamberlain (74 Steven Kenneth Hunt), Bryan Robson (Cap), Anthony Stewart Woodcock (72 Gary Winston Lineker), Luther Loide Blissett, John Charles Bryan Barnes.   Manager: Robert William Robson.

Goals: Mark McGhee (13) / Anthony Woodcock (36)

469. 01.06.1984
FRANCE v SCOTLAND 2-0 (2-0)
Vélodrome, Marseille

Referee: Luigi Agnolin (Italy)   Attendance: 24,641

FRANCE: Joël Bats, Patrick Battiston, Yvon Le Roux, Maxime Bossis, Manuel Amoros, Jean Amadou Tigana, Luis Fernandez (67 Bernard Genghini), Alain Giresse, Michel Platini (Cap), Bernard Lacombe (46 Daniel Bravo), Bruno Bellone (67 Didier Six).   Trainer: Michel Hidalgo.

SCOTLAND: James Leighton, Richard Charles Gough (67 Charles Nicholas), Maurice Daniel Robert Malpas, William Fergus Miller (Cap), Alexander McLeish, Gordon David Strachan (46 Neil Simpson), Raymond Strean McDonald Stewart, James Bett, John Wark, Steven Archibald, Maurice Johnston.   Manager: John Stein.

Goals: Alain Giresse (14), Bernard Lacombe (29)

470. 12.09.1984
SCOTLAND v YUGOSLAVIA 6-1 (3-1)
Hampden Park, Glasgow
Referee: Keith Hackett (England)   Attendance: 18,512
SCOTLAND: James Leighton, Stephen Nicol, Arthur Richard Albiston, William Fergus Miller, Alexander McLeish, James Bett, Graeme James Souness (Cap), John Wark (46 Paul Michael Lyons McStay), David Cooper (60 Charles Nicholas), Kenneth Mathieson Dalglish (55 Paul Whitehead Sturrock), Maurice Johnston.   Manager: John Stein.
YUGOSLAVIA: Dragan Pantelić (46 Ranko Stojić), Branko Miljuš, Mirsad Baljić, Miodrag Ješić, Vladimir Matijević (65 Davor Jozić), Ljubomir Radanović (Cap), Edin Bahtić, Blaž Slišković, Fadilj Vokri (46 Darko Pančev), Petar Georgijevski (46 Nenad Gračan), Zoran Batrović.
Trainer: Miloš Milutinović.
Goals: David Cooper (11), Graeme James Souness (18), Kenneth Dalglish (31), Paul Whitehead Sturrock (64), Maurice Johnston (66), Charles Nicholas (80) / Fadilj Vokri (10)

471. 17.10.1984   13th World Cup Qualifiers
SCOTLAND v ICELAND 3-0 (2-0)
Hampden Park, Glasgow
Referee: Egbert Mulder (Holland)   Attendance: 52,829
SCOTLAND: James Leighton, Stephen Nicol, Arthur Richard Albiston, William Fergus Miller, Alexander McLeish, David Cooper, Graeme James Souness (Cap), Paul Michael Lyons McStay, James Bett, Kenneth Mathieson Dalglish (68 Charles Nicholas), Maurice Johnston.   Manager: John Stein.
ICELAND: Bjarni Sigurðsson, Þorgrímur Þráinsson, Árni Sveinsson, Magnús Bergs, Sævar Jónsson, Janus Guðlaugsson, Pétur Pétursson, Atli Eðvaldsson, Ragnar Margeirsson, Ásgeir Sigurvinsson (Cap), Arnór Guðjohnsen.
Trainer: Anthony Knapp (England).
Goals: Paul Michael Lyons McStay (22, 40), Charles Nicholas (70)

472. 14.11.1984   13th World Cup Qualifiers
SCOTLAND v SPAIN 3-1 (2-0)
Hampden Park, Glasgow
Referee: Adolf Prokop (East Germany)   Attendance: 74,299
SCOTLAND: James Leighton, Stephen Nicol, Arthur Richard Albiston, William Fergus Miller, Alexander McLeish, David Cooper, Graeme James Souness (Cap), Paul Michael Lyons McStay, James Bett, Kenneth Mathieson Dalglish, Maurice Johnston.   Manager: John Stein.
SPAIN: Luis Miguel Arkonada Echarre (Cap), Santiago Urquiaga Pérez Lugar, Andoni Goikoetxea Olaskoaga, Antonio Maceda Francés, José Antonio Camacho Alfaro, Juan Antonio Señor Gómez, Víctor Muñoz Manrique, Rafael Gordillo Vázquez, Carlos Alonso González "Santillana", Ismael Urtubi Aróstegui (80 Francisco José Carrasco Hidalgo), Hipólito Rincón Povedano (46 Emilio Butragueño Santos).
Trainer: Miguel Muñoz Mozún.
Goals: Maurice Johnston (33, 42), Kenneth Dalglish (75) / Andoni Goikoetxea Olaskoaga (65)

473. 27.02.1985   13th World Cup Qualifiers
SPAIN v SCOTLAND 1-0 (0-0)
"Ramón Sánchez Pizjuán", Sevilla
Referee: Michel Vautrot (France)   Attendance: 70,410
SPAIN: Luis Miguel Arkonada Echarre (Cap), Gerardo Miranda Concepción, Andoni Goikoetxea Olaskoaga, Antonio Maceda Francés, José Antonio Camacho Alfaro, Juan Antonio Señor Gómez, Roberto Fernández Bonillo, Ricardo Gallego Redondo (80 Julio Alberto Moreno Casas), Rafael Gordillo Vázquez, Francisco Javier Clos Orozco, Emilio Butragueño Santos.   Trainer: Miguel Muñoz Mozún.
SCOTLAND: James Leighton, Richard Charles Gough, Arthur Richard Albiston, William Fergus Miller, Alexander McLeish, David Cooper, Graeme James Souness (Cap), Paul Michael Lyons McStay (76 Gordon David Strachan), James Bett, Steven Archibald (84 Charles Nicholas), Maurice Johnston.   Manager: John Stein.
Goal: Francisco Javier Clos Orozco (48)

474. 27.03.1985   13th World Cup Qualifiers
SCOTLAND v WALES 0-1 (0-1)
Hampden Park, Glasgow
Referee: Alexis Ponnet (Belgium)   Attendance: 62,424
SCOTLAND: James Leighton, Stephen Nicol, Arthur Richard Albiston (57 Alan David Hansen), William Fergus Miller, Alexander McLeish, David Cooper, Graeme James Souness (Cap), Paul Michael Lyons McStay (75 Charles Nicholas), James Bett, Kenneth Mathieson Dalglish, Maurice Johnston.
Manager: John Stein.
WALES: Neville Southall, Neil John Slatter, Joseph Patrick Jones, Kevin Ratcliffe, Kenneth Francis Jackett, David Owen Phillips, Robert Mark James, Peter Nicholas, Michael Reginald Thomas, Ian James Rush, Leslie Mark Hughes.
Manager: Harold Michael England.
Goal: Ian James Rush (37)

475. 25.05.1985   Stanley Rous Cup
SCOTLAND v ENGLAND 1-0 (0-0)
Hampden Park, Glasgow
Referee: Michel Vautrot (France)   Attendance: 66,489
SCOTLAND: James Leighton, Richard Charles Gough, Maurice Daniel Robert Malpas, William Fergus Miller, Alexander McLeish, Gordon David Strachan (71 Murdo Davidson MacLeod), Graeme James Souness (Cap), Robert Sime Aitken, James Bett, David Robert Speedie, Steven Archibald.   Manager: John Stein.
ENGLAND: Peter Leslie Shilton, Vivian Alexander Anderson, Kenneth Graham Sansom, Terence William Fenwick, Terence Ian Butcher, Glenn Hoddle (80 Gary Winston Lineker), Raymond Colin Wilkins, Bryan Robson (Cap), Trevor John Francis, Mark Wayne Hateley, John Charles Bryan Barnes (63 Christopher Roland Waddle).   Manager: Bobby Robson.

Goal: Richard Charles Gough (68)

476. 28.05.1985   13th World Cup Qualifiers
ICELAND v SCOTLAND 0-1 (0-0)
Laugardalsvöllur, Reykjavík
Referee: Anatoliy Milchenko (Soviet Union)   Att: 15,052
ICELAND: Eggert Guðmundsson, Þorgrímur Þráinsson, Árni Sveinsson, Magnús Bergs, Sævar Jónsson, Janus Guðlaugsson, Pétur Pétursson, Atli Eðvaldsson, Teitur Þórðarson (Cap) (57 Sigurður Grétarsson), Siðurdur Jónsson (25 Ómar Torfason), Guðmundur Þorbjörnsson.   Trainer: Anthony Knapp
SCOTLAND: James Leighton, Richard Charles Gough, Maurice Daniel Robert Malpas, William Fergus Miller, Alexander McLeish, Gordon David Strachan, Graeme James Souness (Cap), Robert Sime Aitken, James Bett, Andrew Mullen Gray (73 Steven Archibald), Graeme Marshall Sharp. Manager: John Stein.

Goal: James Bett (86)

477. 10.09.1985   13th World Cup Qualifiers
WALES v SCOTLAND 1-1 (1-0)
Ninian Park, Cardiff
Referee: Johannes Nicolaas Ignatius "Jan" Keizer (Holland)
Attendance: 39,500
WALES: Neville Southall, Joseph Patrick Jones, Patrick William Roger Van Den Hauwe, Kevin Ratcliffe, Kenneth Francis Jackett, Robert Mark James (80 Stephen John Lovell), David Owen Phillips, Peter Nicholas, Leslie Mark Hughes, Michael Reginald Thomas (83 Clayton Graham Blackmore), Ian James Rush.   Manager: Harold Michael England.
SCOTLAND: James Leighton (46 Alan Roderick Rough), Richard Charles Gough, Maurice Daniel Robert Malpas, William Fergus Miller (Cap), Alexander McLeish, Gordon David Strachan (61 David Cooper), Stephen Nicol, Robert Sime Aitken, James Bett, David Robert Speedie, Graeme Marshall Sharp.   Manager: John Stein.

Goals: Leslie Mark Hughes (13) / David Cooper (81 pen)

478. 16.10.1985
SCOTLAND v EAST GERMANY 0-0
Hampden Park, Glasgow
Referee: Joseph Bertram Worrall (England)   Att: 41,114
SCOTLAND: James Leighton (49 Andrew Lewis Goram), Richard Charles Gough, Arthur Richard Albiston, William Fergus Miller, Alexander McLeish, Stephen Nicol, Graeme James Souness (Cap), Robert Sime Aitken (81 Paul Michael Lyons McStay), David Cooper, Kenneth Mathieson Dalglish, Maurice Johnston (65 David Robert Speedie). Manager: Alexander Ferguson.
EAST GERMANY: René Müller (Cap) (46 Jörg Weißflog), Frank Rohde, Ronald Kreer, Carsten Sänger, Uwe Zötzsche, Hans-Uwe Pilz, Matthias Liebers, Jörg Stübner, Andreas Thom, Ulf Kirsten, Rainer Ernst (70 Andreas Bielau).
Trainer: Bernd Stange.

479. 20.11.1985   13th World Cup Qualifier Play-off
SCOTLAND v AUSTRALIA 2-0 (0-0)
Hampden Park, Glasgow
Referee: Vojtech Christov (Czechoslovakia)   Att: 61,920
SCOTLAND: James Leighton, Stephen Nicol, Maurice Daniel Robert Malpas, William Fergus Miller, Alexander McLeish, Gordon David Strachan (84 James Bett), Graeme James Souness (Cap), Robert Sime Aitken, David Cooper, Kenneth Mathieson Dalglish (72 Graeme Marshall Sharp), Francis McAvennie.   Manager: Alexander Ferguson.
AUSTRALIA: Terry Greedy, Charlie Yankos, Alan Davidson, David Ratcliffe, Steve O'Connor (82 Robbie Dunn), Graham Jennings, Joe Watson (65 Jimmy Patikas), Ken Murphy, Oscar Crino, David Mitchell, John Kosmina.   Trainer: Frank Arok.

Goals: David Cooper (58), Francis McAvennie (60)

480. 04.12.1985   13th World Cup Qualifier Play-off
AUSTRALIA v SCOTLAND 0-0
Olympic Park, Melbourne
Referee: José Roberto Ramiz Wright (Brazil)   Att: 29,500
AUSTRALIA: Terry Greedy, Charlie Yankos, Alan Davidson, David Ratcliffe, Robbie Dunn (75 Frank Farina), Graham Jennings, Jimmy Patikas, Oscar Crino (68 Zarko Odzakov), Ken Murphy, John Kosmina, David Mitchell.
Trainer: Frank Arok.
SCOTLAND: James Leighton, Richard Charles Gough, Maurice Daniel Robert Malpas, William Fergus Miller, Alexander McLeish, Robert Sime Aitken, Graeme James Souness (Cap), Paul Michael Lyons McStay, David Cooper, David Robert Speedie (76 Graeme Marshall Sharp), Francis McAvennie.   Manager: Alexander Ferguson.

481. 28.01.1986
ISRAEL v SCOTLAND 0-1 (0-0)
National, Ramat-Gan, Tel-Aviv
Referee: Albert Rudolf Thomas (Holland)   Att: 7,000
ISRAEL: Avi Ran, Eitan Aharoni, Menashe Shimonov, Avi Cohen I (Rafi Osmo), Zion Marili, Uri Malmilian, Rifat Turk (Eyal Begleivter), Efraim Davidi, Moti Ivanir (Eli Cohen), Zahi Armeli, Eli Ohana (Roni Rosenthal).
Trainer: Yosef Mirmovich.
SCOTLAND: James Leighton, Richard Charles Gough, Maurice Daniel Robert Malpas, David Narey, William Fergus Miller (Cap), Robert Sime Aitken, James Bett, Paul Michael Lyons McStay, Eamonn John Peter Bannon, Graeme Marshall Sharp (68 Paul Whitehead Sturrock), Charles Nicholas.
Manager: Alexander Ferguson.

Goal: Paul Michael Lyons McStay (57)

482. 26.03.1986
SCOTLAND v ROMANIA 3-0 (2-0)
Hampden Park, Glasgow
Referee: Volker Roth (West Germany)   Attendance: 53,589
SCOTLAND: Andrew Lewis Goram, Richard Charles Gough, Maurice Daniel Robert Malpas, David Narey, William Fergus Miller (60 Alan David Hansen), Gordon David Strachan (72 Patrick Kevin Francis Michael Nevin), Robert Sime Aitken, Graeme James Souness, Eamonn John Peter Bannon, Kenneth Mathieson Dalglish (Cap), Graeme Marshall Sharp (46 Charles Nicholas).   Manager: Alexander Ferguson.
ROMANIA: Silviu Lung, Mircea Rednic, Gino Iorgulescu (Cap) (46 Alexandru Nicolae), Lică Movilă, Nicolae Ungureanu, Dorin Mateuț, Ioan Andone (75 Niță Cireașă), Michael Klein, Gheorghe Hagi, Marcel Coraș (70 Romulus Gabor), Rodion Gorun Cămătaru.   Trainer: Mircea Lucescu.

Goals: Gordon David Strachan (18), Richard Gough (27), Robert Sime Aitken (81)

483. 23.04.1986   Stanley Rous Cup
ENGLAND v SCOTLAND 2-1 (2-0)
Wembley, London
Referee: Michel Vautrot (France)   Attendance: 68,357
ENGLAND: Peter Leslie Shilton, Gary Michael Stevens, Kenneth Graham Sansom, Glenn Hoddle, David Watson, Terence Ian Butcher, Raymond Colin Wilkins (Cap) (46 Peter Reid), Trevor John Francis, Mark Wayne Hateley, Stephen Brian Hodge (75 Gary Andrew Stevens), Christopher Roland Waddle.   Manager: Robert William Robson.
SCOTLAND: Alan Roderick Rough, Richard Charles Gough, Maurice Daniel Robert Malpas, William Fergus Miller, Alexander McLeish, Stephen Nicol, Robert Sime Aitken, Graeme James Souness (Cap), Eamonn John Peter Bannon, David Robert Speedie, Charles Nicholas (58 Patrick Kevin Francis Michael Nevin).   Manager: Alexander Ferguson.

Goals: Terence Ian Butcher (27), Glenn Hoddle (39) / Graeme James Souness (57 pen)

484. 29.04.1986
HOLLAND v SCOTLAND 0-0
Philips, Eindhoven
Referee: Helmut Kohl (Austria)   Attendance: 14,500
HOLLAND: Johannes Franciscus van Breukelen (Cap), Dirk Franciscus Blind, Jan Jacobus Silooy, Ronald Koeman, Adrianus Andreas van Tiggelen, Jan Jacobus Wouters, Gerald Mervin Vanenburg, Machiel Valke (72 Wilbert Suvrijn), Johannes Nicolaas van't Schip, Johannes Jacobus Bosman, Robert Leonardus de Wit.   Trainer: Leo Beenhakker.
SCOTLAND: Andrew Lewis Goram, Maurice Daniel Robert Malpas, Arthur Richard Albiston, David Narey, Alexander McLeish, William Fergus Miller (Cap), James Bett, Robert Connor, David Cooper, Alistair Murdoch McCoist, Paul Whitehead Sturrock.   Manager: Alexander Ferguson.

485. 04.06.1986   13th World Cup, 1st Round
DENMARK v SCOTLAND 1-0 (0-0)
Neza, Nezahualcoyotl
Referee: Lajos Németh (Hungary)   Attendance: 18,000
DENMARK: Troels Rasmussen, Søren Busk, Morten Olsen (Cap), Ivan Nielsen, Klaus Berggreen, Frank Arnesen (75 John Sivebæk), Jens Jørn Bertelsen, Søren Lerby, Jesper Olsen (83 Jan Mølby), Michael Laudrup, Preben Elkjær-Larsen.
Trainer: Josef Piontek (West Germany).
SCOTLAND: James Leighton, Richard Charles Gough, Maurice Daniel Robert Malpas, William Fergus Miller, Alexander McLeish, Gordon David Strachan (74 Eamonn John Peter Bannon), Robert Sime Aitken, Graeme James Souness (Cap), Stephen Nicol, Paul Whitehead Sturrock (61 Francis McAvennie), Charles Nicholas.
Manager: Alexander Ferguson.

Goal: Preben Elkjær-Larsen (57)

486. 08.06.1986   13th World Cup, 1st Round
WEST GERMANY v SCOTLAND 2-1 (1-1)
Corregidora, Querétaro
Referee: Ioan Igna (Romania)   Attendance: 30,000
GERMANY: Harald Schumacher (Cap), Thomas Berthold, Klaus Augenthaler, Karlheinz Förster, Hans-Peter Briegel (61 Ditmar Jakobs), Norbert Eder, Lothar Herbert Matthäus, Felix Magath, Pierre Littbarski (75 Karl-Heinz Rummenigge), Rudolf Völler, Klaus Allofs.   Trainer: Franz Beckenbauer.
SCOTLAND: James Leighton, Richard Charles Gough, Maurice Daniel Robert Malpas, David Narey, William Fergus Miller, Gordon David Strachan, Robert Sime Aitken, Graeme James Souness (Cap), Stephen Nicol (59 Francis McAvennie), Eamonn John Peter Bannon (74 David Cooper), Steven Archibald.   Manager: Alexander Ferguson.
Goals: Rudolf Völler (22), Klaus Allofs (50) / Gordon David Strachan (18)

487. 13.06.1986   13th World Cup, 1st Round
URUGUAY v SCOTLAND   0-0
Neza, Nezahualcoyotl
Referee: Joël Quiniou (France)   Attendance: 20,000
URUGUAY: Fernando Harry Alvez, Víctor Hugo Diogo, Eduardo Mario Acevedo, Nelson Daniel Gutiérrez, José Alberto Batista, Alfonso Darío Pereyra, Jorge Walter Barrios (Cap), Sérgio Rodolfo Santín, Enzo Francéscoli (84 Antonio Alzamendi), Venancio Ariel Ramos (71 Mario Daniel Saralegui), Wilmar Rubens Cabrera.   Trainer: Omar Borrás.
SCOTLAND: James Leighton, Richard Charles Gough, Arthur Richard Albiston, David Narey, William Fergus Miller (Cap), Gordon David Strachan, Robert Sime Aitken, Paul Michael Lyons McStay, Stephen Nicol (70 David Cooper), Paul Whitehead Sturrock (70 Charles Nicholas), Graeme Marshall Sharp.   Manager: Alexander Ferguson.

488. 10.09.1986   8th European Champs Qualifiers
SCOTLAND v BULGARIA 0-0
Hampden Park, Glasgow
Referee: Erik Frederiksson (Sweden)   Attendance: 35,076
SCOTLAND: James Leighton, Richard Charles Gough, Maurice Daniel Robert Malpas, David Narey, William Fergus Miller (Cap), Gordon David Strachan, Robert Sime Aitken, Paul Michael Lyons McStay, David Cooper, Maurice Johnston, Charles Nicholas (53 Kenneth Mathieson Dalglish).   Manager: Andrew Roxburgh.
BULGARIA: Borislav Mihailov, Plamen Nikolov, Georgi Dimitrov (Cap), Nikolai Iliev, Petar Petrov, Hristo Kolev, Nasko Sirakov, Plamen Simeonov (78 Georgi Karushev), Anio Sadkov, Petar Aleksandrov (87 Lachezar Tanev), Ilia Voinov.   Trainer: Hristo Mladenov.

489. 15.10.1986   8th European Champs Qualifiers
REPUBLIC OF IRELAND v SCOTLAND   0-0
Lansdowne Road, Dublin
Referee: Einar Halle (Norway)   Attendance: 48,000
REPUBLIC OF IRELAND: Patrick Bonner, David Francis Langan, James Martin Beglin, Michael Joseph McCarthy, Kevin Bernard Moran (71 Gerard Anthony Daly), William Brady, Raymond James Houghton, Paul McGrath, Francis Anthony Stapleton (Cap), John William Aldridge, Kevin Mark Sheedy.   Trainer: John Charlton (England).
SCOTLAND: James Leighton, Richard Charles Gough, Raymond Strean McDonald Stewart, David Narey, Alan David Hansen, Gordon David Strachan, Robert Sime Aitken (Cap), Paul Michael Lyons McStay, Murdo Davidson MacLeod, Graeme Marshall Sharp, Maurice Johnston.   Manager: Andrew Roxburgh.

490. 12.11.1986   8th European Champs Qualifiers
SCOTLAND v LUXEMBOURG 3-0 (2-0)
Hampden Park, Glasgow
Referee: Eysteinn Guðmundsson (Iceland)   Att: 35,078
SCOTLAND: James Leighton, Raymond Strean McDonald Stewart, Murdo Davidson MacLeod (64 Alistair Murdoch McCoist), Alan David Hansen (46 Paul Michael Lyons McStay), Richard Charles Gough, Patrick Kevin Francis Michael Nevin, Robert Sime Aitken (Cap), Brian John McClair, David Cooper, Kenneth Mathieson Dalglish, Maurice Johnston.   Manager: Andrew Roxburgh.
LUXEMBOURG: John van Rijswijck, Marcel Bossi, Gianni Di Pentima, Hubert Meunier, Laurent Schonckert, Guy Hellers, Carlo Weis, Jean-Pierre Barboni, Théo Scholten (89 Jeff Saibene), Théo Malget (79 Gérard Jeitz), Robert Langers.   Trainer: Paul Philipp.
Goals: David Cooper (24 pen, 38), Maurice Johnston (70)

491. 18.02.1987   8th European Champs Qualifiers
SCOTLAND v REPUBLIC OF IRELAND 0-1 (0-1)
Hampden Park, Glasgow
Referee: Henrik van Ettekoven (Holland)   Att: 45,081
SCOTLAND: James Leighton, Raymond Strean McDonald Stewart, Maurice Daniel Robert Malpas (67 Alistair Murdoch McCoist), Alan David Hansen, Richard Charles Gough, Patrick Kevin Francis Michael Nevin, Gordon David Strachan, Robert Sime Aitken (Cap), David Cooper (46 Paul Michael Lyons McStay), Brian John McClair, Maurice Johnston.   Manager: Andrew Roxburgh.
REPUBLIC OF IRELAND: Patrick Bonner, Paul McGrath, Michael Joseph McCarthy, Kevin Bernard Moran, Ronald Andrew Whelan, Raymond James Houghton, Mark Thomas Lawrenson, William Brady (60 John Frederick Byrne), Francis Anthony Stapleton (Cap), John William Aldridge, Anthony Galvin.   Trainer: John Charlton (England).
Goal: Mark Thomas Lawrenson (8)

492. 01.04.1987   8th European Champs Qualifiers
BELGIUM v SCOTLAND 4-1 (1-1)
Parc Astrid, Bruxelles
Referee: Michel Vautrot (France)   Attendance: 26,650
BELGIUM: Jean-Marie Pfaff, Georges Grün, Stéphane Demol, Léo Albert Clijsters, Patrick Vervoort, Vincenzo Scifo (73 Léo Vander Elst), Frank Richard Vander Elst (89 Guy Vandersmissens), Frank Vercauteren, Philippe De Smet, Erwin Vandenbergh, Nicolaas Pieter Claesen.   Trainer: Guy Thys.
SCOTLAND: James Leighton, Richard Charles Gough, Maurice Daniel Robert Malpas, David Narey, Alexander McLeish, James Edward McInally, Paul Michael Lyons McStay, Robert Sime Aitken (Cap), James Bett (80 Patrick Kevin Francis Michael Nevin), Paul Whitehead Sturrock, Alistair Murdoch McCoist.   Manager: Andrew Roxburgh.
Goals: Nicolaas Claesen (9, 55, 86), Frank Vercauteren (75) / Paul Michael Lyons McStay (14)

493. 23.05.1987   Stanley Rous Cup
SCOTLAND v ENGLAND 0-0
Hampden Park, Glasgow
Referee: Dieter Pauly (West Germany)   Attendance: 64,713
SCOTLAND: James Leighton, Richard Charles Gough, Murdo Davidson MacLeod, William Fergus Miller, Alexander McLeish, Paul Michael Lyons McStay, Neil Simpson, Robert Sime Aitken (Cap), Ian William Wilson, Brian John McClair (58 Charles Nicholas), Alistair Murdoch McCoist.   Manager: Andrew Roxburgh.
ENGLAND: Christopher Charles Eric Woods, Gary Michael Stevens, Stuart Pearce, Glenn Hoddle, Mark Wright, Terence Ian Butcher, Bryan Robson (Cap), Stephen Brian Hodge, Mark Wayne Hateley, Peter Andrew Beardsley, Christopher Roland Waddle.   Manager: Robert William Robson.

494. 26.05.1987   Stanley Rous Cup
SCOTLAND v BRAZIL 0-2 (0-0)
Hampden Park, Glasgow
Referee: Luigi Agnolin (Italy)   Attendance: 41,384
SCOTLAND: Andrew Lewis Goram, Richard Charles Gough, Murdo Davidson MacLeod, William Fergus Miller, Alexander McLeish, Paul Michael Lyons McStay, James Edward McInally (59 Brian John McClair), Robert Sime Aitken (Cap), Ian William Wilson, David Cooper, Alistair Murdoch McCoist.   Manager: Andrew Roxburgh.
BRAZIL: Carlos Roberto Gallo, Josimar Higino Pereira, Geraldo Dutra Pereira "Geraldão", Ricardo Roberto Barreto da Rocha "Ricardo Rocha", Nélson Luís Kerschner "Nelsinho", William Douglas Humia Menezes, Raí Souza Vieira de Oliveira, Carlos Eduardo Marangon "Edu Marangon", Luís Antônio Corrêa da Costa "Müller", Francisco Ernândi Lima da Silva "Mirandinha II", Valdo Cândido Filho "Valdo II".   Trainer: Carlos Alberto Silva.
Goals: Raí Souza Vieira de Oliveira (50), "Valdo II" (60)

495. 09.09.1987
SCOTLAND v HUNGARY 2-0 (1-0)
Hampden Park, Glasgow
Referee: Johannes Nicolaas Ignatius "Jan" Keizer (Holland)   Attendance: 21,128
SCOTLAND: James Leighton, Stephen Clarke, Stephen Nicol, William Fergus Miller, Richard Charles Gough, Gordon David Strachan, Paul Michael Lyons McStay (77 James Bett), Robert Sime Aitken (Cap), Iain Durrant, Alistair Murdoch McCoist, Maurice Johnston (71 Eric Black).   Manager: Andrew Roxburgh.
HUNGARY: Péter Disztl, József Csuhay, Árpád Toma, Zoltán Péter, Imre Garaba, Sándor Sallai, György Bognár, József Keller, Ferenc Mészáros, Kálmán Kovács (87 Ferenc Lovász), Gyula Hajszán.   Trainer: József Garami.
Goals: Alistair Murdoch McCoist (34, 62)

496. 14.10.1987   8th European Champs Qualifiers
SCOTLAND v BELGIUM 2-0 (1-0)
Hampden Park, Glasgow
Referee: Paolo Casarin (Italy)   Attendance: 20,052
SCOTLAND: James Leighton, Stephen Clarke, Maurice Daniel Robert Malpas (53 Derek Whyte), Gary Thompson Gillespie, Alexander McLeish, Paul Michael Lyons McStay, Robert Sime Aitken (Cap), Iain Durrant, Ian William Wilson, Alistair Murdoch McCoist, Maurice Johnston (72 Graeme Marshall Sharp).   Manager: Andrew Roxburgh.
BELGIUM: Michel Preud'homme, Eric Gerets, Georges Grün, Léo Albert Clijsters, Patrick Vervoort, Luc Beyens (55 Philippe De Smet), Jan Ceulemans, Frank Richard Vander Elst, Marc Degryse, Frank Vercauteren, Nicolaas Pieter Claesen.   Trainer: Guy Thys.
Goals: Alistair McCoist (14), Paul Michael Lyons McStay (79)

497. 11.11.1987   8th European Champs Qualifiers
BULGARIA v SCOTLAND 0-1 (0-0)
"Vasil Levski", Sofia
Referee: Helmut Kohl (Austria)   Attendance: 49,976
BULGARIA: Borislav Mihailov, Plamen Nikolov, Krasimir Bezinski, Nikolai Iliev, Petar Petrov, Anio Sadkov, Hristo Stoichkov, Plamen Simeonov (87 Liuboslav Penev), Nasko Sirakov (Cap), Petar Aleksandrov (44 Ilia Voinov), Bojidar Iskrenov.   Trainer: Hristo Mladenov.
SCOTLAND: James Leighton, Stephen Clarke, Maurice Daniel Robert Malpas, Gary Thompson Gillespie, Alexander McLeish, Stephen Nicol, Paul Michael Lyons McStay (57 Gary MacKay), Robert Sime Aitken (Cap), Ian William Wilson, Brian John McClair, Graeme Marshall Sharp (71 Gordon Scott Durie).   Manager: Andrew Roxburgh.
Goal: Gary MacKay (87)

498. 02.12.1987   8th European Champs Qualifiers
LUXEMBOURG v SCOTLAND 0-0
Stade de la Frontière, Esch-sur-Alzette
Referee: Manfred Neuner (West Germany)   Att: 2,515
LUXEMBOURG: John van Rijswijck, Hubert Meunier, Marcel Bossi, Carlo Weis, Pierre Petry, Jean-Paul Girres (87 Jeff Saibene), Gérard Jeitz, Jean-Pierre Barboni, Théo Scholten, Robert Langers, Jeannot Reiter (54 Armin Krings).   Trainer: Paul Philipp.
SCOTLAND: James Leighton, Derek Whyte (60 Gary MacKay), Maurice Daniel Robert Malpas, William Fergus Miller, Alexander McLeish (Cap), Patrick Kevin Francis Michael Nevin (60 Eric Black), Paul Michael Lyons McStay, Robert Sime Aitken, Ian William Wilson, Graeme Marshall Sharp, Maurice Johnston.   Manager: Andrew Roxburgh.

499. 17.02.1988
SAUDI ARABIA v SCOTLAND 2-2 (1-0)
"King Fahd" Stadium, Riyadh
Referee: Abdullah Al Nasir (Saudi Arabia)   Att: 35,000
SAUDI ARABIA: Abdullah Al Deayea, Zaki Al Saleh, Ahmed Jamil Madani, Saleh Al Nuaymah, Mohammed Abdul Jawad, Fahd Al Bishi, Bassam Abu Daoud, Khalid Al Muwallid, Youssef Jazaa, Majid Abdullah Mohammed, Hathal Al Dossary (Saad Moubarak).   Trainer: Carlos Alberto Parreira (Brazil).
SCOTLAND: James Leighton (46 Henry George Smith), Stephen Clarke, Maurice Daniel Robert Malpas, William Fergus Miller (46 Alexander McLeish), Richard Charles Gough, Stephen Nicol (46 John Mark Colquhoun), Paul Michael Lyons McStay (63 Gary MacKay), Robert Sime Aitken (Cap), John Angus Paul Collins, Francis McAvennie (81 Robert Connor), Maurice Johnston.   Manager: Andrew Roxburgh.
Goals: Youssef Jazaa (16), Majid Abdullah Mohammed (71) / Maurice Johnston (47), John Angus Paul Collins (49)

500. 22.03.1988
MALTA v SCOTLAND 1-1 (0-1)
National, Ta'Qali
Referee: George Courtney (England)   Attendance: 3,470
MALTA: David Cluett, Edwin Camilleri, Alex Azzopardi, Joseph Brincat, Martin Scicluna, John Buttigieg, Carmel Busuttil, Raymond Vella (Cap), David Carabott, Charles Micallef II (10 Charles Scerri), Michael Degiorgio.   Trainer: Horst Heese (West Germany).
SCOTLAND: James Leighton, Stephen Clarke, Maurice Daniel Robert Malpas, William Fergus Miller, Alexander McLeish, Gary MacKay (55 James Edward McInally), Derek Ferguson, Robert Sime Aitken (Cap), Iain Durrant (75 John Mark Colquhoun), Graeme Marshall Sharp, Alistair Murdoch McCoist (51 Brian John McClair).   Manager: Andrew Roxburgh.
Goals: Carmel Busuttil (55) / Graeme Marshall Sharp (21)

501. 27.04.1988
SPAIN v SCOTLAND 0-0
"Santiago Bernabéu", Madrid
Referee: Carlos Da Silva Valente (Portugal)   Att: 15,000
SPAIN: Andoni Zubizarreta Urreta, Pedro Tomás Reñones Grego, Miguel Soler Sarasols, Manuel Sanchís Hontiyuello, Víctor Muñoz Manrique, Rafael Gordillo Vázquez (Cap), José Miguel González Martín del Campo "Michel", Ricardo Gallego Redondo (46 Miguel Tendillo Belenguer), Rafael Martín Vázquez, Julio Salinas Fernández (78 Eloy José Olaya Prendes), Emilio Butragueño Santos.   Trainer: Miguel Muñoz Mozún.
SCOTLAND: James Leighton, Richard Charles Gough, Stephen Nicol, William Fergus Miller, Alexander McLeish, Gary Thompson Gillespie, Paul Michael Lyons McStay, Robert Sime Aitken (Cap), Iain Durrant, Alistair Murdoch McCoist (69 Brian John McClair), Maurice Johnston.   Manager: Andrew Roxburgh.

502. 17.05.1988   Stanley Rous Cup
SCOTLAND v COLOMBIA 0-0
Hampden Park, Glasgow
Referee: João Martins Pinto Correia (Portugal)   Att: 20,487
SCOTLAND: James Leighton, Richard Charles Gough, Stephen Nicol, William Fergus Miller, Alexander McLeish, Murdo Davidson MacLeod, Paul Michael Lyons McStay, Robert Sime Aitken (Cap), Kevin William Gallacher (67 Andrew Francis Walker), Alistair Murdoch McCoist (59 Derek Ferguson), Maurice Johnston.   Manager: Andrew Roxburgh.
COLOMBIA: José René Higuita, Luis Fernando Herrera, Luis Carlos Perea, Andrés Escobar, Carlos Mario Hoyos, Bernardo Redín, Leonel de Jesús Álvarez, Alexis Enrique García, Carlos Alberto Valderrama (Cap), Arnoldo Alberto Iguarán, John Jairo Tréllez (68 Jaime Arango).
Trainer: Francisco Maturana.

503. 21.05.1988   Stanley Rous Cup
ENGLAND v SCOTLAND 1-0 (1-0)

Wembley, London

Referee: Joël Quiniou (France)   Attendance: 70,480

ENGLAND: Peter Leslie Shilton, Gary Michael Stevens, Kenneth Graham Sansom, Neil John Webb, David Watson, Anthony Alexander Adams, Bryan Robson (Cap), Trevor McGregor Steven (72 Christopher Roland Waddle), Peter Andrew Beardsley, Gary Winston Lineker, John Charles Bryan Barnes.   Manager: Robert William Robson.

SCOTLAND: James Leighton, Richard Charles Gough, Stephen Nicol, William Fergus Miller, Alexander McLeish, Murdo Davidson MacLeod, Neil Simpson (74 Thomas Burns), Paul Michael Lyons McStay, Robert Sime Aitken (Cap), Alistair Murdoch McCoist (77 Kevin William Gallacher), Maurice Johnston.   Manager: Andrew Roxburgh.

Goal: Peter Andrew Beardsley (11)

504. 14.09.1988   14th World Cup Qualifiers
NORWAY v SCOTLAND 1-2 (1-1)

Ullevaal, Oslo

Referee: Luigi Agnolin (Italy)   Attendance: 22,769

NORWAY: Erik Thorstvedt, Hans Hermann Henriksen, Erland Johnsen, Rune Bratseth, Anders Giske, Kjetil Osvold, Sverre Brandhaug, Karl Petter Løken, Gøran Sørloth, Tom Sundby (2 Ørjan Berg (84 Jahn Ivar Jakobsen)), Jan Åge Fjørtoft.   Trainer: Ingvar Stadheim.

SCOTLAND: James Leighton, Stephen Nicol, Maurice Daniel Robert Malpas, William Fergus Miller, Alexander McLeish, Gary Thompson Gillespie, Paul Michael Lyons McStay, Robert Sime Aitken (Cap) (55 Iain Durrant), Brian John McClair, Kevin William Gallacher, Maurice Johnston.   Manager: Andrew Roxburgh.

Goals: Jan Åge Fjørtoft (44) / Paul Michael Lyons McStay (14), Maurice Johnston (63)

505. 19.10.1988   14th World Cup Qualifiers
SCOTLAND v YUGOSLAVIA 1-1 (1-1)

Hampden Park, Glasgow

Referee: Karl-Heinz Tritschler (West Germany)   Att: 42,771

SCOTLAND: Andrew Lewis Goram, Richard Charles Gough, Maurice Daniel Robert Malpas, William Fergus Miller (Cap), Alexander McLeish, Stephen Nicol, Paul Michael Lyons McStay, Robert Sime Aitken (70 David Robert Speedie), James Bett (55 Alistair Murdoch McCoist), Brian John McClair, Maurice Johnston.   Manager: Andrew Roxburgh.

YUGOSLAVIA: Tomislav Ivković, Vujadin Stanojković, Predrag Spasić (83 Dragoljub Brnović), Davor Jozić, Faruk Hadžibegić, Ljubomir Radanović, Dragan Stojković, Srećko Katanec, Borislav Cvetković (89 Refik Šabanadžović), Mehmet Baždarević, Zlatko Vujović (Cap).   Trainer: Ivan Osim.

Goals: Maurice Johnston (19) / Srećko Katanec (37)

506. 22.12.1988
ITALY v SCOTLAND 2-0 (0-0)

Renato Curi, Perugia

Referee: Alain Delmer (France)   Attendance: 20,660

ITALY: Walter Zenga (50 Stefano Tacconi), Giuseppe Bergomi (Cap) (50 Ciro Ferrara), Paolo Maldini, Franco Baresi II, Riccardo Ferri II, Giancarlo Marocchi, Massimo Crippa, Nicola Berti, Gianluca Vialli, Giuseppe Giannini, Aldo Serena.   Trainer: Azeglio Vicini.

SCOTLAND: Andrew Lewis Goram, Richard Charles Gough (87 David Robert Speedie), Maurice Daniel Robert Malpas, David Narey, Alexander McLeish, Murdo Davidson MacLeod, Paul Michael Lyons McStay (56 Brian John McClair), Robert Sime Aitken (Cap), Ian Ferguson (71 Gordon Scott Durie), Kevin William Gallacher, Maurice Johnston.   Manager: Andrew Roxburgh.

Goals: Giuseppe Giannini (48 pen), Nicola Berti (70)

507. 08.02.1989   14th World Cup Qualifiers
CYPRUS v SCOTLAND 2-3 (1-1)

Tsirion, Limassol

Referee: Siegfried Kirschen (East Germany)   Att: 25,000

CYPRUS: Georgios Pantziaras, Charalambos Pittas, Costas Miamiliotis (77 Antonis E. Andrellis), Georgios Christodoulou, Avraam Socratous, Yiannakis Yiangoudakis, Christos Koliantris, Pavlos Savva (39 Costas Petsas), Georgios Savvides, Yiannos Ioannou, Floros Nicolaou.   Trainer: Panikos Iacovou.

SCOTLAND: James Leighton, Richard Charles Gough, Maurice Daniel Robert Malpas, David Narey, Alexander McLeish, Stephen Nicol (10 Ian Ferguson), Paul Michael Lyons McStay, Robert Sime Aitken (Cap), Brian John McClair, David Robert Speedie (78 Alan Bruce McInally), Maurice Johnston.   Manager: Andrew Roxburgh.

Goals: Christos Koliantris (15), Yiannos Ioannou (48) / Maurice Johnston (9), Richard Charles Gough (54, 90)

508. 08.03.1989   14th World Cup Qualifiers
SCOTLAND v FRANCE 2-0 (1-0)

Hampden Park, Glasgow

Referee: Jiří Stiegler (Czechoslovakia)   Attendance: 65,204

SCOTLAND: James Leighton, Richard Charles Gough, Maurice Daniel Robert Malpas, Gary Thompson Gillespie, Alexander McLeish (Cap), Stephen Nicol, Paul Michael Lyons McStay, Robert Sime Aitken, Ian Ferguson (56 Gordon David Strachan), Alistair Murdoch McCoist (69 Brian John McClair), Maurice Johnston.   Manager: Andrew Roxburgh.

FRANCE: Joël Bats, Manuel Amoros (Cap), Frank Silvestre, Luc Sonor, Patrick Battiston, Frank Sauzée, Jean-Philippe Durand (57 Stéphane Paille), Thierry Laurey, Jean-Pierre Papin, Laurent Blanc, Daniel Xuereb (73 Christian Perez).   Trainer: Michel Platini.

Goals: Maurice Johnston (28, 52)

509. 26.04.1989   14th World Cup Qualifiers
SCOTLAND v CYPRUS 2-1 (1-0)
Hampden Park, Glasgow

Referee: Guðmundur Haraldsson (Iceland)   Att: 50,081

SCOTLAND: James Leighton, Richard Charles Gough, Maurice Daniel Robert Malpas, David McPherson, Alexander McLeish, Patrick Kevin Francis Michael Nevin (74 Charles Nicholas), Paul Michael Lyons McStay, Robert Sime Aitken (Cap), Gordon Scott Durie (59 David Robert Speedie), Alistair Murdoch McCoist, Maurice Johnston.
Manager: Andrew Roxburgh.

CYPRUS: Andros Charitou, Spyros Kastanas, Charalambos Pittas (80 Antonis E. Andrellis), Georgios Christodoulou, Avraam Socratous, Yiannakis Yiangoudakis, Costas Petsas, Floros Nicolaou, Georgios Savvides, Yiannos Ioannou, Christos Koliantris.   Trainer: Panikos Iacovou.

Goals: Maurice Johnston (26), Alistair McCoist (63) / Floros Nicolaou (62)

510. 27.05.1989   Stanley Rous Cup
SCOTLAND v ENGLAND 0-2 (0-1)
Hampden Park, Glasgow

Referee: Michel Vautrot (France)   Attendance: 63,282

SCOTLAND: James Leighton, Stewart McKimmie, Maurice Daniel Robert Malpas, David McPherson, Alexander McLeish, Patrick Kevin Francis Michael Nevin, Paul Michael Lyons McStay, Robert Sime Aitken (Cap), Robert Connor (57 Peter Grant), Alistair Murdoch McCoist, Maurice Johnston.
Manager: Andrew Roxburgh.

ENGLAND: Peter Leslie Shilton, Gary Michael Stevens, Desmond Sinclair Walker, Terence Ian Butcher, Stuart Pearce, Trevor McGregor Steven, Neil John Webb, Bryan Robson (Cap), Christopher Roland Waddle, John Fashanu (31 Stephen George Bull), Anthony Richard Cottee (75 Paul John Gascoigne).   Manager: Robert William Robson.

Goals: Christopher Waddle (20), Stephen George Bull (80)

511. 30.05.1989   Stanley Rous Cup
SCOTLAND v CHILE 2-0 (1-0)
Hampden Park, Glasgow

Referee: Alexis Ponnet (Belgium)   Attendance: 9,006

SCOTLAND: James Leighton (Cap), Stewart McKimmie, Maurice Daniel Robert Malpas, Gary Thompson Gillespie (70 Derek Whyte), Alexander McLeish, Peter Grant, Paul Michael Lyons McStay, Robert Sime Aitken, Murdo Davidson MacLeod, David Robert Speedie (46 Maurice Johnston), Alan Bruce McInally.   Manager: Andrew Roxburgh.

CHILE: Roberto Antonio Rojas, Leonel Contreras, Oscar Patricio Reyes, Hugo Armando González, Héctor Eduardo Puebla, Jaime Andrés Vera, Alejandro Manuel Hisis Araya, Jaime Augusto Pizarro, Juvenal Olmos (65 Jaime Patricio Ramírez), Hugo Eduardo Rubio, Juan Covarrubias (46 Juan Carlos Letelier Pizarro).   Trainer: Orlando Aravena.

Goals: Alan McInally (4), Murdo Davidson MacLeod (52)

512. 06.09.1989   14th World Cup Qualifiers
YUGOSLAVIA v SCOTLAND 3-1 (0-1)
Maksimir, Zagreb

Referee: Marcel Van Langenhove (Belgium)   Att: 42,500

YUGOSLAVIA: Tomislav Ivković, Predrag Spasić, Mirsad Baljić, Srećko Katanec, Faruk Hadžibegić, Dragoljub Brnović, Safet Sušić, Mehmet Baždarević, Dragan Jakovljević (74 Dejan Savićević), Dragan Stojković, Zlatko Vujović (Cap).
Trainer: Ivan Osim.

SCOTLAND: James Leighton, Stephen Nicol, Maurice Daniel Robert Malpas, William Fergus Miller, Alexander McLeish, Gary Thompson Gillespie, Paul Michael Lyons McStay, Robert Sime Aitken (Cap), Murdo Davidson MacLeod, Gordon Scott Durie (71 Alan Bruce McInally), Alistair Murdoch McCoist).
Manager: Andrew Roxburgh.

Goals: Srećko Katanec (54), Stephen Nicol (57 own goal), Gary Gillespie (59 own goal) / Gordon Scott Durie (37)

513. 11.10.1989   14th World Cup Qualifiers
FRANCE v SCOTLAND 3-0 (1-0)
Parc des Princes, Paris

Referee: Kurt Röthlisberger (Switzerland)   Att: 25,000

FRANCE: Joël Bats (Cap), Frank Silvestre, Yvon Le Roux (46 Bernard Casoni), Frank Sauzée, Eric Di Meco, Bernard Pardo, Didier Deschamps, Jean-Philippe Durand, Jean-Marc Ferreri, Christian Perez (81 Daniel Bravo), Eric Cantona.
Trainer: Michel Platini.

SCOTLAND: James Leighton, Stephen Nicol, Maurice Daniel Robert Malpas, Richard Charles Gough, Alexander McLeish, Gordon David Strachan (64 Alan Bruce McInally), Paul Michael Lyons McStay, Robert Sime Aitken (Cap), Murdo Davidson MacLeod (75 James Bett), Alistair Murdoch McCoist, Maurice Johnston).   Manager: Andrew Roxburgh.

Sent off: Eric Di Meco (57)

Goals: Didier Deschamps (26), Eric Cantona (63), Stephen Nicol (88 own goal)

514. 15.11.1989   14th World Cup Qualifiers
SCOTLAND v NORWAY 1-1 (1-0)
Hampden Park, Glasgow

Referee: Michał Listkiewicz (Poland)   Attendance: 63,987

SCOTLAND: James Leighton, David McPherson, Maurice Daniel Robert Malpas, William Fergus Miller (67 Murdo Davidson MacLeod), Alexander McLeish, James Bett, Paul Michael Lyons McStay, Robert Sime Aitken (Cap), David Cooper (74 Brian John McClair), Alistair Murdoch McCoist, Maurice Johnston).   Manager: Andrew Roxburgh.

NORWAY: Erik Thorstvedt, Hugo Hansen, Rune Bratseth, Terje Kojedal (82 Jan Halvor Halvorsen), Erland Johnsen, Stig Inge Bjørnebye, Tom Gulbrandsen, Per Egil Ahlsen, Bent Skammelsrud (58 Lars Bohinen), Gøran Sørloth, Jan Åge Fjørtoft.   Trainer: Ingvar Stadheim.

Goals: Alistair Murdoch McCoist (44) / Erland Johnsen (89)

515. 28.03.1990

SCOTLAND v ARGENTINA 1-0 (1-0)

Hampden Park, Glasgow

Referee: Frans Houben (Holland)   Attendance: 51,537

SCOTLAND: James Leighton, Richard Charles Gough, Stewart McKimmie, Craig William Levein, Alexander McLeish (Cap), James Bett (89 Robert Sime Aitken), Stuart Murray McCall, Paul Michael Lyons McStay, Murdo Davidson MacLeod, Robert Fleck, Alan Bruce McInally (74 Brian John McClair).   Manager: Andrew Roxburgh.

ARGENTINA: Nery Alberto Pumpido (Cap), Edgardo Bauza, Roberto Néstor Sensini, Néstor Ariel Fabbri, Oscar Alfredo Ruggeri (60 Pedro Damián Monzón), Sergio Daniel Batista, Gabriel Humberto Calderón, José Horacio Basualdo, Jorge Luis Burruchaga (49 Pedro Antonio Troglio), Jorge Alberto Francisco Valdano (46 Abel Eduardo Balbo), Claudio Paul Caniggia.   Trainer: Dr. Carlos Salvador Bilardo.

Goal: Stewart McKimmie (32)

516. 25.04.1990

SCOTLAND v EAST GERMANY 0-1 (0-0)

Hampden Park, Glasgow

Referee: Neil Midgley (England)   Attendance: 21,868

SCOTLAND: Andrew Lewis Goram, Richard Charles Gough, Gary Thompson Gillespie (57 Paul Michael Lyons McStay), Craig William Levein, Alexander McLeish (Cap), Murdo Davidson MacLeod, Gary McAllister, Stuart Murray McCall, John Angus Paul Collins, Gordon Scott Durie (68 Alistair Murdoch McCoist), Maurice Johnston.   Manager: Andrew Roxburgh.

EAST GERMANY: Perry Bräutigam, Heiko Peschke, Stefan Böger, Hendrik Herzog, Matthias Lindner, Dirk Schuster, Matthias Sammer, Jörg Stübner (85 Steffen Büttner), Rainer Ernst, Ulf Kirsten, Thomas Doll.   Trainer: Eduard Geyer.

Goal: Thomas Doll (73 pen)

517. 16.05.1990

SCOTLAND v EGYPT 1-3 (0-2)

Pittodrie, Aberdeen

Referee: Rune Pedersen (Norway)   Attendance: 23,000

SCOTLAND: Bryan James Gunn, Stewart McKimmie (45 Stuart Murray McCall), Maurice Daniel Robert Malpas, Richard Charles Gough, Alexander McLeish (Cap) (89 Craig William Levein), James Bett, Gary Thompson Gillespie, Paul Michael Lyons McStay, David Cooper, Gordon Scott Durie, Alistair Murdoch McCoist.   Manager: Andrew Roxburgh.

EGYPT: Ahmed Shobair, Ibrahim Hassan Hussein, Hany Guda Ramzy, Hesham Yakan Zaki, Rabie Yassin, Ahmed Megahid Ramzy, Ahmed Abdou El-Kass (46 Tarek Soliman), Ismail Awadallah Youssef, Magdi Abdelghani (60 Alaa Mayhoub), Gamal Abdelhamid, Hossam Ahmad Omar Hussein "Hossam Hassan".   Trainer: Mahmoud El-Gohary.

Goals: Alistair Murdoch McCoist (73) / Gamal Abdelhamid (15), Hossam Ahmad Omar Hussein "Hossam Hassan" (28), Ismail Awadallah Youssef (83)

518. 19.05.1990

SCOTLAND v POLAND 1-1 (1-0)

Hampden Park, Glasgow

Referee: Joseph Bertram Worrall (England)   Att: 25,142

SCOTLAND: Andrew Lewis Goram, Gary Thompson Gillespie, Maurice Daniel Robert Malpas, Craig William Levein, Richard Charles Gough, Murdo Davidson MacLeod (65 John Angus Paul Collins), Robert Sime Aitken (Cap), Stuart Murray McCall, Gary McAllister (83 Paul Michael Lyons McStay), Alistair Murdoch McCoist, Maurice Johnston (73 Alan Bruce McInally).   Manager: Andrew Roxburgh.

POLAND: Jarosław Bako, Dariusz Kubicki, Zbigniew Kaczmarek (Cap), Damian Łukasik (46 Piotr Soczyński), Dariusz Wdowczyk, Waldemar Prusik, Piotr Czachowski, Janusz Nawrocki (70 Leszek Pisz), Jacek Ziober, Dariusz Dziekanowski, Roman Kosecki.   Trainer: Andrzej Strejlau.

Goals: Maurice Johnston (42) / Gary Thompson Gillespie (59 own goal)

519. 28.05.1990

MALTA v SCOTLAND 1-2 (1-1)

National, Ta'Qali

Referee: Carlo Longhi (Italy)   Attendance: 3,938

MALTA: Reginald Cini, Silvio Vella, David Carabott, Joseph Galea (46 Edwin Camilleri), Kristian Laferla, John Buttigieg, Jesmond Zerafa, Raymond Vella (Cap), Martin Gregory (62 Joseph Zarb), Michael Degiorgio, Bernard Licari (77 Charles Scerri).   Trainer: Horst Heese (West Germany).

SCOTLAND: Andrew Lewis Goram (46 James Leighton), David McPherson, Maurice Daniel Robert Malpas, Gary Thompson Gillespie (40 Craig William Levein), Richard Charles Gough, James Bett (46 Gary McAllister), Paul Michael Lyons McStay (80 John Angus Paul Collins), Robert Sime Aitken (Cap), Stuart Murray McCall, Alan Bruce McInally, Maurice Johnston (69 Alistair Murdoch McCoist).   Manager: Andrew Roxburgh.

Goals: Michael Degiorgio (42) / Alan Bruce McInally (5, 81)

520. 11.06.1990   14th World Cup, 1st Round
COSTA RICA v SCOTLAND 1-0 (0-0)

"Luigi Ferraris", Genova

Referee: Juan Carlos Loustau (Argentina)   Att: 30,867

COSTA RICA: Luis Gabelo Conejo Jiménez, Germán José Chavarría Jiménez, Héctor Marchena, Mauricio Montero Chinchilla, Róger Flores Solano (Cap), José Carlos Chaves, Juan Arnaldo Cayasso Reid, Róger Gómez Tenorio, Rónald González Brenes, Claudio Miguel Jara (86 Hernán Evaristo Medford Bryan), Oscar Ramírez Hernández.
Trainer: Bora Milutinović (Yugoslavia).

SCOTLAND: James Leighton, David McPherson, Maurice Daniel Robert Malpas, Richard Charles Gough (46 Stewart McKimmie), Alexander McLeish, James Bett (74 Alistair Murdoch McCoist), Paul Michael Lyons McStay, Robert Sime Aitken (Cap), Stuart Murray McCall, Alan Bruce McInally, Maurice Johnston.   Manager: Andrew Roxburgh.

Goals: Juan Arnaldo Cayasso Reid (49)

521. 16.06.1990   14th World Cup, 1st Round
SCOTLAND v SWEDEN 2-1 (1-0)

"Luigi Ferraris", Genova

Referee: Carlos Alberto Maciel (Paraguay)   Att: 31,823

SCOTLAND: James Leighton, David McPherson, Maurice Daniel Robert Malpas, Craig William Levein, Alexander McLeish, Murdo Davidson MacLeod, Robert Sime Aitken (Cap), Stuart Murray McCall, Gordon Scott Durie (74 Paul Michael Lyons McStay), Robert Fleck (84 Alistair Murdoch McCoist), Maurice Johnston.   Manager: Andrew Roxburgh.

SWEDEN: Thomas Ravelli, Roland Nilsson, Glenn Ingvar Hysén, Peter Larsson (74 Glenn Peter Strömberg), Stefan Schwarz, Klas Ingesson, Jonas Thern, Joakim Nilsson, Anders Erik Limpár, Tomas Brolin, Stefan Pettersson (65 Johnny Ekström).   Trainer: Olle Nordin.

Goals: Stuart McCall (10), Maurice Johnstone (81 pen) / Glenn Peter Strömberg (85)

522. 20.06.1990   14th World Cup, 1st Round
BRAZIL v SCOTLAND 1-0 (0-0)

Delle Alpi, Torino

Referee: Helmut Kohl (Austria)   Attendance: 62,502

BRAZIL: Cláudio André Mergen Taffarel, Jorge de Amorim Campos "Jorginho", Ricardo Roberto Barreto da Rocha "Ricardo Rocha", Mauro Geraldo Galvão, Ricardo Gomes Raymundo (Cap), Ricardo Rogério de Brito "Alemão", Carlos Caetano Bledorn Verri "Dunga", Valdo Cândido Filho "Valdo II", Cláudio Ibrahim Vaz Leal "Branco", Romário de Souza Faria (64 Luís Antônio Corrêa da Costa "Müller"), Antônio de Oliveira Filho "Careca I".   Trainer: Sebastião Lazaroni.

SCOTLAND: James Leighton, Stewart McKimmie, Maurice Daniel Robert Malpas, David McPherson, Alexander McLeish, Murdo Davidson MacLeod (39 Gary Thompson Gillespie), Paul Michael Lyons McStay, Robert Sime Aitken (Cap), Stuart Murray McCall, Alistair Murdoch McCoist (77 Robert Fleck), Maurice Johnston.   Manager: Andrew Roxburgh.

Goal: Luís Antônio Corrêa da Costa "Müller" (81)

523. 12.09.1990   9th European Champs Qualifiers
SCOTLAND v ROMANIA 2-1 (1-1)

Hampden Park, Glasgow

Referee: Ildefonso Urizar Aspitarte (Spain)   Att: 12,801

SCOTLAND: Andrew Lewis Goram, Stewart McKimmie, Maurice Daniel Robert Malpas, Brian Irvine, Alexander McLeish, Murdo Davidson MacLeod, Paul Michael Lyons McStay (Cap), Gary McAllister (73 Patrick Kevin Francis Michael Nevin), Robert Connor (59 Thomas Boyd), John Grant Robertson, Alistair Murdoch McCoist.   Manager: Andrew Roxburgh.

ROMANIA: Silviu Lung (Cap), Dan Petrescu, Emilian Săndoi, Gheorghe Popescu, Michael Klein, Ionuț Angelo Lupescu, Dorin Mateuț (70 Ioan Ovidiu Sabău), Gheorghe Hagi, Iosif Rotariu, Marius Lăcătuș, Rodion Gorun Cămătaru (62 Florin Răducioiu).   Trainer: Gheorghe Constantin.

Goals: John Robertson (37), Alistair Murdoch McCoist (75) / Rodion Gorun Cămătaru (14)

524. 17.10.1990   9th European Champs Qualifiers
SCOTLAND v SWITZERLAND 2-1 (1-0)

Hampden Park, Glasgow

Referee: Esa Palsi (Finland)   Attendance: 27,740

SCOTLAND: Andrew Lewis Goram, Stewart McKimmie, Stephen Nicol, David McPherson, Alexander McLeish (Cap), Murdo Davidson MacLeod, Gary McAllister (79 John Angus Paul Collins), Stuart Murray McCall, Thomas Boyd (68 Gordon Scott Durie), John Grant Robertson, Alistair Murdoch McCoist.   Manager: Andrew Roxburgh.

SWITZERLAND: Philipp Walker, André Egli, Dominique Herr, Peter Schepull (62 Frédéric Chassot), Blaise Piffaretti (80 Beat Sutter), Thomas Bickel, Heinz Hermann, Alain Sutter, Adrian Knup, Kubilay Türkyilmaz, Stéphane Chapuisat.   Trainer: Ulrich Stielike (Germany).

Sent off: André Egli (90)

Goals: John Grant Robertson (34 pen), Gary McAllister (51) / Adrian Knup (64 pen)

525. 14.11.1990   9th European Champs Qualifiers
BULGARIA v SCOTLAND 1-1 (0-1)
"Vasil Levski", Sofia
Referee: Friedrich Kaupe (Austria)   Attendance: 42,000
BULGARIA: Borislav Mihailov, Pavel Dochev, Dimitar Mladenov, Zlatko Yankov, Kalin Bankov, Kostadin Yanchev (55 Nikolai Todorov), Georgi Iordanov, Hristo Stoichkov, Liuboslav Penev, Nasko Sirakov, Krasimir Balakov (73 Emil Kostadinov).   Trainer: Ivan Vutsov.
SCOTLAND: Andrew Lewis Goram, Stewart McKimmie, Maurice Daniel Robert Malpas (Cap), David McPherson, Gary Thompson Gillespie, James Edward McInally, Gary McAllister, Brian John McClair, Thomas Boyd, Gordon Scott Durie (59 Patrick Kevin Francis Michael Nevin), Alistair Murdoch McCoist.   Manager: Andrew Roxburgh.
Goals: Nikolai Todorov (71) / Alistair Murdoch McCoist (9)

526. 06.02.1991
SCOTLAND v SOVIET UNION 0-1 (0-0)
Ibrox Park, Glasgow
Referee: Peter Mikkelsen (Denmark)   Attendance: 20,673
SCOTLAND: Andrew Lewis Goram, Stephen Nicol, Maurice Daniel Robert Malpas, Richard Charles Gough (Cap), Alexander McLeish (46 David McPherson), Gordon David Strachan, Paul Michael Lyons McStay, Stuart Murray McCall (69 Gary McAllister), Thomas Boyd (46 Murdo Davidson MacLeod), Robert Fleck (75 Gordon Scott Durie), Alistair Murdoch McCoist.   Manager: Andrew Roxburgh.
SOVIET UNION: Aleksandr Uvarov, Andrey Chernyshev, Vasiliy Kulkov, Akhrik Tzveyba, Sergey Gorlukovich, Igor Shalimov, Sergey Aleynikov, Andrey Kanchelskis, Aleksandr Mostovoi (69 Dmitriy Kuznetzov), Sergey Yuran (62 Igor Kolyvanov), Igor Dobrovolskiy.   Trainer: Anatoliy Byshovetz.
Goal: Dmitriy Kuznetzov (88)

527. 27.03.1991   9th European Champs Qualifiers
SCOTLAND v BULGARIA 1-1 (0-0)
Hampden Park, Glasgow
Referee: Erik Fredriksson (Sweden)   Attendance: 33,119
SCOTLAND: Andrew Lewis Goram, David McPherson, Maurice Daniel Robert Malpas, Richard Charles Gough, Alexander McLeish (Cap), Gordon David Strachan (80 John Angus Paul Collins), James Edward McInally, Paul Michael Lyons McStay, Brian John McClair, Gordon Scott Durie (80 John Grant Robertson), Alistair Murdoch McCoist.   Manager: Andrew Roxburgh.
BULGARIA: Borislav Mihailov, Pavel Dochev, Trifon Ivanov, Ilian Kiriakov, Nikolai Iliev, Zlatko Yankov, Emil Kostadinov, Nasko Sirakov (87 Petar Aleksandrov), Liuboslav Penev, Georgi Iordanov, Krasimir Balakov (87 Lachezar Tanev).   Trainer: Ivan Vutsov.
Goals: John Angus Paul Collins (83) / Emil Kostadinov (89)

528. 01.05.1991   9th European Champs Qualifiers
SAN MARINO v SCOTLAND 0-2 (0-0)
Olimpico, Serravalle
Referee: Besnik Kaimi (Albania)   Attendance: 3,512
SAN MARINO: Pier Luigi Benedettini, Claudio Canti, Bruno Muccioli, Paolo Daniele Zanotti (62 Ivano Toccaceli), Luca Gobbi, William Guerra, Massimo Ceccoli, Marco Mazza, Paolo Mazza, Fabio Giulio Francini, Waldes Pasolini (78 Ivan Matteoni).   Trainer: Giorgio Leoni.
SCOTLAND: Andrew Lewis Goram, Stewart McKimmie, Maurice Daniel Robert Malpas, Stephen Nicol (74 John Grant Robertson), David McPherson, Gordon David Strachan (Cap), Gary McAllister, Stuart Murray McCall, Brian John McClair (57 Patrick Kevin Francis Michael Nevin), Kevin William Gallacher, Gordon Scott Durie.   Manager: Andrew Roxburgh.
Goals: Gordon Strachan (63 pen), Gordon Scott Durie (66)

529. 11.09.1991   9th European Champs Qualifiers
SWITZERLAND v SCOTLAND 2-2 (2-0)
Wankdorf, Bern
Referee: Tullio Lanese (Italy)   Attendance: 48,000
SWITZERLAND: Stefan Huber, Marc Hottiger, Dominique Herr, Ciriaco Sforza, Christophe Ohrel, Marcel Heldmann (67 Beat Sutter), Heinz Hermann, Alain Sutter (60 Thomas Bickel), Adrian Knup, Kubilay Türkyilmaz, Stéphane Chapuisat.   Trainer: Ulrich Stielike (Germany).
SCOTLAND: Andrew Lewis Goram, Stewart McKimmie (70 Brian John McClair), Maurice Daniel Robert Malpas, Stephen Nicol, David McPherson, Gordon David Strachan (Cap), Stuart Murray McCall, Thomas Boyd, Maurice Johnston (43 Gary McAllister), Gordon Scott Durie, Alistair Murdoch McCoist.   Manager: Andrew Roxburgh.
Goals: Stéphane Chapuisat (30), Heinz Hermann (39) / Gordon Scott Durie (47), Alistair Murdoch McCoist (83)

530. 16.10.1991   9th European Champs Qualifiers
ROMANIA v SCOTLAND 1-0 (0-0)
Steaua, Bucureşti
Referee: Aron Schmidhuber (Germany)   Att: 30,000
ROMANIA: Silviu Lung, Dan Petrescu, Emilian Săndoi, Gheorghe Popescu, Michael Klein, Dorinel Ionel Munteanu, Daniel Timofte (60 Ion Timofte), Gheorghe Hagi (Cap), Ionuţ Angelo Lupescu, Marius Lăcătuş, Florin Răducioiu (75 Ilie Dumitrescu).   Trainer: Mircea Rădulescu.
SCOTLAND: Andrew Lewis Goram, Stewart McKimmie, Maurice Daniel Robert Malpas, David McPherson, Craig William Levein, Gordon David Strachan (Cap), Stuart Murray McCall, Michael Galloway (70 Robert Sime Aitken), Thomas Boyd (58 Kevin William Gallacher), Brian John McClair, Gordon Scott Durie.   Manager: Andrew Roxburgh.
Goal: Gheorghe Hagi (75 pen)

531. 13.11.1991   9th European Champs Qualifiers
SCOTLAND v SAN MARINO 4-0 (3-0)

Hampden Park, Glasgow

Referee: Rune Pedersen (Norway)   Attendance: 35,170

SCOTLAND: Andrew Lewis Goram, David McPherson (46 Maurice Johnston), Maurice Daniel Robert Malpas, Craig William Levein (60 Kevin William Gallacher), Richard Charles Gough (Cap), Paul Michael Lyons McStay, Gary McAllister, Stuart Murray McCall, John Grant Robertson, Gordon Scott Durie, Alistair Murdoch McCoist.
Manager: Andrew Roxburgh.

SAN MARINO: Pier Luigi Benedettini, Claudio Canti, Bruno Muccioli, Marco Mazza, Luca Gobbi (46 Marco Montironi), William Guerra, Loris Zanotti, Massimo Bonini, Paolo Mazza, Fabio Giulio Francini, Waldes Pasolini (66 Pierangelo Manzaroli).   Trainer: Giorgio Leoni.

Goals: Paul Michael Lyons McStay (10), Richard Gough (31), Gordon Scott Durie (37), Alistair Murdoch McCoist (62)

532. 19.02.1992
SCOTLAND v NORTHERN IRELAND 1-0 (1-0)

Hampden Park, Glasgow

Referee: Joseph Bertram Worrall (England)   Att: 13,651

SCOTLAND: Henry George Smith, Stewart McKimmie (46 Gordon Scott Durie), David Robertson, David McPherson, Richard Charles Gough, Gordon David Strachan (Cap), Gary McAllister, Brian John McClair (70 John Angus Paul Collins), Maurice Daniel Robert Malpas, Keith Wright (78 John Grant Robertson), Alistair Murdoch McCoist (46 Kevin William Gallacher).   Manager: Andrew Roxburgh.

NORTHERN IRELAND: Thomas James Wright, Malachy Martin Donaghy, Nigel Worthington, Gerald Paul Taggart (84 Stephen Joseph Morrow), Alan McDonald (Cap), James Magilton, Kingsley Terence Black, Kevin James Wilson (81 Michael Andrew Martin O'Neill), Colin John Clarke (46 Iain Dowie), Daniel Joseph Wilson, Michael Eamonn Hughes.
Manager: William Laurence Bingham.

Goal: Alistair Murdoch McCoist (11)

533. 25.03.1992
SCOTLAND v FINLAND 1-1 (1-1)

Hampden Park, Glasgow

Referee: Anders Frisk (Sweden)   Attendance: 9,275

SCOTLAND: Andrew Lewis Goram, Stewart McKimmie, Maurice Daniel Robert Malpas, Thomas Boyd, David McPherson, Gordon David Strachan (Cap) (65 Gary McAllister), David Bowman, Paul Michael Lyons McStay, John Angus Paul Collins, John Grant Robertson (54 Alistair Murdoch McCoist), Gordon Scott Durie.
Manager: Andrew Roxburgh.

FINLAND: Olavi Huttunen, Jari Rinne (87 Harri Nyyssönen), Ari Heikkinen, Erkka Petäjä, Anders Eriksson, Ilkka Remes, Jari Litmanen, Marko Myyry, Petri Järvinen, Kimmo Tarkkio (69 Jari Vanhala), Mika-Matti Paatelainen.
Trainer: Jukka Vakkila.

Goals: Paul Michael Lyons McStay (24) / Jari Litmanen (41)

534. 17.05.1992
UNITED STATES v SCOTLAND 0-1 (0-1)

High Mile, Denver

Referee: Juan Pablo Escobar López (Guatemala)
Attendance: 24,157

UNITED STATES: Kasey Keller, Desmond Armstrong, Marcelo Luis Balboa, John Joseph Doyle, Fernando Clavijo, Janusz Michallik (70 Zak Ibsen), Brian Quinn, Christopher Joel Henderson, Hugo Pérez, Dominic Kinnear (Cap), Eric Wynalda.   Trainer: Velibor Milutinović (Yugoslavia).

SCOTLAND: Gordon Banks Marshall, Stewart McKimmie, Maurice Daniel Robert Malpas, David McPherson (82 Derek Whyte), Alan McLaren, Gary McAllister, Paul Michael Lyons McStay (Cap) (68 James Edward McInally), Stuart Murray McCall, Patrick Kevin Francis Michael Nevin (50 Duncan Ferguson), Brian John McClair, Alistair Murdoch McCoist (76 David Bowman).   Manager: Andrew Roxburgh.

Goal: Patrick Kevin Francis Michael Nevin (7)

535. 20.05.1992
CANADA v SCOTLAND 1-3 (1-1)

Varsity, Toronto

Referee: Helder Dias (United States)   Attendance: 10,872

CANADA: Craig Forrest, Frank Yallop, Colin Fyfe Miller, Peter Sarantopoulos, Randolph Fitzgerald Samuel, Nick Robert Dasovic, Carl Valentine, John Limniatis (59 Nick Gilbert), Norman Odinga (59 Lyndon Hooper), John Catliff (78 Geoffrey Aunger), Domenic Mobilio (46 Alexander Bunbury).   Trainer: Robert Lenarduzzi.

SCOTLAND: Henry George Smith, David McPherson, Thomas Boyd, Richard Charles Gough (Cap), Alan McLaren, Gary McAllister, Paul Michael Lyons McStay, Stuart Murray McCall (90 Stewart McKimmie), Gordon Scott Durie (78 Maurice Daniel Robert Malpas), Duncan Ferguson (54 Brian John McClair), Alistair Murdoch McCoist.
Manager: Andrew Roxburgh.

Goals: John Catliff (43) /
Gary McAllister (23, 85 pen), Alistair Murdoch McCoist (65)

536. 03.06.1992
NORWAY v SCOTLAND 0-0
Ullevaal, Oslo

Referee: Anders Frisk (Sweden)   Attendance: 8,786

NORWAY: Frode Grodås, Roger Nilsen, Rune Bratseth, Henning Berg, Stig Inge Bjørnebye, Øyvind Leonhardsen, Lars Bohinen (75 Kåre Ingebrigtsen), Jan Ove Pedersen (28 Erik Mykland), Kjetil Rekdal, Tore André Dahlum (72 Jostein Flo), Frank Strandli.   Trainer: Egil Roger Olsen.

SCOTLAND: Andrew Lewis Goram, David McPherson, Maurice Daniel Robert Malpas (Cap) (68 Stewart McKimmie), Richard Charles Gough, Alan McLaren, Gary McAllister (78 James Edward McInally), Paul Michael Lyons McStay, Stuart Murray McCall, Thomas Boyd, Brian John McClair (46 Gordon Scott Durie), Alistair Murdoch McCoist (46 Kevin William Gallacher).   Manager: Andrew Roxburgh.

537. 12.06.1992   9th European Champs, 1st Round
HOLLAND v SCOTLAND 1-0 (0-0)
Nya Ullevi, Göteborg

Referee: Bo Karlsson (Sweden)   Attendance: 35,720

HOLLAND: Johannes Franciscus van Breukelen, Hubertus Aegidius Hermanus van Aerle, Ronald Koeman, Adrianus Andreas van Tiggelen, Ruud Gullit (Cap), Jan Jacobus Wouters (55 Wilhelmus Maria Jonk), Franklin Edmundo Rijkaard, Robert Witschge, Bryan Eduard Steven Roy, Dennis Nicolaas Maria Bergkamp (86 Aron Mohammed Winter), Marcelo van Basten.   Trainer: Marinus Henrikus Bernardus Michels.

SCOTLAND: Andrew Lewis Goram, Stewart McKimmie, Maurice Daniel Robert Malpas, David McPherson, Richard Charles Gough (Cap), Gary McAllister, Paul Michael Lyons McStay, Stuart Murray McCall, Brian John McClair (79 Duncan Ferguson), Gordon Scott Durie, Alistair Murdoch McCoist (73 Kevin William Gallacher).   Manager: Andrew Roxburgh.

Goal: Dennis Nicolaas Maria Bergkamp (77)

538. 15.06.1992   9th European Champs, 1st Round
GERMANY v SCOTLAND 2-0 (1-0)
Idrottsparken, Norrköping

Referee: Guy Goethals (Belgium)   Attendance: 17,800

GERMANY: Bodo Illgner, Manfred Binz, Jürgen Kohler, Guido Buchwald, Thomas Häßler, Stefan Effenberg, Matthias Sammer, Andreas Möller, Andreas Brehme (Cap), Jürgen Klinsmann, Karlheinz Riedle (68 Stefan Reuter (75 Michael Schulz)).   Trainer: Hans-Hubert Vogts.

SCOTLAND: Andrew Lewis Goram, Stewart McKimmie, Maurice Daniel Robert Malpas, David McPherson, Richard Charles Gough (Cap), Gary McAllister, Paul Michael Lyons McStay, Stuart Murray McCall, Brian John McClair, Gordon Scott Durie (54 Patrick Kevin Francis Michael Nevin), Alistair Murdoch McCoist (70 Kevin William Gallacher).   Manager: Andrew Roxburgh.

Goals: Karlheinz Riedle (29), Stefan Effenberg (47)

539. 18.06.1992   9th European Champs, 1st Round
SCOTLAND v C.I.S. 3-0 (2-0)
Idrottsparken, Norrköping

Referee: Kurt Röthlisberger (Switzerland)   Att: 14,660

SCOTLAND: Andrew Lewis Goram, Stewart McKimmie, Thomas Boyd, David McPherson, Richard Charles Gough (Cap), Gary McAllister, Paul Michael Lyons McStay, Stuart Murray McCall, Brian John McClair, Kevin William Gallacher (78 Patrick Kevin Francis Michael Nevin), Alistair Murdoch McCoist (67 James Edward McInally).   Manager: Andrew Roxburgh.

C.I.S.: Dmitriy Kharin, Andrey Chernyshev, Kakhaber Tskhadadze, Viktor Onopko, Oleg Kuznetzov, Sergey Aleynikov (46 Dmitriy Kuznetzov), Andrey Kanchelskis, Aleksey Mikhaylichenko, Sergey Yuran, Sergey Kiryakov (46 Igor Korneev), Igor Dobrovolskiy.   Trainer: Anatoliy Byshovetz.

Goals: Paul Michael Lyons McStay (6), Brian McClair (16), Gary McAllister (83 pen)

540. 09.09.1992   15th World Cup Qualifiers
SWITZERLAND v SCOTLAND 3-1 (1-1)
Wankdorf, Bern

Referee: Mario van der Ende (Holland)   Attendance: 10,000

SWITZERLAND: Marco Pascolo, Marc Hottiger, André Egli, Alain Geiger, Yvan Quentin, Ciriaco Sforza, Georges Brégy (86 Blaise Piffaretti), Christophe Ohrel, Alain Sutter, Adrian Knup (87 Beat Sutter), Stéphane Chapuisat.   Trainer: Roy Hodgson (England).

SCOTLAND: Andrew Lewis Goram, Thomas Boyd (75 Kevin William Gallacher), Maurice Daniel Robert Malpas, David McPherson, Richard Charles Gough (Cap), Gary McAllister, Paul Michael Lyons McStay, Stuart Murray McCall, Brian John McClair (57 Iain Durrant), Gordon Scott Durie, Alistair Murdoch McCoist.   Manager: Andrew Roxburgh.

Sent off: Richard Charles Gough (84)

Goals: Adrian Knup (2, 71), Georges Brégy (81) / Alistair Murdoch McCoist (13)

541. 14.10.1992   15th World Cup Qualifiers
SCOTLAND v PORTUGAL 0-0

Ibrox Park, Glasgow

Referee: Hubert Forstinger (Austria)   Attendance: 22,583

SCOTLAND: Andrew Lewis Goram, Thomas Boyd, Maurice Daniel Robert Malpas, Craig William Levein, Derek Whyte, Gary McAllister, Paul Michael Lyons McStay (Cap), Stuart Murray McCall, John Angus Paul Collins (72 Iain Durrant), Kevin William Gallacher (33 Brian John McClair), Alistair Murdoch McCoist.   Manager: Andrew Roxburgh.

PORTUGAL: Vítor Manuel Martins Baía, João Domingos Silva Pinto (Cap), Hélder Marino Rodrigues Cristóvão, Fernando Manuel Silva Couto, António Augusto da Silva Veloso, Vítor Manuel da Costa Araújo "Paneira", Oceano Andrade da Cruz, António dos Santos Ferreira André, José Orlando Vinha Rocha Semedo (52 Luis Filipe Madeira Caeiro "Figo"), Paulo Jorge dos Santos Futre, Domingos José Paciência Oliveira.   Trainer: Carlos Queiroz.

542. 18.11.1992   15th World Cup Qualifiers
SCOTLAND v ITALY 0-0

Ibrox Park, Glasgow

Referee: Aron Schmidhuber (Germany)   Att: 33,029

SCOTLAND: Andrew Lewis Goram, David McPherson, Maurice Daniel Robert Malpas, Alan McLaren, Derek Whyte, Gary McAllister, Paul Michael Lyons McStay (Cap), Iain Durrant (86 John Grant Robertson), Thomas Boyd, Gordon Scott Durie (71 Eoin Jess), Alistair Murdoch McCoist.   Manager: Andrew Roxburgh.

ITALY: Gianluca Pagliuca, Moreno Mannini, Alberto Di Chiara II (10 Alessandro Costacurta), Alessandro Bianchi, Paolo Maldini, Franco Baresi II (Cap), Stefano Eranio, Demetrio Albertini, Giuseppe Signori (66 Roberto Donadoni), Roberto Baggio I, Gianluigi Lentini.   Trainer: Arrigo Sacchi.

543. 17.02.1993   15th World Cup Qualifiers
SCOTLAND v MALTA 3-0 (1-0)

Ibrox Park, Glasgow

Referee: Ilkka Koho (Finland)   Attendance: 35,490

SCOTLAND: Andrew Lewis Goram, David McPherson (64 John Grant Robertson), Thomas Boyd, Alan McLaren, Alexander McLeish (Cap), Patrick Kevin Francis Michael Nevin, Gary McAllister (72 Ian Ferguson), Paul Michael Lyons McStay, John Angus Paul Collins, Eoin Jess, Alistair Murdoch McCoist.   Manager: Andrew Roxburgh.

MALTA: David Cluett, Silvio Vella, Joseph Galea, Joseph Brincat, John Buttigieg, Richard Buhagiar (84 Edwin Camilleri), Kristian Laferla, Joseph Camilleri, Nicholas Saliba, Stefan Sultana (75 Raymond Vella), Carmel Busuttil (Cap).   Trainer: Philip Psaila.

Goals: Alistair Murdoch McCoist (15, 68), Patrick Kevin Francis Michael Nevin (84)

544. 24.03.1993
SCOTLAND v GERMANY 0-1 (0-1)

Hampden Park, Glasgow

Referee: Leon Schelings (Belgium)   Attendance: 36,400

SCOTLAND: Joseph Nicholas Walker, Stephen Wright (63 Scott Booth), Thomas Boyd, Craig William Levein (Cap), Brian Irvine, Alan McLaren, James Edward McInally, David Bowman, John Angus Paul Collins, John Grant Robertson, Duncan Ferguson.   Manager: Andrew Roxburgh.

GERMANY: Andreas Köpke, Olaf Thon, Guido Buchwald, Jürgen Kohler, Thomas Häßler, Michael Zorc, Lothar Herbert Matthäus (Cap) (88 Matthias Sammer), Thomas Helmer, Thomas Doll (60 Stefan Effenberg), Jürgen Klinsmann, Karlheinz Riedle.   Trainer: Hans-Hubert Vogts.

Goal: Karlheinz Riedle (20)

545. 28.04.1993   15th World Cup Qualifiers
PORTUGAL v SCOTLAND 5-0 (2-0)

da Luz, Lisboa

Referee: Sándor Puhl (Hungary)   Attendance: 28,000

PORTUGAL: Vítor Manuel Martins Baía, Abel Luís Silva Costa Xavier, Fernando Manuel Silva Couto, Jorge Paulo Costa Almeida, José Orlando Vinha Rocha Semedo, Oceano Andrade da Cruz, Rui Gil Soares Barros, Paulo Manuel Carvalho de Sousa, Rui Manuel César Costa (62 António Augusto da Silva Veloso), Paulo Jorge dos Santos Futre (Cap), Jorge Paulo Cadete Santos Reis (80 Domingos José Paciência Oliveira).   Trainer: Carlos Manuel Brito Leal Queiroz.

SCOTLAND: Andrew Lewis Goram, Stewart McKimmie, James Edward McInally, Richard Charles Gough (Cap), David McPherson, Craig William Levein (59 Patrick Kevin Francis Michael Nevin), Paul Michael Lyons McStay, Stuart Murray McCall, John Angus Paul Collins (75 Iain Durrant), Kevin William Gallacher, Alistair Murdoch McCoist.   Manager: Andrew Roxburgh.

Goals: Rui Gil Soares Barros (5, 69), Jorge Paulo Cadete Santos Reis (42, 71), Paulo Jorge dos Santos Futre (66)

546. 19.05.1993   15th World Cup Qualifiers
ESTONIA v SCOTLAND 0-3 (0-1)

Kadriorg, Tallinn

Referee: Tore Hollung (Norway)   Attendance: 5,100

ESTONIA: Mart Poom, Urmas Kaljend, Risto Kallaste, Joanus Veensalu (76 Aleksander Pustov), Marek Lemsalu, Igor Prins, Toomas Kallaste, Marko Kristal (46 Urmas Hepner), Andrei Borisov, Sergei Bragin, Martin Reim.   Trainer: Uno Piir.

SCOTLAND: Bryan James Gunn, Stephen Wright (80 Alan McLaren), Thomas Boyd, Brian Irvine, Edward Colin James Hendry, David Bowman, Paul Michael Lyons McStay (Cap), Brian John McClair, John Angus Paul Collins, John Grant Robertson (61 Scott Booth), Kevin William Gallacher.   Manager: Andrew Roxburgh.

Goals: Kevin Gallacher (43), John Angus Paul Collins (59), Scott Booth (73)

547. 02.06.1993   15th World Cup Qualifiers
SCOTLAND v ESTONIA 3-1 (2-0)

Pittodrie, Aberdeen

Referee: Atanas Uzunov (Bulgaria)   Attendance: 14,309

SCOTLAND: Bryan James Gunn, Alan McLaren (71 Stewart McKimmie), Thomas Boyd, Brian Irvine, Edward Colin James Hendry, Patrick Kevin Francis Michael Nevin, Paul Michael Lyons McStay (Cap), Ian Ferguson (55 Scott Booth), John Angus Paul Collins, Brian John McClair, Kevin William Gallacher.   Manager: Andrew Roxburgh.

ESTONIA: Mart Poom, Urmas Kaljend, Risto Kallaste, Marek Lemsalu (46 Sergei Bragin), Igor Prins, Toomas Kallaste, Marko Kristal, Indro Olumets (73 Joanus Veensalu), Andrei Borisov, Martin Reim, Lembit Rajala.   Trainer: Uno Piir.

Goals: Brian John McClair (18), Patrick Kevin Francis Michael Nevin (27, 72 pen) / Sergei Bragin (57)

548. 08.09.1993   15th World Cup Qualifiers
SCOTLAND v SWITZERLAND 1-1 (0-0)

Pittodrie, Aberdeen

Referee: Joël Quiniou (France)   Attendance: 21,500

SCOTLAND: Bryan James Gunn, Stewart McKimmie, David Robertson, Brian Irvine, Craig William Levein, Patrick Kevin Francis Michael Nevin, David Bowman (75 Philip O'Donnell), Gary McAllister (Cap), John Angus Paul Collins, Scott Booth (70 Eoin Jess), Gordon Scott Durie.   Manager: Andrew Roxburgh.

SWITZERLAND: Marco Pascolo, Régis Rothenbühler (55 Marco Grassi), Dominique Herr, Alain Geiger, Yvan Quentin, Christophe Ohrel, Georges Brégy (70 Martin Rueda), Ciriaco Sforza, Alain Sutter, Adrian Knup, Stéphane Chapuisat.   Trainer: Roy Hodgson (England).

Goals: John Angus Paul Collins (50) / Georges Brégy (69 pen)

549. 13.10.1993   15th World Cup Qualifiers
ITALY v SCOTLAND 3-1 (2-1)

Olimpico, Roma

Referee: Ion Crăciunescu (Romania)   Attendance: 61,178

ITALY: Gianluca Pagliuca, Roberto Mussi (68 Marco Lanna), Antonio Benarrivo, Dino Baggio, Alessandro Costacurta, Franco Baresi II (Cap), Stefano Eranio, Roberto Donadoni, Pier Luigi Casiraghi, Roberto Baggio I, Giovanni Stroppa (90 Gianfranco Zola).   Trainer: Arrigo Sacchi.

SCOTLAND: Bryan James Gunn, Stewart McKimmie, Thomas Boyd, Brian Irvine, Alan McLaren, David Bowman (70 Paul Michael Lyons McStay), Gary McAllister (Cap), Stuart Murray McCall, Gordon Scott Durie, Eoin Jess (46 Iain Durrant), Kevin William Gallacher.   Manager: Andrew Roxburgh.

Goals: Roberto Donadoni (3), Pier Luigi Casiraghi (16), Stefano Eranio (80) / Kevin William Gallacher (18)

550. 17.11.1993   15th World Cup Qualifiers
MALTA v SCOTLAND 0-2 (0-1)

National, Ta'Qali

Referee: Periklis Vassilakis (Greece)   Attendance: 8,900

MALTA: David Cluett, Silvio Vella, Joseph Galea, Joseph Brincat, Richard Buhagiar (46 Nicholas Saliba), John Buttigieg, Michael Spiteri, Kristian Laferla, Carmel Busuttil (Cap), Martin Gregory, Hubert Suda (75 Charles Scerri).   Trainer: Pietro Ghedin (Italy).

SCOTLAND: James Leighton, Alan McLaren, Robert McKinnon, Brian Irvine, Edward Colin James Hendry, Gary McAllister (Cap), Ian Ferguson, William McKinlay (46 Scott Booth), Iain Durrant (74 Thomas Boyd), Patrick Kevin Francis Michael Nevin, Kevin William Gallacher.   Manager: Craig Brown.

Goals: William McKinlay (15), Colin Hendry (74)

551. 23.03.1994
SCOTLAND v HOLLAND 0-1 (0-1)

Hampden Park, Glasgow

Referee: Kim Milton Nielsen (Denmark)   Att: 36,809

SCOTLAND: Andrew Lewis Goram, Stewart McKimmie, David Robertson (65 John Angus Paul Collins), Alan McLaren, Edward Colin James Hendry, Craig William Levein (46 Thomas Boyd), Gary McAllister (Cap), Paul Michael Lyons McStay (46 William McKinlay), Stuart Murray McCall), Patrick Kevin Francis Michael Nevin (67 Eoin Jess), Gordon Scott Durie.   Manager: Craig Brown.

HOLLAND: Eduard Franciscus de Goey, Ulrich van Gobbel, Dirk Franciscus Blind, Franciscus de Boer, Franklin Edmundo Rijkaard (Cap), Wilhelmus Maria Jonk, Robert Witschge, Dennis Nicolaas Maria Bergkamp (46 Johannes Paulus Gillhaus), Johannes Jacobus Bosman (46 Aron Mohammed Winter), Bryan Eduard Steven Roy, Gaston Taument (76 Marc Overmars).   Trainer: Dirk Nicolaas Advocaat.

Goal: Bryan Eduard Steven Roy (23)

552. 20.04.1994
AUSTRIA v SCOTLAND 1-2 (1-1)
"Ernst Happel", Wien
Referee: Hermann Albrecht (Germany)   Attendance: 35,000
AUSTRIA: Franz Wohlfahrt (46 Michael Konsel), Peter Schöttel, Walter Kogler, Walter Hochmaier, Christian Prosenik, Peter Stöger (46 Dietmar Kühbauer), Andreas Herzog, Michael Baur, Adolf Hütter, Harald Cerny, Anton Polster (62 Thomas Weissenberger).   Trainer: Herbert Prohaska.
SCOTLAND: James Leighton, Stewart McKimmie, Thomas Boyd (46 Ian Ferguson), Alan McLaren, Edward Colin James Hendry, Brian Irvine, Gary McAllister (Cap), William McKinlay, John Angus Paul Collins (85 Stuart Murray McCall), John McGinlay (75 Duncan Nichol Shearer), Eoin Jess (84 Patrick Kevin Francis Michael Nevin).
Manager: Craig Brown.

Goals: Adolf Hütter (13) /
John McGinlay (35), William McKinlay (60)

553. 27.05.1994
HOLLAND v SCOTLAND 3-1 (1-0)
Nieuw Galgenwaard, Utrecht
Referee: Juan Ansuátegui Roca (Spain)   Attendance: 22,000
HOLLAND: Eduard Franciscus de Goey, Stanislaus Henricus Christina Valckx, Franciscus de Boer, Jan Jacobus Wouters (Cap), Wilhelmus Maria Jonk, Aron Mohammed Winter, Robert Witschge, Marc Overmars, Ruud Gullit (46 Peter van Vossen), Bryan Eduard Steven Roy (73 Gaston Taument), Ronaldus de Boer (46 Arthur Johannes Numan).   Trainer: Dirk Nicolaas Advocaat.
SCOTLAND: James Leighton (46 Bryan James Gunn), Stephen Clarke, Stewart McKimmie, Brian Irvine, Edward Colin James Hendry, Gary McAllister (Cap), William McKinlay (88 Patrick Kevin Francis Michael Nevin), Stuart Murray McCall, John Angus Paul Collins (61 Ian Ferguson), John McGinlay (76 Duncan Nichol Shearer), Gordon Scott Durie (46 Eoin Jess).   Manager: Craig Brown.

Goals: Bryan Eduard Steven Roy (17), Peter van Vossen (61), Brian Irvine (73 own goal) / Duncan Nichol Shearer (81)

554. 07.09.1994   10th European Champs Qualifiers
FINLAND v SCOTLAND 0-2 (0-1)
Olympiastadion, Helsinki
Referee: Ryszard Wójcik (Poland)   Attendance: 12,845
FINLAND: Petri Jakonen, Janne Mäkelä, Markku Kanerva, Aki Hyryläinen, Antti Heinola (30 Erik Holmgren), Kim Suominen, Rami Rantanen (41 Petri Järvinen), Janne Lindberg, Ari Hjelm (Cap), Jari Litmanen, Mika-Matti Paatelainen.   Trainer: Tommy Lindholm.
SCOTLAND: Andrew Lewis Goram, Stewart McKimmie, Thomas Boyd, Alan McLaren, Edward Colin James Hendry, Craig William Levein (78 Stuart Murray McCall), Gary McAllister (Cap), Paul Michael Lyons McStay, John Angus Paul Collins, Andrew Francis Walker (65 Eoin Jess), Duncan Nichol Shearer.   Manager: Craig Brown.

Goals: Duncan Shearer (29), John Angus Paul Collins (66)

555. 12.10.1994   10th European Champs Qualifiers
SCOTLAND v FAROE ISLANDS 5-1 (3-0)
Hampden Park, Glasgow
Referee: Terje Hauge (Norway)   Attendance: 20,885
SCOTLAND: Andrew Lewis Goram, Stewart McKimmie, Thomas Boyd, Alan McLaren, Edward Colin James Hendry (59 William McKinlay), Craig William Levein, Patrick Kevin Francis Michael Nevin, Paul Michael Lyons McStay (Cap), John Angus Paul Collins, John McGinlay, Scott Booth (70 Andrew Francis Walker).   Manager: Craig Brown.
FAROE ISLANDS: Jens Martin Knudsen, Jens Kristian Hansen, Tummas Eli Hansen, Óli Johannesen, Øssur Hansen, Jan Dam (54 Djoni Joensen), Magni Jarnskor, Kurt Mørkøre (71 Janus Rasmussen), Jan Allan Müller, Todi Jónsson, Henning Jarnskor.
Trainer: Allan Rodenkam Simonsen (Denmark).

Goals: John McGinlay (4), Scott Booth (34), John Collins (40, 72), William McKinlay (61) / Jan Müller (75)

556. 16.11.1994   10th European Champs Qualifiers
SCOTLAND v RUSSIA 1-1 (1-1)
Hampden Park, Glasgow
Referee: Bo Karlsson (Sweden)   Attendance: 31,254
SCOTLAND: Andrew Lewis Goram, Stewart McKimmie, Thomas Boyd, Craig William Levein, Alan McLaren, Gary McAllister (Cap), William McKinlay (83 Patrick Kevin Francis Michael Nevin), Stuart Murray McCall, John Angus Paul Collins, John McGinlay (63 John Spencer), Scott Booth.   Manager: Craig Brown.
RUSSIA: Stanislav Cherchesov, Vasiliy Kulkov, Yuriy Nikiforov, Sergey Gorlukovich, Igor Shalimov, Valeriy Karpin, Viktor Onopko (Cap), Andrey Pyanitskiy (75 Omari Tetradze), Andrey Kanchelskis, Dmitriy Radchenko, Vladislav Radimov.   Trainer: Oleg Romantsev.

Goals: Scott Booth (19) / Dmitriy Radchenko (26)

557. 18.12.1994　10th European Champs Qualifiers
GREECE v SCOTLAND　1-0　(1-0)
Olympiako "Spiros Louis", Athína
Referee: John Blankenstein (Holland)　Attendance: 20,000
GREECE: Ilías Atmatzidis, Efstratios Apostolakis (Cap), Mihális Kasapis, Mihális Vlahos, Giánnis Kalitzakis, Panagiótis Tsalouhidis, Théodoros Zagorakis, Nikolaos Nioplias (88 Theófilos Karasavvidis), Giórgos Toursounidis, Alexandros Alexandris (72 Spyridon Maragos), Nikolaos Mahlas.　Trainer: Konstantinos Polyhroniou.
SCOTLAND: Andrew Lewis Goram (77 James Leighton), Stewart McKimmie, Thomas Boyd, Alan McLaren, Edward Colin James Hendry, Gary McAllister (Cap), William McKinlay (46 John Spencer), Stuart Murray McCall, John Angus Paul Collins, John McGinlay, Duncan Ferguson. Manager: Craig Brown.
Goal: Efstratios Apostolakis (18 pen)

558. 29.03.1995　10th European Champs Qualifiers
RUSSIA v SCOTLAND　0-0
Luzhniki, Moskva
Referee: Hartmut Strampe (Germany)　Attendance: 13,939
RUSSIA: Dmitriy Kharin, Dmitriy Khlestov, Yuriy Nikiforov, Yuriy Kovtun, Igor Shalimov (70 Vladislav Radimov), Valeriy Karpin, Viktor Onopko (Cap), Igor Dobrovolski, Andrey Kanchelskis, Dmitriy Radchenko (56 Nikolay Pisarev), Sergey Kiryakov.　Trainer: Oleg Romantsev.
SCOTLAND: James Leighton, Stewart McKimmie, Thomas Boyd, Alan McLaren, Edward Colin James Hendry, Colin Calderwood, Gary McAllister (Cap), Paul Michael Lyons McStay, John Angus Paul Collins, Darren Jackson (77 Duncan Nichol Shearer), John McGinlay (83 William McKinlay). Manager: Craig Brown.

559. 26.04.1995　10th European Champs Qualifiers
SAN MARINO v SCOTLAND　0-2　(0-1)
Olimpico, Serravalle
Referee: Loizos Loizou (Cyprus)　Attendance: 1,738
SAN MARINO: Pier Luigi Benedettini, Claudio Canti, Mirco Gennari, Marco Mazza, Luca Gobbi, William Guerra, Pierangelo Manzaroli, Pier Domenico Della Valle, Nicola Bacciocchi, Massimo Bonini (46 Ivan Matteoni), Marco Mularoni (71 Davide Gualtieri).　Trainer: Giorgio Leoni.
SCOTLAND: James Leighton, Alan McLaren, Thomas Boyd, Colin Calderwood, Edward Colin James Hendry, Patrick Kevin Francis Michael Nevin (78 William McKinlay), Gary McAllister (Cap), John Angus Paul Collins, Darren Jackson, Duncan Nichol Shearer (67 John Spencer), John McGinlay. Manager: Craig Brown.
Goals: John Angus Paul Collins (19), Colin Calderwood (85)

560. 21.05.1995　Kirin Cup
JAPAN v SCOTLAND　0-0
Big Arch, Hiroshima
Referee: Armando Pérez Hoyos (Colombia)　Att: 24,566
JAPAN: Kazuya Maekawa, Tatsuji Hashiratani (Cap), Masami Ihara, Niorio Omura, Akira Narahashi, Hiroshige Yanagimoto, Ramos (51 Mashiro Fukuda), Motohiro Yamaguchi, Kazuyoshi Miura, Masami Nakayama, Hiroaki Morishima (81 Tsuyoshi Kitazawa).　Trainer: Shu Kamo.
SCOTLAND: James Leighton (Cap), Alan McLaren, Robert McKinnon, Colin Calderwood (79 Derek Whyte), Brian Martin, Scot Gemmill (75 Paul Robert James Bernard), Paul Lambert (37 John Grant Robertson), William McKinlay, Craig William Burley, Darren Jackson, John Spencer. Manager: Craig Brown.
Sent off: John Spencer (34)

561. 24.05.1995　Kirin Cup
ECUADOR v SCOTLAND　1-2　(0-0)
Prefectural Sports Park, Toyama
Referee: Masayoshi Okada (Japan)　Attendance: 5,669
ECUADOR: José Francisco Cevallos, Luis Enrique Capurro, Raúl Alfredo Noriega, Iván Jacinto Hurtado, Wilfrido Enrique Verduga, Juan Helio Guamán, Nixon Aníbal Carcelén, Juan Carlos Garay (46 Agustín Javier Delgado), Hjalmar Zambrano, Diego Rodrigo Herrera (71 José Marcos Mora), Eduardo Hurtado Roa.　Trainer: Francisco Maturana (Colombia).
SCOTLAND: James Leighton (Cap), Alan McLaren, Derek Whyte (76 Paul Lambert), Colin Calderwood, Brian Martin, Scot Gemmill, Paul Robert James Bernard, William McKinlay, Craig William Burley, Darren Jackson (62 Steven Crawford), John Grant Robertson.　Manager: Craig Brown.
Goals: Iván Jacinto Hurtado (79 pen) /
John Grant Robertson (75), Steven Crawford (83)

562. 07.06.1995　10th European Champs Qualifiers
FAROE ISLANDS v SCOTLAND　0-2　(0-2)
Svangaskard, Toftir
Referee: Vladimír Hrinak (Slovakia)　Attendance: 3,881
FAROE ISLANDS: Jens Martin Knudsen, Óli Johannesen, Tummas Eli Hansen, Janus Rasmussen, Jens Kristian Hansen, Øssur Hansen, Magni Jarnskor (62 Allan Joensen), Julian Schantz Johnsson, Henning Jarnskor, Todi Jónsson, Jens Erik Rasmussen (74 Jan Allan Müller).
Trainer: Allan Rodenkam Simonsen (Denmark).
SCOTLAND: James Leighton (Cap), Stewart McKimmie, Robert McKinnon, Colin Calderwood, Alan McLaren, Craig William Burley, William McKinlay, John Angus Paul Collins, Darren Jackson, Duncan Nichol Shearer (86 John Grant Robertson), John McGinlay (75 Scot Gemmill). Manager: Craig Brown.
Goals: William McKinlay (25), John McGinlay (29)

563. 16.08.1995   10th European Champs Qualifiers
SCOTLAND v GREECE 1-0 (0-0)
Hampden Park, Glasgow
Referee: Peter Mikkelsen (Denmark)   Attendance: 34,910
SCOTLAND: James Leighton, Stewart McKimmie, Thomas Valley McKinlay, Colin Calderwood, Thomas Boyd, Gary McAllister (Cap), Craig William Burley, Stuart Murray McCall, John Angus Paul Collins, Darren Jackson (71 John Grant Robertson), Duncan Nichol Shearer (71 Alistair Murdoch McCoist).   Manager: Craig Brown.
GREECE: Ilías Atmatzidis, Efstratios Apostolakis (Cap), Mihális Kasapis, Kiriákos Karataïdis, Nikolaos Dabizas, Giánnis Kalitzakis, Panagiótis Tsalouhidis, Théodoros Zagorakis (79 Giórgos Hrístos Georgiádis), Daniel Lima Batista (49 Alexandros Alexandris), Zísis Vrízas (30 Nikolaos Mahlas), Vasílis Tsiártas.   Trainer: Konstantinos Polyhroniou.
Goal: Alistair Murdoch McCoist (72)

564. 06.09.1995   10th European Champs Qualifiers
SCOTLAND v FINLAND 1-0 (1-0)
Hampden Park, Glasgow
Referee: Vasiliy Melnichuk (Ukraine)   Attendance: 35,505
SCOTLAND: James Leighton, Stewart McKimmie (88 William McKinlay), Thomas Boyd, Alan McLaren, Colin Calderwood, Edward Colin James Hendry, Gary McAllister (Cap), John Angus Paul Collins, Thomas Valley McKinlay, John Spencer (74 Alistair Murdoch McCoist), Scott Booth (80 Darren Jackson).   Manager: Craig Brown.
FINLAND: Kari Laukkanen, Kari Rissanen, Markku Kanerva, Erik Holmgren, Kim Suominen, Janne Lindberg, Rami Nieminen (64 Tommi Grönlund), Marko Myyry, Ari Hjelm (Cap), Jari Litmanen, Petri Järvinen.
Trainer: Jukka Ikäläinen.
Goal: Scott Booth (10)

565. 11.10.1995
SWEDEN v SCOTLAND 2-0 (2-0)
Råsunda, Stockholm
Referee: Manuel Diaz Vega (Spain)   Attendance: 19,121
SWEDEN: Bengt Andersson, Teddy Lucic (90 Pontus Kåmark), Patrik Jonas Andersson, Joachim Björklund, Tomas Brolin, Niklas Gudmundsson (66 Martin Pringle), Stefan Schwarz, Mikael Nilsson, Niclas Alexandersson, Kennet Andersson (81 Magnus Erlingmark), Jörgen Pettersson.
Trainer: Tommy Svensson.
SCOTLAND: James Leighton (73 Andrew Lewis Goram), Stewart McKimmie, Thomas Boyd, Alan McLaren, Colin Calderwood, Edward Colin James Hendry, Gary McAllister (Cap) (60 Darren Jackson), Craig William Burley (46 William McKinlay), John Angus Paul Collins, John McGinlay (46 Eoin Jess), John Grant Robertson (73 Patrick Kevin Francis Michael Nevin).   Manager: Craig Brown.
Goals: Jörgen Pettersson (31), Stefan Schwarz (35)

566. 15.11.1995   10th European Champs Qualifiers
SCOTLAND v SAN MARINO 5-0 (2-0)
Hampden Park, Glasgow
Referee: Karel Bohunek (Czech Republic)   Att: 30,306
SCOTLAND: James Leighton, Alan McLaren, Thomas Boyd, Colin Calderwood, Edward Colin James Hendry, Patrick Kevin Francis Michael Nevin, Scot Gemmill, Gary McAllister (Cap) (48 Alistair Murdoch McCoist), John Angus Paul Collins (58 William McKinlay), Eoin Jess, Scott Booth (65 Darren Jackson).   Manager: Craig Brown.
SAN MARINO: Stefano Muccioli, Federico Moroni, Mirco Gennari, Marco Mazza (81 Pier Domenico Della Valle), Mauro Valentini, William Guerra (70 Paolo Montagna), Pierangelo Manzaroli, Ivan Matteoni, Nicola Bacciocchi, Marco Mularoni (51 Claudio Canti), Fabio Giulio Francini.
Trainer: Giorgio Leoni.
Goals: Eoin Jess (30), Scott Booth (45), Alistair McCoist (49), Patrick Nevin (71), Fabio Francini (90 own goal)

567. 27.03.1996
SCOTLAND v AUSTRALIA 1-0 (0-0)
Hampden Park, Glasgow
Referee: Herman van Dijk (Holland)   Attendance: 20,608
SCOTLAND: James Leighton, Brian O'Neil (46 Kevin William Gallacher), Edward Colin James Hendry, Thomas Boyd, Craig William Burley, Gary McAllister, Paul Michael Lyons McStay (46 Scott Booth), William McKinlay (75 Darren Jackson), John Angus Paul Collins, John Spencer, Alistair Murdoch McCoist (Cap) (80 Patrick Kevin Francis Michael Nevin).   Manager: Craig Brown.
AUSTRALIA: Mark Bosnich, Jason van Blerk, Tony Vidmar, Steve Horvat, Tony Popovic, Alex Tobin (Cap), Aurelio Vidmar, Steve Corica, Robbie Slater, Carl Veart (69 Danny Tiatto), Graham Arnold.   Trainer: Edward Thompson.
Goal: Alistair Murdoch McCoist (53)

568. 24.04.1996
DENMARK v SCOTLAND 2-0 (2-0)
Parken, København
Referee: Jan W. Wegereef (Holland)   Attendance: 23,021
DENMARK: Peter Schmeichel (46 Mogens Krogh), Marc Rieper, Lars Olsen, Jens Risager (81 Jacob Laursen), Thomas Helveg, Claus Thomsen, Michael Laudrup (Cap) (86 Allan Nielsen), Brian Steen Nielsen, Michael Schjønberg, Mikkel Beck, Brian Laudrup.   Trainer: Richard Møller Nielsen.
SCOTLAND: James Leighton (46 Andrew Lewis Goram), Stewart McKimmie, Thomas Boyd, Edward Colin James Hendry (75 William McKinlay), Craig William Burley, Gary McAllister (Cap), Stuart Murray McCall (Scot Gemmill), John Angus Paul Collins, Thomas Valley McKinlay, John Spencer (72 Alistair Murdoch McCoist), Kevin William Gallacher (72 Darren Jackson).   Manager: Craig Brown.
Goal: Michael Laudrup (8), Brian Laudrup (28)

569. 26.05.1996
UNITED STATES v SCOTLAND 2-1 (1-1)
Veteran's Stadium, Willow Brook, New Britain
Referee: Manlio Eduardo Brizio Carter (Mexico) Att: 8,526

UNITED STATES: Juergen Sommer, Mike Burns, Marcelo Luis Balboa, Panayotis Alexi Lalas, Thomas Dooley (53 Jovan Kirovski), John Andrew Harkes, Tabaré Ramos, Jeff Agoos, Cobi Ngai Jones, Claudio Reyna (83 Brian John McBride), Eric Wynalda. Trainer: Steve Sampson.

SCOTLAND: James Leighton (82 Joseph Nicholas Walker), Colin Calderwood, Edward Colin James Hendry (Cap), Derek Whyte, Craig William Burley (60 Stuart Murray McCall), Scot Gemmill (46 Gary McAllister), Darren Jackson (46 John Angus Paul Collins), Eoin Jess, Thomas Boyd, Scott Booth, Gordon Scott Durie (46 John Spencer). Manager: Craig Brown.

Goals: Eric Wynalda (13 pen), Cobi Ngai Jones (72) / Gordon Scott Durie (9)

570. 29.05.1996
COLOMBIA v SCOTLAND 1-0 (0-0)
Orange Bowl, Miami
Referee: Raúl Domínguez (United States) Att: 8,500

COLOMBIA: Farid Camilo Mondragón, Jorge Hernán Bermúdez, Néstor Ortíz (46 Luis Fernando Herrera), Luis Antonio Moreno, Giovanni Cassiani (46 Alexis Antonio Mendoza), Freddy Eusebio Rincón, Andrés Estrada (46 Leonel de Jesús Álvarez), Mauricio Alberto Serna, Edíson Mafla (46 Carlos Alberto Valderrama), José Adolfo Valencia (46 Víctor Hugo Aristizábal), Iván René Valenciano (46 Faustino Hernán Asprilla). Trainer: Hernán Darío Gómez.

SCOTLAND: Andrew Lewis Goram, Stewart McKimmie, Thomas Boyd, Colin Calderwood, Edward Colin James Hendry (46 Craig William Burley), Gary McAllister (Cap), Stuart Murray McCall, John Angus Paul Collins, Thomas Valley McKinlay, John Spencer (69 Eoin Jess), Alistair Murdoch McCoist (61 Kevin William Gallacher). Manager: Craig Brown.

Goal: Faustino Hernán Asprilla (82)

571. 10.06.1996   10th European Champs, 1st Round
HOLLAND v SCOTLAND 0-0
Villa Park, Birmingham
Referee: Leif Sundell (Sweden)   Attendance: 34,363

HOLLAND: Edwin van der Sar, Michael John Reiziger, Johan de Kock, Winston Lloyd Bogarde, Ronaldus de Boer (Cap) (68 Aron Mohammed Winter), Edgar Steven Davids, Clarence Clyde Seedorf, Richard Peter Witschge (78 Phillip John William Cocu), Gaston Taument (63 Patrick Steven Kluivert), Dennis Nicolaas Maria Bergkamp, Johannes Jordi Cruijff. Trainer: Guus Hiddink.

SCOTLAND: Andrew Lewis Goram, Stewart McKimmie (85 Craig William Burley), Thomas Boyd, Colin Calderwood, Edward Colin James Hendry, Stuart Murray McCall, Gary McAllister (Cap), John Angus Paul Collins, Kevin William Gallacher (56 William McKinlay), Scott Booth (46 John Spencer), Gordon Scott Durie. Manager: Craig Brown.

572. 15.06.1996   10th European Champs, 1st Round
ENGLAND v SCOTLAND 2-0 (0-0)
Wembley, London
Referee: Pierluigi Pairetto (Italy)   Attendance: 76,864

ENGLAND: David Andrew Seaman, Gary Alexander Neville, Anthony Alexander Adams (Cap), Gareth Southgate, Stuart Pearce (46 Jamie Frank Redknapp (84 Sulzeer Jeremiah Campbell)), Darren Robert Anderton, Paul Emerson Ince (79 Steven Brian Stone), Paul John Gascoigne, Steve McManaman, Alan Shearer, Edward Paul Sheringham. Manager: Terence Frederick Venables.

SCOTLAND: Andrew Lewis Goram, Stewart McKimmie, Thomas Boyd, Colin Calderwood, Edward Colin James Hendry, Stuart Murray McCall, Gary McAllister (Cap), John Angus Paul Collins, Thomas Valley McKinlay (81 Craig William Burley), John Spencer (66 Alistair Murdoch McCoist), Gordon Scott Durie (84 Eoin Jess). Manager: Craig Brown.

Goals: Alan Shearer (52), Paul John Gascoigne (78)

573. 18.06.1996   10th European Champs, 1st Round
SCOTLAND v SWITZERLAND 1-0 (1-0)
Villa Park, Birmingham
Referee: Václav Krondl (Czech Republic) Att: 34,926

SCOTLAND: Andrew Lewis Goram, Craig William Burley, Thomas Boyd, Colin Calderwood, Edward Colin James Hendry, Stuart Murray McCall, Gary McAllister (Cap), John Angus Paul Collins, Thomas Valley McKinlay (59 Scott Booth), Gordon Scott Durie, Alistair Murdoch McCoist (84 John Spencer). Manager: Craig Brown.

SWITZERLAND: Marco Pascolo, Marc Hottiger, Ramon Vega, Stéphane Henchoz, Yvan Quentin (80 Alexandre Comisetti), Johann Vogel, Marcel Koller (46 Raphaël Wicky), Ciriaco Sforza, Kubilay Türkyilmaz, Christophe Bonvin, Stéphane Chapuisat (46 Sébastien Fournier). Trainer: Artur Jorge Braga Melo Teixeira (Portugal).

Goal: Alistair Murdoch McCoist (37)

574. 31.08.1996   16th World Cup Qualifiers
AUSTRIA v SCOTLAND 0-0
"Ernst Happel", Wien
Referee: Michel Piraux (Belgium)   Attendance: 29,500
AUSTRIA: Michael Konsel, Peter Schöttel, Anton Pfeffer, Wolfgang Feiersinger, Markus Schopp, Dietmar Kühbauer, Andreas Herzog, Andreas Heraf, Stefan Marasek, Dieter Ramusch (77 Andreas Ogris), Anton Polster (68 Herfried Sabitzer).   Trainer: Herbert Prohaska.
SCOTLAND: Andrew Lewis Goram, Craig William Burley, Thomas Boyd, Colin Calderwood, Edward Colin James Hendry, Stuart Murray McCall, Gary McAllister (Cap), John Angus Paul Collins, Thomas Valley McKinlay, Duncan Ferguson, Alistair Murdoch McCoist (69 Gordon Scott Durie).   Manager: Craig Brown.

575. 05.10.1996   16th World Cup Qualifiers
LATVIA v SCOTLAND 0-2 (0-1)
Daugava, Riga
Referee: Jiří Ulrich (Czech Republic)   Attendance: 9,500
LATVIA: Oļegs Karavajevs, Igors Troickis, Vitālijs Astafjevs, Mihails Zemļinskis, Jurijs Ševļakovs, Igors N. Stepanovs, Valerijs Ivanovs, Imants Bleidelis, Vīts Rimkus (78 Rolands Bulders), Vladimirs Babičevs (46 Andrejs Štolcers), Marians Pahars.   Trainer: Jānis Gilis.
SCOTLAND: Andrew Lewis Goram, Craig William Burley, Thomas Boyd, Colin Calderwood, Derek Whyte, Stuart Murray McCall (46 Paul Lambert), Gary McAllister (Cap), John Angus Paul Collins, Thomas Valley McKinlay (80 John McNamara), Darren Jackson, John Spencer (59 William Dodds).   Manager: Craig Brown.
Goals: John Angus Paul Collins (18), Darren Jackson (78)

576. 10.11.1996   16th World Cup Qualifiers
SCOTLAND v SWEDEN 1-0 (1-0)
Ibrox Park, Glasgow
Referee: José-María García Aranda (Spain)   Att: 46,738
SCOTLAND: James Leighton, John McNamara (46 Paul Lambert), Thomas Boyd, Colin Calderwood, Edward Colin James Hendry (Cap), Craig William Burley, William McKinlay, John Angus Paul Collins, Thomas Valley McKinlay, Darren Jackson (78 Kevin William Gallacher), John McGinlay (85 Alistair Murdoch McCoist).   Manager: Craig Brown.
SWEDEN: Thomas Ravelli, Roland Nilsson, Patrik Jonas Andersson, Joachim Björklund, Gary Sundgren, Niclas Alexandersson (68 Henrik Larsson), Jonas Thern, Pär Zetterberg (76 Andreas Andersson), Stefan Schwarz, Jesper Blomqvist, Martin Dahlin (17 Kennet Andersson).   Trainer: Tommy Svensson.
Goal: John McGinlay (8)

577. 11.02.1997   16th World Cup Qualifiers
ESTONIA v SCOTLAND 0-0
"Louis II", Monaco
Referee: Miroslav Radoman (Yugoslavia)   Att: 4,000
ESTONIA: Mart Poom, Marek Lemsalu, Sergei Hohlov-Simson, Urmas Rooba, Urmas Kirs, Viktor Alonen, Meelis Rooba (67 Mati Pari), Marko Kristal, Martin Reim, Liivo Leetma (75 Andres Oper), Indrek Zelinski.
Trainer: Teitur Thórdarson (Iceland).
SCOTLAND: Andrew Lewis Goram, John McNamara (74 Thomas Valley McKinlay), Thomas Boyd, Colin Calderwood, Edward Colin James Hendry, Paul Michael Lyons McStay (63 Ian Ferguson), Gary McAllister (Cap), John Angus Paul Collins, Kevin William Gallacher, John McGinlay (73 Alistair Murdoch McCoist), Duncan Ferguson.
Manager: Craig Brown.

578. 29.03.1997   16th World Cup Qualifiers
SCOTLAND v ESTONIA 2-0 (1-0)
Rugby Park, Kilmarnock
Referee: Bernd Heynemann (Germany)   Att: 17,996
SCOTLAND: James Leighton, Craig William Burley, Thomas Boyd, Colin Calderwood, Edward Colin James Hendry (64 William McKinlay), Scot Gemmill, Paul Michael Lyons McStay, Gary McAllister (Cap), Thomas Valley McKinlay, Darren Jackson (83 John McGinlay), Kevin William Gallacher.   Manager: Craig Brown.
ESTONIA: Mart Poom, Marek Lemsalu, Sergei Hohlov-Simson, Janek Meet, Urmas Kirs, Indrek Zelinski (81 Argo Arbeiter), Marko Kristal, Martin Reim, Mati Pari (55 Meelis Rooba), Kristen Viikmäe (73 Liivo Leetma), Andres Oper.
Trainer: Teitur Thórdarson (Iceland).
Goals: Thomas Boyd (26), Janek Meet (52 own goal)

579. 02.04.1997   16th World Cup Qualifiers
SCOTLAND v AUSTRIA 2-0 (1-0)
Celtic Park, Glasgow
Referee: Nikolay Levnikov (Russia)   Attendance: 43,295
SCOTLAND: James Leighton, Craig William Burley, Thomas Boyd, Colin Calderwood, Edward Colin James Hendry, Gary McAllister (Cap) (88 Paul Michael Lyons McStay), Paul Lambert, John Angus Paul Collins, Thomas Valley McKinlay, Darren Jackson (73 John McGinlay), Kevin William Gallacher (86 Alistair Murdoch McCoist).   Manager: Craig Brown.
AUSTRIA: Michael Konsel, Peter Schöttel (46 Walter Kogler), Anton Pfeffer, Wolfgang Feiersinger, Markus Schopp, Andreas Heraf, Peter Stöger (68 Ivica Vastic), Franz Aigner (81 Andreas Ogris), Arnold Wetl, Andreas Herzog, Anton Polster.   Trainer: Herbert Prohaska.
Goals: Kevin William Gallacher (24, 77)

580. 30.04.1997   16th World Cup Qualifiers
SWEDEN v SCOTLAND 2-1 (1-0)
Ullevi, Göteborg
Referee: Dr. Pierluigi Collina (Italy)   Attendance: 40,302
SWEDEN: Thomas Ravelli, Gary Sundgren, Pontus Kåmark, Patrik Jonas Andersson, Joachim Björklund, Jonas Thern, Pär Zetterberg, Stefan Schwarz (13 Håkan Mild), Andreas Andersson, Kennet Andersson, Martin Dahlin. Trainer: Tommy Svensson.
SCOTLAND: James Leighton, Craig William Burley, Thomas Boyd, Colin Calderwood, Edward Colin James Hendry, Gary McAllister (Cap), Paul Lambert, John Angus Paul Collins, Thomas Valley McKinlay (68 Scot Gemmill), Darren Jackson (66 Gordon Scott Durie), Kevin William Gallacher. Manager: Craig Brown.
Goals: Kennet Andersson (43, 63) / Kevin Gallacher (83)

581. 27.05.1997
SCOTLAND v WALES 0-1 (0-0)
Rugby Park, Kilmarnock
Referee: Alan Snoddy (Northern Ireland)   Att: 8,000
SCOTLAND: Neil Sullivan (80 James Leighton), David Gillespie Weir, Thomas Boyd, Christian Edward Dailly (74 John McNamara), Brian McAllister, Scot Gemmill, Gary McAllister (Cap), Thomas Valley McKinlay, William Dodds, Darren Jackson (46 John Spencer), Kevin William Gallacher (80 Simon Donnelly).   Manager: Craig Brown.
WALES: Andrew Marriott (46 Paul Steven Jones), Stephen Robert Jenkins, Paul Jonathan Trollope, Robert John Page, Christopher Jeremiah Symons, John Robert Campbell Robinson (88 Marcus Trevor Browning), Robert William Savage, Dean Nicholas Saunders (88 Philip Lee Jones), John Hartson (71 Simon Owen Haworth), Mark Anthony Pembridge, Gary Andrew Speed.   Manager: Bobby Gould.
Goal: John Hartson (46)

582. 01.06.1997
MALTA v SCOTLAND 2-3 (1-2)
National, Ta'Qali
Referee: Stefano Braschi (Italy)   Attendance: 3,000
MALTA: Mario Muscat, Lawrence Attard (53 Noel Turner), Silvio Vella (Cap) (76 Stefan Giglio), Darren Debono, Jeffrey Chetcuti, Ivan Zammit, Joseph Brincat, Gilbert Agius (84 David Camilleri), Nicholas Saliba, David Carabott, Hubert Suda (46 Stefan Sultana).   Trainer: Milorad Kosanović (Yugoslavia).
SCOTLAND: James Leighton, Craig William Burley, Thomas Boyd, Christian Edward Dailly, Brian McAllister (46 David Gillespie Weir), Gary McAllister (Cap), David Hopkin (56 Scot Gemmill), John Angus Paul Collins (84 Simon Donnelly), Thomas Valley McKinlay, Darren Jackson, Kevin William Gallacher (56 Gordon Scott Durie).   Manager: Craig Brown.
Goals: Hubert Suda (16), Stefan Sultana (57) / Christian Edward Dailly (4), Darren Jackson (44, 81)

583. 08.06.1997   16th World Cup Qualifiers
BELARUS v SCOTLAND 0-1 (0-0)
Dinamo, Minsk
Referee: Ahmet Çakar (Turkey)   Attendance: 12,000
BELARUS: Andrey Satsunkevich, Andrey Lavrik, Andrey Ostrovskiy, Sergey Shtanyuk, Erik Yakhimovich, Sergey Gurenko, Radislav Orlovskiy (74 Dmitriy Balashov), Andrey Dovnar (55 Valentin Belkevich), Sergey Gerasimets, Andrey Khlebosolov (62 Vladimir Makovskiy), Myroslav Romashchenko.   Trainer: Mikhail Vergeyenko.
SCOTLAND: James Leighton, Craig William Burley, Thomas Boyd, Christian Edward Dailly, Thomas Valley McKinlay (79 Brian McAllister), Gary McAllister (Cap), Paul Lambert, David Hopkin (68 Scot Gemmill), Darren Jackson (87 William Dodds), Gordon Scott Durie, Kevin William Gallacher.   Manager: Craig Brown.
Goal: Gary McAllister (50 pen)

584. 07.09.1997   16th World Cup Qualifiers
SCOTLAND v BELARUS 4-1 (1-0)
Pittodrie, Aberdeen
Referee: Mario van der Ende (Holland)   Attendance: 20,160
SCOTLAND: James Leighton, Craig William Burley, Thomas Boyd, Christian Edward Dailly, Colin Calderwood, Gary McAllister (Cap) (50 David Hopkin), Paul Lambert, John Angus Paul Collins, Thomas Valley McKinlay, Gordon Scott Durie (46 Alistair Murdoch McCoist), Kevin William Gallacher (84 William Dodds).   Manager: Craig Brown.
BELARUS: Valeriy Shantalosov, Andrey Lavrik, Vyacheslav Gerashchenko, Andrey Ostrovskiy, Andrey Dovnar, Sergey Gurenko (51 Radislav Orlovskiy), Valentin Belkevich, Alexandr Kulchiy, Vladimir Zhuravel (63 Oleg Chernyavskiy), Sergey Gerasimets (77 Dmitriy Balashov), Petr Kachuro.   Trainer: Mikhail Vergeyenko.
Goals: Kevin Gallacher (5, 57), David Hopkin (54, 88) / Petr Kachuro (73 pen)

585. 11.10.1997   16th World Cup Qualifiers
SCOTLAND v LATVIA 2-0 (1-0)
Celtic Park, Glasgow
Referee: Sándor Piller (Hungary)   Attendance: 47,613
SCOTLAND: James Leighton, Craig William Burley (89 William McKinlay), Thomas Boyd (81 Thomas Valley McKinlay), Colin Calderwood, Edward Colin James Hendry, Christian Edward Dailly, Gary McAllister (Cap), Paul Lambert, John Angus Paul Collins, Gordon Scott Durie (84 Simon Donnelly), Kevin William Gallacher.   Manager: Craig Brown.
LATVIA: Oļegs Karavajevs, Igors N. Stepanovs, Valentīns Lobaņovs, Mihails Zemļinskis, Jurijs Ševļakovs, Oļegs Blagonadeždins (62 Andrejs Štolcers), Valerijs Ivanovs, Imants Bleidelis, Marians Pahars, Vladimirs Babičevs, Aleksandrs Jeļisejevs (69 Vits Rimkus).   Trainer: Jānis Gilis.
Goals: Kevin Gallacher (43), Gordon Scott Durie (80)

586. 12.11.1997
FRANCE v SCOTLAND 2-1 (1-1)
"Geoffroy Guichard", Saint-Étienne
Referee: Antonio Jesús López Nieto (Spain)   Att: 19,514
FRANCE: Fabien Barthez, Lilian Thuram, Laurent Blanc, Marcel Desailly, Pierre Laigle (79 Vincent Candela), Didier Deschamps (Cap), Ibrahim Ba (80 Franck Gava), Zinedine Zidane, Emmanuel Petit (73 Alain Boghossian), Lilian Laslandes (71 Youri Djorkaeff), Stéphane Guivarc'h. Trainer: Aimé Jacquet.
SCOTLAND: Neil Sullivan, Craig William Burley, Thomas Boyd (Cap) (80 Thomas Valley McKinlay), Colin Calderwood, David Gillespie Weir (76 Matthew Stephen Elliott), Christian Edward Dailly, Gary McAllister, William McKinlay, John Angus Paul Collins, Gordon Scott Durie (89 David Hopkin), Kevin William Gallacher (83 Simon Donnelly). Manager: Craig Brown.
Goals: Pierre Laigle (35), Youri Djorkaeff (78 pen) / Gordon Scott Durie (36)

587. 25.03.1998
SCOTLAND v DENMARK 0-1 (0-1)
Ibrox Park, Glasgow
Referee: Dermot Gallagher (England)   Attendance: 26,468
SCOTLAND: James Leighton (46 Andrew Lewis Goram), John McNamara (59 David Gillespie Weir), Thomas Boyd, Matthew Stephen Elliott, Edward Colin James Hendry (Cap), Colin Calderwood, Scot Gemmill (69 Stuart Murray McCall), William McKinlay, Christian Edward Dailly, Scott Booth (46 Eoin Jess), Darren Jackson (74 Simon Donnelly). Manager: Craig Brown.
DENMARK: Mogens Krogh, Jacob Laursen (46 René Henriksen), Marc Rieper, Michael Schjønberg, Thomas Helveg, Allan Nielsen (62 Per Frandsen), Morten Wieghorst, Jan Heintze, Michael Laudrup (Cap), Peter Møller (74 Martin Jørgensen), Brian Laudrup (80 Bjarne Goldbaek). Trainer: Bo Johansson (Sweden).
Goal: Brian Laudrup (38)

588. 22.04.1998
SCOTLAND v FINLAND 1-1 (1-1)
Easter Road, Edinburgh
Referee: Herman van Dijk (Holland)   Attendance: 14,315
SCOTLAND: James Leighton, Colin Calderwood (71 Gordon Scott Durie), Christian Edward Dailly (87 Thomas Boyd), Matthew Stephen Elliott (46 David Gillespie Weir), Edward Colin James Hendry (Cap), Derek Whyte, Scot Gemmill (76 Paul Lambert), William McKinlay, John Angus Paul Collins, Scott Booth (76 Simon Donnelly), Darren Jackson (46 Kevin William Gallacher). Manager: Craig Brown.
FINLAND: Antti Niemi, Harri Ylönen, Marko Tuomela (65 Tomi Kinnunen), Sami Hyypiä, Jarkko Koskinen, Sami Mahlio, Juha Reini (46 Aarno Turpeinen), Simo Valakari, Antti Sumiala (38 Joonas Kolkka), Jari Litmanen (Cap) (46 Aki Riihilahti), Jonatan Johansson (58 Mika-Matti Paatelainen). Trainer: Richard Møller-Nielsen (Denmark).
Goals: Darren Jackson (15) / Jonatan Johansson (10)

589. 23.05.1998
COLOMBIA v SCOTLAND 2-2 (1-2)
Giants, East Rutherford
Referee: Brian Hall (United States)   Attendance: 56,404
COLOMBIA: Miguel Ángel Calero, José Fernando Santa, Jorge Hernán Bermúdez, Iván Ramiro Córdoba, Wilmer Cabrera, Mauricio Alberto Serna, John Harold Lozano, Freddy Eusebio Rincón, Carlos Alberto Valderrama, José Adolfo Valencia, Faustino Hernán Asprilla. Trainer: Hernán Darío Gómez.
SCOTLAND: Neil Sullivan, John McNamara (71 William McKinlay), Thomas Boyd, Colin Calderwood, Christian Edward Dailly, Edward Colin James Hendry (Cap), Paul Lambert, Craig William Burley, John Angus Paul Collins, Darren Jackson (46 Scott Booth), Gordon Scott Durie (61 Simon Donnelly). Manager: Craig Brown.
Goals: Carlos Valderrama (22 pen), Freddy Rincón (79) / John Angus Paul Collins (24), Craig William Burley (33)

590. 30.05.1998
UNITED STATES v SCOTLAND 0-0
"Robert F. Kennedy" Memorial, Washington D.C.
Referee: Felipe de Jesús Ramos Rizo (Mexico)   Att: 46,037
UNITED STATES: Kasey Keller, George Edward Pope, Thomas Dooley, Mike Burns, David Regis, Chad Deering, Tabaré Ramos (56 Predrag Radosavljevic), Earnest Stewart (82 Panayotis Alexi Lalas), Cobi Ngai Jones, Joseph-Max Moore (69 Jeff Agoos), Roy Wegerle (62 Eric Wynalda). Trainer: Steve Sampson.
SCOTLAND: James Leighton, Christian Edward Dailly, Thomas Boyd, Colin Calderwood, Edward Colin James Hendry (Cap), Paul Lambert, William McKinlay (74 Craig William Burley), John Angus Paul Collins, Thomas Valley McKinlay (60 John McNamara), Darren Jackson, Kevin William Gallacher (82 Simon Donnelly). Manager: Craig Brown.

591. 10.06.1998   16th World Cup, 1st Round
BRAZIL v SCOTLAND 2-1 (1-1)
Stade de France, Saint-Denis, Paris
Referee: José-María García Aranda (Spain)   Att: 80,000
BRAZIL: Cláudio André Mergen Taffarel, Marcos Evangelista de Moraes "Cafu", Aldair Nascimento Santos, Raimundo Ferreira Ramos Júnior "Júnior Baiano", Roberto Carlos da Silva, Carlos Campos César Sampaio, Carlos Caetano Bledorn Verri "Dunga" (Cap), Giovanni Silva de Oliveira (46 Leonardo Nascimento de Araújo "Leonardo I"), Rivaldo Vitor Borba Ferreira, Ronaldo Luís Nazário de Lima, José Roberto Gama de Oliveira "Bebeto" (70 Deníilson de Oliveira).
Trainer: Mário Jorge Lobo Zagallo.
SCOTLAND: James Leighton, Craig William Burley, Thomas Boyd, Colin Calderwood, Edward Colin James Hendry (Cap), Paul Lambert, Darren Jackson (78 William McKinlay), John Angus Paul Collins, Christian Edward Dailly (85 Thomas Valley McKinlay), Gordon Scott Durie, Kevin William Gallacher.   Manager: Craig Brown.
Goals: Carlos César Sampaio (5), Thomas Boyd (73 own goal) / John Angus Paul Collins (38 pen)

592. 16.06.1998   16th World Cup, 1st Round
NORWAY v SCOTLAND 1-1 (0-0)
Parc Lescure, Bordeaux
Referee: László Vágner (Hungary)   Attendance: 30,236
NORWAY: Frode Grodås, Henning Berg (82 Gunnar Halle), Dan Eggen, Ronny Johnsen, Stig Inge Bjørnebye, Håvard Flo (62 Jahn Ivar Jakobsen), Roar Strand, Ståle Solbakken, Kjetil Rekdal, Vidar Riseth (75 Egil Østenstad), Tore André Flo.
Trainer: Egil Roger Olsen.
SCOTLAND: James Leighton, Colin Calderwood (60 David Gillespie Weir), Christian Edward Dailly, Thomas Boyd, Edward Colin James Hendry (Cap), Craig William Burley, Paul Lambert, John Angus Paul Collins, Darren Jackson (62 John McNamara), Gordon Scott Durie, Kevin William Gallacher.   Manager: Craig Brown.
Goals: Håvard Flo (46) / Craig William Burley (66)

593. 23.06.1998   16th World Cup, 1st Round
MOROCCO v SCOTLAND 3-0 (1-0)
Geoffroy Guichard, Saint-Etienne
Referee: Ali Bujsaim (United Arab Emirates)   Att: 35,500
MOROCCO: Driss Benzekri, Abdelilah Saber (72 Youssef Rossi), Noureddine Naybet, Gharib Amzine (76 Rachid Azzouzi), Lahcen Abrami, Tahar El Khalej, Moustafa Hadji, Youssef Chippo (87 Jamal Sellami), Ismaël Triki, Salaheddine Bassir, Abdeljalil Hadda.   Trainer: Henri Michel (France).
SCOTLAND: James Leighton, John McNamara (54 Thomas Valley McKinlay), Thomas Boyd, David Gillespie Weir, Edward Colin James Hendry (Cap), Craig William Burley, Paul Lambert, John Angus Paul Collins, Christian Edward Dailly, Gordon Scott Durie (84 Scott Booth), Kevin William Gallacher.   Manager: Craig Brown.
Sent off: Craig William Burley (54)
Goals: Salaheddine Bassir (22), Abdeljalil Hadda (47), Salaheddine Bassir (84)

594. 05.09.1998   11th European Champs Qualifiers
LITHUANIA v SCOTLAND 0-0
Žalgiris, Vilnius
Referee: Constantin Dan Zotta (Romania)   Att: 4,000
LITHUANIA: Gintaras Staučė (Cap), Andrius Skerla, Deividas Šembaras, Raimondas Žutautas, Virginijus Baltušnikas, Tomas Žvirgždauskas, Gražvydas Mikulėnas (90 Vaidotas Šleksys), Gediminas Sugžda (63 Orestas Buitkus), Aidas Preikšaitis, Aurelijus Skarbalius, Edgaras Jankauskas.
Trainer: Kęstutis Latoža.
SCOTLAND: James Leighton, Colin Calderwood (71 Callum Iain Davidson), Thomas Boyd, Matthew Stephen Elliott, Edward Colin James Hendry (Cap), Paul Lambert, Darren Jackson (56 Barry Ferguson), John Angus Paul Collins, Christian Edward Dailly, Kevin William Gallacher, Alistair Murdoch McCoist (83 Neil McCann).
Manager: Craig Brown.

595. 10.10.1998   11th European Champs Qualifiers
SCOTLAND v ESTONIA 3-2 (0-1)
Tynecastle, Edinburgh
Referee: Joaquim Bento Marques (Portugal)   Att: 16,390
SCOTLAND: James Leighton, Colin Calderwood (57 Simon Donnelly), Thomas Boyd, David Gillespie Weir, Edward Colin James Hendry (Cap), Allan Johnston, William McKinlay, Iain Durrant, Callum Iain Davidson, Kevin William Gallacher (18 Darren Jackson), Alistair Murdoch McCoist (69 William Dodds).   Manager: Craig Brown.
ESTONIA: Mart Poom, Urmas Kirs, Sergei Hohlov-Simson, Martin Reim, Urmas Rooba, Marko Kristal, Maksim Smirnov, Viktor Alonen, Sergei Terehhov, Indrek Zelinski (88 Kristen Viikmäe), Andres Oper.
Trainer: Teitur Thórdarson (Iceland).
Sent off: Marko Kristal (88)
Goals: William Dodds (70, 85), Sergei Hohlov-Simson (77 own goal) / Sergei Hohlov-Simson (35), Maksim Smirnov (76)

596. 14.10.1998   11th European Champs Qualifiers
SCOTLAND v FAROE ISLANDS 2-1 (2-0)
Pittodrie, Aberdeen
Referee: Kostas Kapitanis (Cyprus)   Attendance: 18,517
SCOTLAND: Neil Sullivan, David Gillespie Weir, Thomas Boyd, Matthew Stephen Elliott, Edward Colin James Hendry (Cap), Allan Johnston (79 Stephen Glass), William McKinlay (46 Iain Durrant), Craig William Burley, Callum Iain Davidson, Simon Donnelly, William Dodds. Manager: Craig Brown.
FAROE ISLANDS: Jákup Mikkelsen, Hans Fróði Hansen, Óli Johannesen, Jens Kristian Hansen, Pól Thorsteinsson, Sámal Joensen, Julian Schantz Johnsson, Henning Jarnskor (81 John Hansen), Uni Arge (69 Jákup á Borg), Todi Jónsson, John Petersen. Trainer: Allan Rodenkam Simonsen (Denmark).
Goals: Craig William Burley (21), William Dodds (45) / John Petersen (85 pen)

597. 31.03.1999   11th European Champs Qualifiers
SCOTLAND v CZECH REPUBLIC 1-2 (0-2)
Celtic Park, Glasgow
Referee: Kim Milton Nielsen (Denmark)   Att: 44,513
SCOTLAND: Neil Sullivan, David Gillespie Weir, Callum Iain Davidson (52 Allan Johnston), Matthew Stephen Elliott, Thomas Boyd, David Hopkin, Gary McAllister (Cap) (63 Donald Hutchison), Paul Lambert, Craig William Burley, Neil McCann, Eoin Jess.   Manager: Craig Brown.
CZECH REPUBLIC: Pavel Srníček, Michal Horňák, Tomáš Votava, Jan Suchopárek, Karel Poborský (76 Karel Rada), Martin Hašek, Pavel Nedvěd, Patrik Berger, Jiří Němec (Cap), Vladimír Šmicer (80 Miroslav Baranek), Vratislav Lokvenc (70 Pavel Kuka).   Trainer: Jozef Chovanec.
Goals: Eoin Jess (68) /
Matthew Stephen Elliott (27 own goal), Vladimír Šmicer (36)

598. 28.04.1999
GERMANY v SCOTLAND 0-1 (0-0)
Weser, Bremen
Referee: Urs Meier (Switzerland)   Attendance: 25,000
GERMANY: Jens Lehmann, Christian Wörns, Lothar Herbert Matthäus, Jens Nowotny, Thomas Strunz (88 Carsten Jancker), Dietmar Hamann (60 Michael Ballack), Jens Jeremies (46 Carsten Ramelow), Jörg Heinrich, Olivier Neuville, Oliver Bierhoff (Cap) (60 Ulf Kirsten), Horst Heldt. Trainer: Erich Ribbeck.
SCOTLAND: Neil Sullivan, David Gillespie Weir, Callum Iain Davidson (77 Derek Whyte), Thomas Boyd, Edward Colin James Hendry (Cap) (66 Paul Ritchie), Scot Gemmill (59 Eoin Jess), Paul Lambert (83 Colin Cameron), Iain Durrant (71 Robert Winters), Allan Johnston (86 Brian O'Neil), Donald Hutchison, William Dodds.   Manager: Craig Brown.
Goal: Donald Hutchison (65)

599. 05.06.1999   11th European Champs Qualifiers
FAROE ISLANDS v SCOTLAND 1-1 (0-1)
Svangaskarð, Toftir
Referee: Philippe Kalt (France)   Attendance: 4,100
FAROE ISLANDS: Jákup Mikkelsen, Óli Johannesen, Hans Fróði Hansen, Pól Thorsteinsson, Øssur Hansen (85 John Hansen), Sámal Joensen, Jóhannis Joensen (70 Jákup á Borg), Julian Schantz Johnsson, Todi Jónsson, Allan Mørkøre, John Petersen (82 Uni Arge).
Trainer: Allan Rodenkam Simonsen (Denmark).
SCOTLAND: Neil Sullivan, David Gillespie Weir, Thomas Boyd (Cap), Colin Calderwood, Matthew Stephen Elliott, Allan Johnston (86 Scot Gemmill), Paul Lambert, Iain Durrant (46 Colin Cameron), Callum Iain Davidson, William Dodds, Kevin William Gallacher (89 Eoin Jess).   Manager: Craig Brown.
Goals: Hans Fróði Hansen (86) / Allan Johnston (38)

600. 09.06.1999   11th European Champs Qualifiers
CZECH REPUBLIC v SCOTLAND 3-2 (0-1)
Sparta, Praha
Referee: Hellmut Krug (Germany)   Attendance: 21,000
CZECH REPUBLIC: Pavel Srníček, Jan Suchopárek, Tomáš Řepka, Michal Horňák, Karel Poborský (69 Pavel Kuka), Pavel Nedvěd, Martin Hašek (61 Miroslav Baranek), Patrik Berger, Jiří Němec (Cap), Vratislav Lokvenc (69 Jan Koller), Vladimír Šmicer.   Trainer: Jozef Chovanec.
SCOTLAND: Neil Sullivan, David Gillespie Weir, Thomas Boyd (Cap), Colin Calderwood, Paul Ritchie, Allan Johnston, Paul Lambert, Iain Durrant (70 Eoin Jess), Callum Iain Davidson, William Dodds, Kevin William Gallacher. Manager: Craig Brown.
Goals: Tomáš Řepka (64), Pavel Kuka (74), Jan Koller (87) / Paul Ritchie (30), Allan Johnston (62)

601. 04.09.1999   11th European Champs Qualifiers
BOSNIA-HERZEGOVINA v SCOTLAND 1-2 (1-2)
Koševo, Sarajevo
Referee: Nikolay Levnikov (Russia)   Attendance: 25,000
BOSNIA-HERZEGOVINA: Mirsad Dedić, Omer Joldić (77 Senad Repuh), Muhamed Konjić, Mirsad Hibić, Jasmin Mujdža (77 Enes Demirović), Bakir Beširević, Sead Halilović (62 Edin Mujčin), Meho Kodro, Sergej Barbarez, Marko Topić, Elvir Bolić.   Trainer: Faruk Hadžibegić.
SCOTLAND: Neil Sullivan, David Gillespie Weir, David Hopkin, Colin Calderwood (46 Christian Edward Dailly), Edward Colin James Hendry (Cap), Craig William Burley, Barry Ferguson (70 Iain Durrant), John Angus Paul Collins, Neil McCann (75 Kevin William Gallacher), Donald Hutchison, William Dodds.   Manager: Craig Brown.
Goals: Elvir Bolić (23) /
Donald Hutchison (13), William Dodds (45)

602. 08.09.1999   11th European Champs Qualifiers
ESTONIA v SCOTLAND 0-0
Kadriorg, Tallinn
Referee: Fritz Stuchlik (Austria)   Attendance: 4,500
ESTONIA: Mart Poom, Raio Piiroja, Urmas Kirs, Sergei Hohlov-Simson, Erko Saviauk, Marko Kristal, Aivar Anniste, Martin Reim, Sergei Terehhov, Ivan O'Konnel-Bronin (46 Indrek Zelinski), Andres Oper.
Trainer: Teitur Thórdarson (Iceland).
SCOTLAND: Neil Sullivan, David Gillespie Weir, Callum Iain Davidson, Christian Edward Dailly, Edward Colin James Hendry (Cap), Craig William Burley, Iain Durrant (66 Barry Ferguson), John Angus Paul Collins, Allan Johnston (54 Neil McCann), Donald Hutchison, William Dodds.
Manager: Craig Brown.

603. 05.10.1999   11th European Champs Qualifiers
SCOTLAND v BOSNIA-HERZEGOVINA 1-0 (1-0)
Ibrox Park, Glasgow
Referee: Leif Sundell (Sweden)   Attendance: 30,500
SCOTLAND: Neil Sullivan, David Gillespie Weir, Callum Iain Davidson, Christian Edward Dailly, Edward Colin James Hendry (Cap) (37 Colin Calderwood), Craig William Burley, Paul Lambert, David Hopkin, John Angus Paul Collins, William Dodds (89 Gary McSwegan), Kevin William Gallacher (78 Mark Burchill).   Manager: Craig Brown.
BOSNIA-HERZEGOVINA: Adnan Gušo, Sead Kapetanović, Mirsad Varešanović, Faruk Hujdurović, Bakir Beširević, Faruk Ihtijarević (77 Marko Topić), Sergej Barbarez, Nermin Sabić, Elvir Bolić, Edin Mujčin (84 Alen Avdić), Elvir Baljić.
Trainer: Faruk Hadžibegić.
Goal: John Angus Paul Collins (25 pen)

604. 09.10.1999   11th European Champs Qualifiers
SCOTLAND v LITHUANIA 3-0 (0-0)
Hampden Park, Glasgow
Referee: Stéphane Bré (France)   Attendance: 22,059
SCOTLAND: Jonathan Alan Gould, David Gillespie Weir, Callum Iain Davidson, Brian O'Neil, Paul Ritchie, Craig William Burley (46 Colin Cameron), Paul Lambert (Cap), Donald Hutchison, Christian Edward Dailly, Gary McSwegan (82 Kevin William Gallacher), Mark Burchill (78 William Dodds).   Manager: Craig Brown.
LITHUANIA: Pavelas Leusas, Darius Žutautas, Tomas Žvirgždauskas, Marius Skinderis, Andrius Skerla, Irmantas Stumbrys (54 Donatas Vencevičius), Tomas Ražanauskas, Sakalas Mikalajūnas, Andrijus Tereškinas (Cap) (64 Artūras Fomenka), Vidas Dančenka (54 Darius Maciulevičius), Gražvydas Mikulėnas.   Trainer: Robertas Tautkus.
Goals: Donald Hutchison (48), Gary McSwegan (50), Colin Cameron (88)

605. 13.11.1999   11th Euro Champs Qualifier Play-Off
SCOTLAND v ENGLAND 0-2 (0-2)
Hampden Park, Glasgow
Referee: Manuel Diaz Vega (Spain)   Attendance: 50,132
SCOTLAND: Neil Sullivan, David Gillespie Weir, Paul Ritchie, Christian Edward Dailly, Edward Colin James Hendry (Cap), Craig William Burley, Barry Ferguson, Donald Hutchison, John Angus Paul Collins, William Dodds, Kevin William Gallacher (82 Mark Burchill).   Manager: Craig Brown.
ENGLAND: David Andrew Seaman, Philip John Neville, Martin Raymond Keown, Anthony Alexander Adams, Sulzeer Jeremiah Campbell, David Robert Joseph Beckham, Paul Scholes, Paul Emerson Ince, Jamie Frank Redknapp, Alan Shearer (Cap), Michael James Owen (67 Andrew Alexander Cole).   Manager: Kevin Joseph Keegan.
Goals: Paul Scholes (21, 42)

606. 17.11.1999   11th Euro Champs Qualifier Play-Off
ENGLAND v SCOTLAND 0-1 (0-1)
Wembley, London
Referee: Dr. Pierluigi Collina (Italy)   Attendance: 76,848
SCOTLAND: Neil Sullivan, David Gillespie Weir, Callum Iain Davidson, Christian Edward Dailly, Edward Colin James Hendry (Cap), Craig William Burley, Barry Ferguson, John Angus Paul Collins, Neil McCann (74 Mark Burchill), Donald Hutchison, William Dodds.   Manager: Craig Brown.
ENGLAND: David Andrew Seaman, Philip John Neville, Gareth Southgate, Anthony Alexander Adams, Sulzeer Jeremiah Campbell, David Robert Joseph Beckham, Paul Scholes (90 Raymond Parlour), Paul Emerson Ince, Jamie Frank Redknapp, Alan Shearer (Cap), Michael James Owen (63 Emile William Ivanhoe Heskey).
Manager: Kevin Joseph Keegan.
Goal: Donald Hutchison (38)

607. 29.03.2000
SCOTLAND v FRANCE 0-2 (0-0)
Hampden Park, Glasgow
Referee: Rune Pedersen (Norway)   Attendance: 48,157
SCOTLAND: Neil Sullivan, Paul Norman Telfer (69 Allan Johnston), Paul Ritchie (46 Steven Pressley), Christian Edward Dailly, Edward Colin James Hendry (Cap), Callum Iain Davidson, Barry Ferguson, Donald Hutchison, Colin Cameron (46 Neil McCann), William Dodds, Kevin William Gallacher (80 Mark Burchill).   Manager: Craig Brown.
FRANCE: Ulrich Ramé, Lilian Thuram, Laurent Blanc, Marcel Desailly, Bixente Lizarazu, Didier Deschamps (Cap) (60 Patrick Vieira), Youri Djorkaeff (46 Johan Micoud), Ludovic Giuly (46 Sylvain Wiltord), Emmanuel Petit, Christophe Dugarry (71 Robert Pires), Thierry Henry.
Trainer: Roger Lemmere.
Goals: Sylvain Wiltord (54), Thierry Henry (88)

608. 26.04.2000
HOLLAND v SCOTLAND 0-0
Gelredome, Arnhem

Referee: Hartmut Strampe (Germany)   Attendance: 30,000
HOLLAND: Edwin van der Sar, André Antonius Maria Ooijer, Hubertus Gerard Konterman, Franciscus de Boer (Cap), Arthur Johannes Numan, Paul Bosvelt, Edgar Steven Davids, Marc Overmars (46 Boudewijn Zenden), Jerrel Floyd Hasselbaink (67 Petrus Ferdinandus van Hooijdonk), Rodolfus Antonius Makaay (60 Jeffrey Dennis Talan), Dennis Nicolaas Maria Bergkamp (46 Patrick Steven Kluivert).
Trainer: Franklin Edmundo Rijkaard.

SCOTLAND: Neil Sullivan, David Gillespie Weir, Paul Ritchie, Christian Edward Dailly (85 Brian O'Neil), Matthew Stephen Elliott, John McNamara (66 Mark Burchill), Paul Lambert (Cap), Craig William Burley (46 Iain Durrant), Neil McCann, Donald Hutchison, William Dodds.   Manager: Craig Brown.

609. 30.05.2000
REPUBLIC OF IRELAND v SCOTLAND 1-2 (1-2)
Lansdowne Road, Dublin

Referee: Vítor Manuel Melo Pereira (Portugal)   Att: 30,200
REPUBLIC OF IRELAND: Alan Thomas Kelly, Stephen Carr, Gary Patrick Breen (77 Richard Patrick Dunne), Kevin Daniel Kilbane, Philip Andrew Babb, Mark Kennedy (61 Damien Anthony Duff), Jason Wynn McAteer, Stephen John Finnan, Stephen McPhail (61 Terence Michael Phelan), Niall John Quinn (77 Dominic Joseph Foley), Robert David Keane.
Trainer: Michael Joseph McCarthy.

SCOTLAND: Neil Sullivan, Christian Edward Dailly, Gary Andrew Naysmith (Iain Durrant), Brian O'Neil, Matthew Stephen Elliott, Craig William Burley, Barry Ferguson (84 Colin Cameron), Paul Lambert (Cap) (75 Allan Johnston), Neil McCann (90 Steven Pressley), Donald Hutchison, William Dodds (46 Kevin William Gallacher). Manager: Craig Brown.

Goals: Mark Kennedy (2) /
Donald Hutchison (15), Barry Ferguson (27)

610. 02.09.2000   17th World Cup Qualifiers
LATVIA v SCOTLAND 0-1 (0-0)
Skonto, Riga

Referee: Andreas Schluchter (Switzerland)   Att: 9,500
LATVIA: Aleksandrs Koliņko, Igors N. Stepanovs, Vitālijs Astafjevs, Juris Laizāns, Valentīns Lobaņovs, Oļegs Blagonadeždins, Valerijs Ivanovs, Imants Bleidelis, Marians Pahars, Andrejs Rubins, Andrejs Štolcers.
Trainer: Gary Johnson (England).

SCOTLAND: Neil Sullivan, David Gillespie Weir (46 Colin Cameron), Callum Iain Davidson (46 Gary Andrew Naysmith), Christian Edward Dailly, Edward Colin James Hendry (Cap), Thomas Boyd, Donald Hutchison, Barry Ferguson, Neil McCann, Matthew Stephen Elliott, William Dodds (90 Gary Holt).   Manager: Craig Brown.

Goal: Neil McCann (88)

611. 07.10.2000   17th World Cup Qualifiers
SAN MARINO v SCOTLAND 0-2 (0-0)
Olimpico, Serravalle

Referee: Gylfi Þór Orrason (Iceland)   Attendance: 4,377
SAN MARINO: Federico Gasperoni, Mirco Gennari, Mauro Marani, Luca Gobbi, Ivan Matteoni (72 Vittorio Valentini), Simone Bacciocchi, Ermanno Zonzini (78 Pier Domenico Della Valle), Pierangelo Manzaroli, Paolo Montagna (60 Marco De Luigi), Riccardo Muccioli, Bryan Gasperoni.
Trainer: Gian Paolo Mazza.

SCOTLAND: Neil Sullivan, Christian Edward Dailly (36 David Gillespie Weir), Matthew Stephen Elliott, Edward Colin James Hendry, John McNamara, Gary Andrew Naysmith, Colin Cameron, Donald Hutchison, Neil McCann (46 Allan Johnston), William Dodds, Kevin William Gallacher (Cap) (66 Paul Dickov).   Manager: Craig Brown.

Goals: Matthew Stephen Elliott (71), Donald Hutchison (73)

612. 11.10.2000   17th World Cup Qualifiers
CROATIA v SCOTLAND 1-1 (1-1)
Maksimir, Zagreb

Referee: Gilles Veissière (France)   Attendance: 17,995
CROATIA: Željko Pavlović, Dario Šimić, Igor Štimac, Robert Kovač, Zvonimir Soldo (46 Igor Bišćan), Robert Prosinečki, Niko Kovač, Danijel Šarić, Robert Jarni (46 Boris Živković), Boško Balaban, Alen Bokšić (75 Davor Vugrinec).
Trainer: Miroslav Blažević.

SCOTLAND: Neil Sullivan, David Gillespie Weir, Gary Andrew Naysmith, Matthew Stephen Elliott, Edward Colin James Hendry (Cap), Thomas Boyd, Craig William Burley, Donald Hutchison, Colin Cameron, Allan Johnston (46 Paul Dickov (89 Gary Holt)), Kevin William Gallacher.   Manager: Craig Brown.

Goals: Alen Bokšić (16) / Kevin William Gallacher (24)

613. 15.11.2000
SCOTLAND v AUSTRALIA 0-2 (0-1)
Hampden Park, Glasgow

Referee: Pascal Garibian (France)   Attendance: 30,985
SCOTLAND: Jonathan Alan Gould, Thomas Boyd (Cap), Christian Edward Dailly, Brian O'Neil (58 Edward Colin James Hendry), David Gillespie Weir (46 Matthew Stephen Elliott), Craig William Burley (63 Paul Dickov), Barry Ferguson, Colin Cameron (46 Neil McCann), Dominic Matteo, Donald Hutchison, William Dodds.   Manager: Craig Brown.

AUSTRALIA: Mark Schwarzer, Tony Popovic, Shaun Murphy, Kevin Muscat, Stan Lazaridis, Brett Emerton, Josip Skoko (75 Kasey Wehrman), Paul Okon, Daniel Tiatto (67 Jacob Burns), Paul Agostino (46 Mile Sterjovski), David Zdrillic (89 Clayton Zane).   Trainer: Frank Farina.

Goals: Brett Emerton (12), David Zdrillic (66)

111

614.   24.03.2001   17th World Cup Qualifiers
SCOTLAND v BELGIUM 2-2 (2-0)
Hampden Park, Glasgow

Referee: Kim Milton Nielsen (Denmark)   Att: 37,480

SCOTLAND: Neil Sullivan, David Gillespie Weir, Matthew Stephen Elliott, Edward Colin James Hendry (Cap), Thomas Boyd, Craig William Burley, Barry Ferguson, Paul Lambert, Dominic Matteo, Donald Hutchison, William Dodds (88 Kevin William Gallacher).   Manager: Craig Brown.

BELGIUM: Geert De Vlieger, Eric Deflandre, Joos Valgaeren (58 Daniel Van Buyten), Glen De Boeck, Didier Dheedene, Yves Vanderhaeghe, Marc Wilmots, Bart Goor, Emile Lokonda Mpenza, Walter Baseggio (79 Sven Vermant), Mark Hendrikx (46 Robert Peeters).   Trainer: Robert Waseige.

Goals: William Dodds (2, 29 pen) /
Marc Wilmots (58), Daniel Van Buyten (90)

615.   28.03.2001   17th World Cup Qualifiers
SCOTLAND v SAN MARINO 4-0 (3-0)
Hampden Park, Glasgow

Referee: Petteri Kari (Finland)   Attendance: 27,313

SCOTLAND: Neil Sullivan, David Gillespie Weir, Matthew Stephen Elliott (46 Thomas Boyd), Edward Colin James Hendry (Cap), Craig William Burley, Paul Lambert, Colin Cameron (83 Scot Gemmill), Dominic Matteo (64 Kevin William Gallacher), Allan Johnston, Donald Hutchison, William Dodds.   Manager: Craig Brown.

SAN MARINO: Federico Gasperoni, Simone Della Balda (90 Nicola Albani), Mauro Marani, Simone Bacciocchi, Ivan Matteoni, Luca Gobbi, Riccardo Muccioli, Ermanno Zonzini, Andy Selva, Damiano Vannucci (69 Cristian Selva), Pierangelo Manzaroli (79 Ivan Bugli).   Trainer: Gian Paolo Mazza.

Goals: Edward Colin James Hendry (22, 33), William Dodds (34), Colin Cameron (65)

616.   25.04.2001
POLAND v SCOTLAND 1-1 (0-0)
Zawisza, Bydgoszcz

Referee: Juan Ansuategui Roca (Spain)   Attendance: 18,000

POLAND: Jerzy Dudek, Tomasz Kłos, Tomasz Wałdoch (Cap), Jacek Zieliński (46 Radosław Kałużny), Michał Żewłakow (46 Jacek Krzynówek), Tomasz Iwan, Tomasz Hajto, Tomasz Zdebel (57 Piotr Świerczewski), Marek Koźmiński, Paweł Kryszałowicz (78 Maciej Żurawski), Marcin Żewłakow (63 Marcin Mięciel).   Trainer: Jerzy Engel.

SCOTLAND: Neil Sullivan, Christian Edward Dailly, Thomas Boyd (Cap), Barry Nicholson, Charles Miller (56 Stephen Caldwell), Gavin Paul Rae, John O'Neil (73 Scot Gemmill), Callum Iain Davidson (72 David Gillespie Weir), Colin Cameron (46 Andrew McLaren), Scott Booth (80 Kenneth Miller), William Dodds (46 Steven Crawford).
Manager: Craig Brown.

Sent off: Tomasz Iwan (82)

Goals: Radosław Kałużny (50) / Scott Booth (69 pen)

617.   01.09.2001   17th World Cup Qualifiers
SCOTLAND v CROATIA 0-0
Hampden Park, Glasgow

Referee: Ľuboš Michel (Slovakia)   Attendance: 47,384

SCOTLAND: Neil Sullivan, David Gillespie Weir, Matthew Stephen Elliott, Dominic Matteo, Christian Edward Dailly, Craig William Burley, Paul Lambert (Cap), Gary Andrew Naysmith (85 Scot Gemmill), Donald Hutchison, Scott Booth (71 William Dodds), Neil McCann (52 Colin Cameron).   Manager: Craig Brown.

CROATIA: Stipe Pletikosa, Robert Kovač, Robert Jarni, Zvonimir Soldo, Igor Štimac, Igor Tudor, Stjepan Tomas (84 Igor Bišćan), Robert Prosinečki (78 Davor Vugrinec), Mario Stanić (72 Davor Šuker), Boris Živković, Boško Balaban.
Trainer: Mirko Jozić.

618.   05.09.2001   17th World Cup Qualifiers
BELGIUM v SCOTLAND 2-0 (1-0)
"Roi Baudouin", Bruxelles

Referee: Manuel Mejuto González (Spain)   Att: 43,500

BELGIUM: Geert De Vlieger, Eric Deflandre, Glen De Boeck, Eric Van Meir, Nico Van Kerckhoven, Yves Vanderhaeghe, Marc Wilmots, Bart Goor, Wesley Sonck (82 Robert Peeters), Johan Walem (87 Timmy Simons), Gert Verheyen.
Trainer: Robert Waseige.

SCOTLAND: Neil Sullivan, David Gillespie Weir (66 Colin Cameron), Matthew Stephen Elliott, Thomas Boyd (57 Scott Booth), Christian Edward Dailly, Dominic Matteo, Craig William Burley (82 John McNamara), Paul Lambert (Cap), Gary Andrew Naysmith, Donald Hutchison, William Dodds.
Manager: Craig Brown.

Goals: Nico Van Kerckhoven (28), Bart Goor (90)

619. 06.10.2001   17th World Cup Qualifiers
SCOTLAND v LATVIA 2-1 (1-1)
Hampden Park, Glasgow

Referee: Terje Hauge (Norway)   Attendance: 23,228

SCOTLAND: Neil Sullivan, David Gillespie Weir, Matthew Stephen Elliott (71 Gavin Paul Rae), Christian Edward Dailly, Barry Nicholson (62 Scott Booth), Craig William Burley (Cap), Colin Cameron, Callum Iain Davidson, Donald Hutchison (77 Scott Severin), Neil McCann, Douglas Alan Freedman.
Manager: Craig Brown.

LATVIA: Alesandrs Koliņko, Igors N. Stepanovs, Vitālijs Astafjevs, Artūrs Zakrešvskis, Juris Laizāns, Oļegs Blagonadeždins, Aleksandrs Isakovs, Imants Bleidelis (75 Vladimirs Koļesničenko), Marians Pahars, Andrejs Rubins (83 Viktors Dobrecovs), Māris Verpakovskis.
Trainer: Aleksandrs Starkovs.

Goals: Douglas Alan Freedman (44), David Weir (54) / Andrejs Rubins (21)

620. 27.03.2002
FRANCE v SCOTLAND 5-0 (4-0)
Stade de France, Saint-Denis, Paris

Referee: Jacek Granat (Poland)   Attendance: 80,000

FRANCE: Fabien Barthez, Vincent Candela (58 Christian Karembeu), Frank Leboeuf (64 Philippe Christanval), Marcel Desailly (46 Mikaël Silvestre), Bixente Lizarazu, Patrick Vieira (46 Claude Makélélé), Emmanuel Petit, Zinedine Zidane (81 Youri Djorkaeff), Sylvain Wiltord (57 Steve Marlet), Thierry Henry, David Trézéguet (74 Eric Carrière).
Trainer: Roger Lemmere.

SCOTLAND: Neil Sullivan, David Gillespie Weir, Christian Edward Dailly, Stephen Crainey, Gary Caldwell, Dominic Matteo, Colin Cameron (46 Gary Holt (74 John McNamara)), Paul Lambert (Cap), Neil McCann, Steven Crawford (64 Steven Thompson), Douglas Alan Freedman (46 Scot Gemmill). Manager: Hans-Hubert Vogts (Germany).

Goals: Zinedine Zidane (12), David Trézéguet (23, 42), Thierry Henry (32), Steve Marlet (87)

621. 17.04.2002
SCOTLAND v NIGERIA 1-2 (1-1)
Pittodrie, Aberdeen

Referee: Tom Henning Øvrebø (Norway)   Att: 20,465

SCOTLAND: Robert Douglas, Robert Keith Stockdale (46 Graham Alexander), Stephen Crainey, Paul Lambert (Cap), David Gillespie Weir, Christian Edward Dailly, Kevin McNaughton, Gareth Williams (64 Michael Stewart), Steven Thompson (75 Garry Lawrence O'Connor), Scot Gemmill (46 Gary Caldwell), Neil McCann (78 Allan Johnston).
Manager: Hans-Hubert Vogts (Germany).

NIGERIA: Augustine Amamchukwu Ejide, Joseph Ikpo Yobo, Isaac Okoronkwo, John Chukwudi Utaka (54 Pius Nelson Ikedia), Bartholomew Ogbeche, Augustine Azuka Okocha, Eric Ejiofor, Justice Christopher (78 Mutiu Adepoju), Efetobore Sodje (85 Emeka Ifeajigwa), Nwankwo Christian Kanu, Julius Aghahowa. Trainer: Adegboye Onigbinde.

Goals: Christian Dailly (7) / Julius Aghahowa (41, 67)

622. 10.05.2002
SOUTH KOREA v SCOTLAND 4-1 (1-0)
Asiad Main Stadium, Busan

Referee: Santhan Nagalingam (Singapore)   Att: 52,384

SOUTH KOREA: Kim Byung-Ji, Kim Tae-Young, Hong Myung-Bo (64 Yoon Jung-Hwan), Choi Jin-Cheol (46 Lee Min-Sung), Lee Eul-Yong, Lee Young-Pyo, Song Chong-Gug, Yoo Sang-Cheol, Lee Cheon-Soo (72 Choi Tae-Uk), Hwang Seon-Hong (46 Ahn Jung-Hwan), Park Ji-Sung (72 Cha Doo-Ri). Trainer: Guus Hiddink (Holland).

SCOTLAND: Neil Sullivan, Graham Alexander (63 Robert Keith Stockdale), Maurice Ross, David Gillespie Weir, Christian Edward Dailly (Cap), Gary Caldwell, Allan Johnston (66 Kevin Kyle), Scot Gemmill, Scott Dobie, Michael Stewart (46 Scott Severin), Garry Lawrence O'Connor (46 Gareth Williams). Manager: Hans-Hubert Vogts (Germany).

Goals: Lee Cheon-Soo (14), Ahn Jung-Hwan (56, 86), Yoon Jung-Hwan (66) / Scott Dobie (74)

623. 20.05.2002   Hong Kong Reunification Cup
SOUTH AFRICA v SCOTLAND 2-0 (1-0)
Hong Kong Stadium, Hong Kong

Referee: Chan Siu Kee (Hong Kong)   Attendance: 5,000

SOUTH AFRICA: Hans Vonk, Pierre Issa, Aaron Mokoena (60 Cyril Nzama), Bradley Carnell, Macbeth Sibaya, Jabu Pule (68 McDonald Mukansi), Teboho Mokoena, Lucas Radebe, Quinton Fortune (83 Delron Buckley), Benedict McCarthy, Sibusiso Zuma (81 George Koumantarakis).
Trainer: Jomo Sono.

SCOTLAND: Robert Douglas, Maurice Ross, David Gillespie Weir, Christian Edward Dailly (Cap), Gary Caldwell (46 Lee Wilkie), Allan Johnston (60 James McFadden), Scot Gemmill, Scott Dobie (85 Michael Stewart), Kevin Kyle, Robert Keith Stockdale (68 Graham Alexander), Gareth Williams (77 Scott Severin). Manager: Hans-Hubert Vogts (Germany).

Goals: Teboho Mokoena (20), George Koumantarakis (82)

624. 21.08.2002
SCOTLAND v DENMARK 0-1 (0-1)
Hampden Park, Glasgow
Referee: Leslie Irvine (Republic of Ireland)   Att: 28,766
SCOTLAND: Robert Douglas, Maurice Ross, David Gillespie Weir (78 Scott Severin), Christian Edward Dailly, Robert Keith Stockdale (72 Graham Alexander), Barry Ferguson, Paul Lambert (Cap) (81 Derek John McInnes), Kevin McNaughton (46 Stephen Crainey), Gary Andrew Naysmith (72 Allan Johnston), Kevin Kyle, Steven Thompson (56 Scott Dobie).
Manager: Hans-Hubert Vogts (Germany).
DENMARK: Thomas Sørensen, Kasper Bøgelund (46 Jesper Grønkjær), Martin Laursen (66 Morten Wieghorst), Niclas Jensen, René Henriksen (Cap) (84 Steven Lustü), Christian Bager Poulsen, Thomas Gravesen (46 Claus Jensen), Ebbe Sand, Jon Dahl Tomasson, Dennis Rommedahl (46 Jan Michaelsen), Peter Løvenkrands (73 Michael Silberbauer).
Trainer: Morten Olsen.
Goal: Ebbe Sand (8)

625. 07.09.2002   12th European Champs Qualifiers
FAROE ISLANDS v SCOTLAND 2-2 (2-0)
Svangaskarð, Toftir
Referee: Jacek Granat (Poland)   Attendance: 4,000
FAROE ISLANDS: Jens Martin Knudsen, Óli Johannesen, Jens Kristian Hansen, Pól Thorsteinsson, Jón Rói Jacobsen, Hjalgrím Elttør (90 Heðin á Lakjuni), Fróði Benjaminsen, Julian Schantz Johnsson, Jákup á Borg, John Petersen (79 Andrew av Fløtum), Christian Høgni Jacobsen (74 Rógvi Jacobsen).   Trainer: Henrik Larsen (Denmark).
SCOTLAND: Robert Douglas, Maurice Ross (76 Graham Alexander), Stephen Crainey, Christian Edward Dailly, David Gillespie Weir, Barry Ferguson, Paul Dickov (46 Steven Crawford), Scott Dobie (83 Steven Thompson), Kevin Kyle, Paul Lambert (Cap), Allan Johnston.
Manager: Hans-Hubert Vogts (Germany).
Goals: John Petersen (7, 12) /
Paul Lambert (61), Barry Ferguson (83)

626. 12.10.2002   12th European Champs Qualifiers
ICELAND v SCOTLAND 0-2 (0-1)
Laugardalsvöllur, Reykjavík
Referee: Alain Sars (France)   Attendance: 7,065
ICELAND: Árni Gautur Arason, Bjarni Óskar Þorsteinsson, Lárus Orri Sigurðsson, Hermann Hreiðarsson, Arnar Þór Viðarsson (66 Marel Jóhann Baldvinsson), Brynjar Björn Gunnarsson, Rúnar Kristinsson (Cap), Ívar Ingimarsson, Haukur Ingi Guðnason (75 Bjarni Eggerts Guðjónsson), Helgi Sigurðsson (46 Heiðar Helguson), Eiður Smári Guðjohnsen.
Trainer: Atli Eðvaldsson.

SCOTLAND: Robert Douglas, Maurice Ross, Lee Wilkie, Stephen Pressley, Christian Edward Dailly, Barry Ferguson, John McNamara (23 Callum Iain Davidson), Steven Crawford, Steven Thompson (87 Scott Severin), Paul Lambert (Cap), Gary Andrew Naysmith (90 Russell Anderson).
Manager: Hans-Hubert Vogts (Germany).
Goals: Christian Dailly (7), Gary Andrew Naysmith (63)

627. 15.10.2002
SCOTLAND v CANADA 3-1 (1-1)
Easter Road, Edinburgh
Referee: Luc Huyghe (Belgium)   Attendance: 16,207
SCOTLAND: Paul Gallacher, Maurice Ross (46 Callum Iain Davidson), Christian Edward Dailly (Cap), Steven Pressley, Lee Wilkie (75 Ian William Murray), Russell Anderson, Graham Alexander, Scot Gemmill (66 Scott Severin), Paul John Devlin, Steven Crawford (89 Kevin Kyle), Steven Thompson (81 James McFadden).   Manager: Hans-Hubert Vogts (Germany).
CANADA: Lars Hirschfeld, Paul Fenwick, Richard Corey Hastings, Kevin McKenna, Julián de Guzmán, Christopher Pozniak, Daniel Imhof (81 Davide Xausa), Paul Stalteri, Tamandani Nsaliwa, Tomasz Radzinski, Dwayne De Rosario.
Trainer: Holger Osieck (Germany).
Goals: Steven Crawford (11, 73), Steven Thompson (49) /
Dwayne De Rosario (9 pen)

628. 20.11.2002
PORTUGAL v SCOTLAND 2-0 (2-0)
Primeiro de Maio, Braga
Referee: Viorel Anghelinei (Romania)   Attendance: 8,000
PORTUGAL: Joaquim Manuel Sampaio Silva "Quim" (89 Nélson Alexandre Gomes Pereira), Fernando Manuel Silva Couto (Cap), Rui Jorge de Sousa Dias Macedo de Oliveira (58 Jorge Miguel de Oliveira Ribeiro), Fernando José da Silva Freitas Meira, Ricardo Sérgio Rocha Azevedo, Luis Filipe Madeira Caeiro "Figo" (46 Marco Júlio Castanheira Afonso Alves Ferreira), Rui Manuel César Costa (58 Pedro Miguel da Silva Mendes), Sérgio Paulo Marceneiro Conceição, "Simão" Pedro Fonseca Sabrosa (78 João Alexandre Duarte Fernandes "Neca"), Tiago Cardoso Mendes (83 Nuno Assis Lopes de Almeida), Pedro Miguel Carreiro Resendes "Pauleta" (46 Nuno Miguel Soares Pereira Ribeiro "Nuno Gomes").
Trainer: António Luís Alves Ribeiro Oliveira.
SCOTLAND: Robert Douglas, Russell Anderson (23 Derek John McInnes), Maurice Ross (46 Paul John Devlin), Steven Pressley, Christian Edward Dailly, Lee Wilkie (83 Scott Severin), Graham Alexander, Steven Crawford, Scott Dobie (78 Kevin Kyle), Paul Lambert (Cap) (68 Gareth Williams), Gary Andrew Naysmith.   Manager: Hans-Hubert Vogts (Germany).
Goals: Pedro Miguel Carreiro Resendes "Pauleta" (7, 18)

629. 12.02.2003
SCOTLAND v REPUBLIC OF IRELAND 0-2 (0-2)
Hampden Park, Glasgow
Referee: Eric Braamhaar (Holland)   Attendance: 33,337
SCOTLAND: Neil Sullivan (46 Paul Gallacher), Stephen Caldwell, Russell Anderson, Christian Edward Dailly, Graham Alexander, Paul Lambert (Cap) (46 Scot Gemmill), Barry Ferguson (65 Colin Cameron), Gary Andrew Naysmith, Neil McCann (65 James Smith), Steven Crawford (65 Steven Thompson), Donald Hutchison (46 Paul John Devlin). Manager: Hans-Hubert Vogts (Germany).
REPUBLIC OF IRELAND: Dean Lawrence Kiely (82 Nicholas Vincent Colgan), Stephen Carr, John Francis O'Shea (81 Richard Patrick Dunne), Gary Patrick Breen (90 Andrew James O'Brien), Ian Patrick Harte, Steven John Reid (78 Colin Healy), Matthew Rhys Holland, Mark Anthony Kinsella (78 Lee Kevin Carsley), Kevin Daniel Kilbane, Clinton Hubert Morrison, Gary Michael Thomas Doherty (73 David James Connolly).   Trainer: Brian Kerr.
Goals: Kevin Kilbane (7), Clinton Hubert Morrison (16)

630. 29.03.2003   12th European Champs Qualifiers
SCOTLAND v ICELAND 2-1 (1-0)
Hampden Park, Glasgow
Referee: René Temmink (Holland)   Attendance: 37,938
SCOTLAND: Robert Douglas, Graham Alexander, Lee Wilkie, Christian Edward Dailly, Steven Pressley, Barry Ferguson, Steven Crawford, Paul Lambert (Cap), Kenneth Miller (81 John McNamara), Donald Hutchison (65 Paul John Devlin), Gary Andrew Naysmith. Manager: Hans-Hubert Vogts (Germany).
ICELAND: Árni Gautur Arason, Bjarni Óskar Þorsteinsson, Lárus Orri Sigurðsson, Guðni Bergsson, Ívar Ingimarsson, Arnar Þór Viðarsson (80 Indriði Sigurðsson), Brynjar Björn Gunnarsson (72 Þórður Guðjónsson), Jóhannes Karl Guðjónsson, Arnar Grétarsson, Rúnar Kristinsson (Cap), Eiður Smári Guðjohnsen (85 Tryggvi Guðmundsson). Trainer: Atli Eðvaldsson.
Goals: Kenneth Miller (10), Lee Wilkie (70) / Eiður Smári Guðjohnsen (48)

631. 02.04.2003   12th European Champs Qualifiers
LITHUANIA v SCOTLAND 1-0 (0-0)
S Darius ir S Girenas, Kaunas
Referee: Fritz Stuchlik (Austria)   Attendance: 6,400
LITHUANIA: Gintaras Staučė (Cap), Deividas Šemberas, Ignas Dedura, Nerijus Barasa, Vadimas Petrenka (72 Darius Maciulevičius), Tomas Žvirgždauskas, Igoris Morinas, Saulius Mikalajūnas (90 Orestas Buitkus), Edgaras Jankauskas (62 Arturas Fomenka), Tomas Ražanauskas, Dainius Gleveckas. Trainer: Algimantas Liubinskas.
SCOTLAND: Paul Gallacher, Graham Alexander, Lee Wilkie, Christian Edward Dailly, Steven Pressley, John McNamara (78 Andrew David Gray), Steven Crawford (57 Paul John Devlin), Paul Lambert (Cap), Kenneth Miller, Donald Hutchison (85 Colin Cameron), Gary Andrew Naysmith. Manager: Hans-Hubert Vogts (Germany).
Goal: Tomas Ražanauskas (74 pen)

632. 30.04.2003
SCOTLAND v AUSTRIA 0-2 (0-2)
Hampden Park, Glasgow
Referee: Nicolai Vollquartz (Denmark)   Attendance: 12,189
SCOTLAND: Paul Gallacher, Lee Wilkie, Andrew Webster, Christian Edward Dailly (Cap) (46 Scot Gemmill), Steven Pressley, Craig William Burley (64 Colin Cameron), Paul John Devlin (85 James Smith), Donald Hutchison (62 Kenneth Miller), Steven Thompson (46 Steven Crawford), James McFadden, Gary Andrew Naysmith. Manager: Hans-Hubert Vogts (Germany).
AUSTRIA: Thomas Mandl, Paul Scharner, Anton Ehmann, Martin Stranzl, Ernst Dospel, René Aufhauser, Markus Schopp, Thomas Flögel (89 Mario Hieblinger), Michael Wagner, Roland Kirchler (84 Andreas Herzog), Mario Haas (64 Ronald Brunmayr).   Trainer: Johann Krankl.
Goals: Roland Kirchler (28), Mario Haas (33)

633. 27.05.2003
SCOTLAND v NEW ZEALAND 1-1 (1-0)
Tynecastle Park, Edinburgh
Referee: Martin Ingvarsson (Sweden)   Attendance: 10,016
SCOTLAND: Robert Douglas, Maurice Ross (46 Graham Alexander), Steven Pressley, Andrew Webster, Gary Andrew Naysmith, Paul John Devlin, Christian Edward Dailly (Cap), John McNamara (83 Brian Kerr), James McFadden, Kevin Kyle (60 Andrew David Gray), Steven Crawford. Manager: Hans-Hubert Vogts (Germany).
NEW ZEALAND: Michael Utting (46 Jason Batty), David Mulligan (46 Duncan Oughton), Chris Zoricich (69 Scott Smith), Ryan Nelsen, Gerard Davism, Aaran Lines (81 Chris Bouckenooghe), Chris Jackson (54 Raf de Gregorio), Mark Burton, Simon Elliott, Vaughan Coveny, Noah Hickey. Trainer: Michael Waitt (England).
Goals: Steven Crawford (11) / Ryan Nelsen (48)

634. 07.06.2003   12th European Champs Qualifiers
SCOTLAND v GERMANY 1-1 (0-1)
Hampden Park, Glasgow

Referee: Domenico Messina (Italy)   Attendance: 52,000

SCOTLAND: Robert Douglas, Maurice Ross (73 John McNamara), Gary Andrew Naysmith, Christian Edward Dailly, Steven Pressley, Andrew Webster, Paul John Devlin (59 Gavin Paul Rae), Paul Lambert (Cap), Kenneth Miller (88 Steven Thompson), Steven Crawford, Colin Cameron. Manager: Hans-Hubert Vogts (Germany).

GERMANY: Oliver Kahn, Arne Friedrich, Carsten Ramelow, Christian Wörns, Torsten Frings, Jens Jeremies, Tobias Rau (57 Paul Freier), Bernd Schneider (85 Sebastian Kehl), Michael Ballack, Fredi Bobic, Miroslav Klose (73 Olivier Neuville). Trainer: Rudolf Völler.

Goals: Kenneth Miller (69) / Fredi Bobic (22)

635. 20.08.2003
NORWAY v SCOTLAND 0-0
Ullevall, Oslo

Referee: Mikko Vuorela (Finland)   Attendance: 12,758

NORWAY: Espen Johnsen, Christer Basma (70 Alexander Aas), Henning Berg (Cap) (46 Ronny Johnsen), Claus Lundekvam, André Bergdølmo (69 Steffen Iversen), Ole Gunnar Solskjær, Martin Andresen, Brede Paulsen Hangeland (46 Trond Andersen), Frode Johnsen (46 Jan Gunnar Solli), John Arne Riise, John Alieu Carew (72 Håvard Flo). Trainer: Nils Johan Semb.

SCOTLAND: Robert Douglas, Maurice Ross (60 Darren Barr Fletcher), Gary Andrew Naysmith, Steven Pressley, Andrew Webster, Barry Ferguson, Paul Lambert (Cap), Christian Edward Dailly, Donald Hutchison, Steven Crawford (80 Paul John Devlin), Colin Cameron (85 Gavin Paul Rae). Manager: Hans-Hubert Vogts (Germany).

636. 06.09.2003   12th European Champs Qualifiers
SCOTLAND v FAROE ISLANDS 3-1 (2-1)
Hampden Park, Glasgow

Referee: Darko Čeferin (Slovenia)   Attendance: 40,901

SCOTLAND: Robert Douglas, John McNamara, Gary Andrew Naysmith, Andrew Webster, Lee Wilkie, Barry Ferguson (Cap), Paul John Devlin (58 James McFadden), Colin Cameron, Paul Dickov (67 Gavin Paul Rae), Steven Crawford (75 Steven Thompson), Neil McCann. Manager: Hans-Hubert Vogts (Germany).

FAROE ISLANDS: Jákup Mikkelsen, Jann Ingi Petersen, Pól Thorsteinsson, Jón Rói Jacobsen, Rógvi Jacobsen, Fródi Benjaminsen, Julian Schantz Johnsson (84 Atli Danielsen), Jákup á Borg (84 Christian Lamhauge Holst), John Petersen, Helgi Petersen (65 Tór-Ingar Akselsen), Óli Johannesen. Trainer: Henrik Larsen (Denmark).

Goals: Neil McCann (8), Paul Dickov (45), James McFadden (73) / Julian Schantz Johnsson (35)

637. 10.09.2003   12th European Champs Qualifiers
GERMANY v SCOTLAND 2-1 (1-0)
Westfalen, Dortmund

Referee: Anders Frisk (Sweden)   Attendance: 67,000

GERMANY: Oliver Kahn, Marko Rehmer, Carsten Ramelow, Christian Wörns, Arne Friedrich, Frank Baumann, Tobias Rau, Bernd Schneider (81 Sebastian Kehl), Michael Ballack, Fredi Bobic (76 Miroslav Klose), Kevin Dennis Kurányi. Trainer: Rudolf Völler.

SCOTLAND: Robert Douglas, John McNamara, Gary Andrew Naysmith, Christian Edward Dailly, Steven Pressley, Barry Ferguson, James McFadden (53 Gavin Paul Rae), Colin Cameron, Steven Thompson, Paul Lambert (Cap) (46 Maurice Ross), Neil McCann. Manager: Hans-Hubert Vogts (Germany).

Sent off: Maurice Ross (66)

Goals: Fredi Bobic (25), Michael Ballack (50 pen) / Neil McCann (60)

638. 11.10.2003   12th European Champs Qualifiers
SCOTLAND v LITHUANIA 1-0 (0-0)
Hampden Park, Glasgow

Referee: Claude Colombo (France)   Attendance: 50,343

SCOTLAND: Robert Douglas, John McNamara, Gary Andrew Naysmith, Christian Edward Dailly, Steven Pressley, Barry Ferguson (Cap), Gavin Paul Rae, Colin Cameron (66 Darren Barr Fletcher), Kenneth Miller (66 Donald Hutchison), Steven Crawford, James McFadden (90 Graham Alexander). Manager: Hans-Hubert Vogts (Germany).

LITHUANIA: Gintaras Staučė (Cap), Rolandas Džiaukštas, Ignas Dedura, Nerijus Barasa, Darius Regelskis (87 Ričardas Beniušis), Tomas Žvirgždauskas, Donatas Vencevičius (82 Darius Maciulevičius), Giedrius Barevičius (46 Deividas Česnauskis), Edgaras Jankauskas, Tomas Ražanauskas, Robertas Poškus. Trainer: Algimantas Liubinskas.

Goal: Darren Barr Fletcher (70)

639. 15.11.2003   12th Euro Champs Qualifier Play-Off
SCOTLAND v HOLLAND 1-0 (1-0)
Hampden Park, Glasgow

Referee: Referee: Terje Hauge (Norway)   Att: 50,670

SCOTLAND: Robert Douglas, John McNamara, Gary Andrew Naysmith, Steven Pressley, Lee Wilkie, Barry Ferguson (Cap), Darren Barr Fletcher, Christian Edward Dailly, Paul Dickov (66 Kenneth Miller), James McFadden (90 Donald Hutchison), Neil McCann (71 Stephen Paul Pearson). Manager: Hans-Hubert Vogts (Germany).

HOLLAND: Edwin van der Sar, André Antonius Maria Ooijer, Jacob Stam, Franciscus de Boer (Cap), Giovanni Christiaan van Bronckhorst (46 Clarence Clyde Seedorf), Phillip Cocu, Andy van der Meyde, Edgar Steven Davids (61 Rafael Ferdinand van der Vaart), Rutgerus Johannes Martinus van Nistelrooy, Patrick Steven Kluivert (77 Rodulfus Antonius Makaay), Marc Overmars. Trainer: Dirk Nicolaas Advocaat.

Goal: James McFadden (22)

640. 19.11.2003 12th Euro Champs Qualifier Play-Off
HOLLAND v SCOTLAND 6-0 (3-0)
ArenA, Amsterdam
Referee: Ľuboš Michel (Slovakia)   Attendance: 51,000
HOLLAND: Edwin van der Sar, André Antonius Maria Ooijer (46 Franciscus de Boer), Michael John Reiziger, Wesley Sneijder, Rafael Ferdinand van der Vaart, Phillip Cocu (Cap), Edgar Steven Davids, Marc Overmars, Andy van der Meyde, Wilfred Bouma (69 Clarence Clyde Seedorf), Rutgerus Johannes Martinus van Nistelrooy (78 Patrick Steven Kluivert). Trainer: Dirk Nicolaas Advocaat.
SCOTLAND: Robert Douglas, John McNamara, Gary Andrew Naysmith (46 Maurice Ross), Steven Pressley, Lee Wilkie, Barry Ferguson (Cap), Darren Barr Fletcher, Gavin Paul Rae, Paul Dickov (46 Steven Crawford), James McFadden, Neil McCann (63 Kenneth Miller).
Manager: Hans-Hubert Vogts (Germany).
Goals: Wesley Sneijder (13), André Ooijer (32), Rutgerus Johannes Martinus van Nistelrooy (37, 51, 67), Frank de Boer (65)

641. 18.02.2004
WALES v SCOTLAND 4-0 (2-0)
Millennium, Cardiff
Referee: Michael Ross (Northern Ireland)   Att: 47,124
WALES: Mark Geoffrey Crossley (46 Darren Ward), Robert Edwards, Daniel Leon Gabbidon, Robert John Page, Andrew Roger Melville (87 Christopher Jeremiah Symons), Simon Davies (33 Paul Parry), John Morgan Oster, Gary Andrew Speed (Cap) (72 Carl Phillip Robinson), Robert William Savage (72 Carl Neil Fletcher), Ryan Joseph Giggs (46 Gareth Keith Taylor), Robert Earnshaw.
Manager: Leslie Mark Hughes.
SCOTLAND: Robert Douglas, John McNamara, Gary Andrew Naysmith (46 Graeme Stuart Murty), Christian Edward Dailly (Cap), Stephen Caldwell, Paul Ritchie, Darren Barr Fletcher (85 Andrew Webster), Colin Cameron (67 Paul Gallagher), Stephen Paul Pearson (46 James McFadden), Kenneth Miller, Paul Dickov.
Manager: Hans-Hubert Vogts (Germany).
Goals: Robert Earnshaw (1, 35, 58), Gareth Keith Taylor (78)

642. 31.03.2004
SCOTLAND v ROMANIA 1-2 (0-1)
Hampden Park, Glasgow
Referee: Jouni Hyytia (Finland)   Attendance: 20,433
SCOTLAND: Paul Gallacher, Graham Alexander, John Kennedy (17 Stephen Crainey), Christian Edward Dailly (Cap), Steven Pressley, Gary Caldwell, Gavin Paul Rae, Colin Cameron, Neil McCann, Steven Thompson (62 Steven Crawford), Kenneth Miller (51 James McFadden).
Manager: Hans-Hubert Vogts (Germany).
ROMANIA: Bogdan Stelea (46 Bogdan Ionuț Lobonț), Flavius Vladimir Stoican, Adrian Mihai Iencsi, Cristian Eugen Chivu (Cap), Răzvan Dincă Raț, Florentin Petre (46 Nicolae Mitea), Ovidiu Petre, Daniel Gabriel Pancu (88 Ionel Daniel Dănciulescu), Florin Lucian Cernat (66 Florin Costin Șoavă), Ioan Viorel Ganea (81 Andrei Cristea), Adrian Mutu. Trainer: Anghel Iordănescu.
Goals: James McFadden (58) / Cristian Eugen Chivu (37), Daniel Gabriel Pancu (52)

643. 28.04.2004
DENMARK v SCOTLAND 1-0 (0-0)
Parken, København
Referee: Martin Ingvarsson (Sweden) (Substituted after 46 mins for Stefan Johansson (Sweden))   Attendance: 22,885
DENMARK: Thomas Sørensen, Morten Wieghorst (81 Martin Retov), René Henriksen (Cap) (66 Per Krøldrup), Martin Laursen, Niclas Jensen (46 Asbjørn Sennels), Thomas Helveg, Daniel Jensen, Jesper Grønkjær (84 Thomas Rasmussen), Jon Dahl Tomasson (46 Ebbe Sand), Martin Jørgensen (66 Dennis Rommedahl), Claus Jensen (46 Kenneth Perez). Trainer: Morten Olsen.
SCOTLAND: Paul Gallacher, Gary Caldwell, Stephen Crainey, Christian Edward Dailly (Cap), Malcolm Mackay, Steven Pressley, Darren Barr Fletcher, Gary Holt (17 Peter Canero), Kevin Kyle, James McFadden, Colin Cameron (46 Neil McCann). Manager: Hans-Hubert Vogts (Germany).
Goal: Ebbe Sand (61)

644. 27.05.2004
ESTONIA v SCOTLAND 0-1 (0-0)
A. Le Coq Arena, Tallinn
Referee: Tony Kolbech Poulsen (Denmark)   Att: 4,000
ESTONIA: Martin Kaalma, Teet Allas, Andrei Stepanov, Enar Jääger, Ragnar Klavan, Taavi Rähn, Sergei Terehhov (85 Ott Reinumäe), Martin Reim, Kristen Viikmäe, Andres Oper, Joel Lindpere (75 Tarmo Kink). Trainer: Arnoldus Dick Pijpers
SCOTLAND: Paul Gallacher, David McNamee, Richard Hughes, Gary Caldwell, Malcolm Mackay, Steven Pressley (46 Andrew Webster), Darren Barr Fletcher (Cap), Gary Holt, Kenneth Miller (78 Steven Crawford), James McFadden (89 Brian Kerr), Nigel Francis Quashie.
Manager: Hans-Hubert Vogts (Germany).
Goal: James McFadden (76)

645. 30.05.2004
SCOTLAND v TRINIDAD & TOBAGO 4-1 (4-0)
Easter Road, Edinburgh
Referee: Pieter Vink (Holland)   Attendance: 16,187
SCOTLAND: Craig Sinclair Gordon, John McNamara, Malcolm Mackay (85 Andrew Webster), Steven Pressley (Cap), Jamie McAllister, Nigel Francis Quashie (72 Richard Hughes), Gary Caldwell (80 Stephen Caldwell), Darren Barr Fletcher, Gary Holt (55 Brian Kerr), James McFadden (85 David McNamee), Steven Crawford (69 Kenneth Miller). Manager: Hans-Hubert Vogts (Germany).
TRINIDAD & TOBAGO: Clayton Ince, Ian Cox, Carlos Edwards (90 Densill Theobald), Brent Sancho, Marvin Andrews, Stokely Mason, Angus Eve (82 Kerwyn Jemmot), Kenwyne Jones (46 Marlon Rojas), Arnold Dwarika (75 Jerren Nixon), Stern John, Cornell Glen (29 Andre Boucaud). Trainer: Bertille St. Clair.
Goals: Darren Barr Fletcher (6), Gary Holt (14), Gary Caldwell (23), Nigel Francis Quashie (34) / Stern John (56)

646. 18.08.2004
SCOTLAND v HUNGARY 0-3 (0-1)
Hampden Park, Glasgow
Referee: Laurent Duhamel (France)   Attendance: 15,933
SCOTLAND: David Marshall, Gary Holt, Gary Andrew Naysmith, Andrew Webster, Steven Pressley, Barry Ferguson (Cap) (70 Scott Severin), Darren Barr Fletcher (74 Stephen Paul Pearson), Gary Caldwell (46 Steven Thompson), Nigel Francis Quashie, James McFadden, Kenneth Miller (57 Steven Crawford).   Manager: Hans-Hubert Vogts (Germany).
HUNGARY: Gábor Király, Roland Juhász (84 Gábor Gyepes), Péter Stark, András Tóth, Csaba Fehér (64 Dénes Rósa), László Bodnár, Balázs Molnár, Péter Simek, Szabolcs Huszti (87 Boldizsár Bodor), Zoltán Gera (76 Leandro de Almeida), Sándor Torghelle (25 Péter Kovács).
Trainer: Lothar Herbert Matthäus (Germany).
Goals: Szabolcs Huszti (45 pen, 54), David Marshall (73 own goal)

647. 03.09.2004
SPAIN v SCOTLAND 1-1 (0-1)*
Ciudad de Valencia, Valencia
Referee: Stéphane Bré (France)   Attendance: 11,000
SPAIN: Iker Casillas Fernández, Aitor López Rekarte, Carles Puyol Soforcada, Carlos Marchena López (58 Iván Helguera Bujía), Asier Del Horno Cosgaya, Joaquín Sánchez Rodríguez, Xabier Alonso Olano "Xabi Alonso", Rubén Baraja Vegas (Cap) (46 Juan Carlos Valerón Santana), José Antonio Reyes Calderón, Fernando José Torres Sanz (46 Raúl González Blanco), Raúl Tamudo Montero (46 Vicente Rodríguez Guillem).   Trainer: José Luis Aragones Suárez.
SCOTLAND: Craig Sinclair Gordon, Gary Caldwell, Gary Andrew Naysmith, Andrew Webster, Malcolm Mackay, Barry Ferguson (Cap), Darren Barr Fletcher (57 Colin Cameron), John McNamara, Nigel Francis Quashie, James McFadden (46 Stephen Paul Pearson), Steven Crawford (57 Kenneth Miller).   Manager: Hans-Hubert Vogts (Germany).
Goals: Raúl (57 pen) / Baraja (17 own goal)

* The match was abandoned after 59 mins due to floodlight failure and a waterlogged pitch.

648. 08.09.2004   18th World Cup Qualifiers
SCOTLAND v SLOVENIA 0-0
Hampden Park, Glasgow
Referee: Claus Bo Larsen (Denmark)   Attendance: 38,278
SCOTLAND: Craig Sinclair Gordon, Gary Caldwell, Gary Andrew Naysmith (59 Gary Holt), Andrew Webster, Malcolm Mackay, Barry Ferguson (Cap), Darren Barr Fletcher, John McNamara, Nigel Francis Quashie, James McFadden, Paul Dickov (79 Steven Crawford).
Manager: Hans-Hubert Vogts (Germany).
SLOVENIA: Borut Mavrič, Amir Karič, Matej Mavrič, Aleksander Knavs, Ermin Šiljak (63 Klemen Lavrič), Nastja Čeh, Andrej Komac, Jalen Pokorn, Simon Sešlar, Milenko Ačimovič, Zlatko Dedič (79 Goran Šukalo).
Trainer: Branko Oblak.

649. 09.10.2004   18th World Cup Qualifiers
SCOTLAND v NORWAY 0-1 (0-0)
Hampden Park, Glasgow
Referee: Paul Allaerts (Belgium)   Attendance: 48,882
SCOTLAND: Craig Sinclair Gordon, Gary Caldwell, Gary Andrew Naysmith, Russell Anderson, Andrew Webster, Barry Ferguson (Cap), Darren Barr Fletcher, Gary Holt (79 Steven Thompson), Richard Hughes (62 Stephen Paul Pearson), Paul Dickov (75 Kenneth Miller), James McFadden.   Manager: Hans-Hubert Vogts (Germany).

NORWAY: Thomas Myhre, André Bergdølmo, Erik Hagen, Claus Lundekvam, John Arne Riise, Jan Derek Sørensen (74 Martin Andresen), Jan Gunnar Solli, Magne Hoseth (58 Morten Gamst Pedersen), Tommy Svindal Larsen, John Alieu Carew, Steffen Iversen (89 Frode Johnsen). Trainer: Åge Hareide.

Sent off: James McFadden (53)

Goal: Steffen Iversen (55)

650. 13.10.2004   18th World Cup Qualifiers
MOLDOVA v SCOTLAND 1-1 (1-1)
Republican, Chişinău
Referee: Kristinn Jakobsson (Iceland)   Attendance: 14,000
MOLDOVA: Evgeni Hmaruc, Alexei Savinov, Serghei Laşcencov, Ghenadie Olexici (39 Boris Cebotari), Valeri Catinsus, Iurie Priganiuc, Serghei Covalciuc, Stanislav Ivanov, Iulian Bursuc, Serghei Rogaciov (85 Iurie Miterev), Serghei Dadu.   Trainer: Viktor Pasulko.
SCOTLAND: Craig Sinclair Gordon, Gary Caldwell, Gary Andrew Naysmith (46 Ian William Murray), Stephen Caldwell, Andrew Webster, Barry Ferguson (Cap), Darren Barr Fletcher (66 Kenneth Miller), Gary Holt, Colin Cameron, Steven Thompson (86 Lee Henry McCulloch), Steven Crawford. Manager: Hans-Hubert Vogts (Germany).

Goals: Serghei Dadu (28) / Steven Thompson (31)

651. 17.11.2004
SCOTLAND v SWEDEN 1-4 (0-1)
Easter Road, Edinburgh
Referee: Jaroslav Jara (Czech Republic)   Attendance: 15,071
SCOTLAND: David Marshall, Kevin McNaughton, Ian William Murray, Russell Anderson, Andrew Webster (54 Steven Hammell), John McNamara (Cap) (65 Scott Severin), Barry Nicholson, Nigel Francis Quashie (90 Richard Hughes), Kenneth Miller (71 Steven Crawford), James McFadden, Stephen Paul Pearson.   Manager: Thomas Burns.
SWEDEN: Magnus Hedman, Mikael Nilsson (62 Alexander Östlund), Olof Mellberg (Cap) (46 Petter Hansson), Teddy Lucic, Mikael Dorsin, Anders Andersson, Niclas Alexandersson, Kim Källström, Christian Wilhelmsson (77 Sharbel Touma), Marcus Allback (63 Johan Elmander), Fredrik Berglund.   Trainer: Lars Lagerbäck.

Goals: James McFadden (78 pen) / Marcus Allbäck (27, 49), Johan Elmander (72), Fredrik Berglund (73)

652. 26.03.2005   18th World Cup Qualifiers
ITALY v SCOTLAND 2-0 (1-0)
Giuseppe Meazza, Milano
Referee: Kyros Vassaras (Greece)   Attendance: 40,745
ITALY: Gianluigi Buffon, Daniele Bonera, Fabio Cannavaro (Cap), Marco Materazzi, Giorgio Chiellini, Mauro Camoranesi, Andrea Pirlo, Gennaro Gattuso, Francesco Totti (72 Daniele De Rossi), Alberto Gilardino, Antonio Cassano (83 Luca Toni). Trainer: Marcello Lippi.
SCOTLAND: Robert Douglas (39 Craig Sinclair Gordon), John McNamara, Gary Andrew Naysmith, Steven Pressley, Gary Caldwell, David Gillespie Weir, Paul James Hartley (76 Neil McCann), Nigel Francis Quashie, Kenneth Miller (85 Garry Lawrence O'Connor), Barry Ferguson (Cap), Lee Henry McCulloch.   Manager: Walter Smith.

Goals: Andrea Pirlo (35, 85)

653. 04.06.2005   18th World Cup Qualifiers
SCOTLAND v MOLDOVA 2-0 (0-0)
Hampden Park, Glasgow
Referee: Frederikus Johannes Braamhaar (Holland) Attendance: 45,317
SCOTLAND: Craig Sinclair Gordon, Graham Alexander, John McNamara (26 Christian Edward Dailly), Steven Pressley, David Gillespie Weir, Barry Ferguson (Cap), Darren Barr Fletcher, Andrew Webster, Kenneth Miller, Paul James Hartley, Lee Henry McCulloch (74 James McFadden). Manager: Walter Smith.
MOLDOVA: Evgeni Hmaruc, Alexei Savinov, Serghei Laşcencov (46 Alexandru Covalenco), Ghenadie Olexici, Valeri Catînsus (Cap) (60 Serghei Covalciuc), Iurie Priganiuc, Vadim Boreţ, Stanislav Ivanov, Serghei Dadu, Alexandru Epureanu, Serghei Rogaciov (82 Viorel Frunză). Trainer: Viktor Pasulko.

Goals: Christian Edward Dailly (53), James McFadden (89)

654. 08.06.2005   18th World Cup Qualifiers
BELARUS v SCOTLAND 0-0
Dinamo, Minsk
Referee: Olegário Manuel Bártolo Faustino Benquerença (Portugal)   Attendance: 28,287
BELARUS: Yuriy Zhevnov, Sergey Omelyanchuk, Sergey Yaskovich, Sergey Shtanyuk, Sergey Gurenko (Cap), Timofei Kalachev (61 Vyacheslav Hleb), Denis Kovba, Valentin Belkevich, Vitaliy Bulyga (86 Alexandr Kulchiy), Alexandr Hleb, Sergey Kornilenko.   Trainer: Anatoliy Baydachniy.
SCOTLAND: Craig Sinclair Gordon, Graham Alexander, Steven Pressley, David Gillespie Weir, Barry Ferguson (Cap), Darren Barr Fletcher, Andrew Webster, Kenneth Miller, Gary Caldwell, Christian Edward Dailly, Lee Henry McCulloch (76 James McFadden).   Manager: Walter Smith.

655. 17.08.2005
AUSTRIA v SCOTLAND 2-2 (0-2)
"Arnold Schwarzenegger", Graz
Referee: Selçuk Dereli (Turkey)   Attendance: 13,800
AUSTRIA: Helge Payer (46 Andreas Schranz), Ernst Dospel (54 Joachim Standfest), Anton Ehmann, Emanuel Pogatetz, Ronald Gercaliu, Markus Schopp (68 Andreas Ibertsberger), Dietmar Kühbauer (78 Jürgen Säumel), René Aufhauser, Andreas Ivanschitz, Christian Mayrleb (63 Muhammet Akagündüz), Ivica Vastic (63 Sanel Kuljic).
Trainer: Johann Krankl.
SCOTLAND: Craig Sinclair Gordon (46 Robert Douglas), John McNamara, Graham Alexander, Steven Pressley (46 Russell Anderson), Stephen Caldwell, Andrew Webster, Kenneth Miller (46 Derek George Riordan), Christian Edward Dailly (Cap), Garry Lawrence O'Connor, Brian O'Neil (46 Scott Severin), Nigel Francis Quashie (73 Richard Hughes).
Manager: Walter Smith.
Goals: Andreas Ibertsberger (83), Joachim Standfest (87) / Kenneth Miller (3), Garry Lawrence O'Connor (38).

656. 03.09.2005   18th World Cup Qualifiers
SCOTLAND v ITALY 1-1 (1-0)
Hampden Park, Glasgow
Referee: Ľuboš Michel (Slovakia)   Attendance: 50,185
SCOTLAND: Craig Sinclair Gordon, John McNamara, Andrew Webster, Christian Edward Dailly, David Gillespie Weir, Barry Ferguson (Cap), Darren Barr Fletcher, Graham Alexander, Kenneth Miller (75 Craig Beattie), Paul James Hartley, Nigel Francis Quashie (66 Neil McCann).
Manager: Walter Smith.
ITALY: Angelo Peruzzi, Cristian Zaccardo (46 Fabio Grosso), Alessandro Nesta, Fabio Cannavaro (Cap), Gianluca Zambrotta, Gennaro Gattuso, Daniele De Rossi (60 Mauro Camoranesi), Andrea Pirlo, Francesco Totti, Vincenzo Iaquinta (71 Luca Toni), Christian Vieri. Trainer: Marcello Lippi.
Goals: Kenneth Miller (12) / Fabio Grosso (75)

657. 07.09.2005   18th World Cup Qualifiers
NORWAY v SCOTLAND 1-2 (0-2)
Ullevaal, Oslo
Referee: Alain Hamer (Luxembourg)   Attendance: 24,904
NORWAY: Thomas Myhre, Jan Gunnar Solli (46 Kristofer Kruger Hæstad), Vidar Riseth, Claus Lundekvam, André Bergdølmo, Martin Andresen, Christian Grindheim, Alex Valencia (46 Daniel Omoya Braaten), Egil Østenstad (46 Ole Martin Årst), John Arne Riise, John Alieu Carew.
Trainer: Åge Hareide.
SCOTLAND: Craig Sinclair Gordon, John McNamara, Andrew Webster, Steven Pressley, David Gillespie Weir, Barry Ferguson (Cap), Darren Barr Fletcher, Graham Alexander, Kenneth Miller (40 Neil McCann), Paul James Hartley, James McFadden (71 Craig Beattie). Manager: Walter Smith.
Goals: Ole Martin Årst (89) / Kenneth Miller (21, 31)

658. 08.10.2005   18th World Cup Qualifiers
SCOTLAND v BELARUS 0-1 (0-1)
Hampden Park, Glasgow
Referee: Zsolt Szabó (Hungary)   Attendance: 51,105
SCOTLAND: Craig Sinclair Gordon, Graham Alexander, Ian William Murray (46 Shaun Richard Maloney), Steven Pressley, David Gillespie Weir, Barry Ferguson (Cap), Darren Barr Fletcher, Christian Edward Dailly, Kenneth Miller, Paul James Hartley, Lee Henry McCulloch.   Manager: Walter Smith.
BELARUS: Vasiliy Khomutovskiy, Vladimir Korytko, Igor Tarlovskiy, Andrey Ostrovskiy, Andrey Lavrik (Cap), Timofei Kalachev, Alexandr Kulchiy, Denis Kovba, Alexandr Hleb, Vitaliy Bulyga (88 Denis Sashcheko), Vitaliy Kutuzov.
Trainer: Anatoliy Baydachniy.
Goal: Vitaliy Kutuzov (5)

659. 12.10.2005   18th World Cup Qualifiers
SLOVENIA v SCOTLAND 0-3 (0-1)
Športni Park "Arena Petrol", Celje
Referee: René J. Temmink (Holland)   Attendance: 9,100
SLOVENIA: Samir Handanovič, Matej Mavrič (26 Andrej Pečnik (56 Branko Ilič)), Boštjan Cesar, Aleksander Knavs, Robert Koren, Nastja Čeh, Andrej Komac, Anton Žlogar, Sebastjan Cimirotič, Aleksandar Rodić (54 Ermin Šiljak), Milenko Ačimovič.   Trainer: Branko Oblak.
SCOTLAND: Craig Sinclair Gordon, Christian Edward Dailly (Cap), Graham Alexander, Steven Pressley (46 Gary Caldwell), David Gillespie Weir, Andrew Webster, Darren Barr Fletcher, Nigel Francis Quashie (71 Stephen Caldwell), Kenneth Miller (46 Garry Lawrence O'Connor), Paul James Hartley, James McFadden. Manager: Walter Smith.
Goals: Darren Barr Fletcher (3), James McFadden (47), Paul James Hartley (83)

660. 12.11.2005
SCOTLAND v UNITED STATES 1-1 (1-1)
Hampden Park, Glasgow
Referee: Alberto Undiano Mallenco (Spain)   Att: 26,708
SCOTLAND: Craig Sinclair Gordon, Christian Edward Dailly (Cap), Graham Alexander, Steven Pressley (46 Stephen Caldwell), Andrew Webster, David Gillespie Weir (46 Gary Caldwell), Darren Barr Fletcher, Paul James Hartley, Gary O'Connor (73 Shaun Richard Maloney), Nigel Francis Quashie (73 Scott Brown), Neil McCann (62 James McFadden).
Manager: Walter Smith.
UNITED STATES: Kasey Keller (Cap), Steven Cherundolo, Carlos Bocanegra (80 James Conrad), Gregg Berhalter, Jonathan Spector, Brian Michael Carroll, Kerry Zavagnin (46 Benjamin Robert Olsen), Eddie Gaven (46 Santino Quaranta), DaMarcus Lamont Beasley (77 Heath Pearce), Joshua David Wolff (58 Christopher Rolfe), Brian Ching.
Trainer: Bruce Arena.
Goals: Andrew Webster (38) / Joshua David Wolff (9 pen)

661. 01.03.2006
SCOTLAND v SWITZERLAND 1-3 (0-2)
Hampden Park, Glasgow
Referee: Bruno Coué (France)   Attendance: 20,952
SCOTLAND: Craig Sinclair Gordon (46 Neil Alexander), Christian Edward Dailly, Graham Alexander, David Gillespie Weir (46 Stephen Caldwell), Andrew Webster, Barry Ferguson (Cap) (46 Gary Stewart Teale), Darren Barr Fletcher, Gary Caldwell, Kenneth Miller, Nigel Francis Quashie, James McFadden.   Manager: Walter Smith.

SWITZERLAND: Pascal Zuberbühler (50 Fabio Coltorti), Philipp Degen, Philippe Senderos (73 Boris Smiljanic), Stéphane Grichting, Valon Behrami (50 Johannes Djourou), Johann Vogel (81 Blerim Dzemaili), Tranquillo Barnetta, Ricardo Cabanas, Raphaël Wicky (50 Johan Vonlanthen), Daniel Gygax, Marco Streller (73 Mauro Lustrinelli).   Trainer: Jakob Kühn.

Goals: Kenneth Miller (54) / Tranquillo Barnetta (21), Daniel Gygax (41), Ricardo Cabanas (69)

662. 11.05.2006   Kirin Cup
SCOTLAND v BULGARIA 5-1 (2-1)
"Kobe Wing" Stadium, Kobe
Referee: Toru Kamikawa (Japan)   Attendance: 5,780
SCOTLAND: Neil Alexander, Graeme Stuart Murty (82 David McNamee), Gary Caldwell, David Gillespie Weir (Cap), Russell Anderson, Gary Andrew Naysmith, Darren Barr Fletcher, Scott Severin (69 Gavin Paul Rae), Lee Henry McCulloch (78 Ian William Murray), Gary Stewart Teale (74 Chris Burke), Kris Boyd (52 James McFadden).   Manager: Walter Smith.

BULGARIA: Stoian Kolev (72 Nikolai Mihailov), Stanislav Angelov, Rosen Kirilov, Elin Topuzakov, Asen Karaslavov (56 Hristo Yanev), Lúcio Wagner, Yordan Todorov, Dimitar Telkiyski, Martin Petrov (Cap), Svetoslav Todorov (72 Tsvetan Genkov), Valeri Domovchiyski (72 Georgi Iliev Rusev).   Trainer: Hristo Stoichkov.

Goals: Kris Boyd (12, 43), James McFadden (69), Chris Burke (76, 88) / Yordan Todorov (26)

663. 13.05.2006   Kirin Cup
JAPAN v SCOTLAND 0-0
Saitama Stadium 2002, Saitama
Referee: Eduardo Iturrálde González (Spain)   Att: 58,648
JAPAN: Yoshikatsu Kawaguchi, Tsuneyasu Miyeamoto, Alessandro dos Santos, Yuji Nakazawa (50 Keisuke Tsuboi), Akira Kaji, Takashi Fukunishi, Mitsuo Ogasawara, Shinji Ono, Yasuhito Endo (72 Hisato Sato), Tatsuhiko Kubo (82 Seiichiro Maki), Keiji Tamada.
Trainer: Arthur Antunes Coimbra "Zico" (Brazil).

SCOTLAND: Neil Alexander, Graeme Stuart Murty (79 David McNamee), Gary Caldwell, David Gillespie Weir (Cap), Russell Anderson, Gary Andrew Naysmith (46 Ian William Murray), Darren Barr Fletcher, Scott Severin (46 Gavin Paul Rae), Lee Henry McCulloch (69 Lee Miller), Gary Stewart Teale (59 Chris Burke), James McFadden (59 Kris Boyd).   Manager: Walter Smith.

664. 02.09.2006   13th European Champs Qualifiers
SCOTLAND v FAROE ISLANDS 6-0 (5-0)
Celtic Park, Glasgow
Referee: Igor Yegorov (Russia)   Attendance: 50,059
SCOTLAND: Craig Sinclair Gordon, Christian Edward Dailly, David Gillespie Weir (Cap), Steven Pressley, Gary Andrew Naysmith, Darren Barr Fletcher (46 Gary Stewart Teale), Paul James Hartley, Nigel Francis Quashie (84 Scott Severin), Kenneth Miller (62 Garry Lawrence O'Connor), Kris Boyd, James McFadden.   Manager: Walter Smith.

FAROE ISLANDS: Jákup Mikkelsen, Pauli G. Hansen, Óli Johannesen (Cap), Atli Danielsen, Janus Mouritsarson Joensen, Fróði Benjaminsen, Julian Schantz Johnsson (76 Símun Samuelsen), Jákup á Borg, Jónhard Frederiksberg (60 Hanus Thorleifson), Rógvi Jacobsen (84 Kári Nielsen), Christian Høgni Jacobsen.   Trainer: Jógvan Martin Olsen.

Goals: Darren Barr Fletcher (6), James McFadden (10), Kris Boyd (24 pen, 38), Kenneth Miller (30 pen), Garry Lawrence O'Connor (85)

665. 06.09.2006   13th European Champs Qualifiers
LITHUANIA v SCOTLAND 1-2 (0-0)
S Darius & S Girenas, Kaunas
Referee: Vladimír Hriňák (Slovakia)   Attendance: 6,500
LITHUANIA: Žydrūnas Karčemarskas, Marius Stankevičius, Rolandas Džiaukštas, Andrius Skerla, Tomas Žvirždauskas, Aidas Preikšaitis (82 Darius Miceika), Mantas Savėnas (50 Tomas Tamošauskas), Saulius Mikoliūnas (67 Tadas Labukas), Mindaugas Kalonas, Tomas Danilevičius (Cap), Robertas Poškus.   Trainer: Algimantas Liubinskas.

SCOTLAND: Craig Sinclair Gordon, Christian Edward Dailly, Gary Andrew Naysmith, Steven Pressley, David Gillespie Weir (Cap), Gary Caldwell, Darren Barr Fletcher, Paul James Hartley (88 Scott Severin), Kenneth Miller, Nigel Francis Quashie (42 Kris Boyd), James McFadden (22 Graham Alexander).   Manager: Walter Smith.

Goals: Darius Miceika (85) / Christian Edward Dailly (47), Kenneth Miller (61)

666. 07.10.2006   13th European Champs Qualifiers
SCOTLAND v FRANCE   1-0 (0-0)
Hampden Park, Glasgow
Referee: Massimo Busacca (Switzerland)   Att: 50,456
SCOTLAND: Craig Sinclair Gordon, Christian Edward Dailly, Gary Caldwell, Steven Pressley, David Gillespie Weir, Graham Alexander, Barry Ferguson (Cap), Paul James Hartley, Darren Barr Fletcher, Lee Henry McCulloch (57 Gary Stewart Teale), James McFadden (71 Garry Lawrence O'Connor). Manager: Walter Smith.
FRANCE: Grégory Coupet, Willy Sagnol, Lilian Thuram, Jean-Alain Boumsong, Éric Abidal, Franck Ribéry (74 Sylvain Wiltord), Patrick Vieira (Cap), Claude Makélélé, Florent Malouda, David Trézéguet (62 Louis Laurent Saha), Thierry Henry.   Trainer: Raymond Domenech.
Goal: Gary Caldwell (67)

667. 11.10.2006   13th European Champs Qualifiers
UKRAINE v SCOTLAND   2-0 (0-0)
Olympiyskiy, Kyiv
Referee: Martin Hansson (Sweden)   Attendance: 40,000
UKRAINE: Oleksandr Shovkovskiy, Andriy Nesmachniy, Vyacheslav Sviderskiy, Oleksandr Kucher, Andriy Rusol, Anatoliy Tymoschuk, Oleh Gusev (62 Artem Milevskiy), Oleh Shelayev, Maxym Kalynychenko (76 Andriy Vorobey), Andriy Voronin (90+3 Bohdan Shershun), Andriy Shevchenko (Cap). Trainer: Oleh Blokhin.
SCOTLAND: Craig Sinclair Gordon, Robert Neilson (89 Stephen McManus), Gary Caldwell, Steven Pressle, David Gillespie Weir, Graham Alexander, Barry Ferguson (Cap), Paul James Hartley, Darren Barr Fletcher, James McFadden (73 Kris Boyd), Kenneth Miller.   Manager: Walter Smith.
Sent off: Steven Pressley (86)
Goals: Oleksandr Kucher (60), Andriy Shevchenko (90 pen)

668. 24.03.2007   13th European Champs Qualifiers
SCOTLAND v GEORGIA   2-1 (1-1)
Hampden Park, Glasgow
Referee: Nicolai Vollquartz (Denmark)   Attendance: 50,850
SCOTLAND: Craig Sinclair Gordon, Gary Andrew Naysmith, Stephen McManus, David Gillespie Weir, Graham Alexander, Paul James Hartley, Barry Ferguson (Cap), Gary Stewart Teale (60 Scott Brown), Kris Boyd (76 Craig Beattie), Kenneth Miller (90 Shaun Richard Maloney), Lee Henry McCulloch. Manager: Alexander McLeish.
GEORGIA: Giorgi Lomaia, Giorgi Shashiashvili, Lasha Salukvadze, Zurab Khizanishvili, Zaal Eliava, Vladimir Burduli (56 David Siradze), Zurab Menteshashvili (46 Gogita Gogua), Levan Tskitishvili (90+2 David Mujiri), Levan Kobiashvili, Giorgi Demetradze, Shota Arveladze.
Trainer: Klaus Toppmöller (Germany).
Goals: Kris Boyd (11), Craig Beattie (89) / Shota Arveladze (41)

669. 28.03.2007   13th European Champs Qualifiers
ITALY v SCOTLAND   2-0 (1-0)
San Nicola, Bari
Referee: Frank De Bleeckere (Belgium)   Attendance: 37,500
ITALY: Gianluigi Buffon, Massimo Oddo, Fabio Cannavaro, Marco Materazzi, Gianluca Zambrotta, Gennaro Gattuso, Daniele De Rossi, Mauro Camoranesi, Simone Perrotta (77 Andrea Pirlo), Antonio Di Natale (66 Alessandro Del Piero), Luca Toni (87 Fabio Quagliarella).
Trainer: Roberto Donadoni.
SCOTLAND: Craig Sinclair Gordon, Gary Andrew Naysmith, Stephen McManus, David Gillespie Weir, Graham Alexander, Paul James Hartley, Barry Ferguson (Cap), Gary Stewart Teale (66 Shaun Richard Maloney), Scott Brown (86 Craig Beattie), Kenneth Miller, Lee Henry McCulloch (81 Kris Boyd). Manager: Alexander McLeish.
Goals: Luca Toni (12, 70)

670. 30.05.2007
AUSTRIA v SCOTLAND   0-1 (0-0)
"Gerhard Hanappi", Wien
Referee: Zsolt Szabó (Hungary)   Attendance: 13,200
AUSTRIA: Helge Payer, Joachim Standfest, Martin Hiden (89 Sebastian Prödl), Jürgen Patocka, Christian Fuchs (74 Markus Katzer), Andreas Ivanschitz (Cap), René Aufhauser (74 Yüksel Sariyar), Jürgen Säumel, Christoph Leitgeb, Roland Linz, Mario Haas (60 Sanel Kuljic).   Trainer: Josef Hickersberger.
SCOTLAND: Allan James McGregor (46 Craig Sinclair Gordon), David Gillespie Weir (46 Christian Edward Dailly), Gary Caldwell, Graham Alexander (71 Alan Hutton), Gary Andrew Naysmith, Barry Ferguson (Cap), Lee Henry McCulloch (46 Paul James Hartley), Darren Barr Fletcher, Shaun Richard Maloney (67 Charles Graham Adam), Kris Boyd, Garry Lawrence O'Connor (86 Stephen McManus). Manager: Alexander McLeish.
Goal: Garry Lawrence O'Connor (58)

671. 06.06.2007   13th European Champs Qualifiers
FAROE ISLANDS v SCOTLAND   0-2 (0-2)
Svangaskarð, Toftir
Referee: Georgios Kasnaferis (Greece)   Attendance: 4,600
FAROE ISLANDS: Jákup Mikkelsen, Atli Danielsen, Jón Rói Jacobsen, Óli Johannesen (Cap) (36 Marni Djurhuus (77 Símun Samuelsen)), Fróði Benjaminsen, Mikkjal Thomassen, Jákup á Borg (82 Andrew av Fløtum), Súni Olsen, Christian Lamhauge Holst, Rógvi Jacobsen, Christian Høgni Jacobsen. Trainer: Jógvan Martin Olsen.
SCOTLAND: Craig Sinclair Gordon, Graham Alexander, David Gillespie Weir, Stephen McManus, Gary Andrew Naysmith, Paul James Hartley, Barry Ferguson (Cap), Darren Barr Fletcher (68 Gary Stewart Teale), Shaun Richard Maloney (77 Charles Graham Adam), Garry Lawrence O'Connor, Kris Boyd (83 Steven John Naismith).   Manager: A. McLeish.
Goals: Shaun Maloney (31), Garry Lawrence O'Connor (35)

672. 22.08.2007
SCOTLAND v SOUTH AFRICA 1-0 (0-0)
Pittodrie, Aberdeen

Referee: Martin Atkinson (England)   Attendance: 13,723

SCOTLAND: Craig Sinclair Gordon, Alan Hutton, James Michael McEveley, Stephen McManus, Russell Anderson, Scott Brown (72 Gary Stewart Teale), Gary Caldwell (56 Barry Robson), Darren Barr Fletcher (Cap), James McFadden (46 Stephen Paul Pearson), Garry Lawrence O'Connor (68 Craig Beattie), Kenneth Miller (68 Kris Boyd).
Manager: Alexander McLeish.

SOUTH AFRICA: Rowen Fernandez, Cyril Nzama (83 Vuyo Mere), Aaron Mokoena (Cap), Benson Mhlongo, Bradley Carnell, Steven Pienaar, Papi Zothwane (75 Teko Modise), Macbeth Sibaya, Delron Buckley (75 Dillon Sheppard), Siyabonga Nkosi (75 Thembinkosi Fanteni), Sibusiso Zuma (12 Siyabonga Nomvethe).   Trainer: Carlos Alberto Parreira

Goal: Kris Boyd (71)

673. 08.09.2007   13th European Champs Qualifiers
SCOTLAND v LITHUANIA 3-1 (1-0)
Hampden Park, Glasgow

Referee: Damir Skomina (Slovenia)   Attendance: 51,349

SCOTLAND: Craig Sinclair Gordon, Alan Hutton, James Michael McEveley, Stephen McManus, David Gillespie Weir, Scott Brown, Darren Barr Fletcher (Cap), Lee Henry McCulloch (76 Shaun Richard Maloney), Gary Stewart Teale (69 James McFadden), Kris Boyd, Garry Lawrence O'Connor (76 Craig Beattie).   Manager: Alexander McLeish.

LITHUANIA: Žydrūnas Karčemarskas, Arūnas Klimavičius, Andrius Skerla, Tomas Žvirgždauskas, Marius Stankevičius (56 Edgaras Jankauskas), Deividas Šemberas, Igoris Morinas (47 Saulius Mikoliūnas), Deividas Česnauskis, Mindaugas Kalonas, Tomas Danilevičius (Cap), Andrius Velička (47 Audrius Kšanavičius).   Trainer: Algimantas Liubinskas.

Goals: Kris Boyd (31), Stephen McManus (77), James McFadden (83) / Tomas Danilevičius (61 pen)

674. 12.09.2007   13th European Champs Qualifiers
FRANCE v SCOTLAND 0-1 (0-0)
Stade de France, Saint-Denis, Paris

Referee: Konrad Plautz (Austria)   Attendance: 42,000

FRANCE: Mickaël Landreau, Lassana Diarra, Lilian Thuram, Julien Escudé, Éric Abidal (76 Karim Benzema), Franck Ribéry, Patrick Vieira (Cap) (69 Samir Nasri), Claude Makélélé, Florent Malouda, David Trézéguet, Nicolas Sébastien Anelka.   Trainer: Raymond Domenech.

SCOTLAND: Craig Sinclair Gordon, Alan Hutton, Graham Alexander, Stephen McManus, David Gillespie Weir, Lee Henry McCulloch, Barry Ferguson (Cap), Darren Barr Fletcher (26 Stephen Paul Pearson), Scott Brown, Paul James Hartley, James McFadden (76 Garry Lawrence O'Connor). Manager: Alexander McLeish.

Goal: James McFadden (64)

675. 13.10.2007   13th European Champs Qualifiers
SCOTLAND v UKRAINE 3-1 (2-1)
Hampden Park, Glasgow

Referee: Pieter Vink (Holland)   Attendance: 51,366

SCOTLAND: Craig Sinclair Gordon, Alan Hutton, David Gillespie Weir, Stephen McManus, Gary Andrew Naysmith, Scott Brown (76 Shaun Richard Maloney), Barry Ferguson (Cap), Stephen Paul Pearson, Lee Henry McCulloch (60 Christian Edward Dailly), James McFadden (80 Garry Lawrence O'Connor), Kenneth Miller.
Manager: Alexander McLeish.

UKRAINE: Oleksandr Shovkovskiy, Andriy Nesmachniy, Andriy Rusol, Dmytro Chyhrynskiy, Olexandr Kucher, Oleh Gusev (46 Ruslan Rotan), Anatoliy Tymoschuk (73 Oleh Shelayev), Olexandr Gladkiy, Andriy Vorobey (62 Serhiy Nazarenko), Andriy Shevchenko (Cap), Andriy Voronin.
Trainer: Oleh Blokhin.

Goals: Kenneth Miller (4), Lee Henry McCulloch (10), James McFadden (88) / Andriy Shevchenko (24)

676. 17.10.2007   13th European Champs Qualifiers
GEORGIA v SCOTLAND 2-0 (1-0)
"Boris Paichadze", Tbilisi

Referee: Knut Kircher (Germany)   Attendance: 55,500

GEORGIA: Giorgi Makaridze, Giorgi Shashiashvili, Lasha Salukvadze, Malkhaz Asatiani, Zurab Khizanishvili, Jaba Kankava, Zurab Menteshashvili, Levan Kenia (79 Ilia Kandelaki), David Kvirkvelia, David Siradze (89 Lasha Jakobia), Levan Mchedlidze (85 Aleksandre Kvakhadze).
Trainer: Klaus Toppmöller (Germany).

SCOTLAND: Craig Sinclair Gordon, Graeme Stuart Murty, Graham Alexander, Stephen McManus, David Gillespie Weir, Darren Barr Fletcher, Barry Ferguson (Cap), Stephen Paul Pearson (66 Kris Boyd), Shaun Richard Maloney, James McFadden, Kenneth Miller (66 Craig Beattie).
Manager: Alexander McLeish.

Goals: Levan Mchedlidze (16), David Siradze (64)

677. 17.11.2007   13th European Champs Qualifiers
SCOTLAND v ITALY 1-2 (0-1)
Hampden Park, Glasgow

Referee: Manuel Enrique Mejuto González (Spain)
Attendance: 53,301

SCOTLAND: Craig Sinclair Gordon, Alan Hutton, David Gillespie Weir, Stephen McManus, Gary Andrew Naysmith, Scott Brown (74 Kenneth Miller), Darren Barr Fletcher, Paul James Hartley, Barry Ferguson (Cap), Lee Henry McCulloch (90+2 Kris Boyd), James McFadden.
Manager: Alexander McLeish.

ITALY: Gianluigi Buffon, Christian Panucci, Fabio Cannavaro, Andrea Barzagli, Gianluca Zambrotta, Mauro Camoranesi (83 Giorgio Chiellini), Gennaro Gattuso (87 Daniele De Rossi), Andrea Pirlo, Massimo Ambrosini, Antonio Di Natale (68 Vincenzo Iaquinta), Luca Toni.   Trainer: Roberto Donadoni.

Goals: Barry Ferguson (65) /
Luca Toni (2), Christian Panucci (90+1)

678. 26.03.2008
SCOTLAND v CROATIA 1-1 (1-1)
Hampden Park, Glasgow

Referee: Terje Hauge (Norway)   Attendance: 28,821

SCOTLAND: Craig Sinclair Gordon, Alan Hutton, Gary Caldwell (70 Russell Anderson), Stephen McManus (Cap), Gary Andrew Naysmith (62 James Michael McEveley), Shaun Richard Maloney (72 Kris Boyd), Paul James Hartley, Darren Barr Fletcher (90 Graham Alexander), Scott Brown (65 Gary Stewart Teale), Kenneth Miller, Steven Kenneth Fletcher (46 Gavin Paul Rae).   Manager: George Elder Burley.

CROATIA: Stipe Pletikosa, Vedran Ćorluka (85 Dario Šimić), Robert Kovač (73 Dario Knežević), Josip Šimunić, Danijel Pranjić, Darijo Srna (63 Jerko Leko), Niko Kovač (Cap) (46 Ognjen Vukojević), Luka Modrić, Niko Kranjčar, Mladen Petrić (58 Ivan Klasnić), Ivica Olić (58 Igor Budan).
Trainer: Slaven Bilić.

Goals: Kenneth Miller (30) / Niko Kranjčar (10)

679. 30.05.2008
CZECH REPUBLIC v SCOTLAND 3-1 (0-0)
AXA Arena, Praha

Referee: Eric Bramhaar (Holland)   Attendance: 11,314

CZECH REPUBLIC: Petr Čech, Zdeněk Pospěch (74 Tomáš Sivok), Tomáš Ujfaluši (46 David Rozehnal), Radoslav Kováč, Marek Jankulovski (46 Michal Kadlec), Jan Polák, Tomáš Galásek, Marek Matějovský (46 David Jarolím), Libor Sionko, Rudolf Skácel (46 Jaroslav Plašil), Jan Koller (46 Václav Svěrkoš).   Trainer: Karel Brückner.

SCOTLAND: Craig Sinclair Gordon, Kevin McNaughton (90 Christoph Diddier Bera), Gary Caldwell, Stephen McManus (Cap) (56 Christian Edward Dailly), Gary Andrew Naysmith, Barry Robson (81 Ross McCormack), Gavin Paul Rae (71 David Clarkson), James Clark Morrison (67 Shaun Richard Maloney), Darren Barr Fletcher, Kenneth Miller.
Manager: George Elder Burley.

Goals: Libor Sionko (60, 89), Michal Kadlec (84) /
David Clarkson (85)

680. 20.08.2008
SCOTLAND v NORTHERN IRELAND 0-0
Hampden Park, Glasgow

Referee: Nicolai Vollquartz (Denmark)   Attendance: 28,072

SCOTLAND: Craig Sinclair Gordon (46 Allan James McGregor), Graham Alexander, Stephen McManus (Cap) (46 Darren Barr), David Gillespie Weir (72 Christoph Diddier Bera), Gary Andrew Naysmith, Scott Brown, Darren Barr Fletcher (69 Michael Stewart), Kevin Thomson (46 Barry Robson), James Clark Morrison (62 Kristian Arron Commons), James McFadden, Kenneth Miller.
Manager: George Elder Burley.

NORTHERN IRELAND: Maik Stefan Taylor, Gareth McAuley (76 Michael James Duff), Ryan McGivern, Jonathan Evans, Stephen James Craigan, Samuel Clingan (59 Michael O'Connor), Christopher Patrick Baird, Steven Davis, David Jonathan Healy, Martin Paterson (46 Dean Shiels), Christopher Brunt (56 Warren Feeney).
Manager: Nigel Worthington.

681. 06.09.2008   19th World Cup Qualifiers
MACEDONIA v SCOTLAND 1-0 (1-0)
Gradski, Skopje

Referee: Pavel Královec (Czech Republic)   Att: 9,000

MACEDONIA: Petar Miloševski, Nikolče Noveski, Goce Sedloski (Cap), Igor Mitreski, Vlade Lazarevski, Robert Petrov (79 Boban Grnčarov), Vlatko Grozdanovski, Veliče Šumulikoski, Goran Maznov, Goran Pandev (83 Darko Tasevski), Ilčo Naumoski (69 Vančo Trajanov).
Trainer: Srečko Katanec (Slovenia).

SCOTLAND: Craig Sinclair Gordon, Graham Alexander, Gary Andrew Naysmith, Stephen McManus (Cap), Gary Caldwell, Paul James Hartley (65 Kristian Arron Commons), Darren Barr Fletcher, Scott Brown, Kenneth Miller (80 Kris Boyd), James McFadden, Barry Robson (76 Shaun Richard Maloney).   Manager: George Elder Burley.

Goal: Ilčo Naumoski (5)

682. 10.09.2008   19th World Cup Qualifiers
ICELAND v SCOTLAND 1-2 (0-1)

Laugardalsvöllur, Reykjavík

Referee: Serge Gumienny (Belgium)   Attendance: 9,764

ICELAND: Kjartan Sturluson, Bjarni Ólafur Eiríksson (46 Indriði Sigurðsson), Hermann Hreiðarsson (Cap), Kristján Örn Sigurðsson, Grétar Rafn Steinsson, Birkir Már Sævarsson (78 Veigar Páll Gunnarsson), Stefán Gíslason, Aron Einar Gunnarsson (64 Pálmi Rafn Pálmason), Emil Hallfreðsson, Eiður Smári Guðjohnsen, Heiðar Helguson.
Trainer: Ólafur Davíð Jóhanesson.

SCOTLAND: Craig Sinclair Gordon, Kirk Broadfoot, Gary Andrew Naysmith, Stephen McManus (Cap), Gary Caldwell, Scott Brown, Darren Barr Fletcher, Shaun Richard Maloney (78 Graham Alexander), James McFadden (80 Paul James Hartley), Kristian Arron Commons (62 Kenneth Miller), Barry Robson.   Manager: George Elder Burley.

Sent off: Stephen McManus (76)

Goals: Eiður Smári Guðjohnsen (77 pen) / Kirk Broadfoot (18), James McFadden (59)

683. 11.10.2008   19th World Cup Qualifiers
SCOTLAND v NORWAY 0-0

Hampden Park, Glasgow

Referee: Massimo Busacca (Switzerland)   Att: 51,300

SCOTLAND: Craig Sinclair Gordon, Kirk Broadfoot, Gary Andrew Naysmith, David Gillespie Weir, Gary Caldwell, Scott Brown, Darren Barr Fletcher (Cap), James Clark Morrison (56 Steven Kenneth Fletcher), James McFadden (56 Christopher Robert Iwelumo), Barry Robson, Shaun Richard Maloney.
Manager: George Elder Burley.

NORWAY: Jon Knudsen, Jon Inge Høiland, Kjetil Wæhler, Brede Paulsen Hangeland (Cap), John Arne Riise, Bjørn Helge Riise (56 Daniel Omoya Braaten), Christian Grindheim, Fredrik Winsnes, Fredrik Strømstad (77 Morten Gamst Pedersen), John Alieu Carew, Steffen Iversen.
Trainer: Åge Hareide.

684. 19.11.2008
SCOTLAND v ARGENTINA 0-1 (0-1)

Hampden Park, Glasgow

Referee: Dr. Felix Brych (Germany)   Attendance: 32,492

SCOTLAND: Allan James McGregor, Kirk Broadfoot, Alan Hutton, Stephen McManus (75 Christoph Diddier Bera), Gary Caldwell, Scott Brown (63 Graham Alexander), Paul James Hartley (59 Shaun Richard Maloney), Barry Ferguson (59 Scott Robertson), James McFadden (67 David Clarkson), Christopher Robert Iwelumo (46 Lee Miller), Kristian Arron Commons.   Manager: George Elder Burley.

ARGENTINA: Juan Pablo Carrizo, Javier Adelmar Zanetti, Martín Gastón Demichelis, Gabriel Iván Heinze, Fernando Rubén Gago, Javier Alejandro Mascherano, Jonás Manuel Gutiérrez (71 Luis Oscar González), Emiliano Ramiro Papa (86 Daniel Alberto Díaz), Maximiliano Rubén Rodríguez (90 José Ernesto Sosa), Ezequiel Iván Lavezzi (75 Germán Gustavo Denis), Carlos Alberto Tévez.
Trainer: Diego Armando Maradona.

Goal: Maximiliano Rubén Rodríguez (12)

685. 28.03.2009   19th World Cup Qualifier
NETHERLANDS v SCOTLAND 3-0 (2-0)

Amsterdam ArenA, Amsterdam

Referee: Laurent Duhamel (France)   Attendance: 49,552

NETHERLANDS: Maarten Stekelenburg, Gregory van der Wiel, André Ooijer, Joris Mathijsen, Giovanni van Bronckhorst, Mark van Bommel, Nigel de Jong (79 Stijn Schaars), Robin van Persie (64 Wesley Sneijder), Arjen Robben, Dirk Kuyt, Klaas-Jan Huntelaar (79 Ibrahim Afellay).
Manager: Bert van Marwijk

SCOTLAND: Allan McGregor, Graham Alexander (73 Alan Hutton), Gary Naysmith, Christophe Berra, Gary Caldwell, Barry Ferguson, Gary Teale (84 James Morrison), Darren Fletcher, Scott Brown, Kenny Miller (71 Steven Fletcher), Ross McCormack.   Manager: George Burley

Goals: Klaas-Jan Huntelaar (30), Robin van Persie (45+1), Dirk Kuyt (77 pen)

686. 01.04.2009   19th World Cup Qualifier
SCOTLAND v ICELAND 2-1 (1-0)

Hampden Park, Glasgow

Referee: Thomas Einwaller (Austria)   Attendance: 42,259

SCOTLAND: Craig Gordon, Gary Naysmith, Stephen McManus, Alan Hutton, Gary Caldwell, James Morrison (90 Gavin Rae), Darren Fletcher, Scott Brown, Kenny Miller, Steven Fletcher (78 Gary Teale), Ross McCormack.
Manager: George Burley

ICELAND: Gunnleifur Gunnleifsson, Helgi Daníelsson, Kristján Orn Sigurdsson, Indridi Sigurdsson (81 Ármann Smári Björnsson), Bjarni Eiríksson, Grétar Steinsson, Aron Gunnarsson (70 Eggert Jónsson), Hermann Hreidarsson, Pálmi Pálmason, Eidur Gudjohnsen, Arnór Smárason.
Manager: Ólafur Jóhannesson

Goals: Ross McCormack (39), Steven Fletcher (65) / Indridi Sigurdsson (54)

687. 12.08.2009   19th World Cup Qualifier
NORWAY v SCOTLAND 4-0 (2-0)
Ullevaal Stadion, Oslo

Referee: Alain Hamer (Luxembourg)   Attendance: 24,493

NORWAY: Jon Knudsen, Tom Høgli, Kjetil Wæhler, John Arne Riise, Brede Hangeland, Magne Hoseth, Erik Huseklepp (76 Steffen Iversen), Bjørn Helge Riise (84 Per Cilijan Skjelbred), Christian Grindheim, Morten Pedersen, John Carew (85 Thorstein Helstad).   Manager: Egil Olsen

SCOTLAND: David Marshall, Callum Davidson, Alan Hutton, Steven Caldwell (48 James McFadden), Gary Caldwell, Graham Alexander, Darren Fletcher, Kris Commons, Scott Brown, Kenny Miller, Ross McCormack (37 Christophe Berra, 79 Steven Whittaker).   Manager: George Burley

Sent off: Gary Caldwell (34)

Goals: John Arne Riise (36), Morten Pedersen (45, 90), Erik Huseklepp (60)

688. 05.09.2009   19th World Cup Qualifier
SCOTLAND v MACEDONIA 2-0 (0-0)
Hampden Park, Glasgow

Referee: Wolfgang Stark (Germany)   Attendance: 50,214

SCOTLAND: Craig Gordon, Stephen McManus, Alan Hutton, Callum Davidson (14 Steven Whittaker), Graham Alexander, David Weir, Darren Fletcher, Scott Brown (73 Paul Hartley), Kenny Miller, James McFadden, Steven Fletcher (68 Shaun Maloney).   Manager: George Burley

MACEDONIA: Jane Nikoloski, Goce Sedloski, Nikolce Noveski, Igor Mitreski, Slavco Georgievski (69 Vlatko Grozdanovski), Goran Popov, Filip Despotovski, Velice Sumulikoski, Ilco Naumoski (65 Darko Tasevski), Aco Stojkov (80 Besart Ibraimi), Goran Pandev.   Manager: Mirsad Jonuz

Goals: Scott Brown (56), James McFadden (81)

689. 09.09.2009   19th World Cup Qualifier
SCOTLAND v NETHERLANDS 0-1 (0-0)
Hampden Park, Glasgow

Referee: Claus Bo Larsen (Denmark)   Attendance: 51,230

SCOTLAND: David Marshall, Steven Whittaker, Stephen McManus, Alan Hutton, David Weir, Steven Naismith, Paul Hartley (66 Kris Commons), Darren Fletcher, Scott Brown, Shaun Maloney (81 Gary O'Connor), Kenny Miller.   Manager: George Burley

NETHERLANDS: Michel Vorm, Gregory van der Wiel, André Ooijer, Joris Mathijsen, Demy de Zeeuw, Giovanni van Bronckhorst, Nigel de Jong, Wesley Sneijder (77 Rafael van der Vaart), Robin van Persie (84 Klaas-Jan Huntelaar), Arjen Robben (72 Eljero Elia), Dirk Kuyt.
Manager: Bert van Marwijk

Goal: Eljero Elia (81)

690. 10.10.2009
JAPAN v SCOTLAND 2-0 (0-0)
Nissan Stadium, Yokohama

Referee: Sang-woo Kim (South Korea)   Attendance: 61,285

JAPAN: Eiji Kawashima, Daika Iwamasa, Atsuto Uchida (65 Yuhei Tokunaga), Naohiro Ishikawa (65 Daisuke Matsui), Hideo Hashimoto (65 Yoshito Okubo), Kengo Nakamura, Vasuyuki Konno, Junichi Inamoto (81 Yuichi Komano), Keisuke Honda, Yuki Abe, Ryoichi Maeda (56 Takayuki Morimoto).   Manager: Takeshi Okada

SCOTLAND: Craig Gordon, Steven Whittaker, Lee Wallace, Stephen McManus, Christophe Berra, Gary Caldwell, Ross Wallace (46 Don Cowie), Graham Dorrans, Charlie Adam (67 Stephen Hughes), Craig Conway (74 Derek Riordan), Lee Miller (46 Steven Fletcher).   Manager: George Burley

Goals: Christophe Berra (82 og), Keisuke Honda (90)

691. 14.11.2009
WALES v SCOTLAND 3-0 (3-0)
Millennium, Cardiff

Referee: Cyril Zimmermann (Switzerland)   Att: 13,844

WALES: Wayne Hennessey, Sam Ricketts, Lewin Nyatanga (60 Daniel Gabbidon), Craig Morgan, Ashley Williams, Aaron Ramsey (56 Joe Allen), Joe Ledley (80 Andy King), Dave Edwards (88 David Cotterill), Gareth Bale, Ched Evans (46 Sam Vokes), Simon Church (46 Robert Earnshaw).
Manager: John Toshack

SCOTLAND: David Marshall, Alan Hutton, Danny Fox (54 Lee Wallace), Stephen McManus, Gary Caldwell, Steven Naismith (62 Kevin Kyle), Darren Fletcher, Graham Dorrans (71 Barry Robson), Don Cowie (78 Derek Riordan), Kenny Miller (55 Steven Fletcher), James McFadden (62 Ross McCormack).   Manager: George Burley

Goals: Dave Edwards (17), Simon Church (32), Aaron Ramsey (35)

692. 03.03.2010
SCOTLAND v CZECH REPUBLIC 1-0 (0-0)
Hampden Park, Glasgow

Referee: Fredy Fautrel (France)   Attendance: 26,530

SCOTLAND: Craig Gordon, Andy Webster (46 Christophe Berra), Lee Wallace, Alan Hutton, Gary Caldwell, Barry Robson (69 Charlie Adam), Scott Brown, Kevin Thomson (46 Paul Hartley), Darren Fletcher (83 Steven Whittaker), Graham Dorrans, Kenny Miller (63 Kris Boyd).   Manager: Craig Levein

CZECH REPUBLIC: Jaroslav Drobny, Ondrej Kusnír (86 Daniel Pudil), Michal Kadlec, Tomás Hübschman (79 Jan Morávek), Roman Hubník, Tomás Sivok, Mario Holek, Tomás Rosicky (66 Rudi Skácel), Jaroslav Plasil (79 Jan Rajnoch), Václav Sverkos (67 Jan Blazek), Tomás Necid (67 Michal Papadopulos).   Manager: Michel Bílek

Goal: Scott Brown (62)

693.   11.08.2010
SWEDEN v SCOTLAND 3-0 (2-0)

Råsunda Stadion, Solna

Referee: Gianluca Rocchi (Italy)   Attendance: 25,249

SWEDEN: Andreas Isaksson, Olof Mellberg, Daniel Majstorovic, Behrang Safari, Mikael Lustig (46 Kim Källström), Anders Svensson (73 Oscar Wendt), Emir Bajrami (64 Christian Wilhelmsson), Pontus Wernbloom (46 Sebastian Larsson), Zlatan Ibrahimovic (59 Tobias Hysén), Johan Elmander (78 Marcus Berg), Ola Toivonen.
Manager: Erik Hamrén

SCOTLAND: Allan McGregor, Gary Kenneth, Kirk Broadfoot (75 Steven Whittaker), Christophe Berra, Lee Wallace, Barry Robson (80 Chris Iwelumo), Darren Fletcher, Charlie Adam (65 James Morrison), Kevin Thomson (54 Scott Robertson), James McFadden, Steven Fletcher (64 Kris Boyd).
Manager: Craig Levein

Goals: Zlatan Ibrahimovic (4), Emir Bajrami (39), Ola Toivonen (56)

694.   03.09.2010   14th European Champs Qualifier
LITHUANIA v SCOTLAND 0-0

Dariaus ir Giréno, Kaunas

Referee: Cüneyt Çakir (Turkey)   Attendance: 5,248

LITHUANIA: Zydrūnas Karcemarskas, Marius Stankevicius, Andrius Skerla, Deividas Semberas, Tadas Kijanskas, Darvydas Sernas (80 Vytautas Luksa), Ramūnas Radavicius, Mindaugas Panka, Saulius Mikoliūnas (71 Robertas Poskus), Edgaras Cesnauskis, Tomas Danilevicius (90 Kestutis Ivaskevicius).   Manager: Raimondas Zutautas

SCOTLAND: Allan McGregor, Steven Whittaker (90 Christophe Berra), David Weir, Stephen McManus, Alan Hutton, Barry Robson (69 James McFadden), Steven Naismith, Darren Fletcher, Scott Brown (76 James Morrison), Kenny Miller, Lee McCulloch.   Manager: Craig Levein

695.   07.09.2010   14th European Champs Qualifier
SCOTLAND v LIECHTENSTEIN 2-1 (0-0)

Hampden Park, Glasgow

Referee: Viktor Shvetkov (Ukraine)   Attendance: 37,050

SCOTLAND: Allan McGregor, David Weir, Lee Wallace (55 Barry Robson), Stephen McManus, Alan Hutton, Darren Fletcher, Scott Brown, Kenny Miller, James McFadden (46 James Morrison), Lee McCulloch, Kris Boyd (66 Steven Naismith).   Manager: Craig Levein

LIECHTENSTEIN: Peter Jehle, Michael Stocklasa, Martin Stocklasa, Martin Rechsteiner, Yves Oehri, Michele Polverino, Franz Burgmeier, Sandro Wieser (71 Ronny Büchel), David Hasler (90 Nicolas Hasler), Mario Frick (79 Fabio D'Elia), Philippe Erne.   Manager: Hans-Peter Zaugg

Goals: Kenny Miller (62), S. McManus (90) / Mario Frick (46)

696.   08.10.2010   14th Euro Champs Qualifier
CZECH REPUBLIC v SCOTLAND 1-0 (0-0)

Synot Tip Aréna, Praha

Referee: Ivan Bebek (Croatia)   Attendance: 14,922

CZECH REPUBLIC: Petr Cech, Zdenek Pospech, Michal Kadlec, Tomás Hübschmann, Roman Hubník, Marek Suchy, Tomás Rosicky, Jan Polák, Jaroslav Plasil (90+3 Jan Rajnoch), Tomás Necid (84 Mario Holek), Lukás Magera (59 Roman Bednár).   Manager: Michal Bílek

SCOTLAND: Allan McGregor, Steven Whittaker, David Weir, Stephen McManus, Alan Hutton, Gary Caldwell (76 Kenny Miller), Steven Naismith, James Morrison (84 Barry Robson), Darren Fletcher, Graham Dorrans, Jamie Mackie (76 Chris Iwelumo).   Manager: Craig Levein

Goal: Roman Hubník (69)

697.   12.10.2010   14th European Champs Qualifier
SCOTLAND v SPAIN 2-3 (0-1)

Hampden Park, Glasgow

Referee: Massimo Busacca (Switzerland)   Att: 51,322

SCOTLAND: Allan McGregor, Steven Whittaker, David Weir, Stephen McManus, Phil Bardsley, Steven Naismith, James Morrison (88 Shaun Maloney), Darren Fletcher, Graham Dorrans (80 Jamie Mackie), Kenny Miller, Lee McCulloch (46 Chris Adam).   Manager: Craig Levein

SPAIN: IKER CASILLAS Fernández, Joan CAPDEVILLA Méndez, SERGIO RAMOS García, Carles PUYOL Saforcada, Gerard PIQUÉ i Bernabéu, Xabier "Xabi" ALONSO Olano, Andrés INIESTA Luján, DAVID Jiménez SILVA (76 Fernando LLORENTE Torres), Santiago "Santi" CAZORLA González (71 PABLO HERNÁNDEZ Domínguez), Sergio BUSQUETS Burgos (90 Carlos MARCHENA López), DAVID VILLA Sánchez.   Manager: Vicente DEL BOSQUE González

Sent off: Steven Whittaker (89)

Goals: S. Naismith (58), Gerard PIQUÉ i Bernabéu (66 og) / DAVID VILLA Sánchez (44 pen), Andrés INIESTA Luján (55), Fernando LLORENTE Torres (79)

127

698. 16.11.2010
SCOTLAND v FAROE ISLANDS 3-0 (3-0)
Pittodrie Stadium, Aberdeen
Referee: Pol van Boekel (Netherlands)   Attendance: 10,873
SCOTLAND: Craig Gordon (68 Cammy Bell), Stephen Crainey, Phil Bardsley (71 Steven Saunders), Danny Wilson (61 Gary Kenneth), Steven Caldwell, Darren Fletcher (68 Craig Bryson), Kris Commons (76 David Goodwillie), Barry Bannan, Charlie Adam (55 James McArthur), Shaun Maloney, Jamie Mackie.   Manager: Craig Levein
FAROE ISLANDS: Gunnar Nielsen (68 Tórdur Thomsen), Erling Jacobsen, Atli Gregersen, Jóhan Davidsen, Jónas Næs, Bogi Løkin (78 Levi Hanssen), Christian Holst (56 Rógvi Poulsen), Hjalgrim Elttør, Jóan Edmundsson, Jann Ingi Petersen (60 Christian Mouritsen), Daniel Udsen (86 Pól Justinussen).   Manager: Brian Kerr
Goals: Danny Wilson (24), Kris Commons (31), Jamie Mackie (45)

699. 09.02.2011   Nations Cup
NORTHERN IRELAND v SCOTLAND 0-3 (0-2)
Aviva Stadium, Dublin
Referee: Tomas Connolly (Republic of Ireland)   Att: 18,742
NORTHERN IRELAND: Jonny Tuffey, Rory McArdle (46 Lee Hodson), Stephen Craigan (66 Adam Thompson), Chris Baird, Gareth McAuley, Pat McCourt, Grant McCann (46 David Healy), Corry Evans, Steven Davis (58 Oliver Norwood), Niall McGinn (72 Liam Boyce), Rory Patterson.   Manager: Nigel Worthington
SCOTLAND: Allan McGregor, Steven Caldwell, Christophe Berra, Phil Bardsley (57 Mark Wilson), Alan Hutton, Kris Commons (72 Craig Conway), Charlie Adam (57 Barry Bannan), Steven Naismith (58 Robert Snodgrass), James Morrison (79 Chris Maguire), James McArthur, Kenny Miller (89 Danny Wilson).   Manager: Craig Levein
Goals: Kenny Miller (19), James McArthur (32), Kris Commons (51)

700. 27.03.2011
BRAZIL v SCOTLAND 2-0 (1-0)
Emirates Stadium, London
Referee: Howard Webb (England)   Attendance: 53,087
BRAZIL: JÚLIO CÉSAR Soares Espíndola, ANDRÉ Clarindo dos SANTOS, THIAGO Emiliano SILVA, Lucimar da Silva Ferreira "Lúcio", Daniel "Dani" ALVES da Silva, RAMIRES Santos do Nascimento, LUCAS Pezzini LEIVA (86 SANDRO Ranieri Guimarães Cordeiro), JÁDSON Rodrigues da Silva (72 LUCAS Rodrigues Moura da Silva), ELANO Ralph Blumer (83 ELÍAS Mendes Trindade), LEANDRO DAMIÃO da Silva dos Santos (79 JONAS Gonçalves Oliveira), NEYMAR da Silva Santos Júnior (90 RENATO Soares de Oliveira AUGUSTO).   Manager: Luiz Antonio Venker "Mano" MENEZES

SCOTLAND: Allan McGregor, Steven Whittaker (65 Kris Commons), Alan Hutton, Stephen Crainey, Gary Caldwell, Christophe Berra (73 Danny Wilson), Charlie Adam (78 Robert Snodgrass), James Morrison (90+2 Don Cowie), James McArthur (57 Barry Bannan), Scott Brown, Kenny Miller (86 Craig Mackail-Smith).   Manager: Craig Levein
Goals: NEYMAR da Silva Santos Júnior (43, 77 pen)

701. 25.05.2011   Nations Cup
WALES v SCOTLAND 1-3 (1-0)
Aviva Stadium, Dublin
Referee: Raymond Crangle (Northern Ireland)   Att: 6,036
WALES: Glyn Oliver "Boaz" Myhill, Neil Taylor (46 Chris Gunter), Craig Morgan, Neal Eardley (61 Adam Matthews), Owain Tudur-Jones (72 David Vaughan), Andy King (61 Aaron Ramsey), Andy Dorman (61 David Cotterill), Darcy Blake, Sam Vokes (73 Steve Morison), Jermaine Easter, Robert Earnshaw.   Manager: Gary Speed
SCOTLAND: Allan McGregor, Steven Whittaker (80 Phil Bardsley), Stephen Crainey (81 Russell Martin), Gary Caldwell (86 Grant Hanley), Christophe Berra, Steven Naismith, James Morrison (74 Barry Robson), Scott Brown, Charlie Adam (88 James McArthur), Kenny Miller, Ross McCormack (74 Barry Bannan).   Manager: Craig Levein
Goals: Robert Earnshaw (36) / James Morrison (56), Kenny Miller (65), Christophe Berra (71)

702. 29.05.2011   Nations Cup
REPUBLIC OF IRELAND v SCOTLAND 1-0 (1-0)
Aviva Stadium, Dublin
Referee: Mark Whitby (Wales)   Attendance: 17,694
REPUBLIC OF IRELAND: Shay Given, Darren O'Dea (66 Kevin Foley), Paul McShane, Stephen Kelly, Stephen Ward, Keith Fahey, Keith Andrews, Liam Lawrence (62 Séamus Coleman), Stephen Hunt, Robbie Keane (83 Keith Treacy), Simon Cox.   Manager: Giovanni Trapattoni
SCOTLAND: Allan McGregor, Christophe Berra, Phil Bardsley, Steven Whittaker, Grant Hanley, Charlie Adam (63 Barry Bannan), Barry Robson (75 Chris Maguire), Steven Naismith, Scott Brown, Kenny Miller, James Forrest (85 Ross McCormack).   Manager: Craig Levein
Goal: Robbie Keane (23)

703. 10.08.2011
SCOTLAND v DENMARK 2-1 (2-1)
Hampden Park, Glasgow
Referee: Marco Borg (Malta)   Attendance: 17,582
SCOTLAND: Allan McGregor, Stephen Crainey, Gary Caldwell, Phil Bardsley, Danny Wilson, Steven Naismith (74 James Forrest), James Morrison (67 Barry Bannan), Scott Brown (19 Don Cowie), Charlie Adam (58 Graham Dorrans), Robert Snodgrass (88 Grant Hanley), Kenny Miller (57 Craig Mackail-Smith).   Manager: Craig Levein
DENMARK: Thomas Sørensen, Nicolai Boilesen, William Kvist, Simon Kjær, Lars Jacobsen (73 Michael Silberbauer), Daniel Agger (58 Mathias Jørgensen), Christian Poulsen (46 Lasse Schöne), Michael Krohn-Dehli (76 Bashkim Kadrii), Christian Eriksen, Nicklas Bendtner (46 Nicklas Pedersen), Dennis Rommedahl (46 Niki Zimling).
Manager: Morten Olsen
Goals: William Kvist (22 og), Robert Snodgrass (44) / Christian Eriksen (31)

704. 03.09.2011   14th European Champs Qualifier
SCOTLAND v CZECH REPUBLIC 2-2 (1-0)
Hampden Park, Glasgow
Referee: Kevin Blom (Netherlands)   Attendance: 51,457
SCOTLAND: Allan McGregor, Alan Hutton, Christophe Berra, Gary Caldwell, Phil Bardsley (76 Danny Wilson), Scott Brown, Charlie Adam (79 Don Cowie), Steven Naismith (87 Barry Robson), James Morrison, Kenny Miller, Steven Fletcher.   Manager: Craig Levein
CZECH REPUBLIC: Jan Lastuvka, Jan Rajnoch, Michal Kadlec, Tomás Hübschmann, Roman Hubník, Tomás Sivok, Tomás Rosicky, Jaroslav Plasil, Petr Jirácek (78 Tomás Pekhart), Milan Petrzela (56 Jan Rezek), Milan Baros (90+1 Kamil Vacek).   Manager: Michal Bílek
Goals: Kenny Miller (44), Steven Fletcher (82) / Jaroslav Plasil (78), Michal Kadlec (90 pen)

705. 06.09.2011   14th European Champs Qualifier
SCOTLAND v LITHUANIA 1-0 (0-0)
Hampden Park, Glasgow
Referee: Kristinn Jakobsson (Iceland)   Attendance: 34,071
SCOTLAND: Allan McGregor, Steven Whittaker, Christophe Berra, Gary Caldwell, Phil Bardsley (70 Stephen Crainey), Steven Naismith, James Morrison (79 Graham Dorrans), Darren Fletcher, Don Cowie, Barry Bannan (84 Robert Snodgrass), David Goodwillie.   Manager: Craig Levein

LITHUANIA: Zydrūnas Karcemarskas, Deividas Semberas, Arūnas Klimavicius, Tadas Kijanskas (61 Tomas Danilevicius), Marius Zaliūkas, Darvydas Sernas, Ramūnas Radavicius, Linas Pilibaitis, Saulius Mikoliūnas (77 Ricardas Beniusis), Deividas Cesnauskis, Tadas Labukas (46 Arvydas Novikovas).
Manager: Raimondas Zutautas
Goal: Steven Naismith (50)

Darren Fletcher missed a penalty kick in the 45th minute.

706. 08.10.2011   14th European Champs Qualifier
LIECHTENSTEIN v SCOTLAND 0-1 (0-1)
Rheinpark, Vaduz
Referee: Tom Hagen (Norway)   Attendance: 5,636
LIECHTENSTEIN: Peter Jehle, Martin Stocklasa, Marco Ritzberger, Martin Rechsteiner, Daniel Kaufmann, Michele Polverino, Nicolas Hasler, Rony Hanselmann (75 Lucas Eberle), Martin Büchel (71 Wolfgang Kieber), Mario Frick, Thomas Beck.   Manager: Hans-Peter Zaugg
SCOTLAND: Allan McGregor, Alan Hutton, Christophe Berra, Gary Caldwell, Phil Bardsley, Steven Naismith, James Morrison, Darren Fletcher, Barry Bannan (73 James Forrest), Charlie Adam (76 Don Cowie), Craig Mackail-Smith.
Manager: Craig Levein
Goal: Craig Mackail-Smith (32)

707. 11.10.2011   14th European Champs Qualifier
SPAIN v SCOTLAND 3-1 (2-0)
Estadio José Rico Pérez, Alicante
Referee: Stefan Johannesson (Sweden)   Attendance: 27,559
SPAIN: VÍCTOR VALDÉS Arribas, JORDI ALBA Ramos, SERGIO RAMOS García, Carles PUYOL Saforcada (46 Álvaro ARBELOA Coca), Gerard PIQUÉ i Bernabéu, Xavier Hernández i Creus "Xavi" (64 Fernando LLORENTE Torres), DAVID Jiménez SILVA (55 THIAGO Alcântara do Nascimento), Santiago "Santi" CAZORLA González, Sergio BUSQUETS Burgos, PEDRO Eliezer Rodríguez Ledesma, DAVID VILLA Sánchez.
Manager: Vicente DEL BOSQUE González
SCOTLAND: Allan McGregor, Alan Hutton, Christophe Berra, Gary Caldwell, Phil Bardsley, Steven Naismith, James Morrison, Darren Fletcher (85 Don Cowie), Barry Bannan (64 David Goodwillie), Charlie Adam (64 James Forrest), Craig Mackail-Smith.   Manager: Craig Levein
Goals: DAVID Jiménez SILVA (6, 44), DAVID VILLA (54) / David Goodwillie (66 pen)

129

708. 11.11.2011
CYPRUS v SCOTLAND 1-2 (0-1)
Stadio Antonis Papadopoulos, Larnaca
Referee: Meir Levi (Israel)   Attendance: 1,360
CYPRUS: Antonis Georgallides (46 Tasos Kissas), Stelios Parpas (58 Mários Nikolaou), Jason Demetriou (46 Valentinos Sielis), Giorgios Merkis, Athos Solomou, Marinos Satsias, Giorgos Efrem, Sinisa Dobrasinovic (74 Giorgos Vasiliou), Dimitris Christofi, Nektarios Alexandrou (69 Antonis Katsis), Andreas Avraam (46 Nestoras Mitidis). Manager: Nikos Nioplias
SCOTLAND: Allan McGregor, Steven Whittaker, Gary Caldwell, Christophe Berra, Phil Bardsley (74 Stephen Crainey), Darren Fletcher (63 James McArthur), Barry Robson (80 Craig Conway), James Morrison, Jamie Mackie (87 Jordan Rhodes), Don Cowie, Kenny Miller (63 Craig Mackail-Smith). Manager: Craig Levein
Goals: Dimitris Christofi (60) / Kenny Miller (23), Jamie Mackie (57)

709. 29.02.2012
SLOVENIA v SCOTLAND 1-1 (1-1)
SRC Bonifika, Koper
Referee: Aleksandar Stavrev (Macedonia)   Att: 4,190
SLOVENIA: Samir Handanovic, Marko Suler, Bojan Jokic, Bostjan Cesar, Miso Brecko, Aleksander Radosavljevic, Rene Krhin (85 Darijan Matic), Andraz Kirm (89 Nejc Pecnik), Josep Ilicic (68 Dare Vrsic), Zlatko Dedic (83 Zlatan Ljubijankic), Valter Birsa (61 Haris Vuckic). Manager: Slavisa Stojanovic
SCOTLAND: Allan McGregor, Charlie Mulgrew, Gary Caldwell, Christophe Berra, James Morrison (72 Graham Dorrans), James McArthur, Russell Martin, Jamie Mackie (81 Kenny Miller), Charlie Adam (46 Barry Bannan), Craig Mackail-Smith (61 Robert Snodgrass), James Forrest (87 Barry Robson). Manager: Craig Levein
Goals: Andraz Kirm (33) / Christophe Berra (39)

710. 27.05.2012
USA v SCOTLAND 5-1 (2-1)
EverBank Field, Jacksonville
Referee: Elmer Bonilla (El Salvador)   Attendance: 44,438
USA: Tim Howard (71 Brad Guzan), Fabian Johnson (73 Edgar Castillo), Steven Cherundolo, Carlos Bocanegra (63 Oguchi Onyewu), Landon Donovan, José Francisco Torres (68 Joe Corona), Jermaine Jones, Maurice Edu (64 Kyle Beckerman), Geoff Cameron, Michael Bradley, Terrence Boyd (64 Hérculez Gómez). Manager: Jürgen Klinsmann

SCOTLAND: Allan McGregor, Andy Webster (82 Christophe Berra), Charlie Mulgrew (76 Lee Wallace), Gary Caldwell, Phil Bardsley (59 Russell Martin), Matt Phillips, James McArthur (59 Steven Whittaker), Shaun Maloney (83 Craig Mackail-Smith), Scott Brown, Barry Bannan (51 Don Cowie), Kenny Miller. Manager: Craig Levein
Goals: Landon Donovan (3, 60, 65), Michael Bradley (11), Jermaine Jones (70) / Geoff Cameron (15 og)

711. 15.08.2012
SCOTLAND v AUSTRALIA 3-1 (1-1)
Easter Road Stadium, Edinburgh
Referee: Tom Hagen (Norway)   Attendance: 11,110
SCOTLAND: Allan McGregor (23 Matt Gilks), Allan Hutton (68 Russell Martin), Danny Fox (70 Charlie Mulgrew), Gary Caldwell (87 Ian Black), Christophe Berra, Andy Webster, Charlie Adam, James Morrison (27 Shaun Maloney), Robert Snodgrass, Steven Naismith, Jordan Rhodes (67 Ross McCormack). Manager: Craig Levein
AUSTRALIA: Mark Schwarzer (46 Adam Federici), Rhys Williams, Sasa Ognenovski (79 Ryan McGowan), Lucas Neill, Brett Holman (46 Scott McDonald), David Carney (60 Jason Davidson), Mark Bresciano (46 Mile Jedinak), Carl Valeri, Luke Wilkshire, Alex Brosque (85 Archie Thompson), Robbie Kruse. Manager: Holger Osieck
Goals: Jordan Rhodes (28), Jason Davidson (63 og), Ross McCormack (76) / Mark Bresciano (18)

712. 08.09.2012   20th World Cup Qualifier
SCOTLAND v SERBIA 0-0
Hampden Park, Glasgow
Referee: Jonas Eriksson (Sweden)   Attendance: 47,369
SCOTLAND: Allan McGregor, Allan Hutton, Paul Dixon, Gary Caldwell, Christophe Berra, Andy Webster, Steven Naismith, James Morrison (81 Jamie Mackie), Charlie Adam, Robert Snodgrass (69 James Forrest), Kenny Miller (81 Jordan Rhodes). Manager: Craig Levein
SERBIA: Vladimir Stojkovic, Matija Nastasic, Aleksandar Kolarov, Branislav Ivanovic, Milan Bisevac, Milos Ninkovic, Srdan Mijailovic (46 Ljubomir Fejsa), Darko Lazovic (58 Dusan Tadic), Aleksandar Ignjovski, Filip Djuricic (83 Dejan Lekic), Zoran Tosic. Manager: Sinisa Mihajlovic

713. 11.09.2012   20th World Cup Qualifier
SCOTLAND v MACEDONIA 1-1 (1-1)
Hampden Park, Glasgow

Referee: Sergey Karasev (Russia)   Attendance: 32,430

SCOTLAND: Allan McGregor, Andy Webster, Allan Hutton, Paul Dixon, Gary Caldwell, Christophe Berra, James Morrison (66 Jordan Rhodes), Shaun Maloney, Jamie Mackie (77 Steven Naismith), Kenny Miller (58 Charlie Adam), James Forrest. Manager: Craig Levein

MACEDONIA: Martin Bogatinov, Vance Shikov, Goran Popov, Nikolce Noveski, Daniel Georgievski, Nikola Gligorov (70 Velice Sumulikoski), Muhamed Demiri, Ivan Trichkovski (38 Ferhan Hasani), Goran Pandev, Mirko Ivanovski, Agim Ibraimi (89 Darko Tasevski).   Manager: Cedomir Janevski

Goals: Kenny Miller (43) / Nikolce Noveski (11)

714. 12.10.2012   20th World Cup Qualifier
WALES v SCOTLAND 2-1 (0-1)
Cardiff City Stadium, Cardiff

Referee: Florian Meyer (Germany)   Attendance: 23,249

WALES: Lewis Price, Ashley Williams, Chris Gunter, Darcy Blake, Ben Davies, David Vaughan, Aaron Ramsey, Joe Ledley (71 Hal Robson-Kanu), Joe Allen, Gareth Bale, Steve Morison (65 Craig Davies).   Manager: Chris Coleman

SCOTLAND: Allan McGregor, Allan Hutton, Danny Fox, Gary Caldwell, Christophe Berra, James Morrison (85 Kenny Miller), Shaun Maloney, Darren Fletcher, Kris Commons (84 Jamie Mackie), Scott Brown (46 Charlie Adam), Steven Fletcher.   Manager: Craig Levein

Goals: Gareth Bale (81 pen, 89) / James Morrison (27)

715. 16.10.2012   20th World Cup Qualifier
BELGIUM v SCOTLAND 2-0 (0-0)
Stade Roi Baudouin, Brussels

Referee: Tom Hagen (Norway)   Attendance: 44,132

BELGIUM: Thibaut Courtois, Jan Vertonghen, Thomas Vermaelen, Vincent Kompany, Toby Alderweireld, Axel Witsel, Dries Mertens (56 Kevin Mirallas), Mousa Dembélé (46 Eden Hazard), Kevin De Bruyne, Nacer Chadli, Christian Benteke (87 Ilombe M'Boyo).   Manager: Marc Wilmots

SCOTLAND: Allan McGregor, Allan Hutton, Danny Fox, Gary Caldwell, Christophe Berra, James Morrison (80 Matt Phillips), James McArthur, Shaun Maloney, Darren Fletcher, Kris Commons (46 Jamie Mackie), Steven Fletcher (76 Kenny Miller).   Manager: Craig Levein

Goals: Christian Benteke (68), Vincent Kompany (71)

716. 14.11.2012
LUXEMBOURG v SCOTLAND 1-2 (0-2)
Stade Josy Barthel, Luxembourg

Referee: Cyril Zimmermann (Switzerland)   Att: 2,521

LUXEMBOURG: Jonathan Joubert, Tom Schnell, Mathias Jänisch (53 Daniël Alves Da Mota), Ante Bukvic, Guy Blaise, Gilles Bettmer (71 David Turpel), Ben Payal (46 René Peters), Charles Leweck (76 Tom Laterza), Lars Gerson, Mario Mutsch, Maurice Deville (64 Stefano Bensi).   Manager: Luc Holtz

SCOTLAND: Matt Gilks, Grant Hanley, Christophe Berra, Paul Dixon, Steven Whittaker, Charlie Mulgrew (46 Liam Kelly), Andrew Shinnie (70 Leigh Griffiths), Darren Fletcher, Steven Naismith, Jordan Rhodes (90+1 Murray Davidson), Kenny Miller.   Manager: Billy Stark

Goals: Lars Gerson (47) / Jordan Rhodes (11, 23)

717. 06.02.2013
SCOTLAND v ESTONIA 1-0 (1-0)
Pittodrie Stadium, Aberdeen

Referee: Clément Turpin (France)   Attendance: 16,102

SCOTLAND: Allan McGregor, Andy Webster, Charlie Mulgrew, Alan Hutton, Christophe Berra, Steven Naismith (74 Kris Commons), Shaun Maloney (46 Jordan Rhodes), Chris Burke (46 Robert Snodgrass), Scott Brown (62 James Morrison), Charlie Adam (62 James McArthur), Steven Fletcher (67 Kenny Miller).   Manager: Gordon Strachan

ESTONIA: Sergei Pareiko, Igor Morozov, Ragnar Klavan, Enar Jääger, Konstantin Vassiljev, Sander Puri (59 Ats Purje), Sergei Mosnikov, Taijo Teniste, Andres Oper (47 Jarmo Ahjupera), Henrik Ojamaa (73 Gert Kams), Tarmo Kink (58 Siim Luts).   Manager: Tarmo Rüütli

Goal: Charlie Mulgrew (39)

718. 22.03.2013   20th World Cup Qualifier
SCOTLAND v WALES 1-2 (1-0)
Hampden Park, Glasgow

Referee: Antony Gautier (France)   Attendance: 39,365

SCOTLAND: Allan McGregor, Grant Hanley, Gary Caldwell, Charlie Mulgrew, Alan Hutton, Graham Dorrans (64 Charlie Adam), Chris Burke (86 Jordan Rhodes), Robert Snodgrass, James McArthur, Shaun Maloney, Steven Fletcher (4 Kenny Miller).   Manager: Gordon Strachan

WALES: Glyn Oliver "Boaz" Myhill, Chris Gunter, Ben Davies, Ashley Williams, Sam Ricketts, Jack Collison (58 Andy King), Aaron Ramsey, Joe Ledley (89 Simon Church), Gareth Bale (46 Jonathan Williams), Craig Bellamy, Hal Robson-Kanu.   Manager: Chris Coleman

Sent off: Robert Snodgrass (72), Aaron Ramsey (90+4)

Goals: Grant Hanley (45+1) / Aaron Ramsey (72 pen), Hal Robson-Kanu (74)

719. 26.03.2013   20th World Cup Qualifier
SERBIA v SCOTLAND 2-0 (0-0)
Stadion Karadjordje, Novi Sad
Referee: István Vad (Hungary)   Attendance: 5,000
SERBIA: Vladimir Stojkovic, Nenad Tomovic, Neven Subotic, Matija Nastasic, Branislav Ivanovic, Dusan Basta, Zoran Tosic (90+3 Alen Stevanovic), Dusan Tadic (69 Filip Djordevic), Ljubomir Fejsa (85 Radoslav Petrovic), Filip Djuricic, Luka Milivojevic.   Manager: Sinisa Mihajlovic
SCOTLAND: David Marshall, Steven Whittaker, Alan Hutton, Grant Hanley, Gary Caldwell, Steven Naismith, James McArthur (46 Charlie Adam), Shaun Maloney (80 Chris Burke), Liam Bridcutt, George Boyd, Jordan Rhodes (80 Kenny Miller).   Manager: Gordon Strachan
Goals: Filip Djuricic (59, 65)

720. 07.06.2013   20th World Cup Qualifier
CROATIA v SCOTLAND 0-1 (0-1)
Stadion Maksimir, Zagreb
Referee: David Fernández Borbalán (Spain)   Attendance: 25,016
CROATIA: Stipe Pletikosa, Ivan Strinic (70 Nikola Kalinic), Darijo Srna, Josip Simunic, Gordon Schildenfeld, Jorge SAMMIR Cruz Campos, Ivan Rakitic, Ivan Perisic (56 EDUARDO Alves da Silva), Mateo Kovacic, Ivica Olic, Mario Mandzukic (88 Niko Kranjcar).   Manager: Igor Stimac
SCOTLAND: Allan McGregor, Steven Whittaker, Alan Hutton, Grant Hanley, Robert Snodgrass, James Morrison, James McArthur, Russell Martin, Shaun Maloney (75 Craig Conway), Barry Bannan (63 Steven Naismith), Leigh Griffiths (64 Jordan Rhodes).   Manager: Gordon Strachan
Goal: Robert Snodgrass (26)

721. 14.08.2013
ENGLAND v SCOTLAND 3-2 (1-1)
Wembley, London
Referee: Dr. Felix Brych (Germany)   Attendance: 80,485
ENGLAND: Joe Hart, Phil Jagielka (84 Phil Jones), Gary Cahill, Leighton Baines, Kyle Walker, Steven Gerrard (62 Alex Oxlade-Chamberlain), Tom Cleverley (67 James Milner), Jack Wilshere (46 Frank Lampard), Wayne Rooney (67 Rickie Lambert), Danny Welbeck, Theo Walcott (75 Wilfried Zaha).   Manager: Roy Hodgson
SCOTLAND: Allan McGregor, Alan Hutton, Steven Whittaker, Grant Hanley, James Morrison (82 Jordan Rhodes), Russell Martin, Shaun Maloney (86 Steven Naismith), Scott Brown, Robert Snodgrass (68 Craig Conway), Kenny Miller (73 Leigh Griffiths), James Forrest (67 Charlie Mulgrew).   Manager: Gordon Strachan
Goals: T. Walcott (29), D. Welbeck (53), Rickie Lambert (70) / James Morrison (12), Kenny Miller (50)

722. 06.09.2013   20th World Cup Qualifier
SCOTLAND v BELGIUM 0-2 (0-1)
Hampden Park, Glasgow
Referee: Paolo Tagliavento (Italy)   Attendance: 40,284
SCOTLAND: David Marshall, Alan Hutton, Grant Hanley, Steven Whittaker, Charlie Mulgrew, Scott Brown, Robert Snodgrass (59 Ikechi Anya), Russell Martin, Shaun Maloney, James Forrest (86 Ross McCormack), Leigh Griffiths (67 Jordan Rhodes).   Manager: Gordon Strachan
BELGIUM: Thibaut Courtois, Daniel Van Buyten, Jan Vertonghen, Nicolas Lombaerts (77 Sébastien Pocognoli), Toby Alderweireld, Axel Witsel, Marouane Fellaini (68 Kevin Mirallas), Steven Defour (87 Mousa Dembélé), Kevin De Bruyne, Nacer Chadli, Christian Benteke.   Manager: Marc Wilmots
Goals: Steven Defour (38), Kevin Mirallas (89)

723. 10.09.2013   20th World Cup Qualifier
MACEDONIA v SCOTLAND 1-2 (0-0)
Filip II. Makedonski, Skopje
Referee: Fredy Fautrel (France)   Attendance: 14,093
MACEDONIA: Tome Pachovski, Vance Shikov, Nikolce Noveski, Daniel Georgievski, Ostoja Stjepanovic, Stefan Ristovski, David Badunski (42 Darko Tasevski), Ivan Trichkovski, Aleksandar Trajkovski (57 Mirko Ivanovski), Goran Pandev, Adis Jahovic (83 Jovan Kostovski).   Manager: Cedomir Janevski
SCOTLAND: David Marshall (46 Matt Gilks), Steven Whittaker (80 Lee Wallace), Charlie Mulgrew, Alan Hutton, Grant Hanley, Steven Naismith, Russell Martin, Shaun Maloney, Scott Brown, Barry Bannan (79 James McArthur), Ikechi Anya.   Manager: Gordon Strachan
Goals: Jovan Kostovski (84) / Ikechi Anya (60), Shaun Maloney (89)

724. 15.10.2013   20th World Cup Qualifier
SCOTLAND v CROATIA 2-0 (1-0)
Hampden Park, Glasgow
Referee: Ovidiu Hategan (Romania)   Attendance: 30,172
SCOTLAND: Allan McGregor, Charlie Mulgrew, Alan Hutton, Grant Hanley, Robert Snodgrass (82 James McArthur), Steven Naismith, James Morrison, Russell Martin, Scott Brown, Barry Bannan (89 Chris Burke), Ikechi Anya (77 Graham Dorrans).   Manager: Gordon Strachan
CROATIA: Stipe Pletikosa, Domagoj Vida, Ivan Strinic, Darijo Srna, Dejan Lovren, Vedran Corluka, Niko Kranjcar (68 Ivan Perisic), Ognjen Vukojevic, Luka Modric, Nikola Kalinic (59 EDUARDO Alves da Silva), Mario Mandzukic (80 Nikica Jelavic).   Manager: Igor Stimac
Goals: Robert Snodgrass (28), Steven Naismith (73)

Barry Bannan missed a penalty kick in the 73rd minute.

725. 15.11.2013
SCOTLAND v USA 0-0
Hampden Park, Glasgow
Referee: Michael Oliver (England)   Attendance: 21,079
SCOTLAND: David Marshall, Grant Hanley, Steven Whittaker (69 Lee Wallace), Charlie Mulgrew, Alan Hutton, Gordon Greer, Robert Snodgrass (69 Ross McCormack), Craig Conway (84 Gary Mackay-Steven), Scott Brown, Barry Bannan (81 Steven Naismith), Steven Fletcher.
Manager: Gordon Strachan
USA: Tim Howard, Omar González, Geoff Cameron, Sacha Kljestan (62 Aron Jóhannsson), Jermaine Jones (62 Mix Diskerud), Brad Evans (72 Eric Lichaj), Michael Bradley, Alejandro Bedoya (81 Chris Wondolowski), DaMarcus Beasley, Eddie Johnson (62 Brek Shea), Jozy Altodore (90 Terrence Boyd).   Manager: Jürgen Klinsmann

726. 19.11.2013
NORWAY v SCOTLAND 0-1 (0-0)
Aker Stadion, Molde
Referee: Martin Strömbergsson (Sweden)   Att: 9,751
NORWAY: Ørjan Nyland, Tore Reginiussen (65 Stefan Strandberg), Tom Høgli, Vegard Forren, Omar Elabdellaoui (60 Martin Linnes), Per Skjelbred (67 Mats Møller Dæhli), Morten Pedersen, Ruben Jenssen, Magnus Eikrem (80 Anders Konradsen), Marcus Pedersen (87 Tarik Elyounoussi), Ola Kamara (46 Mohammed Abdellaoue).
Manager: Per-Mathias Høgmo
SCOTLAND: David Marshall, Steven Whittaker, Alan Hutton, Gordon Greer, Craig Bryson (46 Barry Bannan), Ikechi Anya (51 Craig Conway), Robert Snodgrass, Steven Naismith (90+4 Christophe Berra), Russell Martin, Scott Brown, Charlie Adam (65 James McArthur).   Manager: Gordon Strachan
Goal: Scott Brown (61)

727. 05.03.2014
POLAND v SCOTLAND 0-1 (0-0)
Stadion Narodowy, Warszawa
Referee: Alain Bieri (Swtizerland)   Attendance: 41,642
POLAND: Wojciech Szczesny, Tomasz Brzyski (90+2 Marcin Komorowski), Lukasz Szukala, Grzegorz Krychowiak (88 Tomasz Jodlowiec), Kamil Glik, Lukasz Piszczek, Mateusz Klich (82 Lukasz Teodorczyk), Waldemar Sobota (89 Michal Maslowski), Ludovic Obraniak (74 Marcin Robak), Slawomir Peszko (74 Eugen Polanski), Arkadiusz Milik.
Manager: Adam Nawalka
SCOTLAND: David Marshall, Charlie Mulgrew, Alan Hutton (67 Phil Bardsley), Gordon Greer, Steven Fletcher (46 Steven Naismith), Scott Brown, Barry Bannan (67 Andrew Robertson), Ikechi Anya (90+2 Chris Burke), James Morrison (46 Darren Fletcher), Russell Martin, Ross McCormack (77 Charlie Adam).   Manager: Gordon Strachan
Goal: Scott Brown (77)

728. 28.05.2014
NIGERIA v SCOTLAND 2-2 (1-1)
Craven Cottage, London
Referee: Lee Probert (England)   Attendance: 24,000
NIGERIA: Austin Ejide, Ebenezer Kunle (75 Efe Ambrose), Elderson Echiéjilé, Azubuike Egwuekwe, Joseph Yobo, Joel Obi (54 Nosa Igiebor), Reuben Shalu Gabriel, Michel Babatunde (66 Nnamdi Oduamadi), Ejike Uzoenyi (62 Victor Moses), Shola Ameobi (62 Uche Nwofor), Michael Uchebo (55 Peter Odemwingie).   Manager: Stephen Keshi
SCOTLAND: Allan McGregor, Grant Hanley, Gordon Greer, Andrew Robertson (77 Craig Forsyth), Charlie Mulgrew, Alan Hutton, Scott Brown, Ikechi Anya (84 Steven Whittaker), Shaun Maloney, Steven Naismith (46 Chris Martin), James Morrison (63 George Boyd).   Manager: Gordon Strachan
Goals: Michael Uchebo (41), Uche Nwofor (90) / Charlie Mulgrew (10), Azubuike Egwuekwe (52 og)

729. 07.09.2014   15th European Champs Qualifier
GERMANY v SCOTLAND 2-1 (1-0)
Signal-Iduna-Park, Dortmund
Referee: Svein Moen (Norway)   Attendance: 60,209
GERMANY: Manuel Neuer, Benedikt Höwedes, Erik Durm, Jérôme Boateng, Sebastian Rudy, Marco Reus (90+2 Matthias Ginter), Toni Kroos, Christoph Kramer, Mario Götze, André Schürrle (84 Lukas Podolski), Thomas Müller.
Manager: Joachim Löw
SCOTLAND: David Marshall, Steven Whittaker, Charlie Mulgrew, Alan Hutton, Grant Hanley, Steven Naismith (82 Shaun Maloney), James Morrison, Russell Martin, Darren Fletcher (58 James McArthur), Barry Bannan (58 Steven Fletcher), Ikechi Anya.   Manager: Gordon Strachan
Sent off: Charlie Mulgrew (90+4)
Goals: Thomas Müller (18, 70) / Ikechi Anya (66)

730. 11.10.2014   15th European Champs Qualifier
SCOTLAND v GEORGIA 1-0 (1-0)
Ibrox Stadium, Glasgow
Referee: Miroslav Zelinka (Czech Republic)   Att: 34,719
SCOTLAND: David Marshall, Andrew Robertson, Alan Hutton, Grant Hanley, Steven Naismith (80 James McArthur), James Morrison, Russell Martin, Shaun Maloney, Scott Brown, Ikechi Anya, Steven Fletcher (90 Chris Martin).
Manager: Gordon Strachan
GEORGIA: Giorgi Loria, Ucha Lobzhanidze, Dato Kvirkvelia (46 Tornike Okriashvili), Solomon Kverkvelia, Akaki Khubutia, Gia Grigalava, Giorgi Papava (70 Irakli Dzaria), Jaba Kankava, Murtaz Daushvili, Valeri Qazaishvili (80 Giorgi Chanturia), Nikoloz Gelashvili.   Manager: Temur Ketsbaia
Goal: Akaki Khubutia (28 og)

731. 14.10.2014   15th European Champs Qualifier
POLAND v SCOTLAND 2-2 (1-1)

Stadion Narodowy, Warszawa

Referee: Alberto Undiano Mallenco (Spain)   Attendance: 55.197

POLAND: Wojciech Szczesny, Lukasz Szukala, Lukasz Piszczek, Grzegorz Krychowiak, Artur Jedrzejczyk, Kamil Glik, Waldemar Sobota (63 Sebastian Mila), Krzysztof Maczynski, Arkadiusz Milik, Robert Lewandowski, Kamil Grosicki (89 Michal Zyro).   Manager: Adam Nawalka

SCOTLAND: David Marshall, Steven Whittaker, Alan Hutton, Gordon Greer, Steven Naismith (71 Chris Martin), James Morrison, Russell Martin, Shaun Maloney, Scott Brown, Ikechi Anya, Steven Fletcher (71 Darren Fletcher).   Manager: Gordon Strachan

Goals: Krzysztof Maczynski (11), Arkadiusz Milik (76) / Shaun Maloney (18), Steven Naismith (57)

732. 18.11.2014   15th European Champs Qualifier
SCOTLAND v REPUBLIC OF IRELAND 1-0 (0-0)

Celtic Park, Glasgow

Referee: Milorad Mazic (Serbia)   Attendance: 59,239

SCOTLAND: David Marshall, Charlie Mulgrew, Grant Hanley, Steven Whittaker, Andrew Robertson, Russell Martin, Shaun Maloney, Scott Brown, Ikechi Anya (88 Darren Fletcher), Steven Naismith, Steven Fletcher (56 Chris Martin).   Manager: Gordon Strachan

REPUBLIC OF IRELAND: David Forde, John O'Shea, Richard Keogh, Séamus Coleman, Stephen Ward, Aiden McGeady, Jeff Hendrick (78 Robbie Keane), Darron Gibson (69 Stephen Quinn), James McClean, Shane Long (68 Robbie Brady), Jon Walters.   Manager: Martin O'Neill

Goal: Shaun Maloney (74)

733. 18.11.2014
SCOTLAND v ENGLAND 1-3 (0-1)

Celtic Park, Glasgow

Referee: Jonas Eriksson (Sweden)   Attendance: 49,506

SCOTLAND: David Marshall (46 Craig Gordon), Steven Whittaker, Andrew Robertson, Charlie Mulgrew, Grant Hanley (66 Stevie May), Steven Naismith, Russell Martin, Shaun Maloney (81 Johnny Russell), Scott Brown (46 Darren Fletcher), Ikechi Anya (61 Barry Bannan), Chris Martin (46 James Morrison).   Manager: Gordon Strachan

ENGLAND: Fraser Forster, Chris Smalling, Luke Shaw (66 Kieran Gibbs), Nathaniel Clyne, Gary Cahill (46 Phil Jagielka), Stewart Downing (46 Adam Lallana), Jack Wilshere (87 Ross Barkley), Alex Oxlade-Chamberlain (80 Rickie Lambert), James Milner, Danny Welbeck (66 Raheem Sterling), Wayne Rooney.   Manager: Roy Hodgson

Goals: Andrew Robertson (83) / Alex Oxlade-Chamberlain (32), Wayne Rooney (47, 85)

734. 25.03.2015
SCOTLAND v NORTHERN IRELAND 1-0 (0-0)

Hampdon Park, Glasgow

Referee: Martin Atkinson (England)   Attendance: 30,000

SCOTLAND: Craig Gordon (46 Allan McGregor), Steven Whittaker (78 Johnny Russell), Gordon Greer, Craig Forsyth, Matt Ritchie, James McArthur (62 James Morrison), Russell Martin (46 Christophe Berra), Shaun Maloney (46 Steven Naismith), Darren Fletcher, Ikechi Anya, Steven Fletcher (63 Jordan Rhodes).   Manager: Gordon Strachan

NORTHERN IRELAND: Michael McGovern, Ben Reeves (70 Ryan McLaughlin), Daniel Lafferty, Aaron Hughes, Jonny Evans (81 Luke McCullough), Oliver Norwood (69 Steven Davis), Stuart Dallas, Paddy McNair, Chris Baird (58 Lee Hodson), Josh Magennis (75 Billy McKay), Will Grigg (58 Pat McCourt).   Manager: Michael O'Neill

Goal: Christophe Berra (85)

735. 29.03.2015   15th European Champs Qualifier
SCOTLAND v GIBRALTAR 6-1 (4-1)

Hampden Park, Glasgow

Referee: Mattias Gestranius (Finland)   Attendance: 34,255

SCOTLAND: David Marshall, Andrew Robertson, Alan Hutton, Matt Ritchie (46 Gordon Greer), Steven Naismith (66 Jordan Rhodes), James Morrison, Russell Martin, Shaun Maloney, Scott Brown, Ikechi Anya (74 Barry Bannan), Steven Fletcher.   Manager: Gordon Strachan

GIBRALTAR: Jamie Robba, Scott Wiseman, Roy Chipolina (73 Jake Gosling), Joseph Chipolina, Ryan Casciaro, David Artell (53 Jean Garcia), Liam Walker, Aaron Payas, Anthony Bardon (82 Daniel Duarte), Adam Priestley, Lee Casciaro.   Manager: Dave Wilson

Goals: S. Maloney (18 pen, 34 pen), S. Fletcher (29, 77, 90), Steven Naismith (39) / Lee Casciaro (19)

736. 05.06.2015
SCOTLAND v QATAR 1-0 (1-0)

Easter Road Stadium, Edinburgh

Referee: Sebastien Delferière (Belgium)   Att: 14,270

SCOTLAND: David Marshall (46 Craig Gordon), Charlie Mulgrew, Gordon Greer, Craig Forsyth, Ikechi Anya, Matt Ritchie, James McArthur (46 James Morrison), Shaun Maloney (60 Charlie Adam), James Forrest (74 Johnny Russell), Scott Brown (60 Darren Fletcher), Steven Naismith (59 Leigh Griffiths).   Manager: Gordon Strachan

QATAR: Amine Lecomte-Addani, Ahmed Yasser, Mohammed Kasola, Abdelaziz Hatem (54 Ali Al Mahdi), Ahmed El Sayed, Mohammed Muntari (78 Abdulgadir Ilyas Bakur), Abdelkarim Hassan, Karim Boudiaf, Ali Assadalla (66 Abdulrahman Mohd Hussain), Hasan Al Haidos (86 Moayad Hassan), Mohammed Trésor Abdullah (78 Hamid Ismail).   Manager: José Daniel Carreño

Goal: Matt Ritchie (41)

737. 13.06.2015   15th European Champs Qualifier
REPUBLIC OF IRELAND v SCOTLAND 1-1 (1-0)
Aviva Stadium, Dublin
Referee: Nicola Rizzoli (Italy)   Attendance: 49,063
REPUBLIC OF IRELAND: Shay Given, Marc Wilson, John O'Shea, Séamus Coleman, Robbie Brady, Glenn Whelan (68 James McClean), James McCarthy, Wes Hoolahan (73 Robbie Keane), Jeff Hendrick, Jon Walters, Daryl Murphy (80 Shane Long).   Manager: Martin O'Neill
SCOTLAND: David Marshall, Charlie Mulgrew, Alan Hutton, Craig Forsyth, Matt Ritchie (46 Ikechi Anya), Steven Naismith (90+2 Christophe Berra), James Morrison, Russell Martin, Shaun Maloney, Scott Brown (85 James McArthur), Steven Fletcher.   Manager: Gordon Strachan
Goals: Jon Walters (38) / John O'Shea (47 og)

738. 04.09.2015   15th European Champs Qualifier
GEORGIA v SCOTLAND 1-0 (1-0)
Boris Paichadze Dinamo Arena, Tbilisi
Referee: Ovidiu Hategan (Romania)   Attendance: 23,000
GEORGIA: Nukri Revishvili, Ucha Lobzhanidze, Solomon Kverkvelia, Guram Kashia, Aleksandr Amisulashvili, Giorgi Navalovski, Jaba Kankava, Jano Ananidze (82 Murtaz Daushvili), Valeri Qazaishvili, Tornike Okriashvili (71 Giorgi Merebashvili), Levan Mchedlidze (90+3 Mate Vatsadze).   Manager: Kakhaber Tskhadadze
SCOTLAND: David Marshall, Andrew Robertson (59 Grant Hanley), Charlie Mulgrew, Alan Hutton, Steven Naismith (60 James Forrest), James Morrison, Russell Martin, Shaun Maloney, Scott Brown, Ikechi Anya (75 Leigh Griffiths), Steven Fletcher.   Manager: Gordon Strachan
Goal: Valeri Qazaishvili (38)

739. 07.09.2015   15th European Champs Qualifier
SCOTLAND v GERMANY 2-3 (2-2)
Hampden Park, Glasgow
Referee: Björn Kuipers (Netherlands)   Attendance: 50,753
SCOTLAND: David Marshall, Charlie Mulgrew, Alan Hutton, Grant Hanley, James Morrison, James McArthur, Russell Martin, Shaun Maloney (60 Ikechi Anya), James Forrest (81 Matt Ritchie), Scott Brown (81 Chris Martin), Steven Fletcher.   Manager: Gordon Strachan
GERMANY: Manuel Neuer, Jérôme Boateng, Mats Hummels, Jonas Hector, Emre Can, Bastian Schweinsteiger, Ilkay Gündogan, Mesut Özil (90+2 Christoph Kramer), Toni Kroos, Mario Götze (86 André Schürrle), Thomas Müller.   Manager: Joachim Löw
Goals: Mats Hummels (28 og), James McArthur (43) / Thomas Müller (18, 34), Ilkay Gündogan (54)

740. 08.10.2015   15th European Champs Qualifier
SCOTLAND v POLAND 2-2 (1-1)
Hampden Park, Glasgow
Referee: Viktor Kassai (Hungary)   Attendance: 49,359
SCOTLAND: David Marshall, Steven Whittaker, Alan Hutton, Grant Hanley, Matt Ritchie, Steven Naismith (69 Shaun Maloney), Russell Martin, James Forrest (84 Graham Dorrans), Darren Fletcher (74 James McArthur), Scott Brown, Steven Fletcher.   Manager: Gordon Strachan
POLAND: Lukasz Fabianski, Lukasz Piszczek, Michal Pazdan, Grzegorz Krychowiak, Kamil Glik, Maciej Rybus (71 Jakub Wawrzyniak), Krzysztof Maczynski, Jakub Blaszczykowski (83 Pawel Olkowski), Arkadiusz Milik (63 Tomasz Jodlowiec), Robert Lewandowski, Kamil Grosicki.   Manager: Adam Nawalka
Goals: Matt Ritchie (45), Steven Fletcher (62) / Robert Lewandowski (3, 90+4)

741. 11.10.2015   15th European Champs Qualifier
GIBRALTAR v SCOTLAND 0-6 (0-2)
Estádio do Algarve, Faro-Loulé (Portugal)
Referee: Aleksey Kulbakov (Belarus)   Attendance: 12,401
GIBRALTAR: Jamie Robba, Jean Garcia, Roy Chipolina, Joseph Chipolina, Ryan Casciaro, Erin Barnett, Liam Walker, Daniel Duarte (57 Brian Perez), Kyle Casciaro (89 Michael Yome), Anthony Bardon, Lee Casciaro (82 John-Paul Duarte).   Manager: Jeff Wood
SCOTLAND: Allan McGregor, Andrew Robertson, Alan Hutton, Gordon Greer, Christophe Berra, Matt Ritchie (64 Johnny Russell), Shaun Maloney, Graham Dorrans, Scott Brown (63 Darren Fletcher), Chris Martin (76 Steven Naismith), Steven Fletcher.   Manager: Gordon Strachan
Goals: Chris Martin (25), Shaun Maloney (39), Steven Fletcher (52, 56, 85), Steven Naismith (90+1)

742. 24.03.2016
CZECH REPUBLIC v SCOTLAND 0-1 (0-1)
Generali Arena, Praha
Referee: Paul McLaughlin (Republic of Ireland)   Att: 14,580
CZECH REPUBLIC: Tomás Koubek, David Limbersky, Michal Kadlec, Tomás Sivok, Pavel Kaderábek, Kamil Vacek (78 Lukás Marecek), Borek Dockal (65 Daniel Kolár), Vladimír Darida (87 Jakub Rada), Josef Sural (78 Daniel Pudil), Martin Frydek (46 Jirí Skalák), Tomás Necid (65 Matej Vydra).   Manager: Pavel Vrba
SCOTLAND: Allan McGregor, Andrew Robertson (58 Barry Bannan), Charlie Mulgrew, Russell Martin, Alan Hutton, Christophe Berra, Robert Snodgrass, Kenny McLean (58 Matt Phillips), Darren Fletcher, Ikechi Anya (87 Paul Caddis), Ross McCormack (78 Anthony Watt).   Manager: Gordon Strachan
Goal: Ikechi Anya (10)

743. 29.03.2016
SCOTLAND v DENMARK 1-0 (1-0)
Hampden Park, Glasgow
Referee: Svein Moen (Norway)   Attendance: 18,385
SCOTLAND: Craig Gordon, Steven Whittaker, Kieran Tierney (46 Charlie Mulgrew), Grant Hanley, Gordon Greer, Matt Ritchie (82 Oliver Burke), John McGinn, Shaun Maloney (69 Liam Bridcutt), Scott Brown, Leigh Griffiths (60 Chris Martin), Steven Fletcher (46 Ikechi Anya).
Manager: Gordon Strachan
DENMARK: Kasper Schmeichel (46 Jonas Lössl), Simon Kjær, Riza Durmisi, Andreas Christensen, Daniel Agger (64 Erik Sviatchenko), Pierre-Emile Højbjerg, Christian Eriksen (81 Lasse Schöne), Thomas Delaney, Yussuf Poulsen (46 Martin Braithwaite), Nicolai Jørgensen, Henrik Dalsgaard.
Manager: Åge Hareide
Goal: Matt Ritchie (8)

744. 29.05.2016
ITALY v SCOTLAND 1-0 (0-0)
Ta'Qali National Stadium, Ta'Qali (Malta)
Referee: Alan Sant (Malta)   Attendance: 8,000
ITALY: Gianluigi Buffon, Andrea Barzagli, Giorgio Chiellini, Leonardo Bonucci, Matteo Darmian (60 Federico Bernardeschi), Alessandro Florenzi, Daniele De Rossi (67 Filho Jorge Luiz Frello "JORGINHO"), Antonio Candreva (62 Marco Parolo), Emanuele Giaccherini (80 Giacomo Bonaventura), Graziano Pellè (71 Simone Zaza), ÉDER Citadin Martins (59 Lorenzo Insigne).   Manager: Antonio Conte
SCOTLAND: David Marshall, Callum Paterson (46 Christophe Berra), Charlie Mulgrew, Russell Martin, Grant Hanley, Ikechi Anya (71 Steven Naismith), Matt Ritchie, Matt Phillips (71 Oliver Burke), James McArthur (83 Craig Bryson), Darren Fletcher, Ross McCormack (46 Steven Fletcher).
Manager: Gordon Strachan
Goal: Graziano Pellè (57)

745. 04.06.2016
FRANCE v SCOTLAND 3-0 (3-0)
Stade Saint-Symphorien, Longeville-lès-Metz
Referee: Sebastien Delferrière (Belgium)   Att: 25,057
FRANCE: Hugo Lloris, Bacary Sagna, Adil Rami, Laurent Koscielny, Patrice Evra (83 Lucas Digne), Paul Pogba, Blaise Matuidi (69 Yohan Cabaye), N'Golo Kanté (88 Moussa Sissoko), Olivier Giroud (63 André-Pierre Gignac), Kingsley Coman (46 Antoine Griezmann), Dimitri Payet (46 Anthony Martial).   Manager: Didier Deschamps

SCOTLAND: David Marshall, Andrew Robertson (46 Charlie Mulgrew), Russell Martin, Grant Hanley, Gordon Greer, Robert Snodgrass (66 Stephen Kingsley), Matt Ritchie, James McArthur (84 Barrie McKay), Shaun Maloney (46 Ikechi Anya), Darren Fletcher, Steven Fletcher (58 Steven Naismith).
Manager: Gordon Strachan
Goals: Olivier Giroud (8, 35), Laurent Koscielny (39)

746. 04.09.2016   21st World Cup Qualifier
MALTA v SCOTLAND 1-5 (1-1)
Ta'Qali National Stadium, Ta'Qali
Referee: Evgen Aranovskiy (Ukraine)   Attendance: 15,069
MALTA: Andrew Hogg, Joseph Zerafa, Jonathan Caruana, Steve Borg, Andrei Agius, Ryan Scicluna (79 Ryan Camilleri), Gareth Sciberras, Luke Gambin, Paul Fenech, André Schembri (66 Roderick Briffa), Alfred Effiong (89 Michael Mifsud).
Manager: Pietro Ghedin
SCOTLAND: David Marshall, Andrew Robertson, Callum Paterson, Russell Martin, Grant Hanley, Robert Snodgrass, Matt Ritchie (86 Ikechi Anya), Darren Fletcher, Barry Bannan, Oliver Burke (66 James Forrest), Chris Martin (69 Steven Fletcher).   Manager: Gordon Strachan
Sent off: Jonathan Caruana (59), Luke Gambin (90+1)
Goals: Alfred Effiong (14) / Robert Snodgrass (9, 61 pen, 84), Chris Martin (53), Steven Fletcher (78)

747. 08.10.2016   21st World Cup Qualifier
SCOTLAND v LITHUANIA 1-1 (0-0)
Hampden Park, Glasgow
Referee: Tobias Stieler (Germany)   Attendance: 35,966
SCOTLAND: David Marshall, Andrew Robertson, Callum Paterson, Russell Martin, Grant Hanley, Robert Snodgrass, Matt Ritchie (71 Leigh Griffiths), Darren Fletcher (46 James McArthur), Barry Bannan, Oliver Burke (57 James Forrest), Chris Martin.   Manager: Gordon Strachan
LITHUANIA: Ernestas Setkus, Egidijus Vaitkūnas, Edvinas Girdvainis, Georgas Freidgeimas, Vaidas Slavickas (64 Vytautas Andriuskevicius), Artūras Zulpa (65 Karolis Chvedukas), Vykintas Slivka, Mantas Kuklys, Nerijus Valskis (85 Mindaugas Grigaravicius), Arvydas Novikovas, Fiodor Cernych.   Manager: Edgaras Jankauskas
Goals: James McArthur (89) / Fiodor Cernych (59)

748. 11.10.2016   21st World Cup Qualifier
SLOVAKIA v SCOTLAND 3-0 (1-0)
Stadión Antona Malatinského, Trnava
Referee: Martin Strömbergsson (Sweden)   Att: 11,098
SLOVAKIA: Matús Kozácik, Martin Skrtel, Ján Durica, Milan Skriniar, Erik Sabo, Juraj Kucka, Jakub Holúbek, Marek Hamsík (87 Filip Kiss), Adam Nemec (69 Marek Bakos), Michal Duris, Róbert Mak (80 Dusan Svento).
Manager: Ján Kozák
SCOTLAND: David Marshall, Kieran Tierney, Callum Paterson, Russell Martin, Grant Hanley, Robert Snodgrass, Matt Ritchie (64 Ikechi Anya), James McArthur, Darren Fletcher (64 Leigh Griffiths), Barry Bannan, Steven Fletcher (76 John McGinn).   Manager: Gordon Strachan
Goals: Róbert Mak (18, 56), Adam Nemec (68)

749. 11.11.2016   21st World Cup Qualifier
ENGLAND v SCOTLAND 3-0 (1-0)
Wembley, London
Referee: Cüneyt Çakir (Turkey)   Attendance: 87,258
ENGLAND: Joe Hart, Gary Cahill, Kyle Walker, John Stones, Danny Rose, Raheem Sterling, Adam Lallana, Jordan Henderson, Eric Dier, Daniel Sturridge (75 Jamie Vardy), Wayne Rooney.   Manager: Gareth Southgate
SCOTLAND: Craig Gordon, Christophe Berra, Lee Wallace, Grant Hanley, Ikechi Anya (79 Callum Paterson), Robert Snodgrass (82 Matt Ritchie), James Morrison (66 James McArthur), James Forrest, Darren Fletcher, Scott Brown, Leigh Griffiths.   Manager: Gordon Strachan
Goals: Daniel Sturridge (24), Adam Lallana (50), Gary Cahill (61)

750. 22.03.2017
SCOTLAND v CANADA 1-1 (1-1)
Easter Road Stadium, Edinburgh
Referee: Jakob Kehlet (Denmark)   Attendance: 9.158
SCOTLAND: Allan McGregor, Lee Wallace (46 Andrew Robertson), Charlie Mulgrew, Christophe Berra, Robert Snodgrass, Darren Fletcher, Tom Cairney (76 John McGinn), Oliver Burke (46 Barry Bannan), Ikechi Anya, Steven Naismith (62 Jordan Rhodes), Chris Martin (62 Leigh Griffiths).
Manager: Gordon Strachan
CANADA: Simon Thomas (46 Jayson Leutwiler), Maxim Tissot (68 La'Vere Corbin-Ong), Adam Straith, Manjrekar James, Fraser Aird, Nicolas Ledgerwood, Samuel Piette, Junior Hoilett, Marco Bustos, Scott Arfield (90+4 Charlie Trafford), Simeon Jackson (76 Ben Fisk).   Manager: Octavio Zambrano
Goals: Steven Naismith (35) / Fraser Aird (11)

751. 26.03.2017   21st World Cup Qualifier
SCOTLAND v SLOVENIA 1-0 (0-0)
Hampden Park, Glasgow
Referee: Björn Kuipers (Netherlands)   Attendance: 20,435
SCOTLAND: Craig Gordon, Kieran Tierney, Andrew Robertson, Charlie Mulgrew, Russell Martin, Robert Snodgrass (75 Ikechi Anya), James Morrison (82 Chris Martin), James Forrest, Scott Brown, Stuart Armstrong, Leigh Griffiths (49 Steven Naismith).   Manager: Gordon Strachan
SLOVENIA: Jan Oblak, Aljaz Struna, Miral Samardzic, Bojan Jokic, Bostjan Cesar, Jasmin Kurtic, Rene Krhin, Kevin Kampl (87 Nik Omladic), Josip Ilicic, Valter Birsa (69 Robert Beric), Roman Bezjak (58 Benjamin Verbic).
Manager: Srecko Katanec
Goal: Chris Martin (88)

752. 10.06.2017   21st World Cup Qualifier
SCOTLAND v ENGLAND 2-2 (0-0)
Hampden Park, Glasgow
Referee: Paolo Tagliavento (Italy)   Attendance: 48,520
SCOTLAND: Craig Gordon, Kieran Tierney, Andrew Robertson, Charlie Mulgrew, Christophe Berra, Robert Snodgrass (67 Ryan Fraser), James Morrison (46 James McArthur), Scott Brown, Stuart Armstrong, Ikechi Anya (81 Chris Martin), Leigh Griffiths.   Manager: Gordon Strachan
ENGLAND: Joe Hart, Kyle Walker, Chris Smalling, Gary Cahill, Ryan Bertrand, Jake Livermore (90+2 Jermain Defoe), Adam Lallana, Dele Alli (84 Raheem Sterling), Eric Dier, Marcus Rashford (65 Alex Oxlade-Chamberlain), Harry Kane.   Manager: Gareth Southgate
Goals: Leigh Griffiths (87, 90) /
Alex Oxlade-Chamberlain (70), Harry Kane (90+3)

753. 01.09.2017   21st World Cup Qualifier
LITHUANIA v SCOTLAND 0-3 (0-2)
LFF Stadium, Vilnius
Referee: Carlos Del Cerro Grande (Spain)   Att: 5,067
LITHUANIA: Ernestas Setkus, Egidijus Vaitkūnas, Tadas Kijanskas, Georgas Freidgeimas, Valdemars Borovskis, Artūras Zulpa (68 Lukas Spalvis), Vykintas Slivka (79 Ovidijus Verbickas), Darvydas Sernas (82 Deivydas Matulevicius), Mantas Kuklys, Arvydas Novikovas, Fiodor Cernych.
Manager: Edgaras Jankauskas
SCOTLAND: Craig Gordon, Kieran Tierney, Andrew Robertson, Charlie Mulgrew, Christophe Berra, Matt Phillips, James McArthur, James Forrest (66 Matt Ritchie), Scott Brown, Stuart Armstrong (85 John McGinn), Leigh Griffiths (79 Chris Martin).   Manager: Gordon Strachan
Goals: Stuart Armstrong (25), Andrew Robertson (30), James McArthur (72)

754. 04.09.2017   21st World Cup Qualifier
SCOTLAND v MALTA 2-0 (1-0)
Hampden Park, Glasgow
Referee: Jakob Kehlet (Denmark)   Attendance: 26,371
SCOTLAND: Craig Gordon, Kieran Tierney, Andrew Robertson, Charlie Mulgrew (56 Grant Hanley), Christophe Berra, Matt Phillips, James McArthur (46 James Morrison), James Forrest, Scott Brown, Stuart Armstrong, Leigh Griffiths (70 Chris Martin).   Manager: Gordon Strachan
MALTA: Andrew Hogg, Joseph Zerafa, Samuel Magri, Steve Borg (86 Alex Muscat), Andrei Agius, Zach Muscat, Bjorn Kristensen (85 Paul Fenech), Ryan Fenech, André Schembri (71 Luke Gambin), Stephen Pisani, Alfred Effiong.   Manager: Pietro Ghedin
Goals: Christophe Berra (9), Leigh Griffiths (49).

755. 05.10.2017   21st World Cup Qualifier
SCOTLAND v SLOVAKIA 1-0 (0-0)
Hampden Park, Glasgow
Referee: Milorad Mazic (Serbia)   Attendance: 46,733
SCOTLAND: Craig Gordon, Kieran Tierney (82 Ikechi Anya), Andrew Robertson, Charlie Mulgrew, Christophe Berra, Matt Phillips, James Morrison, James Forrest (61 Chris Martin), Darren Fletcher (79 James McArthur), Barry Bannan, Leigh Griffiths.   Manager: Gordon Strachan
SLOVAKIA: Martin Dúbravka, Martin Skrtel, Peter Pekarík, Tomás Hubocan, Ján Durica, Stanislav Lobotka, Juraj Kucka (80 Norbert Gyömbér), Marek Hamsík (79 Ondrej Duda), Ján Gregus, Adam Nemec (79 Vladimír Weiss), Róbert Mak.   Manager: Ján Kozák
Sent off: Róbert Mak (23)
Goal: Martin Skrtel (89 og)

756. 08.10.2017   21st World Cup Qualifier
SLOVENIA v SCOTLAND 2-2 (0-1)
Stozice Stadium, Ljubljana
Referee: Jonas Eriksson (Sweden)   Attendance: 11,123
SLOVENIA: Jan Oblak, Aljaz Struna (46 Nejc Skubic), Miha Mevlja, Bojan Jokic, Bostjan Cesar, Rajko Rotman, Jan Repas (46 Roman Bezjak), Jasmin Kurtic, Josip Ilicic, Benjamin Verbic, Tim Matavz (89 Amedej Vetrih).   Manager: Srecko Katanec
SCOTLAND: Craig Gordon, Kieran Tierney (80 Steven Fletcher), Andrew Robertson, Charlie Mulgrew, Christophe Berra, Matt Phillips, James McArthur (79 Robert Snodgrass), Darren Fletcher, Barry Bannan, Chris Martin (53 Ikechi Anya), Leigh Griffiths.   Manager: Gordon Strachan
Sent off: Bostjan Cesar (90+2)
Goals: Roman Bezjak (52, 72) / Leigh Griffiths (32), Robert Snodgrass (87)

757. 09.11.2017
SCOTLAND v NETHERLANDS 0-1 (0-1)
Pittodrie Stadium, Aberdeen
Referee: Ruddy Buquet (France)   Attendance: 17,883
SCOTLAND: Craig Gordon, Andrew Robertson, Christophe Berra (46 Charlie Mulgrew), Kieran Tierney, Matt Phillips, Kenny McLean, Callum McGregor (87 Jason Cummings), John McGinn, James Forrest (71 Ryan Fraser), Ryan Christie, Ryan Jack.   Manager: Malky Mackay
NETHERLANDS: Jasper Cillessen, Virgil van Dijk, Karim Rekik, Timothy Fosu-Mensah (72 Joël Veltman), Nathan Aké, Daley Blind, Georginio Wijnaldum, Kevin Strootman, Quincy Promes (76 Steven Berghuis), Memphis Depay, Ryan Babel.   Manager: Dick Advocaat
Goal: Memphis Depay (40)

758. 23.03.2018
SCOTLAND v COSTA RICA 0-1 (0-1)
Hampden Park, Glasgow
Referee: Tobias Stieler (Germany)   Attendance: 20,488
SCOTLAND: Allan McGregor, Charlie Mulgrew (82 John McGinn), Grant Hanley, Andrew Robertson, Callum Paterson, Scott McKenna, Kevin McDonald, Matt Ritchie (87 Jamie Murphy), Tom Cairney (58 Callum McGregor), Scott McTominay (58 Stuart Armstrong), Oliver McBurnie (77 Matt Phillips).   Manager: Alex McLeish
COSTA RICA: KEYLOR Antonio NAVAS Gamboa, BRYAN Josué OVIEDO Jiménez (77 FRANCISCO Javier CALVO Quesada), ÓSCAR Esau DUARTE Gaitán, CRISTIAN Esteban GAMBOA Luna (75 IAN Rey SMITH Quiros), GIANCARLO GONZÁLEZ Castro, JOHNNY ACOSTA Zamora, CELSO BORGES Mora, DAVID Alberto GUZMÁN Pérez (55 YELTSIN Ignacio TEJEDA Valverde), BRYAN RUIZ González, MARCO Danilo UREÑA Porras (68 YENDRICK Alberto RUIZ González), DANIEL COLINDRES Solera (62 RODNEY WALLACE Burns).   Manager: ÓSCAR Antonio RAMÍREZ Hernández
Goal: MARCO Danilo UREÑA Porras (14)

759. 27.03.2018
HUNGARY v SCOTLAND 0-1 (0-0)
Groupama Aréna, Budapest
Referee: Harald Lechner (Austria)   Attendance: 8,942

HUNGARY: Péter Gulácsi, Richárd Guzmics, Attila Fiola, Kenneth Otigba, Szilveszter Hangya (46 János Szabó), Balász Dzsudzsák (58 Krisztián Németh), Ádám Pintér (46 Ákos Elek), Ádám Szalai (77 Dániel Böde), Gergö Lovrencsics, László Kleinheisler (67 Máté Pátkai), Roland Varga (83 Nemanja Nikolics).   Manager: Georges Leekens

SCOTLAND: Allan McGregor, Charlie Mulgrew, Andrew Robertson (67 Barry Douglas), Scott McKenna, Jack Hendry, Matt Phillips (84 Oliver McBurnie), Stuart Armstrong (70 Kenny McLean), Ryan Fraser (82 Callum Paterson), John McGinn, James Forrest (77 Ryan Christie), Callum McGregor (90+3 Jason Cummings).   Manager: Alex McLeish

Goal: Matt Phillips (48)

760. 29.05.2018
PERU v SCOTLAND 2-0 (1-0)
Estadio Nacional de Lima, Lima
Referee: FERNANDO GUERRERO Ramírez (Mexico)
Attendance: 40,000

PERU: JOSÉ Aurelio CARVALLO Alonso, ALBERTO Junior RODRÍGUEZ Valdelomar, Christian Guillermo Martín RAMOS Garagay, LUIS Jan Piers ADVÍNCULA Castrillón (87 ALDO Sebastián CORZO Chávez), MIGUEL Ángel TRAUCO Saavedra, JEFFERSON Agustín FARFÁN Guadalupe (81 Christopher PAOLO César HURTADO Huertas), Víctor YOSHIMAR YOTÚN Flores (69 RAÚL Mario RUIDÍAZ Misitich), CHRISTIAN Alberto CUEVA Bravo (80 PEDRO Jesús AQUINO Sánchez), ANDRÉ Martín CARRILLO Díaz (69 ANDY Jorman POLO Andrade), RENATO Fabrizio TAPIA Cortijo (84 WILDER José CARTAGENA Mendoza), ÉDISON Michael FLORES Peralta.
Manager: RICARDO Alberto GARECA Nardi

SCOTLAND: Jordan Archer, Lewis Stevenson, Charlie Mulgrew, Stephen O'Donnell, Scott McKenna, Jamie Murphy (63 Oliver McBurnie), Matt Phillips (72 Lewis Morgan), Kenny McLean (87 Chris Cadden), Dylan McGeouch (76 Graeme Shinnie), John McGinn (63 Callum Paterson), Scott McTominay.   Manager: Alex McLeish

Goals: CHRISTIAN Alberto CUEVA Bravo (37 pen), JEFFERSON Agustín FARFÁN Guadalupe (47)

761. 02.06.2018
MEXICO v SCOTLAND 1-0 (1-0)
Estadio Azteca, Mexico City
Referee: HENRY Alberto BEJARANO Matarrita (Costa Rica)
Attendance: 70,993

MEXICO: Francisco GUILLERMO OCHOA Magaña, HUGO AYALA Castro, MIGUEL Arturo LAYÚN Prado, CARLOS Joel SALCEDO Hernández (46 RAFAEL MÁRQUEZ Álvarez), EDSON Omar ÁLVAREZ Velázquez, HÉCTOR Miguel HERRERA López (58 MARCO Jhonfai FABIÁN De La Mora), JESÚS Daniel GALLARDO Vasconcelos, CARLOS Alberto VELA Garrido (63 JAVIER Ignacio AQUINO Carmona), GIOVANI DOS SANTOS Ramírez (57 JONATHAN DOS SANTOS Ramírez), RAÚL Alonso JIMÉNEZ Rodríguez (57 ORIBE PERALTA Morones), HIRVING Rodrigo LOZANO Bahena (73 JESÚS Manuel CORONA Ruíz).
Manager: Juan Carlos OSORIO Arbeláez

SCOTLAND: Jon McLaughlin (46 Scott Bain), Graeme Shinnie, Stephen O'Donnell, Callum Paterson (55 Charlie Mulgrew), Scott McKenna, Jack Hendry, Kenny McLean (55 Chris Cadden), Dylan McGeouch, Ryan Christie (55 John McGinn), Johnny Russell, Oliver McBurnie (80 Lewis Morgan).   Manager: Alex McLeish

Goal: GIOVANI DOS SANTOS Ramírez (13)

762. 07.09.2018
SCOTLAND v BELGIUM 0-4 (0-1)
Hampden Park, Glasgow
Referee: Luca Banti (Italy)   Attendance: 20,196

SCOTLAND: Craig Gordon, John Souttar, Charlie Mulgrew (68 Stephen O'Donnell), Kieran Tierney, Ryan Fraser, Andrew Robertson, John McGinn (73 Graeme Shinnie), Kevin McDonald (53 Robert Snodgrass), Callum McGregor (68 Johnny Russell), Leigh Griffiths (46 Steven Naismith), Stuart Armstrong (53 Ryan Jack).   Manager: Alex McLeish

BELGIUM: Thibaut Courtois, Vincent Kompany (46 Thomas Vermaelen), Jan Vertonghen, Dedryck Boyata, Timothy Castagne (46 Thomas Meunier), Mousa Dembélé (85 Birger Verstraete), Youri Tielemans, Eden Hazard (56 Hans Vanaken), Romelu Lukaku (46 Michy Batshuayi), Thorgan Hazard, Dries Mertens (46 Yannick Carrasco).
Manager: ROBERTO MARTÍNEZ Montoliú

Goals: Romelu Lukaku (28), Eden Hazard (46), Michy Batshuayi (52, 60)

763. 10.09.2018   UEFA Nations League Group C1
SCOTLAND v ALBANIA 2-0 (0-0)
Hampden Park, Glasgow

Referee: Matej Jug (Slovenia)   Attendance: 17,455

SCOTLAND: Allan McGregor, Charlie Mulgrew, Stephen O'Donnell, Andrew Robertson, John Souttar, Kieran Tierney, Kevin McDonald (46 Stuart Armstrong), Callum McGregor (79 Scott McTominay), Steven Naismith, John McGinn, Johnny Russell (70 Leigh Griffiths).   Manager: Alex McLeish

ALBANIA: Thomas Strakosha, Freddie Veseli (90+1 Enea Mihaj), Elseid Hysaj, Berat Gjimshiti, Egzon Binaku, Sabien Lilaj, Ledian Menushaj, Taulant Xhaka, Enis Gavazaj (46 Herdi Prenga), Emanuele Ndoj (66 Rey Manaj), Bekim Balaj.   Manager: Christian Panucci

Goals: Berat Gjimshiti (47 og), Steven Naismith (68)

764. 11.10.2018   UEFA Nations League Group C1
ISRAEL v SCOTLAND 2-1 (0-1)
Sammy Ofer Stadium, Haifa

Referee: Daniel Stefanski (Poland)   Attendance: 10,234

ISRAEL: Ariel Harush, Shiran Yeini, Taleb Tawatha (76 Eliran Atar), Omri Ben Harush, Eytan Tibi, Eli Dasa, Bibras Natcho, Beram Kayal (82 Dan Einbinder), Dor Peretz, Ben Sahar (46 Dia Seba), Moanes Dabour.   Manager: Andreas Herzog

SCOTLAND: Allan McGregor, Charlie Mulgrew (46 Scott McKenna), Stephen O'Donnell, Andrew Robertson, John Souttar, Kieran Tierney, Kevin McDonald, Callum McGregor, John McGinn, Steven Naismith (76 Oliver McBurnie), Johnny Russell (67 James Forrest).   Manager: Alex McLeish

Goals: Dor Peretz (52), Kieran Tierney (74 og) /
Charlie Mulgrew (25 pen)

Sent off: John Souttar (61)

765. 14.10.2018
SCOTLAND v PORTUGAL 1-3 (0-1)
Hampden Park, Glasgow

Referee: Ruddy Buquet (France)   Attendance: 19,684

SCOTLAND: Craig Gordon, Stephen O'Donnell, Andrew Robertson, Scott McKenna, Jack Hendry, James Forrest, Stuart Armstrong (77 Kevin McDonald), Callum McGregor, John McGinn (67 Graeme Shinnie), Oliver McBurnie (76 Gary Mackay-Steven), Steven Naismith.   Manager: Alex McLeish

PORTUGAL: António Alberto Bastos Pimparel "BETO" (86' CLÁUDIO Pires Morais RAMOS), LUÍS Carlos Novo NETO, CÉDRIC Ricardo Alves SOARES, KÉVIN Manuel RODRIGUES, RÚBEN Diogo da Silva NEVES (57 PEDRO Filipe Teodósio MENDES), SÉRGIO Miguel Relvas de OLIVEIRA (56 RENATO Júnior Luz SANCHES), DANILO Luís Hélio PEREIRA (90+1 WILLIAM Silva de CARVALHO), BRUNO Miguel Borges FERNANDES (68 GEDSON Carvalho FERNANDES), Ederzito António "ÉDER" Macedo Lopes, HÉLDER Wander Sousa Azevedo COSTA, Armindo Tué Na Bangna "BRUMA" (90+1 Rafael Alexandre "RAFA" Fernandes Ferreira SILVA).
Manager: FERNANDO Manuel Fernandes da Costa SANTOS

Goals: Steven Naismith (90+3) /
Hélder Costa (43), Eder (74), Bruma (84)

766. 17.11.2018   UEFA Nations League Group C1
ALBANIA v SCOTLAND 0-4 (0-2)
Loro Boriçi Stadiumi, Shkodër

Referee: Vladislav Bezborodov (Russia)   Attendance: 8,632

ALBANIA: Etrit Berisha, Mërgim Mavraj, Freddie Veseli, Berat Gjimshiti (52 Kastriot Dermaku), Egzon Binaku, Ledian Menushaj, Taulant Xhaka, Ergys Kaçe (27 Ardian Ismajli), Eros Grezda, Myrto Uzuni, Rey Manaj (62 Bekim Balaj).   Manager: Christian Panucci

SCOTLAND: Allan McGregor, Andrew Robertson, Callum Paterson, David Bates, Scott McKenna, James Forrest, Stuart Armstrong (61 Scott McTominay), Callum McGregor, Ryan Fraser (73 Johnny Russell), Ryan Christie, Steven Fletcher (68 Matt Phillips).   Manager: Alex McLeish

Goals: Ryan Fraser (14), Steven Fletcher (45+2 pen), James Forrest (55, 67)

Sent off: Mërgim Mavraj (21)

767. 20.11.2018   UEFA Nations League Group C1
SCOTLAND v ISRAEL 3-2 (2-1)
Hampden Park, Glasgow

Referee: Tobias Welz (Germany)   Attendance: 21,281

SCOTLAND: Allan McGregor, Andrew Robertson, Callum Paterson, David Bates, Scott McKenna, James Forrest, Stuart Armstrong (76 Matt Phillips), Callum McGregor, Ryan Fraser, Ryan Christie (76 Graeme Shinnie), Steven Fletcher (87 Scott McTominay).   Manager: Alex McLeish

ISRAEL: Ariel Harush, Shiran Yeini, Taleb Tawatha (85 Tomer Hemed), Omri Ben Harush, Loai Taha (67 Almog Cohen), Eli Dasa, Bibras Natcho, Eran Zahavi, Beram Kayal, Dor Peretz (73 Dia Seba), Moanes Dabour.
Manager: Andreas Herzog

Goals: James Forrest (34, 43, 64) /
Beram Kayal (9), Eran Zahavi (75)

768. 21.03.2019 16th European Champs Qualifiers
KAZAKHSTAN v SCOTLAND 3-0 (2-0)

Astana Arena, Nur-Sultan

Referee: Srdjan Jovanovic (Serbia) Attendance: 27,641

KAZAKHSTAN: Dmytro Nepohodov, Sergey Malyi, Yevgeniy Postnikov, Gafurzhan Suyumbayev, Temirlan Yerlanov (81 Yeldos Akhmetov), Islambek Kuat, Aleksandr Merkel, Yan Vorogovskiy, Baktiyor Zainutdinov (84 Serikzhan Muzhikov), Yuriy Pertsukh, Roman Murtazayev (68 Bayurzhan Turysbek). Manager: Michal Bílek

SCOTLAND: Scott Bain, Graeme Shinnie, David Bates, Scott McKenna, James Forrest (81 Marc McNulty), Liam Palmer, Stuart Armstrong, Callum McGregor, John McGinn (69 Scott McTominay), Oliver Burke, Oliver McBurnie (61 Johnny Russell).   Manager: Alex McLeish

Goals: Yuriy Pertsukh (6), Yan Vorogovskiy (10), Baktiyor Zainutdinov (51)

769. 24.03.2019 16th European Champs Qualifiers
SAN MARINO v SCOTLAND 0-2 (0-1)

Stadio Olimpico di Serravalle, Serravalle

Referee: Manuel Schüttengruber (Austria) Att: 4,077

SAN MARINO: Elia Benedettini, Mirko Palazzi, Davide Simoncini (86 Lorenzo Lunadei), Manuel Battistini, Michele Cevoli, Enrico Golinucci, Adolfo José Hirsch (77 Andrea Grandoni), Alessandro Golinucci, Marcello Mularoni, Filippo Berardi, Matteo Vitaioli (60 Nicola Nanni).
Manager: Franco Varrella

SCOTLAND: Scott Bain, Stephen O'Donnell, Andrew Robertson, Callum Paterson (37 Marc McNulty), David Bates, Scott McKenna, Kenny McLean, Stuart Armstrong (71 James Forrest), Callum McGregor (56 Scott McTominay), Ryan Fraser, Johnny Russell.   Manager: Alex McLeish

Goals: Kenny McLean (4), Johnny Russell (74)

770. 08.06.2019 16th European Champs Qualifiers
SCOTLAND v CYPRUS 2-1 (0-0)

Hampden Park, Glasgow

Referee: Ola Hobber Nilsen (Norway) Attendance: 31,277

SCOTLAND: David Marshall, Charlie Mulgrew, Stephen O'Donnell, Andrew Robertson, Scott McKenna, James Forrest, Kenny McLean, Ryan Fraser, Callum McGregor (88 Stuart Armstrong), John McGinn (79 Scott McTominay), Eamonn Brophy (73 Oliver Burke).   Manager: Steve Clarke

CYPRUS: Urko Pardo, Konstantinos Laifis, Nicolas Ioannou, Ioannis Kousoulos, Giorgos Efraim, Renato Matgaça, Kostakis Artymatas, Mihalis Ioannou (66 Anthony Georgiou), Pieros Sotiriou, Andreas Makris (80 Ioannis Pittas), Matija Spoljaric (70 Ioannis Kosti).   Manager: Ran Ben Shimon

Goals: Andrew Robertson (61), Oliver Burke (89) / Ioannis Kousoulos (87)

771. 11.06.2019 16th European Champs Qualifiers
BELGIUM v SCOTLAND 3-0 (1-0)

Stade Roi Baudouin, Brussels

Referee: Petr Ardelaenu (Czech Republic)
Attendance: 32,482

BELGIUM: Thibaut Courtois, Vincent Kompany (90 Thomas Vermaelen), Jan Vertonghen, Toby Alderweireld, Thomas Meunier, Axel Witsel, Kevin De Bruyne, Youri Tielemans (78 Dries Mertens), Eden Hazard, Romelu Lukaku, Thorgan Hazard (90 Yannick Carrasco).
Manager: ROBERTO MARTÍNEZ Montoliú

SCOTLAND: David Marshall, Charlie Mulgrew, Stephen O'Donnell, Scott McKenna, Greg Taylor, Kenny McLean, Stuart Armstrong (32 Ryan Fraser), Callum McGregor, Oliver Burke, Scott McTominay, Johnny Russell (67 James Forrest). Manager: Steve Clarke

Goals: Romelu Lukaku (45+1, 57), Kevin De Bruyne (90+2)

772. 06.09.2019 16th European Champs Qualifiers
SCOTLAND v RUSSIA 1-2 (1-1)

Hampden Park, Glasgow

Referee: Anastasios Sidiropoulos (Greece)
Attendance: 32,432

SCOTLAND: David Marshall, Charlie Mulgrew, Liam Cooper, Stephen O'Donnell, Andrew Robertson, James Forrest (62 Kenny McLean), Callum McGregor, Ryan Fraser, John McGinn (62 Ryan Christie), Scott McTominay (78 Matt Phillips), Oliver McBurnie.   Manager: Steve Clarke

RUSSIA: GUILHERME Alvim MARINATO, Fyodor Kudryashov, Andrey Semyonov, MÁRIO Figueira FERNANDES, Georgiy Dzhikiya, Yuriy Zhirkov, Aleksey Ionov (80 Aleksandr Yerokhin), Magomed Ozdoyev, Roman Zobnin (66 Dmitriy Barinov), Aleksandr Golovin (89 Ilzat Akhmetov), Artyom Dzyuba. Manager: Stanislav Cherchesov

Goals: John McGinn (11) /
Artyom Dzyuba (40), Stephen O'Donnell (59 og)

773. 09.09.2019   16th European Champs Qualifiers
SCOTLAND v BELGIUM 0-4 (0-3)

Hampden Park, Glasgow

Referee: Pawel Gil (Poland)   Attendance: 25,524

SCOTLAND: David Marshall, Charlie Mulgrew, Liam Cooper, Stephen O'Donnell, Andrew Robertson, Robert Snodgrass, Matt Phillips (77 Johnny Russell), Kenny McLean, Callum McGregor (68 Stuart Armstrong), Scott McTominay, Ryan Christie (86 John McGinn).   Manager: Steve Clarke

BELGIUM: Thibaut Courtois, Toby Alderweireld, Thomas Vermaelen, Jan Vertonghen, Thomas Meunier (90 Benito Raman), Nacer Chadli (77 Yannick Carrasco), Kevin De Bruyne, Leander Dendoncker, Youri Tielemans (86 Yari Verschaeren), Dries Mertens, Romelu Lukaku. Manager: ROBERTO MARTÍNEZ Montoliú

Goals: Romelu Lukaku (9), Thomas Vermaelen (24), Toby Alderweireld (32), Kevin De Bruyne (82)

774. 10.10.2019   16th European Champs Qualifiers
RUSSIA v SCOTLAND 4-0 (0-0)

Grand Sports Arena of the Luzhniki Olympic Complex, Moscow

Referee: Jakob Kehlet (Denmark)   Attendance: 65,703

RUSSIA: GUILHERME Alvim MARINATO, Fyodor Kudryashov, Andrey Semyonov, MÁRIO Figueira FERNANDES, Georgiy Dzhikiya, Yuriy Zhirkov (66 Denis Cheryshev), Aleksey Ionov (79 Ilzat Akhmetov), Dmitriy Barinov, Aleksandr Golovin, Magomed Ozdoyev, Artyom Dzyuba (86 Nikolay Komlichenko).
Manager: Stanislav Cherchesov

SCOTLAND: David Marshall, Charlie Mulgrew, Michael Devlin, Andrew Robertson, Robert Snodgrass, John Fleck (81 Stuart Armstrong), Liam Palmer, Callum McGregor, Ryan Fraser (68 Ryan Christie), John McGinn, Oliver Burke (46 Lawrence Shankland).   Manager: Steve Clarke

Goals: Artyom Dzyuba (57, 70), Magomed Ozdoyev (60), Aleksandr Golovin (84)

775. 13.10.2019   16th European Champs Qualifiers
SCOTLAND v SAN MARINO 6-0 (3-0)

Hampden Park, Glasgow

Referee: Jérôme Brisard (France)   Attendance: 20,699

SCOTLAND: Jon McLaughlin, Michael Devlin, Stuart Findlay, Andrew Robertson, James Forrest, Liam Palmer, Callum McGregor (70 Johnny Russell), John McGinn (70 Stuart Armstrong), Scott McTominay, Ryan Christie, Lawrence Shankland.   Manager: Steve Clarke

SAN MARINO: Aldo Simoncini, Cristian Brolli, Manuel Battistini, Alessandro D'Addario (46 Andrea Grandoni), Alex Gasperoni, Mattia Giardi (46 Adolfo José Hirsch), Alessandro Golinucci, Luca Censoni, Marcello Mularoni, Filippo Berardi (80 Luca Ceccaroli), Nicola Nanni.   Manager: Franco Varrella

Goals: J. McGinn (12, 27, 45+1), Lawrence Shankland (65), Stuart Findlay (67), Stuart Armstrong (86)

776. 16.11.2019   16th European Champs Qualifiers
CYPRUS v SCOTLAND 1-2 (0-1)

GSP Stadium, Strovolos

Referee: Harald Lechner (Austria)   Attendance: 7,595

CYPRUS: Urko Pardo, Nicolas Ioannou, Giorgos Merkis, Ioannis Kousoulos, Andreas Karo (42 Grigoris Kastanos), Haralambos Kyriakou (77 Dimitris Theodorou), Giorgos Efraim (74 Matija Spoljaric), Jason Dimitriou, Fotis Papoulis, Ioannis Kosti, Pieros Sotiriou.   Manager: Ran Ben Shimon

SCOTLAND: David Marshall, Declan Gallagher, Scott McKenna, Greg Taylor, Ryan Jack, James Forrest (72 Oliver Burke), Liam Palmer, Callum McGregor, John McGinn, Ryan Christie (90+2 Michael Devlin), Steven Naismith (62 Oliver McBurnie).   Manager: Steve Clarke

Goals: Giorgos Efraim (47) / Ryan Christie (12), John McGinn (53)

777. 19.11.2019   16th European Champs Qualifiers
SCOTLAND v KAZAKHSTAN 3-1 (0-1)

Hampden Park, Glasgow

Referee: Bas Nijhuis (Netherlands)   Attendance: 19,515

SCOTLAND: David Marshall, Declan Gallagher, Scott McKenna, Greg Taylor, Ryan Jack, James Forrest, Liam Palmer, Callum McGregor, John McGinn (90+2 Stuart Armstrong), Ryan Christie (83 John Fleck), Steven Naismith (77 Oliver Burke).   Manager: Steve Clarke

KAZAKHSTAN: Dmytro Nepohodov, Yuriy Logvinenko, Dmitriy Shomko, Sergey Malyi, Gafurzhan Suyumbayev, Aleksandr Marochkin, Aybol Abiken, Baktiyor Zainutdinov, Bauyrzhan Islamkhan (74 Maxim Fedin), Yuriy Pertsukh (74 Islambek Kuat), Aleksey Shchetkin (83 Abat Aymbetov). Manager: Michal Bílek

Goals: John McGinn (48, 90+1), Steven Naismith (64) / Baktiyor Zainutdinov (34)

778. 04.09.2020   UEFA Nations League – Group B2
SCOTLAND v ISRAEL 1-1 (1-0)
Hampden Park, Glasgow
Referee: Slavko Vincic (Slovenia)   Attendance: 0

SCOTLAND: David Marshall, Andrew Robertson, Scott McKenna, Kieran Tierney, Ryan Jack, James Forrest, Callum McGregor, John McGinn (79 Stuart Armstrong), Ryan Christie, Scott McTominay, Lyndon Dykes (74 Oliver Burke).   Manager: Steve Clarke

ISRAEL: Ofir Marciano, Taleb Tawatha, Eitan Tibi, Hatem Abd Elhamed, Eli Dasa, Bibras Natcho, Nir Bitton, Dor Peretz (72 Yonatan Cohen), Eran Zahavi, Moanes Dabour (79 Shon Weissman), Manor Solomon (90 Dan Glazer).   Manager: Willibald Ruttensteiner

Goals: Ryan Christie (45 pen) / Eran Zahavi (73)

779. 07.09.2020   UEFA Nations League – Group B2
CZECH REPUBLIC v SCOTLAND 1-2 (1-1)
Andruv Stadion, Olomouc
Referee: Serdar Gözübüyük (Netherlands)   Attendance: 0

CZECH REPUBLIC: Ales Mandous, Roman Hubník, Jaroslav Zelený, Tomás Holes, Adam János, Václav Jemelka, Marek Havlík (81 Antonín Rusek), Lukás Budínský (55 Radim Breite), Tomás Malinský, Jakub Pesek (76 Roman Potocný), Stanislav Tecl.   Manager: Jaroslav Silhavý

SCOTLAND: David Marshall, Liam Cooper, Andrew Robertson, Scott McKenna, John Fleck (71 John McGinn), Kenny McLean, Liam Palmer, Stuart Armstrong (80 Callum McGregor), Scott McTominay, Ryan Christie, Lyndon Dykes (67 Callum Paterson).   Manager: Steve Clarke

Goals: Jakub Pesek (12) / Lyndon Dykes (27), Ryan Christie (52 pen)

780. 08.10.2020   16th European Champs Qualifiers – Play-off
SCOTLAND v ISRAEL 0-0 (AET)
Hampden Park, Glasgow
Referee: Ovidiu Alin Hategan (Romania)   Attendance: 0

SCOTLAND: David Marshall, Liam Cooper, Declan Gallagher, Stephen O'Donnell (113 Kenny McLean), Andrew Robertson, Ryan Jack (83 Ryan Fraser), Callum McGregor, John McGinn, Scott McTominay, Oliver McBurnie (73 Lawrence Shankland), Lyndon Dykes (91 Callum Paterson).   Manager: Steve Clarke

ISRAEL: Ofir Marciano, Sheran Yeini, Eitan Tibi, Hatem Abd Elhamed, Eli Dasa, Bibras Natcho (69 Mohammad Abu Fani), Manor Solomon, Nir Bitton, Eyal Golasa (101 Ilay Elmkies), Eran Zahavi, Moanes Dabour (83 Shon Weissman).   Manager: Willibald Ruttensteiner

Penalties: 1-0 John McGinn, Eran Zahavi (missed), 2-0 Callum McGregor, 2-1 Nir Bitton, 3-1 Scott McTominay, 3-2 Shon Weissman, 4-2 Lawrence Shankland, 4-3 Mohammad Abu Fani, 5-3 Kenny McLean

781. 08.10.2020   UEFA Nations League – Group B2
SCOTLAND v SLOVAKIA 1-0 (0-0)
Hampden Park, Glasgow
Referee: Davide Massa (Italy)   Attendance: 0

SCOTLAND: David Marshall, Andrew Considine, Declan Gallagher, Stephen O'Donnell, Andrew Robertson, John Fleck (72 Callum McGregor), Kenny McLean, Ryan Fraser (85 Callum Paterson), Scott McTominay, Lyndon Dykes (72 Oliver McBurnie), John McGinn (89 Ryan Jack).   Manager: Steve Clarke

SLOVAKIA: Dusan Kuciak, Jakub Holúbek, Branislav Ninaj, Martin Valjent, Martin Koscelník, Ján Gregus, Marek Hamsík (62 Juraj Kucka), Matús Bero (22 Ondrej Duda), Ivan Schranz (62 Róbert Mak), Lukás Haraslín (76 Albert Rusnák), Róbert Bozeník (76 Pavol Safranko).   Manager: Pavel Hapal

Goal: Lyndon Dykes (54)

782. 14.10.2020   UEFA Nations League – Group B2
SCOTLAND v CZECH REPUBLIC 1-0 (1-0)
Hampden Park, Glasgow
Referee: Felix Zwayer (Germany)   Attendance: 0

SCOTLAND: David Marshall, Andrew Considine, Declan Gallagher, Stephen O'Donnell, Greg Taylor (79 Paul Hanlon), Ryan Jack, Callum McGregor, Ryan Fraser (70 Kenny McLean), John McGinn (79 Callum Paterson), Scott McTominay, Lyndon Dykes (65 Oliver McBurnie).   Manager: Steve Clarke

CZECH REPUBLIC: Tomás Vaclík, Ondrej Kúdela, Ondrej Celustka (20 David Hovorka), Jan Boríl, Vladimír Coufal, Vladimír Darida, Lukás Masopust (65 Tomás Poznar), Lukás Provod (65 Petr Sevcík), Tomás Soucek, Matej Vydra (77 Michael Rabusic), Alex Král (77 Pavel Kaderábek).   Manager: Jaroslav Silhavý

Goal: Ryan Fraser (6)

783.   12.11.2020   16th European Champs Qualifiers – Play-off Final
SERBIA v SCOTLAND 1-1 (0-0, 1-1) (AET)
Stadion Rajko Mitic, Beograd
Referee: Antonio Miguel Mateu Lahoz (Spain)   Attendance: 0
SERBIA: Predrag Rajkovic, Stefan Mitrovic (108 Uros Spajic), Nikola Milenkovic, Darko Lazovic, Nemanja Gudelj, Filip Kostic (59 Filip Mladenovic), Sasa Lukic, Sergej Milinkovic-Savic (70 Aleksandar Katai), Nemanja Maksimovic (70 Luka Jovic), Dusan Tadic, Aleksandar Mitrovic.
Manager: Ljubisa Tumbakovic
SCOTLAND: David Marshall, Declan Gallagher, Stephen O'Donnell (118 Leigh Griffiths), Andrew Robertson, Kieran Tierney, Ryan Jack, Callum McGregor, John McGinn (83 Kenny McLean), Ryan Christie (87 Callum Paterson), Scott McTominay, Lyndon Dykes (82 Oliver McBurnie).
Manager: Steve Clarke

Goals: Luka Jovic (90) / Ryan Christie (52)

Penalties: 1-0 Leigh Griffiths, 1-1 Dusan Tadic, 2-1 Callum McGregor, 2-2 Luka Jovic, 3-2 Scott McTominay, 3-3 Nemanja Gudelj, 4-3 Oliver McBurnie, 4-4 Aleksandar Katai, 5-4 Kenny McLean, Aleksandar Mitrovic (missed)

784.   15.11.2020   UEFA Nations League – Group B2
SLOVAKIA v SCOTLAND 1-0 (1-0)
Stadion Antona Malatinského, Trnava
Referee: István Kovács (Romania)   Attendance: 0
SLOVAKIA: Marek Rodák, Peter Pekarík, Róbert Mazán, Lubomír Satka, Milan Skriniar, Marek Hamsík (68 Albert Rusnák), Juraj Kucka (61 Stanislav Lobotka), Ján Gregus, Patrik Hrosovský, Ondrej Duda, Michal Duris (90+3 Pavol Safranko).   Manager: Stefan Tarkovic
SCOTLAND: Craig Gordon, Andrew Considine (68 Leigh Griffiths), Liam Cooper, Scott McKenna, Kieran Tierney, Kenny McLean, Liam Palmer, Stuart Armstrong (87 Lawrence Shankland), John McGinn, Ryan Christie, Oliver McBurnie.
Manager: Steve Clarke

Goal: Ján Gregus (32)

785.   18.11.2020   UEFA Nations League – Group B2
ISRAEL v SCOTLAND 1-0 (1-0)
Netanya Stadium, Netanya
Referee: Pawel Raczkowski (Poland)   Attendance: 0
ISRAEL: Ofir Marciano, Sheran Yeini (78 Orel Dgani), Eitan Tibi, Eli Dasa, Sun Menachem, Bibras Natcho (62 Eyal Golasa), Nir Bitton, Manor Solomon (84 Yonatan Cohen), Eran Zahavi, Shon Weissman, Neta Lavi (78 Mohammed Abu Fani).
Manager: Willibald Ruttensteiner
SCOTLAND: David Marshall, Declan Gallagher (73 Scott McKenna), Stephen O'Donnell (73 Oliver Burke), Andrew Robertson, Kieran Tierney, Ryan Jack, Callum McGregor (82 Kenny McLean), John McGinn (61 Leigh Griffiths), Ryan Christie, Scott McTominay, Lyndon Dykes (61 Oliver McBurnie).   Manager: Steve Clarke

Goal: Manor Solomon (44)